WAR AND SOCIETY

A Yearbook of Military History

WAR AND SOCIETY

A Yearbook of Military History

Edited by

BRIAN BOND *and* IAN ROY

CROOM HELM LONDON

Croom Helm Ltd
2-10 St John's Road London SW 11

ISBN   0-85664-292-4

Printed and bound in Great Britain by
Redwood Burn Limited
Trowbridge & Esher

CONTENTS

FOREWORD

This is the first issue of the Yearbook, *War and Society*. It has long been felt that a place exists for a new outlet in the historical study of war and armed forces, and their relationship with society. It is hoped that the Yearbook will provide a forum for the publication of research in the field, and for the discussion of recent published work. No chronological or geographical limits will be set. The contributions to this volume range from the Renaissance to the era of Total War, and it is intended that future issues will be equally wide-ranging. The Yearbook will aim to trace the developing interests and new directions of historians in the field, to integrate military history and other disciplines, where these will add to our understanding of war, historically considered, and to persuade historians and students in general of the need to give proper emphasis, where appropriate, to the military factor in history.

Future issues will include an extensive review section, which will survey current literature.

Three of the essays printed below are versions of papers first delivered at King's College, London, in the Michaelmas and Lent Terms, 1974-5, as part of the public lecture series, 'War and Society: from Feudalism to Total War'. We are grateful to the authors, Professor Hale, Mr Howard, and Dr Roy, for allowing their publication here, and to the Principal, the College, and the Departments of History and War Studies for providing facilities and funds to ensure the success of this course, which coincided with and was a stimulus in the preparation of the Yearbook.

May 1975   B.J.B
                                                               I.R.

MEN AND WEAPONS: THE FIGHTING POTENTIAL OF SIXTEENTH-CENTURY VENETIAN GALLEYS*

J. R. Hale

The Venetian oared fighting vessel has attracted considerable, sometimes rapt, attention from historians.[1] There has not yet, however,
been an attempt to estimate its overall effectiveness in attack or defence. Hesitation in making such an attempt is all too justified. Fire has
devoured, and occupying forces (French and Austrian) have dispersed,
the greater part of the archival sources dealing with the fitting out,
manning and supplying of Venetian warships. The nonchalance of men
who took for granted what we long to know has impaired the useful-
ness of many of the documents that survive. There are more records
saying what should have been done than what was done or how it was
done. The shortage of crew lists, punishment sheets and take-home pay
slips, let alone of supporting biographical information, prejudices one
of the very topics with which this publication is concerned — the links
between a fighting unit and the society from which it is manned. It is
difficult for the historian to believe that it is better to travel hopefully
than to arrive, but it is necessarily in this spirit that the following ob-
servations, limited to crewing, armament and morale, and ignoring tactical practices and strategic intention, are made.

That a ship is a microcosm of society is so much a cliche that it needs
to be demonstrated. Here, then, is a list (of 1601) of those who crewed
the most populous of Venetian warships, a great galley flagship.[2]

	No. on board	Venetian term	Approx. trans.	Wage (*lire* per 'month' of 11 p.a.)
1	1	Capitano	Commanding officer	620
2	2	Capellan	Chaplain	20
3	4	Nobeli	Patrician volunteers	62
4	1	Fisico	Physician	60
5	1	Segretario	Correspondence clerk	36
6	1	Rasonato	Book-keeper	49½
7	1	Armiraglio	Chief navigating officer	72
8	1	Comito	For'ard deck officer	60
9	1	Huomo da Conseglio	Navigating officer	48

1

No. on board		Venetian term	Approx. trans.	Wage (*lire* per 'month' of 11 p.a.)
9	1	Huomo da Conseglio	Navigating officer	48
10	1	Paron	Aft deck officer	40
11	2	Pedotti	Pilots	40
12	1	Ceroico	Surgeon	31
13	1	Capo di Bombardieri	Chief gunner	30*[3]
14	8	Sotto capi di Bombardieri	Gunners' mates	24*
15	12	Bombardieri	Gunners	18*
16	1	Marangon	Carpenter	24*
17	1	Calafao	Caulker	24*
18	1	Remer	Oar-wright	24*
19	4	Penesi	Storesmen	24*
20	2	Compagni di stendardo	Masters-at-arms	20*
21	36	Compagni d'alboro	A.B.s	20*
22	1	Botter	Cooper	18*
23	1	Corazzier	Armourer	18*
24	1	Scrivanello	Copy-clerk	15
25	2	Barberotti	Barber-medical aides	12
26	2	Capitanei di soldati	Captains of soldiers	90
27	130	Soldati	Soldiers	12*
28	1	Patron di gondolieri	Chief longboatman	36*
29	12	Gondolieri	Longboatmen	12*
30	10	Prouieri	Strokesmen	12*
31	4	Fanti del marangon et calafao	Carpenter's and caulker's mates	12*
32	12	Mocci	Cabinboys	6
33	290	Galeotti, 25 de respetto	Oarsmen, incl. 25 reserves	10
34	1	Mistro de casa	Chief steward	28
35	1	Scalco	Steward	21
36	1	Cuogo	Cook	21
37	1	Sotto cuogo	Asst. cook	18
38	1	Canever	Wine steward	21
39	1	Spenditor	Purser	21
40	1	Caneverolo	Asst. wine steward	18
41	4	Servatori del Capitano	Personal assistants/servants	21

2

No. on board		Venetian term	Approx. trans.	Wage (*lire* per 'month' of 11 p.a.)
42	2	Servatori de nobeli	Personal assistants/servants	21
43	1	Servatore del fisico	Personal assistants/servants	21
44	1	Servatore del Segretario	Personal assistants/servants	21
45	1	Servatore del Rasanato	Personal assistants/servants	21
46	1	Aguzin	Crewminder	31*
47	4	Trombetti	Trumpeters	24*
48	2	Fanti dell' armiraglio	Chief navigating officer's assts.	10

572

With an annual wage and food bill of 31,929 ducats, it was essential that the great majority of the crew, not just the gunners and soldiers, should be able to fight the ship. Here Venice was able to call upon a long tradition of trusting subjects with arms and training them in their use. In 1506, when ordering the reconstruction of shooting yards, so that men from each *sestriere* could practise regularly with bow and crossbow for the periodical shooting competitions on the Lido, the Council of Ten stressed the need for all classes — patricians, citizens and workers — to be ready to defend the city.[4] The threat of invasion from the land was then very much in mind, from Maximilian's Austria, from the Turkish Balkans through Friuli, but the tradition originated in the custom of requiring evidence of military competence from those who wished to sail in merchant galleys (and obtain the perquisites of a niche of freight free cargo space and customs exemption) whether as oarsmen, craftsmen, mariners or deck officers; the positions reserved for young patrician traders were, indicatively, called *balestrerie*, crossbowman's places.[5] Merchant galleys were seldom convoyed. They had the benefit of naval galley squadrons patrolling the red sectors, as it were, of their routes, the 'Christian' corsair area south of Istria, the Turkish corsair zone in the southern Adriatic, the waters off Crete, but for the most part they were on their own, and cargo privileges had, literally, to be fought for. When, in 1509, the allies of Cambrai rolled Venice's armies towards the brink of the lagoon, this sea tradition came ashore. Patricians, mariners and craftsmen from the *arsenale* (the Venetian dockyard) were sent to defend positions the government felt to be too crucial to be entrusted to mercenaries: the town gates of Venice's nearest subject cities, Padua and Treviso.[6] The tradition continued throughout the sixteenth century, whether on great galleys, or on the far more numerous light galleys (150 or 160 oarsmen); clerical, ecclesiastical and medical staff apart, practically every man on board was expected to fight when occasion demanded. The patrician commander directed his vessel in armour,[7] crossbow in hand. Craftsmen and storekeepers were expected to be qualified marksmen.[8] Oarsmen rowed into action wearing sallets and reinforced canvas jacks, one third with swords at hand for the moment of boarding or repelling boarders.[9] A.B.s were ordered to have arquebus and morion 'as the *scapoli* do'.[10]

Scapolo was a chameleon-like term. There are traces of its earlier sense of 'volunteer'. It was occasionally used to describe all crew members in receipt of food allowances above the basic ration (the asterisked items on the crew list above) who were not clerks, chaplains or senior officers. But the technical significance of *scapoli* is best expressed as 'marines', the fighting men ('homini da spada' was a frequent synonym) enlisted as part of a galley's normal complement; and – except in the later crew lists of great galleys, where the distinction is seldom made – *scapoli* are to be clearly distinguished from *soldati*, the supplementary troops raised in time of war, with amphibious operations and full-scale combat at sea in mind.[11]

Up to 1542 the number of marines on a light galley was set at forty-two. From then until 1550 two marines were to be replaced by mariners, to mitigate the unemployment caused by the demobilisation that followed the Turkish war of 1537-40.[12] In 1565 there was another reduction of two, this time to increase the opportunities for young gunners to obtain sea experience,[13] but by the end of the century the standard number was forty-four.[14] These were peacetime numbers, calculated in terms of anti-corsair patrol, harbour guard and on-board discipline. They were increased when especially notorious corsair squadrons were known to be cruising,[15] in vessels serving in the Usock-ridden headwaters of the Adriatic, or when galleys were carrying cash from Venice for the payment of salaries *da mar*. On the other hand, Donato Gianotti, writing in 1525-6,[16] had suggested 80-100. A generation later Cristoforo da Canal, a serving naval commander, reckoned seventy to be necessary for patrol duty.[17] One hundred was the number recommended in a treatise of 1614 largely based on Venetian example.[18]

The discrepancy between the ideal and the actual is partly to be explained in terms of space and expense, but also in terms of the difficulty of recruiting sufficient men. The pay was low – 120-132 lire a year[19] – and remained constant throughout the century. Any proposals to alter it deliberately ignored the upward creep of prices and, by suggesting an increase in pay coupled with the abolition of the ration allowance, threatened a reduction in take-home pay.[20] The official free ration allowance (on top of biscuit) does not sound so bad on paper. Sunday, Monday, Tuesday and Thursday, six *onze* of meat and two glasses of 'honestly' watered wine; Wednesday and Friday, two sardines with oil and vinegar, plus soup; Saturday three *onze* of cheese and soup.[21] To purchase this, captains were advanced a sum roughly equivalent to a marine's cash pay.[22] But when in 1573 Venice was having a hard time recruiting marines and turned to the Mantovano, the Senate was forced to admit the justice of rumours that captains were not honouring their obligations, and not only to offer fifteen lire instead of twelve, but to suggest to the Duke of Mantua that galleys chiefly crewed by his oarsmen and marines should be commanded by Mantuan nobles who could ensure that rations were issued in accordance with regulations.[23] It was, doubtless, the persistent defaulting of Venetian captains in this respect that led marines to jump ship in the War of Gradisca (1615-17) in order to join the republic's land army.[24]

Information regarding the recruitment of marines is scanty. Though Venice maintained in readiness a militia on the *terra ferma* that from 1560 numbered 20,000 men, the government was reluctant to draw on it for service at sea.[25] There was more drafting of men from the militias of the ports and islands *da mar*, but here too the militia organisation was seen as an essential supplement to the republic's small core of professional troops in garrison. There is an occasional reference to recruiting drives by individual *entrepreneurs*,[26] but for the most part the government seems to have relied on volunteers, and the loan of arms and armour to newly joining marines suggests that many of these men were not among the roaming professional or semi-professional soldiers who made up the bulk of land armies. From a bare handful of references the chief recruitment areas can just about be guessed at: Venice itself, the *terra ferma*, Romagna, Apulia, Dalmatia and Albania, Crete; there was the odd northerner — 'Zuane Springal, fiamingo'.[27]

Before turning to the other straightforwardly military component of a normal galley crew (i.e. a crew not supplemented with additional professional soldiers), the gunners, it would be as well to consider the armament for which they were responsible by means of some typical equipment orders.

Light galleys

1540[28]	1571[31]	1600[32]
1 culverin of 50[29]	1 cannon of 50	1 cannon of 50
2 sackers of 12	2 asps of 12	1 falcon of 6
6 asps of 12	3 falcons of 6	1 falconet of 3

4 falconets of 3	3 falconets of 3	10 perriers of 6
1 musket 'da zuogo'[30]	3 perriers of 6	8 perriers of 3
36 muskets 'da braga'	12 perriers of 3	

Great Galleys

1570[33]	1587[34]	(weight in lb.)[35]
2 culverins of 50	2 culverins of 60	10,407
2 culverins of 30		10,282
2 culverins of 20	2 culverins of 30	5,832
4 culverins of 14		5,773
4 cannons of 30	4 cannons of 30	5,976
4 falcons of 6		4,876
2 falconets of 3		3,831
2 perriers of 30		3,920
12 perriers of 3	6 cannons of 20	3,420
		3,210
		3,072
		2,989
		2,939
		2,918
	4 culverins of 14	3,212
		3,211
		3,185
		3,181
	5 perriers of 3	About 150 each

From these and other inventories some generalisations may cautiously be made.

The types of artillery of a calibre equivalent to more than a single pound ball numbered twenty-one. Allowing that guns of similar calibre, though different types, could share projectiles, this leaves twelve varying weights of ball. Seventy balls was standardised as the issue for each piece of artillery in 1617.[36] In sieges, each side reckoned to recover by night a proportion of the balls fired during the day; armies could receive fresh supplies; navies, however, lost every shot fired and could place much less reliance on receiving more. The growing cost of metal and powder led to suggestions towards the end of the sixteenth century that both in fortresses and at sea Venice should concentrate on smaller guns from two to fourteen calibres;[37] no mention was made of the inconvenience involved in having so many sorts of incompatible missiles, but it must at times have been formidable. The liveliest debate concerning naval armament was about the substitution of breech- for muzzle-loading guns in the interest of giving gunners less occasion for exposing themselves to enemy short range fire.[38]

More important is the lack of contemporary discussion (to my knowledge) about the purpose of naval artillery: to what extent was it intended to sink the enemy at a distance, how far to maim his vessel and his crew during closing and grappling?

By applying a crude arithmetical test to a sample of equipment orders between 1540 and 1600, and taking point-blank ranges,[39] we get the following distribution of weapons:

Long range	(300 *passi*[40] and over)	42
Medium	(200-300 *passi*)	145
Medium-short	(100-200 *passi*)	112
Short	(0-100 *passi*)	62

Short range weapons must, of course, be supplemented by muskets, arquebuses, bows and projectile incendiary weapons, but ship artillery seems concentrated on the hope of sinking or disabling at 100 *passi* plus. There are supplementary pieces of evidence that point in the same direction. In 1537, at the beginning of the Turkish war, when the reserve of guns and metal was low, the Arsenal was nevertheless ordered to concentrate on cannons and culverins of fifty[41] and the Duke of Ferrara was asked to loan fifty pieces of forty and fifty.[42] In 1590 it was proposed that all cannons and culverins of fifty to one hundred should be transferred from the *terra ferma* to the fleet.[43] And in 1607, orders to replace perriers of six with a new type of falcon of six, replaced a short with a medium range weapon.[44]

The men in charge of the choice and production of naval guns, as *proveditori* of artillery or of the manning and armament of ships or as members of *ad hoc* committees to supervise the testing of new weapons,[45] were, on the whole, men with sea experience of their own. Changes in gun design were, perhaps, slow in being adopted, but experimentation was constant and the Republic's dynasties of gunfounders — Alberghetti, de Conti — were among the most progressive in Europe. At Lepanto, a booty of some 225 Turkish guns had been sent back to Venice. These the Arsenal had melted down and recast 'al moderno' until, in 1601, the Senate decreed that the thirty-four still left should be preserved 'to keep alive the memory of so worthy and famous an event'.[46] We may assume that naval armament, if conservative, was the result of practical and frequently reviewed experience.

We may also assume that, as in the matter of fortifications, the Venetian government was readier to invest in hardware than in manpower. The armament of galleys was not only as numerous and powerful as the vessels' manner of construction could well bear, but it demanded a variety of skills: calculating the charges for different calibres,[47] manipulating heavy guns recoiling on sleds (which could only be aimed by moving the ship as a whole) as well as the lighter swivel guns, loading some weapons by the muzzle, others at the breech, timing each shot with reference to the vessel's motion. Yet

7

manning never approached even a one man per gun basis. In light galleys, with a minimum armament of eleven three-pounders and up, the number of gunners of all ranks was seldom more than eight. In great galleys, where such pieces varied between twenty-two and forty-two, gunners seldom exceeded the twenty-one given on our crew list. And these figures take no account of the non-portable versions of the *moschetto*. To load and fire these, and to get the heavy guns back into position after recoil, recourse must have been had to non-specialists, from cabin boys to officers' and master craftsmen's servants. In 1533, when there was still considerable competition from craftsmen in the Arsenal to go on trading voyages, carpenters, oarwrights, caulkers and sailmakers (*filacanevi*) had first to qualify as prentice gunners;[48] it is doubtful how long this regulation remained effective.

Graded by pay and responsibility into three ranks, *capi, sotto capi* and *scolari*, gunners were drawn from artillery companies which, since the establishment of the *Scuola* of St Barbara in Venice in 1500, had been set up in nearly all the cities of the *terra ferma* and in many of the islands and fortified ports of the empire *da mar*. Volunteers were attracted by exemption from personal taxation, the right to carry arms and exemption from sales taxes on certain quantities of grain, wine and wood. Attendance at training periods under full-time chief gunners was encouraged by prizes for marksmanship, patrician military governors (*capitani*) were required to keep an eye on the efficiency of their local company, general army officers to examine them during tours of inspection. As a precaution against slack training in the *terra ferma* all gunners coming to serve on galleys were in 1534 ordered to be re-examined in Venice. As a result of this system, gunners both full and part-time were looked on as the most reliable of the military components in warship crews, and from 1556 fines of 500 ducats were to be imposed on any official who tried to detach them from ship- to shore-based duties.[49] Gunners were responsible not only for a ship's artillery but for signal rockets and for incendiary devices. There was, however, some difficulty in recruiting men for naval, as opposed to trading voyages. In 1539 the Council of Ten (responsible as they were until 1588 — when control passed to the Senate — for gunners as well as for artillery) ordered that prior service of at least two years in the army or in a naval squadron was a prerequisite for obtaining a place on a trading vessel.[50] The order to ships' captains of 1565 to take two extra gunners in place of two marines arose from fears of a shortage of men with sea experience. The 'monthly' wage of a chief gunner remained constant at thirty lire plus food from at least 1531;[51] that of a gunner's mate is obscured by conflicting terminology; the ordinary gunner continued to get eighteen lire plus food throughout the century. All the same, the problem of recruiting only became really serious late in the century when Spain and Austria became consistently hostile to Venice. In order that the fortress towns of the *terra ferma* should not be left vulnerable by drafting gunners to the fleet, urgent but not entirely successful attempts were made to keep up the numbers and intensify the training of the artillery companies.[52]

Far graver than the problem of recruiting marines and gunners was that of obtaining enough oarsmen. The numbers involved were large. From 1537 Venice decided to have 100 light galleys at sea or in readiness: this would require some 16,000 oarsmen. The 106 light and 6 great galleys at Lepanto in 1571 were rowed by about 18,140 oarsmen; an even larger force was envisaged by the treaty of 1573 with Spain and the Papacy.[53] And these figures take no account of *fuste, briganti* and oared galleons.

In 1522 it was decided that even with the manpower of Dalmatia and the Mediterranean islands to draw on, swift mobilisation required a reserve of local oarsmen. On 18 March[54] the Senate decided to enroll 6,000 men in the cities and territories of the *terra ferma* who would be liable, when called upon, for paid galley service. Targets for volunteers from between 18 and 40 years of age were set for each administrative centre.[55] The inducements offered were these: freedom for life from personal taxation,[56] permission to wear arms (a much coveted privilege for reasons not only of status but personal safety),[57] freedom during service and for six months afterwards from prosecution for debt.[58] Once enrolled, the men were to be given and taught to use firearms (the *schioppo*, a simpler version of the arquebus) 'which will be of great benefit to us in time of need both by land and sea', though their chief contribution would be to the motive force of the galleys they were called up to. It was anticipated that this measure would enable the Republic to crew fifty galleys from the city of Venice and the *terra ferma*. The initial response, however, was so poor that the government accepted an offer by a *condottiere*, Giulio de Bruna, to raise 1,200 men himself; there were to be eight companies of 150 men each with an ensign in charge of it and six corporals. On being called up, the ensigns would serve as gunners (one per galley), the corporals as *schioppettieri* (six per galley), the rank and file as oarsmen. This blueprint for a private enterprise system of raising *scapoli* and oarsmen together seems to have come to nothing, and though sporadic attempts were made in subsequent years to enroll the 'Ordinanza da Mar', in September 1534 it was acknowledged to have been a failure.[59]

A number of men, noted the Senate, had been raised, but they had been put aboard in groups of forty or fifty 'together with Dalmatians who had treated them badly', and they had been made to winter abroad, as a consequence of which 'many had died and the rest had undergone much suffering'. These experiences had discouraged others from coming forward. The Senate then voted the reimposition of the scheme of 18 March 1522, with two changes: men from one area were to form the entire rowing crew (150) of one galley under a prominent local resident who would command the vessel, and they were to serve only for six months at a time. It was also decided that men already enrolled in the militia of arquebusiers (24,000 strong at that time) could change to the sea militia, but this provision was cancelled later in the year and, more important, the first note of true conscription was sounded. Provincial military governors were to spread enrolment equally among families in each community, to forbid enrolled men to change their place of residence without permission, and to transfer those whose ineptness with pike or firearm disqualified them from serving usefully in the militia of arquebusiers to the sea militia.[60]

In February 1537, half of the 6,000 were called up, the rest in September as mobilisation for war against the Turks got under way.[61] In the same month the balance between the land and sea militias was radically changed and conscription for the latter carried further.[62] The militia of arquebusiers was to be reduced to 15,000. From the 9,000 men discharged and the 6,000 already enrolled in the sea militia, 12,000 of the most suitable were to be enrolled in an enlarged sea militia. The burden was to be spread equally among all communities on the *terra ferma* (Venice had inherited the feudal right to exact labour and military service from the territories it had conquered piecemeal in the preceding centuries), though no community could be called on twice until all the others had already sent men to galley service. The men would have the tax exemptions of 1522 and the right to bear arms from call-up until six months after discharge. Among those enrolled, men who volunteered on call-up would be paid two ducats a month (by their communities), the rest would be chosen by lot. In this way the manning of sixty-six galleys should be assured.

Again, however, the government's hopes were disappointed by the negligence of provincial governors, by the disinclination of local communities to pay the two ducats to volunteers, and by the draft-dodging ingenuity of individuals. When a general mobilisation of the whole sea militia was put in motion in the war scare year 1545, it was found that there were still only 6,000 men enrolled. The Collegio was then ordered to increase it to 8,000 and in 1561 — population growth having led the arquebus militia to be increased from 15,000 to 20,000 — to 10,000:[63] 30,000 in both militias at a time when the total number of adult males fit for active service on the *terra ferma* was reckoned at around 200.000.[64]

The Turkish war of 1537-40 put such a strain on the recruitment of of oarsmen, that on 20 June 1539, the *scuole* (fraternities), craft associations and guilds of Venice and the islands and coastal villages of the lagoon were called on to enroll 4,000 potential oarsmen. The perquisites offered were these: on their return oarsmen could be accepted for full membership of their occupational organisation without paying the usual fee; they would have priority in filling vacant places in the city's numerous ferry services (*traghetti*) and for certain jobs such as watchmen, customs guards and warehousemen; each period of naval service would gain them the right to go on a merchant voyage, with its attendant freight- and custom-free allowance.[65] By 1594 a bonus of ten ducats had been added as an additional incentive.[66] In 1595 the regulations of 1539 were to be printed and distributed to the organisations concerned, with a number of additions.[67] To raise crews of 160 for fifty light galleys, plus an on-board reserve of 1,000 between them, the enrolment of 4,000 was to be increased to 9,000. To this end names were to be submitted (they came to 23,095)[68] from which the 9,000 would be chosen either as volunteers, or as the result of choices made or lots cast by individual organisations or, as a last resort, by lots cast by the presidents of the College of the *Milizia da Mar*, the age limits being 18-45. The cash incentive was increased to twenty-five ducats in addition to normal pay (provided by the organisations, not by the government), and during their time of service and for six months afterwards, oarsmen could not 'save in grave circumstances' be taken to law.[69]

Nevertheless, neither the *terra ferma* nor the city system proved adequate to provide oarsmen in sufficient numbers or of adequate quality in times of war. Faulty administration, legal quibbles concerning exemption, the possibility of using, or faking, substitutes, simple draft-dodging — these were among the reasons which had caused the Senate in 1539 to invite petitions from outlaws and prisoners to have their sentences remitted if they volunteered to row in war galleys,[70] and which led the government in 1570-1 to seek 2-3,000 oarsmen among the Swiss,[71] to ask the permission of the Duke of Ferrara to recruit among his subjects,[72] and to debate the propriety of contracting for 600 and upward from the Swiss canton of Graubünden.[73]

Lepanto, the greatest Mediterranean naval victory of the century, was not regarded by the Venetians as conclusive. The following two years saw larger fleets aimed for and achieved amidst a flurry of expedients. The goverment's proposal in 1572 to winter galleys crewed by oarsmen from the *terra ferma* abroad was challenged as illegal and unwise within the Senate, but was passed nevertheless — fear of the delays caused by assembling new crews for the spring junction with the Spanish and Papal fleets over-riding the dismay with which this decision would be greeted.[74]

The government's optimistic view that additional oarsmen would be lured from Dalmatia by the prospect of loot in the continuing action against the Turk, who could at last be represented as on the defensive,[75] was not, as it turned out, shared by men on the spot and in February 1572 the Senate authorised negotiations with a Swiss entrepreneur for the supply of at least 600 oarsmen from Graubünden 'or others, as long as they are Catholic [this was meant to be an orthodox holy war] and live "catholicamente" and are not our own subjects'. They were to be paid the inflated 'Mantuan' rate of fifteen lire a month plus basic rations.[76] In August a more radical note was struck. All those who had been using Turkish captives as slaves after Lepanto and the coastal skirmishes that followed it, were to send them, for a compensation of twenty ducats or more, depending on their quality, to be chained oarsmen.[77] In November the fleet commanders were ordered to recruit Turkish subjects, voluntarily if possible, or by force, though still paying them as though they were volunteers.[78] And the accounts kept by Captain General Giacomo Foscarini record purchases of slaves at sums varying between ten and twenty-five ducats (for Mustafa da Constantinopoli, among others).[79]

For the mobilisation of 1573 recourse was again had to the Duke of Mantua, with the promise that his subjects would be discharged without fail in October.[80] Another Swiss entrepreneur, Colonel Mechior Lusi, with a long-standing contract to supply troops to Venice, was now asked to supply 1,200 oarsmen — at a price that had crept up to sixteen lire a month plus travel allowance and on his condition that the bargain should include the same number of infantry;[81] when Venice, disillusioned as to the militancy of its allies, edged its way out of the Christian League in March, the oarsmen were dismissed with a *douceur* of two ducats each while the troops, lesss amenable to summary dismissal, were apportioned among the *terra ferma* garrisons.[82] More revealing still of Venice's shortage of manpower was the response in the following year to rumours from Constantinople that yet another Turkish fleet was fitting out. Lusi was asked to raise another 1,200 oarsmen from his canton, Unterwalden — where few, if any, men had been in a boat let alone seen the sea. The rumour was denied within a few days, and a courier sent to overtake the contract,[83] but the episode reveals the disadvantages of a dependence on oared warships.

Apart from the years immediately following Lepanto, the Venetians did not use slaves as oarsmen. Nor do slave raids at other times appear to have been adopted as a deliberate means of filling the benches, and what have been taken to be such raids[84] were probably the result of bribes, promises of pardon for offences[85] or of exemption from militia or pioneer services, pressures just inside the letter of the law. However, some thirty years before, in 1542, the difficulty of obtaining volunteers was thought to justify the use of chained criminals, men who would otherwise have been imprisoned. From 1545 *galee de condannati* were regularly sent to sea and by 1579 vessels manned in this way were referred to by the Council of Ten as 'the chief sinew (*il principal nervo*) of our fleet'.[86] In 1615 an offer from the Duke of Bavaria to export criminals from his gaols to serve as oarsmen was gratefully accepted.[87] In 1616 orders were given to the commissioners with the army in Friuli to send archducal prisoners of war to the galleys,[88] but the decision was reversed in the following year as counter to Christian duty and to the charitable nature of the republic.[89] Perhaps it had not been put into effect. Certainly it would have compromised ransom settlements and exchanges of prisoners of war at the end of hostilities.

Chained oarsmen received no wage. They were given the oarsman's basic ration: soup made from vegetables or rice, or from stale bread or crushed biscuit with a little oil, plus ship's biscuit on its own.[90] Like the free oarsmen they were charged for clothing, paliasses and medical services and if they could not raise cash they had to row on past the conclusion of their sentences until they were judged to have paid for them.[91] The free oarsman's 'monthly' wage of twelve lire for the first four months and nine thereafter[92] was changed in 1524 to a flat ten lire a month,[93] and, as our crew list shows, so it remained throughout the century. What the government thought about the conditions of service at the oar is clear from a law of 1548 which pronounced transfer to the sea militia as the sentence for breaches of certain regulations concerning the arquebus militia.[94] All the same, motley as their origin and grim as their lives on board might have been, thanks to the poverty and hardships that for many were the alternatives ashore, to the wide disciplinary powers granted to commanders and the group discipline imposed by the three, four or five men to an oar system which gradually gained ground from the 1570s,[95] there were few complaints about oarsmen being unable to propel galleys adequately in combat.

Oarsmen, moreover, both chained and free, were issued with weapons and were expected to use them. From December, 1518, the Council of Ten's order that arquebuses were to replace crossbows on galleys[96] was quickly taken up in Senate equipment orders. In addition to the firearms issued to marines, A.B.s and craftsmen, it was ordered in 1528 that each light galley should take fifty for use by rowers. Each craft was to have enough ammunition to allow for six practice shots a month and the men were to be encouraged by three prizes worth ten ducats each.[97] When the Arsenal's experimental quinquereme was being fitted out in the following year, 100 arquebuses were to be provided for its oarsmen.[98] Cristoforo da Canal claimed, however, to have been the first to have trained oarsmen to use the arquebus; he had borrowed weapons from the Arsenal and had fifty of them trained by a professional soldier ('whom I called the "captain of the oarsmen-arquebusiers" ' and who received an extra ducat per pay) whenever the vessel touched land. The aim was not so much to produce accurate marksmen as men who could fire, reload and blaze away again at short range, while archers filled in the reloading periods. He had had, he claimed, as many as 500 of these oarsmen-arquebusiers in his squadron. Unlike the marines, whose weapons were stored in a central magazine, they kept their weapons in chests fastened down between the benches. But, aside from the arquebus, he went on, oarsmen should be fully involved both in attack and defence. The inboard member of each bench should have a short pike; the middleman a 'long bow of the sort used by our country folk' which he should stand on the bench to use, the outboard oarsmen, hampered between his fellows and the portable defences (the *pavesata* of wooden shuttering mounted on the gunwale), could at least throw stones and lumps of lead from the pile under his bench. And, he concluded, chained prisoners were as useful as free oarsmen. The most trustworthy could be released in combat and promised liberty in exchange for gallant service, the others could handle weapons in self-defence as far as their chains allowed and, unlike free men, could not jump overboard when the odds against them seemed too threatening.[99] In the mid-1570s an ex-chained oarsman with long experience in the galleys of Tuscany remarked that of all the Christian governments operating in the Mediterranean, the Venetians got the most fighting service out of their oarsmen.[100]

The arquebus did not displace the bow. The crossbow does appear to have dropped out of use apart from its largely symbolic role in the hands of a commander, but the longbow held its ground sturdily. We have seen them used to cover the arquebusiers' loading periods in da Canal's description. Galleys arming in Crete in 1538 were to take on 'good, reliable and skilled archers';[101] an inventory of 1556 lists twenty arquebuses firing half-ounce (*oncia*) balls, together with twenty of the older hand guns (*schioppi*) and fifty bows.[102] As the musket came to rival, though not supplant, the arquebus on land, it was employed increasingly at sea, partly because its weight could be steadied on top of, or in, the ambrasures of the temporary combat defences built up at prow and poop and (unlike the practice in Turkish or Spanish vessels) along the sides. The Venetian war galley in action was like a self-propelled fortress and could use the weapons appropriate to curtain and bastion. Each great galley in 1617 was to have 100 muskets.[103] Even so it was as late as this year that the Senate still found it necessary to inveigh against the continuing use of 'bows and arrows, which are useless and superfluous weapons'.[104] For defence against missiles and handstrokes, oarsmen wore helmets and flexible jacks (*corrazzine, curazine*), which allowed freedom of movement, while marines and other crewmen-combatants used the stouter cuirass (*corsaletto*) of plate. Armour for thighs, legs and arms is seldom mentioned, presumably because, as Pantero Pantera remarked, at sea it was necessary 'to fly, as it were, from one vessel to another', full armour only being appropriate for the commander and the captain of *soldati* who remained exposed while giving orders throughout an engagement.[105]

With *soldati* we come to the last and most purely military element in a galley's complement, the soldiers recruited to reinforce the marines in time of threatened or actual war. Their numbers were not simply determined by the needs of large-scale sea battles. These were few and undertaken with reluctance. Numbers were also conditioned by the potentially amphibious nature of naval operations. During the Apulian campaign of 1528-9, the bombardment of ports from the sea, the landing of raiding parties or of the entire military component of a fleet to reinforce land armies, had all played an important part in Venetian strategy.[106] During that campaign, as in the Turkish war of 1537-40, warships were on occasion used straightforwardly as troop transports, to land an army and then sail away, But troops might at any time be needed to distract the enemy's recruiting activities, relieve a siege, strengthen a threatened garrison or take back a captured port. In 1570-3 Venice's vessels had to match the military component in Turkish fleets manned for the conquest and occupation of her Adriatic bases as well as for the domination of her trade and military supply routes. And, as Sebastiano Venier wrote with reference to an attempt to destroy the fort built by the Turks in 1572 to block the entrance to the Venetian base at Cattaro (Kotor), guns were not enough. Galleys, he pointed out, are at a disadvantage when engaged in an artillery duel with a fortress, 'because, being in movement, they shoot awry, and when they do score a hit it is on a stone bastion or a thick and stout earthwork, whereas shots from the land strike thin, vulnerable wood or human flesh'.[107] He says nothing of the difficulties confronting the land gunner: the problem of aiming consistently at small, thin, moving targets at a level below his own platform; but the moral, that galleys needed landing parties as well as guns, was in any case established doctrine. Nor was it shaken by the war of 1615-17, when not only formal combined operations but the temporary borrowing of naval troops by land forces were constant themes.[108]

During March and April 1570, Venice contracted for 11,600 infantry to join the fleet,[109] enough to guarantee the bare minimum of eighty fighting men per light galley quickly, and to build towards the number thought necessary — 100.[110] In 1572 12,000 fighting men (the distinction between marines and soldiers tended to be ignored in wartime) was fixed as Venice's contribution to the Christian League's fleet, and efforts were made to select from newly enrolled men, and from those serving in garrisons, those who would best stand the conditions of sea service[111] — in the winter of 1570-71 the wastage, primarily due to privation, had amounted to some 5,000.[112] Possession of the full complement of marines and soldiers was considered of paramount importance; Marc' Antonio Colonna justified his inaction against the Turkish fleet in 1570, which led to the fall of Nicosia, by saying that, with fewer troops per vessel, the Venetians would have been unlikely to have won.[113]

Soldati for the fleet were raised, as for the land forces, by contract with mercenary captains. There were almost always gaps in their numbers when mustered before embarkation, always losses thereafter from sickness and desertion. The difficulty of keeping numbers up is reflected in the measures taken in 1570-72: peasant volunteers from the *terra ferma* were offered four years of exemption from personal taxation from the end of their service, outlaws (*banditi*) were offered amnesties, patrician volunteers were not to be inhibited by any legal proceedings in which they were involved, naval commanders were allowed to recruit members of the militias of Dalmatia and Albania.[114] By means such as these, any means short — legally, at least — of actual conscription or the press gang, Venice accumulated a floating army. Paruta later stigmatised it as composed of 'men for the most part unused to military service'.[115] This was an exaggeration. The floating army at Lepanto was probably not much less experienced, taken as a whole, than land armies of the period, and its inexperienced elements were to some extent compensated for by the restricted need for tactical discipline on shipboard, the impossibility of flight, and the terror of falling captive to the Turk.

Terror was, indeed, the keynote of Pantero Pantera's graphic account of the special demands made on the morale of troops by naval service. First the soldier had to become accustomed to the vessel's constant movement, then to exposure to squalls of rain, finally to visual horrors: the flashing cannon,

'the havoc wrought among human limbs now by iron now by fire (which is not so terrifying in land battles), the sight of this man torn to shreds and in the same moment another burned up, another drowned, another pierced by an arquebus ball, yet another split into wretched pieces by the artillery. On top of this there is the terror caused by the sight of a vessel swallowed up by the sea with all hands without the remotest possibility of rescue, to see the crew, half alive, half burned, sink miserably to the bottom while the sea changes colour and turns red with human blood, covered the while with arms and with scraps and fragments of broken ships.'[116]

How far this passage, a recruiting officer's nightmare, represented the popular view of military service at sea, can only be guessed at. The normal hazards of land service, disease, food shortages, rough living, arrears of pay, harsh discipline, were well known. Among the voluminous series of petitions, often including *curricula vitarum*, addressed by soldiers to the government, there is no hint that service at sea gave rise to any special grievance or sense of alarm. Indeed, it is generally referred to (not, of course, necessarily sincerely) with pride. Venice paid no more for sea than for land service,[117] and the system of stoppages for food, armour and weapons and replacement clothing was roughly comparable. Certain contracts with military entrepreneurs specifically excluded service at sea, but these related exclusively to Swiss troops; men recruited *da mar* and the 'foreign' Italian troops on which Venice chiefly relied, as well as the *terra ferma* volunteers she increasingly came to rely on, were aware that they were signing on for service on land or at sea according to the orders given their captain. The difficulty Venice had in amassing troops for the War of Gradisca, which led to the amassing of the most cosmopolitan, desertion- and sickness-prone and fractious of all her armies, applied equally to land and sea service. It would be incorrect to suggest as a general rule that the quality or quantity of soldiers in galleys was such as seriously to impede the aims of those who had designed and armed them.

These aims were to build (as cheaply as possible, with the wage bills of large crews in mind) long, narrow, low, fast and, as necessary, self-propelled vessels, to equip them with a formidable variety of weapons, and to cram them with men trained in their use. In spite of the problems of firing from a moving platform, long and medium range artillery continued to be mounted in the hope of successful attack at a distance. As the range shortened, loopholed portable defences provided cover for men using firearms and bows, while temporary platforms gave vantage points for the most skilled marksmen. At contact, sword and pole-arms came into play, together with such incendiary materials as had not been affected by damp.[118] At each of the three stages the military potential of the ship's company was progressively augmented; first the gunners, then the marines and soldiers, finally all those mates, craftsmen, seamen and oarsmen who were not engaged in keeping the vessel locked to windward of the enemy in order to clear the decks of smoke and reduce the danger of fire.

And the commanders? There is no space here to discuss the effectiveness of the command structure of a fleet,[119] or to do more than note that though, numerically, the patriciate which supplied the commanders of individual ships and the captains of squadrons and fleets was becoming progressively more land- than sea-centred, the system of office-holding which switched men from naval commands to military responsibilities on land and *vice versa*,[120] continued to provide a leadership which soldiers, as well as sailors, appeared to respect.

Notes

N.B. In this, and following note sections, place of publication of books cited is London, unless otherwise stated.

* This article owes much to the unstinted generosity with references and advice of Dr Marco Morin, and to the encouragement of Professor Frederic C. Lane, whose sequel to the article on seamen cited in note 1 will greatly supplement the information given here.

1. Notably, Frederic C. Lane, *Navires et constructeurs à Venise pendant la Renaissance* (Paris, 1965), *Venice and history* (Baltimore, 1966) Nos. 11 and 12, and 'Venetian seamen in the nautical revolution of the middle ages', in *Venezia e il Levante fino al secolo XV* (Florence, 1973); Alberto Tenenti, *Cristoforo da Canal; la marine Vénitienne avant Lépante* (Paris, 1962) and *Piracy and the decline of Venice, 1580-1615* (Berkeley U.P., 1967); G. Giomo and F. Visentini, *Le grosse galere veneziane nel 1593* (Venice, 1895). More generally, R. G. Anderson, *Oared fighting ships* (1962); John Francis Guilmartin Jr., *Gunpowder and galleys* (1974); W. L. Rodgers, *Naval warfare under oars, 4th to 16th centuries* (Annapolis, 1939). For additional works, see the bibliographies to Lane's *Venice, a maritime republic* (Baltimore, 1973) and Tenenti's *Cristoforo da Canal*.

2. S[enato], M[ar], D[eliberationi], R[egistro] 61, ff. 46-46ᵛ. All manuscript references are to Archivio di Stato, Venice, unless another source is given.

3. Asterisks denote men who were given food above the basic ration of biscuit and soup.

4. Council of Ten (henceforward Cl. X.) Misti, D.R. 31,2 f.23ᵛ, 19 May.

5. Even when the crossbow was replaced by the arquebus in 1518. These positions, for patricians between the ages of 12 and 30, increasingly became sinecures, bartered for cash, and in 1551 their numbers were limited to fifty in any one year (S.M.D.R. 31,ff.81-81ᵛ). From 1571 the 'nobeli di galea' who appear on crew lists were patricians who volunteered for military duties out of patriotism and for a wage. Eight were killed and five wounded at Lepanto (Archivi propri, Pinelli, 1-2, f.13ᵛ).

6. 'Homeni maritimi' who had served at Padua were to be offered priority places on the next merchant galleys going to Beirut and Alexandria, S.M.D.R. 17, f.64ᵛ, 20 Oct. 1509. The same practice was observed, scare by scare. E.g. on 12 Nov. 1526 'homeni di le maistranze di l'arsenale' were sent to defend Padua; Marino Sanuto, *Diarii* (Venice, 1879-1903), xliii, col. 221.

7. For Cristoforo da Canal, killed in action in 1552, see *Della milizia da mar* [c. 1540], ed. M. Nani Mocenigo (Rome, 1930) 12. The seventy-five-year-old Sebastiano Venier, at Lepanto, 'stava armata d'una corazza all'antica, in pianelle, con un balestra in mano'; P. Molmenti, 'Sebastiano Veniero dopo la battaglia di Lepanto', *Nuovo Archivio Veneto* (1915), 10-11.

8. This, at least, is how I read a reference to 'i balestrieri de maestranze et tutte gl'altri tolti al bersaglio' in Pinelli, 1-2, n.p., 'da mandare galie in ponente', item 45. The reference is to merchant galleys.

9. Arsenal inventory of 1544. Archivi propri, Secreta, G. Contarini, 25-6: 'Corazine et zellade et spade bone per galliotti' (9,000, 2,000 and 1,200 respectively) with a note that each [light] galley was to be issued with 150 jacks and

sallets, i.e. one of each per oarsmen, and thirty swords. This last figure had been amended to fifty by 1556, a figure confirmed by an issue in 1582. (da Canal, ed. cit., notes on pp. 102 and 107. Cl.X.C[omune].D. R. 36, f.121^v, 3 July.)

10.   A late reference, but this is unlikely to be an innovation. S.M.D.R. 62.f.144.

11.   E.g., 'Gente da remo, homini da spada et soldati'. S. S[ecreta] D.R. 78,f. 166^v, 3 Jan. 1573 [all dates in these notes are modernised] ; 'cosi alli scapoli ordinarii come alli soldati estraordinarii' (pay regulations, S.M.D.R. 37,f.191^r, 23 Sept. 1566. And see below, pp. 15-16.

12.   S.M.D.R. 31,f.66^r.

13.   *Ibid.*, R.37,ff.22^v-25^r. All galley commanders (*sopracomiti* and *governatori*) raising crews in Venice or in Dalmatia, Albania or Crete, are to take two extra gunners from those enrolled for at least two years in an artillery company on the *terra ferma* or *da mar*.

14.   At the turn of the century there was a proposal (unimplemented) to reduce this number to thirty-two in the interest of economy. Materie Miste Notabili, 29. Unpaginated proposal to the Doge from the Presidents of the Collegio della Milizia da Mar ('Prima scrittufa').

15.   Especially, at mid-century, that of Dragut. E.g., twenty extra marines per galley; S.M.D.R. 30, 107-107^v. On smaller oared vessels, *fuste* and *brigantini*, figures for patrol and combat were respectively 8, 24 ; 4. 10. S.M.D.R. 23, f.168; *ibid.*, 27, ff.27^v-28; *ibid.*, 28, ff.117-18.

16.   *Libro della repubblica di Veneziani* (Florence, 1850), ii, 161-2.

17.   Ed. cit., 119-20. He gives a valuably specific account of the positions around the galley taken up by *scappoli* on guard duty, and their relief system.

18.   Pantero Pantera, *L'armata navale* (Rome, 1614), 168.

19.   Depending on whether it was calculated at ten lire per calendar month, or twelve lire an 'Arsenal' month (eleven to the year).

20.   On 12 March 1587, a petition signed by twelve *sopracomiti* protested that these cheeseparing moves would rob the service of efficient and loyal marines. Materie Miste Notabili, 29, n.p., endorsed 'in lettere del Prov.^{e} dell'Armada, 27 Aprile'.

21.   S.S. Filze, 24 Jan. 1573.

22.   Materie Miste Notabili 29, *parte* of 12 Mar. 1587.

23.   S.S.D.R. 78, ff.173^v-174.

24.   S.M.D.R. 74, f.80^v-81. The offence was to be punishable with death.

25.   The *Collegio* was authorised to call up 10,000 men, however, in 1520 and 1566; Sanuto, xxviii, 559 and S.M.D.R. 37, 174^v. In each case the war scare passed before more than a proportion of the men (1,500 in 1566) had been mobilised.

26.   E.g., S.M.D.R. 21, f.154, 22 Sept. 1529.

27.   S.M.D.R. 33, f.169; *ibid.*, 42 ff.63^v, 105.

28.   Cl.X.C.D.R. 13, 10 Oct., F.216.

29.   Artillery was calibrated according to the weight of the proving shot in pounds. From 12 lb. down, however, the proof ball was of lead, whereas iron balls, a third lighter, were used in action. Perriers were proved with stone balls, and used them in action.

30.   Bronze light artillery, not to be confused with the portable *moschetto*. The musket 'da zuogo' (380-400 lb.) was bedded in a heavy wooden base; the musket 'da braga' (80-120 lb.) had an iron stirrup welded into a bronze barrel and was charged through removable chambers fitting into the stirrup.

31.   C.X.C.D.R. 30, f.49^v.

32.   Tenenti, *Piracy*, 188, where 'mortars' are misleadingly given for perriers.

In 1558 the following armament was given as 'customary' for light galleys: 1 cannon of 50; 1 falcon of 6; 3 falconets of 3; 2 perriers of 6; 4 perriers of 3. Materie Miste Notabili, 13, f.16.^{V}.

33. Proveditori all'Artiglieria, 36, no. 4. A typical example from 11; the other totals were 28, 26, 23, 42, 37, 33, 22, 40, 40, 35.

34. *Ibid.*

35. Given because the weight of individual guns issued to a galley is seldom found and can make it easier to appreciate a vessel's firepower. I do not know whether the 'heavy' Venetian lb. (= 1.05 English lb.) or the 'light' Venetian lb. (= 0.66 English lb.) is meant; most probably the former.

36. S.M.D.R. 75, f.45^V.

37. S.S.R.R. 87, f.26^V and Collegio, Secreta, Relazioni, 52, 17 July 1590.

38. Materie Miste Notabili, 22, 6 Apr. 1589 and S.M.D.R. 51, f.101. S.M.D.R. 61, f.8, 7 Apr. 1601, for adoption of breech-loaders.

39. Alessandro Capobianco, *Corona e palma militaire di artiglieria* (Venice, c. 1598), 34. His ranges square with trials described in e.g. Archivi Propri Contarini, 25, 1 Sept. 1544.

40. The Venetian *passo* = 5.5 English feet.

41. Cl.X.C.D.R. 12, 7 June, f.35-35^V.

42. *Ibid.*, 13 Sept. 1537, f.37^V.

43. Collegio, *doc. cit.*

44. Savio alla Scrittura, 193, 3 Feb.

45. Tests of a new type of breech-loader on the Lido range in 1590 were attended not only by the *proveditori* of artillery, the *patroni* of the Arsenal and the professional superintendent of fortifications, but all 'li nobili nostri che si trovano al presente in città che hanno fin hora portato fanò' – i.e. served as galley commanders. S.M.D.R. 51, f.101.

46. S.M.D.R. 61, f.8.

47. While there are references to 'prepackaged' fustian cartridges (*scartozzi*) – e.g., Cl.X.C.D.R. 21 Mar. 1566, f.93^V – it seems unlikely that sufficient quantities were made up in advance, given the damp conditions of naval gunnery.

48. Scuole Piccole, 257, Capitolare, 20 Oct.

49. *Ibid.*, 20 June.

50. Cl.X.C.D.R. 13, f.13^V.

51. S.M.D.R. 22, f.58 (a useful crew list for a 'galion grande'), confirmed by the crew list for a great galley in 1538, S.M.D.R. 24, f.103^V-104.

52. E.g., Savio alla Scritture, 193, 8 Aug. 1607.

53. S.S.D.R. 78, ff.187-8^V. Venice had agreed to raise her contribution to 130, 'computate le grosse a una per due sottili'. 160 is the number of oarsmen for a light galley that appears most frequently.

54. S.M.D.R. 20, ff.7-8^V.

55. Padua 800, Vicenza 800, Verona (and Colognese) 800. Brescia (and Salò and Riviera) 1,200, Crema 200, Bergamo 600, Udine (and Friuli as a whole) 700, Treviso 800, Rovigo and the Polesine 200.

56. 'da ogni gravezze, si personale come real per quello pagano sopra li estimi della persona sua, a le qual gravezze mai in alcun caso possuno essere astretti etiam che fosse statuito ed ordinato che exempti havessero a contribuire'.

57. The Council of Ten, responsible for public order, subsequently cut this down to the times when men were actually going to join, or were returning from their vessels.

58. 'exceptuanda li debiti de afficti et livelli che stimo de lire 50 de pizoli in suso'.

59. S.M.D.R. 23, ff.39^V-40.

60. S. T[erra] D.R. 28, ff.94^V-95^V.

61.   S.M.D.R. 23, ff. 182^V-183; S.T.D.R. 29, f.158.
62.   S.M.D.R. 24, ff.53-54.
63.   *Ibid.*, 35, ff.65-69^V, 22 March.
64.   Marciana Library, Venice, MSS, It. VII, 1213 (8656) f.62^V. On f.65^r there is a 'Carrata de Terra ferma per homini 8,000 per armar galie 50 a 160 per galia' which itemises the men enrolled in each territory. The exact total is 8,026. The manuscript is undated but appears to be c.1550.
65.   Provisions listed on ff.203-205 of the *doc. cit.* in n. 67.
66.   S.M.D.R. 55, ff.62-62^V. Eight were to be given along with pay on board, two witheld until debts incurred on board (e.g. treatment from *barbiero*) had been settled.
67.   S.M.D.R. 55, ff.200-202^V.
68.   Mentioned in S.M.D.R. 65, ff.4-4^V.
69.   A complete list (126 items) of the organisations and lagunar communities subject to these provisions is given in S.M.D.R. 61, ff.44-46.
70.   Cl.X.C.D.R. 13, f.3.
71.   S.S.D.R. 77, ff.31^V.
72.   S.M.D.R. 39, ff.295-295^V. Pointing out to the Duke that the fleet would be operating to the advantage of Christianity as a whole.
73.   S.S.D.R. 77, f.7^V. Voting on this proposal dragged on irresolutely from February to April 1571.
74.   S.S.D.R. 78, ff.56^V-57.
75.   *Ibid.*, ff.56^V-57.
76.   S.S.D.R. 78, ff.63^V-64.
77.   *Ibid.*, ff.123-123^V. Some Lepanto captives were still at the oar in 1616, when a merciful government released them to almshouses — because they had become Christians. S.M.D.R. 74, f.20^V.
78.   *Ibid.*, f.140.
79.   Procuratori di S Marco, 190, e.g. ff.3^V and 12. I owe this reference to Dr R. Muller.
80.   S.S.D.R. 78, ff.168^V-169^V.
81.   *Ibid.*, ff. 171^V-172 and 186^V.
82.   S.S.D.R. 79, 4 Apr.
83.   *Ibid.*, ff.100^V-102^V.
84.   E.g., when R. C. Anderson, *Naval wars in the Levant 1559-1853* (Princeton, 1952), 31, speaks with reference to 1570 of 'the time-honoured method of sending a division of galleys to raid the Archipelago . . . and a good haul of slaves secured'.
85.   E.g., in 1532 the *capitano general del mar* was allowed to accept volunteer *banditi* from Corfu, Dalmatia, Albania and Istria, and to determine when their sentences should be cancelled. S.M.D.R. 22, f.116.
86.   Cl.X.C.D., 8 Feb. 1579, ff.54-54^V.
87.   S.S.D.R. 105, ff.177-177^V.
88.   *Ibid.*, 106, ff.244-244^V.
89.   S.T.D.R. 87, ff.117-117^V. To these pious reasons was added the belief that 'ne conferire finalemente al nostro servitio'.
90.   S.S. Filze, 24 Jan. 1573.
91.   These debts were sometimes paid by the state, e.g. S.M.D.R. 33, f.70^r, more frequently by relatives, but in times when oarsmen were desperately in short supply, as during the War of Gradisca, the right to pay their debts in cash was suspended, and they were forced to row them off; S.M.D.R. 74, ff.55^V-56.
92.   S.M.D.R. 20, f.7^V. This provision of the sea militia ordinance of 18 March 1522 contradicts a decison of 1519 that the wage should be reduced to eight lire for the first four months and six thereafter.

93. Lane, *Venice, a maritime republic*, 366.
94. S.T.D.R. 35, ff.179bis-182.
95. One man per oar was probably the rule in the first half of the century, as the terms trireme, and quadrireme suggest. Writing in 1593 Francesco Duodo, noting that one oar per bench had proved more effective for light galleys, urged the adoption of the same principle for great galleys. Archivi propri, Contarini, 25, no. 1. For the adoption of this suggestion, S.M.D.R. 74, ff.85ᵛ-86ᵛ.
96. Cl.X.Misti D.R. 42, f.143. The word used is 'schiopeto', but the terminology used for firearms in this period was not yet standardised.
97. S.M.D.R. 21, ff.121ᵛ-122.
98. *Ibid.*, 24, f.141ᵛ.
99. *Ed. cit.*, 125-149.
100. 'Le memorie di un uomo da remo' [Aurelio Scetti], *Rivista Marittima* (1884), 217.
101. 'Buoni et sufficienti et periti arcierii'. S.M.D.R. 24, f.89ᵛ.
102. Da Canal, *ed. cit.*, 177, note. 50 bows were recorded, again in a light galley inventory, in 1574. S.M.D.R. 42, f.3-3ᵛ.
103. *Ibid.*, 75, f.29.
104. *Ibid.*, f.87; 'archi et frezzie, quale sono armi inutili et superflue'. Great galleys in 1570 had been issued with sixty arquebuses, twenty-five *archibusoni* and 100 bows — double stringed, so that two arrows could be discharged at once, saturation compensating for reduced accuracy. *Ibid.*, 39, f.165ᵛ
105. *Op. cit.* (Rome, 1614), 166-7.
106. V. Vitale, 'L'impresa di Puglio degli anni 1528-9', *Nuovo Archivio Veneto* (1907). See especially 162-3 for the capture of Molfetta.
107. Molmenti, 25.
108. E.g., S.S.D.R. 107, f.57.
109. Summarised in S.M.D.R. 37, f.149ᵛ.
110. S.S.D.R. 76, ff. 65-65ᵛ; *ibid.*, 78, f.1.
111. *Ibid.*, 78, ff.91ᵛ-92 and 85ᵛ.
112. S.M.D.R. 39, f.228, 12 Sept. 1570, on the effects of cold and rain on men unhardened to service in open galleys. Five thousand additional troops were raised, but could not get past the Turkish fleet blockading the mouth of the Adriatic to join the Venetian fleet off Messina in July-August 1571. Venice was forced, humiliatingly, to bring numbers up to 100 fighting men per galley by borrowing troops from Don Giovanni, thus giving a most unwelcome extra weight to his influence on strategic decisons.
113. Capi di Guerra, 1. 29 Sept. 1570.
114. Paolo Paruta, *Dell. historia venetiana 'ella guerra di Cipro* (Venice, 1645), 104-5; Collegio, Notatorio, R.38, ff.199ᵛ, 200ᵛ, 223ᵛ-224; Molmenti, *op. cit.*, 84.
115. Paruta, *op. cit.*, 148-9.
116. *Op. cit.*, 154-5.
117. Soldiers in galleys in 1570 got three ducats per 'month' (eleven per year), of which one third was stopped against loans and expenses over and above the basic ration; S.S.D.R. 76, f.66. At this time troops serving in garrisons *da mar* were being paid three ducats per calendar month; sea pay was brought into line with this in 1572; S.S.D.R. 78, f.154. By 1605, soldiers 'chi siano di questa citta, o Albanesi, Crovati, Greci, Dalmatini et de subditi dello stato nostro' were to get four ducats a calendar month; S.M.D.R. 65, f.24ᵛ. Four ducats (twenty-eight lire) was still the monthly rate in 1617; S.M.D.R. 75, ff.32ᵛ-33. I have not been able to find what effect these rates had on marines' pay in wartime.
118. Most commonly: *trombe* and *pignate*, i.e. wooden-cased iron tubes using an explosive charge to project flaming material, and fire bombs. E.g., S.M.D.R. 42,

ff.3-3^v, for eight *trombe* and sixty *pignate da fuoco* on a light galley.

119.   S.S.D.R. 76, ff.78-80 for a careful spelling out of the relations between naval commanders (*proveditori*, captain general, captains of the great galley and Gulf squadrons) and the military governor general of the troops in the galleys; 15 April 1570.

120.   As when Giacomo Foscarini, *Proveditore Generale* in Dalmatia (responsible for infantry, cavalry and fortifications), was switched in January 1572 to being captain general of the fleet (in association with Sebastiano Venier, the victor of Lepanto). S.S.D.R. 78, f.60^v.

THE ENGLISH CIVIL WAR AND ENGLISH SOCIETY

Ian Roy

The launching of a new publication in which the relationship between war and society will be examined may be thought a convenient point at which to review some of the more familiar territory in military history. The English Civil War is one such. Dr Gentles, in the article which follows this, offers a fresh interpretation of a famous event of the period, the revolt of the New Model Army in 1647. By relating the material grievances of the rank and file to the deteriorating political and economic situation of post-Civil War England, he and other historians are uncovering some of the ways in which the impact of the wars was absorbed by the community, and the ways the community responded to army mutinies and discontent. In these studies the rank and file of the armies hold the centre of the stage, alongside the common people of the localities.

Was there as much disorder on the part of the soldiery, and an equally violent response on the part of the civilian population, during the Civil War proper, as immediately afterwards? The materials to provide an answer to this question lie at the grass-roots level, and it is from the perspective of local history that the most satisfactory explanations will in future be provided. The object of this paper is to say something generally about the character of the Civil War, with these questions in mind, and to examine in greater detail the impact of invading forces in one locality at one moment of the war — the siege of Gloucester by the King's army in August-September 1643. A case study of this event may, it is hoped, throw some light on the question of popular participation in the Civil War.

At earlier crises in English history, when the government has been challenged, the common people have found a role. Historians of Tudor rebellion may debate the exact responsibility of the 'Commons', but they are in no danger of overlooking the non-gentry population altogether. The military history of the Great Rebellion has not yet made this breakthrough. Why not? One explanation is undoubtedly the influence still exerted on military history of the conventional kind by the master military theorist, Clausewitz. Military historians are still inclined to see even such a complicated, localised and 'popular' war as the English Civil War in terms of strategy and tactics; to depict armies as smooth military machines rolling over a neutral terrain; and to describe the war as almost exclusively a series of battles and sieges. The Olympian view adopted by Clausewitz and his disciples can hardly be expected to take much notice of popular involvement in the war at ground level. The perspective of the local historian is different. He sees mainly those elements of particularism and civilian obduracy which get in the way of generals' grand strategy. Some of the highest concepts of military theory dissolve into thin air when subjected to closer examination. Viewed at ground level the grand strategy of the Civil War, so dear to military theory, seems a mere chimera. To the historians of Staffordshire the movement of troops in the county appears to have as much direction as 'ducks on a pond'.[1] Altogether too much military precision has been given to the hurly burly of England's 'civil broils'.

Perhaps the time has come for a new model of military history to replace the old Clausewitzian type. It has recently been suggested[2] that a better set of references would be provided by the modern theory of revolutionary warfare, and that this would be the most appropriate model to use in the study of 'popular' wars, such as the Civil War and the War of American Independence. This proposal at least has the merit of inviting the historian of war to alter his traditional stance and see war in a social context.

Whether influenced by this interesting suggestion or not, American historians have adopted a more integrated approach to the War of Independence. For the historian of the Civil War it is instructive to see the progress made in this direction in the work reviewed below by Professor Stuart. In the books he discusses and the articles he refers to, the war is broadly conceived, and is closely related to the structure of colonial society. The involvement of the colonial population, assemblies and militia, and the popular response to the armies waging the war, are of prime importance to these historians. The political and military history of the American War is more closely integrated, and as a result, the War is better understood than the English Civil War.

That public opinion will play an influential role in the conduct of the Civil War comparable to that of colonial opinion in the later war, is virtually guaranteed by the character of the wars which were fought in an age — before Clausewitz, so to speak — when military organisation was relatively primitive and armies could not depend on the regular satisfaction of all their needs by the High Command. Seventeenth-century soldiery took what they needed, more often than not, from the countryside, in free quarter and pillage. The forces put in the field for most of the Civil War were not self-sufficient, well paid, competently officered 'barracks armies'. They could not be carefully screened from civil society. They were not mercenaries imported from abroad, but were recruited directly from the ranks of the civilian population, on whose resources they were dependent for their continuance. In other words there was a close and abiding relationship between the armies and the society that supported them, so close that the civil and military functions of the county committees, and the status of the soldier and that of the civilian, can only with difficulty be distinguished. The immunity of the non-combatant was very imperfectly recognised, despite the claims of both sides that they wished to protect lives and property.

The Commons had played an active part in the events which preceded the outbreak of the war. Popular unrest accompanied the constitutional crisis of 1641-2, when London apprentices rioted against the bishops. Fed by fears aroused by the Irish rebellion, and the suspicion of Catholic plotting in England, waves of anti-Papist and anti-Cavalier hysteria swept the country, and there were numerous attacks on the houses of recusant gentry. Depression in the cloth industry gave a sharper edge to the complaints of the West Riding towns, and parts of the West Country. Several pro-Royalist landlords found themselves opposed by their tenants when sides had to be taken. Some of the King's greatest supporters, appearing at the start of the war to rally support in the areas where they customarily exercised most influence, were dismayed to find strong opposition by the Commons. The Marquess of Hertford, at the head of the Royalist gentry of Somerset, was faced by the massed ranks of the country farmers and weavers, and was forced to flee.

Equally well known are the demonstrations for peace and of neutrality which took place towards the end of the war. In 1645 there was widespread civil disturbance as the population began to rebel against the burdens placed on it by the war. The Clubmen, a popular movement which affected several western counties, was strong and well organised. Ten to fifteen thousand men appeared in Hertfordshire to oppose the Royalist Governor of Hereford garrison. In Somerset and Dorset primitive armies were organised to work for peace, and defend property, which were strong enough to treat with the New Model Army itself. At this stage of the war, the Clubmen tended to support that side which could win a quick victory and a lasting peace, and which maintained the best control over its troops. When the war was over, resistance to the continuance of the armies of Parliament rose to new heights, coinciding, as it did, with a major subsistence crisis. The hostility society felt towards the soldiers, and the unwillingness of the political authorities to settle their arrears, increased the resentment of the rank and file. 'In several counties . . . fighting broke out between soldiers and armed civilian bands.'[3] A vicious circle of disorderly behaviour by the troops increased their unpopularity and provoked civilian resistance, which in turn moved the soldiery to more deperate measures, mutinies and attacks on county committeemen. These were the circumstances influencing provincial armies as well as the New Model Army in 1647. Can we assume that during the middle years of the war popular agitation, so manifest before and after, was neutralised or contained? The evidence is unclear. It is certainly true that conservative elements in the Parliamentarian leadership, increasingly alarmed at the strength of popular feeling, grew lukewarm in espousing the popular cause. In the shires, the moderate gentry on both sides got together to calm things down, and in some counties to make pacts of neutrality. The majority of the people, once the war had broken out, were shown to be not firm partisans of one side or the other; few were determined on a fight to the finish. The cry of 'Peace, Peace' by London women crowding Palace Yard, Westminster, as early as December 1642, was echoed by the 'old song of "Home, Home" ' sung by Waller's London troops, apprentices on campaign, in the summer of 1644. Failures of leadership at London and Oxford may have deflated hopes raised earlier, and allowed the peasantry to lapse into a sullen neutralism.[4] If this reasoning is correct, and there was a decline in party allegiance, there would consequently be room for a response, owing more to self-interest than political or religious commitment, to the facts of the war itself, the domination of one army or another, and to the way each side conducted the war. Attitudes to political authority, as well as the authority itself, would be transformed by the great changes brought about by Civil War, and to these we must now pay some attention.

For most Englishmen war was a novel experience. England in the 1630s was not a premier military power in Europe, and possessed neither a standing army nor an establishment capable of supporting one. The training of ordinary citizens in the militia was not taken seriously, except in the artillery gardens of the capital. The means whereby the government might raise troops in an emergency, or for foreign expeditions, was rusty. The assembling of the armies to oppose the Scots in 1638-40 seemed almost beyond the capacity of the nation, too hard a task for the government. Charles I had met political resistance in his attempts to reform the militia; political traditions and the Common Law ran counter, and the Grand Remonstrance even objected to the modest activities of the saltpetremen, as inimical to English liberty.

When a resort to arms became inevitable in 1642, therefore, both sides would have to enter new and unfamiliar territory, create armies where none had existed before, abandon cherished principles in order to impose huge and novel burdens on society. The needs of the Civil War transformed England within a decade from a militarily backward and pacific kingdom into an army dominated republic in the forefront of European affairs, with armed forces which matched those of her Continental rivals. Calculations of numbers cannot be precise, but it may be estimated that fewer than 1,000 were in the military service of Charles I before the Civil War, even if the servants of the Ordnance Office at the Tower are included. If we take the broadest view possible, and include those subjects of the King in foreign pay, such as the soldiers of the Anglo-Dutch brigade and the recently increased government army in Ireland (many of whom were Welsh, and later native Irish), the number will not exceed 10,000. When men were needed for the armies of the Scots Wars, 1638-40, they had to be pressed by the county lieutenancy, and they were speedily disbanded in 1641. Within a year of the start of the war, however, conscription had been introduced and there were probably over 110,000 in arms throughout England, fighting on one side or the other. We must remember that a civil war needs twice as many soldiers as a normal war. The peacetime establishment was not just doubled or trebled, but increased 110-fold. A major alteration had been effected in English life. The nation achieved, at a stroke, a high proportion of soldiers to civilians — a proportion comparable to that maintained by Revolutionary and Napoleonic France, though falling short of the figures reached in the era of Total War in the twentieth century. The vast majority of those who now joined up had no previous military experience — like the King and Cromwell themselves. The soldiers of the early years of the Civil War were simply citizens in arms, anxious to return to their homes as soon as possible. Although both sides called in a small number of foreign military experts there was no separate officer caste or the nucleus of a professional army which could be mobilised and expanded by slow stages, and so save the people the trouble of fighting. It was all to do.

The key to army size is finance. Justices in the shires, and MPs at Westminster, during the years of peace, had bitterly resisted the military demands, modest though they were, of the government. The same men, now in their places on the county committees running the war, the Long Parliament or the King's Counter-Parliament at Oxford, were obliged to consent to war taxation on a massive scale. Novel, un-English and thoroughly detested imposts, such as a realistically assessed land tax, and the excise ('that damned Dutch device'), were introduced, and soon both sides were confiscating the goods and estates of those who refused to pay. At Westminster, Pym guided these controversial measures through Parliament with great skill, exploiting the distrust felt for the King. At Oxford the Royalists persuaded or forced those counties within their power to enter into agreements to pay 'Contribution', a tax based on the German *Kontribution* system in operation during the Thirty Years War. Huge sums were raised in this way. Wealthier Parliamentarian counties, such as Suffolk and Kent, paid over £¼ million each in assessment over the war years. But this was only the half of it; an equal or larger sum was expended in free quarter for the troops.[5] Royalist demands were even heavier, for the area they controlled was poorer. Oxfordshire paid £61,000 p.a. under the terms of the contribution treaty of 1643; this was seventeen times higher than the ship money level at its height, and ten times as onerous as the 1641 Parliamentary subsidy. When the King's forces took Gloucestershire, £6,000 a month was demanded of the county. Step by step the King kept pace with Parliament, introducing the same measures, over-riding property rights without Parliamentary consent.[6]

For the ordinary individual the war was difficult to avoid. Men were dragged from the plough or the harvest wagon, for campaigns took place in the summer season, at the height of the farming year. Lord Fairfax in Yorkshire remarked on the reluctance of men to enlist during harvest time: Royalist Commissioners at Swansea, on the other hand, feared that the harvest there could not be brought in, the country having been 'so gleaned of people' on the King's behalf.[7]

The farmers' draught animals were seized, their houses and goods pillaged, their produce and transport waylaid on the way to market. Not only the taxpayer and the pressed man but the householder and the innkeeper (required to quarter troops), the agricultural labourer and artisan (obliged to work on the defences of the nearest garrison or fortified house), were involved. Even women and maids aided in the building of fortifications and in defence of their homes: they are mentioned as playing an active part during several sieges. The demands on the populace were backed up by force where necessary: cavalry – 'an unsanctified troop of horse' as one officer threatened[8] – were sent to enforce military orders which were not immediately obeyed. The condition of the hard-pressed parish official, torn between the intolerable demands of the soldiery and the unwillingness of the country people to obey, was pitiable. A warrant from the Governor of Devizes to a Wiltshire constable survives: on the back the unhappy man has scrawled, 'Woe is me, poor Ba[stard].' Many local officials ran away; others were murdered.[9]

Men's livelihoods were endangered by the interruption of communications by river and road, the stoppage of trade, the deliberate seizure of transport. Trade between London and Newcastle, between Bristol and the towns on the Severn, between the West and the capital (Royalist garrisons sat athwart the main roads), and many drove roads, such as that from North Wales to Shrewsbury, were either closed for long periods during the war, or were subject to frequent interruption. The sufferings of those dependent on the exchange of agricultural produce or manufactured goods by these routes were great. As the Civil War was a host of little wars, local marketing was also disrupted.

While the war was sporadic rather than continuous, and affected some regions much more than others, no region was completely free from political or military conflict. Even countries distant from the battleground, such as Norfolk or Kent, contained active minorities at odds with the dominant military command, and endured local risings, bloodily suppressed. It is a common error to think of any class, town or county as politically monolithic during the course of this great political crisis, through years of high political excitement. It was this internecine quality of the war which gave it its special terror in the eyes of contemporaries. In divided counties rival garrisons raided each other, attempted to lay waste the countryside round about and so destroy the economy on which the other depended. Newark and Nottingham, Ashby-de-la-Zouch and Derby, Abingdon and Oxford (in 1645) all engaged in local skirmishing of this kind.

There was considerable destruction which was not directly due to enemy action, but was related to the conditions imposed by the war. There were terrible accidents attributable to the disruptive presence of troops, such as the fire at Oxford in 1644 caused by a soldier overheating a stolen pig. Several flourishing towns paid the penalty for pre-war expansion beyond their ancient walls: whole suburbs were pulled down by the inhabitants in the interests of defence. At Gloucester one fifth of the city's stock of houses (including 'very large and fair buildings', altogether valued at over £28,000) were lost in this way.[10] Examples of severe damage due to the fighting abound. Two thirds of Taunton was destroyed in the siege of 1645. It did, however, escape being captured. Some of the richest towns in the country were 'miserably sackt' during the war, and in terms of personal loss this must have been the worst fate of all.

It was fortunate for the country that the war years were marked by good harvests. Food prices remained low, and it was not till the end of the war that poor harvests reinforced the economic disruption caused by the fighting and led to a food crisis. The considerable margin of spare or underused labour in the seventeenth-century economy may have helped to absorb the bad effect of the diversion of labour from agriculture and industry into the war effort. The prosperity of the 1650s repaired much of the damage of the 1640s, and made good losses suffered in the Civil War. For these reasons the real cost of the war was concealed.

Was the Civil War correspondingly bloody? In terms of battle-connected casualties the answer must be 'No'. But as with most wars until the present age, the majority of those who died were the victims of disease and seventeenth-century medicine. Lives were at risk not only by the frequent disorders which accompanied the passage or the presence of armies, but by the diseases which the soldiery brought with them as certainly as their baggage trains and their whores. From

30

classical times armies have been associated with the spreading of epidemics. Overcrowded camps and garrisons were pestilential in the Civil War: Oxford in most summers, Banbury in 1644, Bristol in 1645. As well as frequent visitations of the plague, the war saw outbreaks of typhus, a form of the disease known as 'morbus campestris', smallpox and the 'bloody flux' (bacillary dysentery). It was the latter which forced the Royalist garrison to surrender Arundel Castle at Christmas 1643. It was an attack of typhus which halted both Royalist and Parliamentarian armies at Reading in April 1643. The burial registers of several garrisons show a huge leap in mortality in the three middle years of the war. In Banbury the permanent garrison was small, about 600 men. In the years 1642-5 the death rate among the soldiery was over 10 per cent p.a. For the civilian population of the town the mortality rate was probably trebled during the war. These figures can be matched by Oxford, Bristol, Exeter and other places.[11]

There were, therefore, few innocent bystanders in the English Civil War, few spectators of this great drama who were not to some degree themselves involved. This is why I am doubtful of the apocryphal tale of the ploughman who stumbles on the rival armies drawn up on Marston Moor for the imminent battle, and who remarks, when it is explained to him that King and Parliament are about to fight, 'What! Are them two fallen out again?'

The prime danger in these circumstances was that the presence of the armies and the heavy demands they made, would be resisted: that one side or the other would fail in the task of gaining and keeping the obedience of the populace in these matters. A battle developed for the political support of the Commons. To fight this campaign both sides used the weapons of political persuasion in addition to the ultimate sanction of force. A propaganda barrage had begun before the opening shots of the Civil War itself, and continued as a 'paper war' during the fighting. Apologists for King or Parliament set forth their case in newspapers, printed sermons and pamphlets. The propaganda war took also more exotic and ephemeral forms, such as political pageantry (as at funeral processions and orations, public fanfares and pronouncements by the heralds), the staging of mock battles with a political message, political mottoes woven on regimental colours, and astrological predictions of a partisan character.

To win adherents both sides had to make concessions, while at the same time, paradoxically, they were making greater demands on the goodwill of the population than ever before. To gain and keep support they had to offer inducements, such as protection, a share in the spoils of war, even a voice in decision making. On Parliament's side commanders courted popularity by taking an oath 'to live and die' with their common soldiers. It is probably significant that the King's camp

considered this both ridiculous and foolish.[12] And it may not be
irrelevant in this context, where reference has already been made to
the participation of the Commons in earlier English disturbances, to
note that the phrase was employed in the Pilgrimage of Grace, when
the Commons of Sleaford persuaded Lord Hussey to take such an oath.

An important part of the campaign to sway public opinion was the
well-publicised concern of both sides for the welfare of the subject
during the war. The 'needless effusion of Christian blood and treasure'
was constantly deplored. Both sides took whatever political advantage
could be obtained by proposing treaties of peace, and continuing them
as long as possible. The King's concern for the casualties after a battle
extended to the soldiers of Parliament, according to Royalist news-
books. Charles, despite the poor reputation he has in these matters,
kept continuously in mind during the war the importance of a 'good
press'. The Oxford Royalist newspaper was one of the best of the war.
The editor was primed with good stories and told how to handle them
to the best effect. The King publicly reminded Rupert that military
methods appropriate to Germany must not be used in England. He frequently counselled his commanders on the importance of winning
public support. Through his secretary he wrote to the governor of one
garrison to thank him for restoring teams of horses to their rightful
owners: 'This kind of treating the country will not only win reputation to yourself, but hearts to His Majesty and affections to his service.'[13] What is this but the winning of the hearts and minds of the
people, thought so essential to success in modern revolutionary warfare?

Some commanders managed to achieve popularity in the districts
where they held command, or at least to gain the acquiesence of the
existing civil authority and most of the civilian population. By respecting the accredited representatives of the county, by tempering his military demands, and by keeping good discipline among his troops, a
governor or provincial general might win the active cooperation of the
people, without which his operation in the area would suffer. Hopton,
in Somerset with his forces in June 1643, found the county 'not re-
lucting at free-quarter soberly taken'.[14] The New Model Army in the
west in 1645 surprised the country people by paying its way and exer-
cising strict discipline over its rank and file; in return they supplied
necessary food and billets.

But the possibility of resistance by the Commons remained. Historians are agreed that there was a notable increase in political and social
insubordination in the Civil War. Where rival powers competed for the
support of the people, resorted to political weapons and made political
concessions, there was probably a decline in unthinking obedience by
the subject. The appeals of King and Parliament in 1641-2 heightened

political awareness and encouraged an independent spirit among those who had existed previously only to be ruled. The war saw a weakening of social and political ties, as pressures increased on the existing framework of legal and political authority. There were fewer meetings of the assize courts, of the J.P.s in Quarter Sessions and of the church courts. The surviving records of the normal judicial processes indicate widespread disruption and neglect. Like supreme political authority itself, the great law courts were weakened by being divided between London and Oxford, and by the general uncertainty of the times. A murder case at Weymouth illustrates this decline in keeping the peace. A householder was accused of killing his lodger, a wealthy merchant, and dumping his body in the new earthworks of the town. At his trial it was alleged that he had said to his wife, 'It was no matter for killing of a man now 'twas time of war.'[15]

But insubordination was not necessarily partisan, nor directed to the furtherance of the cause of one side or the other. It has already been suggested that the popular agitation in favour of Parliament had subsided under the impact of the war by 1643. If there was a weakening of political obedience because of the fragmentation of recognised authority, there was a strengthening of the military power. The creation of armies tilted the balance, not in favour of the old order in church and state, but the new authorities, county committee and Council of War, against popular disturbance. If political persuasion failed, the newly armed powers could compel obedience. The Marquess of Hertford, rejected in Somerset at the start of the war, returned at the head of an army; he was joined by Hopton's Cornish forces, and together they could subdue the area. The heavy demands made by the armies, discussed above, were hard to bear, and increased civil-military antagonism; but even if the army orders were only half obeyed, the acquisition of men, money and resources, and so power and authority, by the military command, would increase its security against popular attack. Commanders could transfer forces raised in loyal areas to those still recalcitrant, and crush the opposition. Much military policy had this end in view. To quell resistance Royalist garrisons were planted on Puritan Newbury ('a factious town') and Banbury, famous for dissent; and Puritan Birmingham was sacked by Rupert.

If recruitment was successful the ranks of the civilian population were thinned, the power of the military increased. Account must be taken, in assessing the apparent decline of political commitment, of the humbling and disillusioning experience which service in the armies of the day had on some eager partisans.[16] The first armies raised by Parliament were far from saintly. They served as a school for robbery and deceit, rather than religious devotion. The conduct of some Parliamentary garrisons in previously sympathetic areas must have had the same effect on a wider scale. Successive Governors of Berkeley Castle for Parliament, a Scotsman and an Irishman, plundered this Puritan neighbourhood with impunity. Did its political sympathies survive this harsh treatment?

There were of course dangers in this course of action, as those who argued for peaceable persuasion recognised. High handed behaviour by the military might provoke a much more organised and sustained resistance on the part of the Commons. If ill feeling between soldiers and civilians degenerates into violence, the former, dependent on the countryside for supply, are not necessarily in an unassailable position. Much will depend on the mood of the people, the quality of the generalship, the discipline of the soldiery, even the nature of the terrain. If the violence becomes widespread, the military command might find itself facing a hostile and armed population, capable of defending themselves. Groups of partisans, protected and supported by society, might even be better weaponed than the soldiery: clumsy matchlocks in the hands of poorly trained troops would be inferior to the fowling pieces the hunting squirearchy, their tenants and servants, more expertly handled. Personal arms, including firearms, were probably more commonly owned by householders in the seventeenth century than in the twentieth.[17] Better regulated armies than those of the Civil War have failed to deal effectively with parties of well armed farmers, equipped with a good knowledge of the local terrain and drawing support from a sympathetic population. In these circumstances the model of modern guerrilla warfare is distinctly more useful to the historian than the categories and definitions of Clausewitz.

Disorder and insubordination at this time might well come from the soldiery, rather than the civilian population. The loud lamentations of the nobility and gentry immediately before the war and during the first months of fighting, concerning the behaviour of the hydra-headed multitude, were replaced by their complaints against the upstart military men, now enjoying their houses and estates under cover of military necessity. The world was turned upside down, but now by the soldiers rather than the Commons. 'God of His mercy amend it; or the soldiers will have all; for they are masters of all', wrote the Earl of Middlesex's steward.[18] The civilian population began to obey the greater power, the military, at the expense of the weaker, the civil. Tenants, hard pressed by the military exactions imposed on them, withheld rent from their landlords and tithe payments from the church. Others followed the soldiers' example and seized what they could, taking advantage of the general disorder to free themselves of longstanding and vexatious obligations, and to settle private scores. The tenantry of the Cecils followed the marauding Royalist troops into Cranborne House in Dorset, in May 1643, and destroyed the court rolls which contained the

34

records of their copyhold tenures.[19]

If the opportunity arose, however, the actions of the Commons would go beyond casual looting and the occasional murder. The acceptance or rejection by the civilian population of the military authority imposed on them would depend on local conditions; and there might be particular circumstances which would favour their resistance to army demands, in spite of a prevailing neutralism after a year of war. The situation in August 1643, when the Royalists had taken Bristol and laid plans for the siege of Gloucester, provided that opportunity, and this important crisis of the war deserves a closer study.

The Royalist army was supreme at this juncture. With the conquest of Bristol, 'the King's country reached from the utmost Cornwall to the borders of Scotland', as John Corbet, a Puritan minister in Gloucester and chaplain to Governor Massey, said with pardonable exaggeration.[20] None of the Parliamentarian leaders of the region remained in the area after the Royalist triumph: several were at Westminster. The last vestiges of organised resistance from Parliamentarian outposts were quickly extinguished, and Gloucester stood alone. If the city could be taken the whole region, the richest the King's forces had yet seen, would fall to the Royalists: and they looked forward to exacting a high price for its former disobedience: 'a rich and populous county . . .' wrote Clarendon, 'might be wholly in the King's quarters; and by how much it had offended and disquieted the King more than any other counties, by so much the more money might be raised upon them'.[21]

In the military events which followed the capture of Bristol the political and economic background of the area is of the first importance. The country near Bristol and Gloucester consisted of the much enclosed, fertile dairy farming vales of Gloucester and Berkeley, and, beyond, the cold plateau of the Cotswolds, with their extensive sheep walks. To the west, over the Severn, lay the different countryside, of woodland, iron working and coal mining, of the Forest of Dean. In the events we are to describe, the northern parts of Somerset and Wiltshire, which bordered this region, were also involved. These areas were indeed 'rich and populous', producing butter and cheese, and with the by-employment of clothmaking. Farms were held by single families, whose outlook was independent in politics and religion. Because of enclosure traditional manorial control was absent: there was less gentry dominance than in most areas of England. The dairymen, graziers, part-time farmers and workers in industry in this region constituted a fairly representative sample of what contemporaries described as the 'middling sort'. And it is worth recalling that it was in the still afforested areas that royal monopolists and enclosing landlords had met most resistance: in the West Country, the revolt of 'Lady Skimmington' ten years before. The woodlanders and free miners of the Forest of Dean were notoriously lawless.

The politics of the dairy farmers were largely Parliamentarian, their religion Puritan. John Aubrey, their neighbour and a severe critic, believed their dairy produce ('Milke meates') was responsible: it was too easy to produce, giving the farmers both material prosperity and the leisure to think for themselves: it made their bodies 'plump and foggy' and 'cooled their brains too much'.[22] Another of their countrymen, the pious Royalist gentleman and captain in Maurice's army, Richard Atkyns, observed: 'The parts about Gloucester . . . happened to be most unanimous for the Parliament.'[23] Although Waller had his doubts, it was generally thought the vast majority were active Parliamentarians.[24]

This was the reputation the region enjoyed among Royalists: but, as has already been argued, no area of England was unanimous for one side or the other. Despite the evidence of Captain Atkyns, Gloucestershire proves on closer examination to be no exception to this rule. There were Royalists in Puritan Gloucester. A list of 104 citizens, 'reputed to be loyall', was drawn up in the King's camp, no doubt to identify potential fifth columnists in the coming siege, or those to be protected when the town was stormed.[25] The majority of the inhabitants, 'ten for one' according to the Governor, Massey, were 'averse' to the military government and the Puritan magistracy which held power in the city.[26] Massey's own loyalty to Parliament was suspect, and the city fathers were divided. It was only after long debate that they decided to resist the impressive forces of the King, fresh from their triumph at Bristol. In the county as a whole the gentry, said Clarendon, 'for the most part were well affected' to the King, and if they had not already done so, hastened to aid the Royalist forces when they over-ran the region.[27]

The chronicler of these events in Gloucester, John Corbet, although himself a committed Parliamentarian, recognised that, as within the city, so beyond its walls, the majority were moved by expediency, and in the interests of self-preservation would prefer to make terms with the King, as the dominant party. Further resistance would lead to the general destruction of their corn and cattle. 'Whereas if the enemy should prevail, they were sure to rest in the heart of the King's countrey, farre from spoile and plunder, and have as free and ample trade as in times of peace.'[28] A petition to the King from Gloucestershire clothiers for resumption of their trade, badly hit by the war, is indicative of this mood.[29] Anxious for peace, even at the price of Royalist domination, the county's first reaction to Gloucester's decision to resist was outright dismay: 'the whole countrey forsook us', wrote Corbet.[30] If the Royalist troops had treated the country people well, as Hopton had done earlier when he had made terms with Somerset, self-interest alone on their part would have led them to cooperate with the victorious army in their midst.

But the Royalist army was difficult to control; particularly after it had won a victory. It must be remembered that few armies of the period were well paid, and certainly none in the Civil War before the foundation of the New Model Army in 1645. The promise of 'constant pay' to that body was not fulfilled, as Dr Gentles makes clear. In lieu of regular pay the soldier and sailor could look forward only to prizes; in the case of the military it was the expectation of the pillage of captured cities and defeated armies which was an inducement to remain with the colours when pay was not forthcoming. The military law of the day laid down rules for the taking of plunder, and attempted to regulate this important matter. But the laws of war were seldom carried out to the letter, and whatever the efforts of the commanders might be to protect a captured city from wholesale pillage and indiscriminate destruction, rioting troops usually had the upper hand. Rupert was as helpless at Bristol as Essex had been at Reading, or Tilly at Magdeburg. In spite of the safeguards for the citizens embodied in the terms of the surrender treaty, Bristol was given up to looting for two days. The King's generals ordered some units out of the city to distant quarters, but this solution was frustrated by the desertion of officers and men who feared to lose their share in the plunder of the city.[31] The effect of their sudden success on a badly paid and ill-disciplined army was calamitous, as it was to be in very similar circumstances at Leicester in 1645. Atkyns, who was at Bristol, remarked that the failure to keep the articles of surrender 'did moulder two gallant armies', the Oxford and the Cornish; the latter took no further part in this campaign.[32]

Once finished with the city the Royalist forces turned their attention to the country nearby, which lay at their feet. As the High Command debated whether to attack Gloucester, and strove to restore discipline to their forces for this purpose, the soldiery broke into the countryside. The apparent hostility of the inhabitants, and their seemingly defenceless state, encouraged the King's men to treat the populace as they had treated the citizens of Bristol. Clarendon explained the situation: 'A very great license broke into the army, both amongst officers and soldiers; the malignity of those parts being thought excuse for the exercise of any rapine or severity amongst the inhabitants; . . . all which brought great clamour upon the discipline of the army and justice of the officers, and made them likewise less prepared for the service they were to expect.'[33] One reason for the breakdown of military discipline was the bitter quarrel in the High Command over the Governorship of Bristol, and the resulting delays in giving orders to the army: another was the conduct of the regimental officers, who hardly

37

set their men a good example, busying themselves in arresting and ransoming the rich clothiers and farmers — 'the yeomanry', as Clarendon said, 'who had been most forward and seditious, being very wealthy and able to redeem their delinquency at a high price' — and running protection rackets.[34] Several of the protections sold to Gloucestershire inhabitants who could afford them survive in the county's archives.[35]

Among other evidence of the depredations of the King's forces we have five recently discovered proclamations, which show that the commanders were desperately attempting to restore discipline in the army.[36] In the time and circumstances none of these could be printed, but copies were made in the writing office of the Secretary-at-War and circulated among the units. That they were widely distributed in the area may be indicated by the finding of one in the last century behind the wainscoting of an old house in Tewkesbury! At frequent intervals (the five were issued in the period 6-30 August 1643) they prohibited desertion and straggling, plunder and the robbery of country people bringing their goods to market, and the sending out of exorbitant demands. The last was a common device to give legal sanction to robbery. Warrants making impossible demands on the local inhabitants were issued: the country people inevitably failed to comply: the army then distrained their goods with impunity. The implication of these orders is clear enough. They are a catalogue of the more persistent crimes of the soldiery during the time of the siege, and provide an insistent commentary on their outrageous behaviour.

The tone and content of the proclamations to the troops before Gloucester are well caught in that of 12 August, issued from Matson House, the King's Headquarters, which is worth reproducing here for the first time in its entirety.[37]

'We being informed that divers soldiers both of horse and foot and others pretending themselves to be of our army do wander about the country robbing and spoiling our subjects and taking away provisions of victual coming for the use of our army before Gloucester, do straightly require and command the chief officers of our horse to cause all such as shall be found so offending to be apprehended and hanged without mercy; and to send forth parties to perform the same. And further to give straight charge and command that no officer or soldier under their command shall plunder, rob or spoil any of our subjects or take away any provision of victual of what kind soever coming to the commissary of the victuals, or for the use of our army, upon pain of death. This we require them to publish in all the horse quarters of our army, that it may be observed accordingly. 12 August, Matson.'

[spelling modernised]

The outrages of the soldiery tipped the political balance in the region against an accommodation with the Royalists. The neutralist majority could not remain indifferent to the destruction of their property and the injury of their families. Even those who had bought protections, willingly or not, from the King's officers, found they gave no guarantee of immunity against the undistinguishing troops. They too would have to defend themselves and side with the Puritan minority, who now no doubt took the lead in organising resistance. The example of Gloucester's decision to fight, and — as the month wore on — its success in doing so, although resented at first, must have influenced many.

If resistance might now be the wished for course of action, could it be successful? The country people in the vale around Gloucester did have one important factor in their favour. A letter from the Royalist General, Sir Arthur Aston, stationed at Painswick, to Prince Rupert, explained what this was:[38]

> 'I am forced to keep our horse upon perpetual duty for the want of foot, the country being so generally evil affected unto his Majesty, and besides so full of hedges and enclosures that our horse are not able to do anything against them, albeit the country people do themselves assault some of our quarters . . . But if I can by any means light upon them they shall pay dear for it . . . and indeed there is scarcely one of all these clothiers but have both lent money, and do maintain soldiers upon their own charges against his Majesty.'

The hedges and ditches of the enclosed dairy farming country (enclosed to keep the cattle in, ditched to drain the heavy clays of the valley) were the secret weapon, as it might be called, which safeguarded civilian resistance.

The other important advantage the local populace had was the poor discipline of the invaders, which had provoked their resistance in the first place, and the separation of the horse and foot, which Aston refers to. The natural defences of the terrain, better known to the country people than to the Royalist soldiers, was a major factor; equally crucial were the loss of the army's cohesion; its spawning of a host of runaways, laden with the booty of Bristol, stragglers and hangers-on, impossible to restrain; the dispersal of its quarters over a wide area, difficult to defend; and — the result of all these — the separation of the cavalry from the infantry. They needed each other: the horse to bring in provisions for the foot in camp, and for scouting; the foot to line the hedges and guard the passages for the horse, otherwise exposed to ambush. Now this vital cooperation, always under strain in the Royalist forces, snapped completely. The farmers were given their opportunity. They counterattacked with great determination and ferocity.

There spread in the month following the fall of Bristol, while the

King's army invested Gloucester, a wide insurgent movement, secret, violent and terrible; so that the area witnessed for some weeks a form of guerrilla warfare. The whole countryside was aflame. The depredations of the soldiery provoked resistance by the local population, which was punished by reprisals on the part of the military, which in turn led to more determined resistance. The pattern is familiar. It was a second war which the Royalists were forced to wage while at the same time they attempted to take Gloucester, a second war never referred to in the history books.

Strong parties of armed farmers roamed the countryside. The Governor of Berkeley Castle described to Rupert his increasingly desperate situation in early September:[39]

> 'The Country people have so augmented their former baseness that notwithstanding your Highness's warrants for victuals of the Castle I can't get any. The reason is they know, I have no forces but foot, and these I dare not send out, because they knock them down . . . the Country within six miles of this Castle did rise upon a troop of your Highness's horse, and killed six of them.'

To ambush an eighty-strong troop of the crack cavalry of the King's forces was a bold step, and must have required a party of men heavily armed and equally strong. The Governor's letter is an indication of the size and determination of the armed bands harassing the Royalists.

Civilian resistance took other forms than outright attack. The local people were in a strong position to deny vital supplies to the Royalist commissaries; to withhold information needed by the army; to ambush messengers, scouts and convoys of provisions — to interdict almost all the essential activities which maintain an army in the field. Even the poor woodmen and miners of the Forest of Dean had something valuable which they could withhold — their labour. The Sheriff of Gloucestershire, ordered to provide miners for the works at Gloucester (the Royalists were busy in mid-August undermining the city's defences on the southeast side), was met with refusals and desertion, as he confessed to the King's General of Artillery. Those he had summoned had fled home, and his officers were now pursuing them with 'strict orders . . . to bring them away by force . . . and burn the houses of those that resist or refuse instantly to come with them'.[40] Eventually miners were recruited, but from more distant South Wales, and too late to affect the course of the siege.

The general hostility of the region continued unabated as the siege progressed, and may even have increased as the cycle of resistance, reprisal and further resistance deepened. No doubt news of the Royalists' difficulties reached the besieged and encouraged them in the struggle, which had been so uncertainly begun. So the resistance of the one fortified the other. Not even the Royalists' use of a primitive form of tank, invented by the eminent Anglican divine, Dr William Chilling-worth, could bring success nearer: they were as far from capturing the city on 5 September, when Essex's relieving force was seen on Prestbury Hill, overlooking Gloucester, and they were forced to withdraw, as they had been when they summoned it on 10 August. They raised the siege, in an atmosphere of mutual recrimination which did lasting harm to the King's cause.

Yet this sorry episode, from the Royalist point of view, was not quite over. To relieve Gloucester the Parliamentarians had traversed an area stripped bare of foodstuffs, and their own supplies were exhausted. The King's Generals hoped to benefit from this situation, perhaps by surprising the enemy as they scattered in search of provisions. But again the country people took a hand in shaping events. They had one final indignity to administer to the Royalist forces at whose hands they had suffered. Clarendon tells what he called 'as wonderful as any part of the story'. The Parliamentarians, having reached Gloucester, 'caused all necessary provisions to be brought in to them out of those very quarters in which the King's army had been sustained, and which they conceived to be entirely spent: so solicitous were the people to conceal what they had, and to reserve it for them'.[41] Clarendon suspected cor-ruption in the royal officials, and certainly their sale of protections allowed stores to remain in 'enemy' hands. But clearly, too, the armed resistance of the farmers had had some success in keeping much needed supplies from the Royalist forces.

All historians, from Clarendon to the present day, agree that the King's failure to take Gloucester was a genuine turning point in the war. Essex's army, having supplied the city, fought its way past the Royalists at Newbury and returned in triumph to London. The best chance that the King had had of winning the war was lost. Gloucester remained a permanent impediment to the consolidation of the King's power in the western half of England, and an obstacle to the traffic, on which the Royalists depended, between South Wales and Oxford, and Bristol and Worcester. In the region itself Gloucestershire fell to Parliament by mid-1644, and remained in its hands thereafter. The Royalists continued dominant in Somerset and Wiltshire, however, Hopton at Bristol re-covering by gentler means what had been lost during the siege of Glou-cester. But the invasion of another rapacious Royalist army, under Goring, committing 'horrid outrages and barbarities' still remembered in Somerset a century later, finally alienated the country people. They were willing to support the New Model Army in July 1645 and so contributed to Goring's defeat at Langport.[42]

Viewed in the context of the war, the events of August-September 1643 were not untypical. The exact circumstances were not repeated, but parallel cases — like that of Goring in Somerset — were common. The King's army had met resistance on its march through the West Midlands in October 1642, from hostile country people who 'carried away or hid all their provisions'.[43] The Royalists' inability to obtain supplies was a factor in their decision to stand and fight at Edgehill. Essex's forces found themselves in worse case when they marched into Cornwall in summer 1644. The country people were inclined to Royalism, and considered the Parliamentarians invaders and disturbers of the peace. They harassed the troops, picked off stragglers and withheld supplies. As the army became weaker and more disorderly so the hostility of the Commons escalated. Cooped up by the King's forces at Lostwithiel the Parliamentarians surrendered. In each of these cases the armies were to some degree dependent on the cooperation of the populace, and its withdrawal contributed to their defeat.

If we apply these findings more generally we may obtain a clearer picture of what has remained as obscure and secret as the clandestine warfare of the summer of 1643. Beneath the surface of the grand strategy of the Civil War there existed a subterranean form of conflict, the disorder of the rank and file of the contending armies and the hostility of the civilian population to the troops. Multiplied over a wide area this conflict might hinder the operation of the armies themselves, and so alter the course of the war. This form of action and reaction by the Commons may be the bridge which links the agitation of the pre-Civil War years with the more organised civilian resistance of 1645 and beyond.

Notes

1.   D. H. Pennington and I. A. Roots (eds.), *The Committee at Stafford* (Manchester, 1957), 1xi.
2.   By Professor Dominick Graham, at the International Colloquy of Military History, R.M.A., Sandhurst, September 1974.
3.   J. S. Morrill, 'Mutiny and Discontent in English Provincial Armies, 1645-1647', *Past and Present*, 56 (1972), 73;
4.   The best account of this is B. S. Manning, 'Neutrals and Neutralism in the English Civil War, 1642-1646', unpub. Oxon. D.Phil. thesis, 1957.
5.   Morrill. *loc. cit.*, 51-2.
6.   Evidence to support these and other remarks concerning the Royalists will be given in full in my forthcoming study, *The Royalist Army*.
7.   Results and Orders of the Glamorgan Commissioners, 1643-44, National Library of Wales, Ll.MB.17, p. 32.
8.   B. Whitelocke, *Memorials of the English Affairs* (1853), I, 540.
9.   G. A. Harrison, 'Royalist Organisation in Wiltshire', unpub. London Ph.D. thesis, 1963, 342.
10.   J. Washbourn (ed.), *Bibliotheca Gloucestrensis* (1825), 379-85; see also Clarendon, *History of the Great Rebellion*, ed. W. D. Macray (1888), VII, § 163 (cited hereafter as Clarendon).

11.   J. S. Gibson (ed.), *Baptism and Burial Register of Banbury*, I (Banbury Historical Society, Vol. 7, 1965-6), *passim*.

12.   See the remarks made to Lady Verney in 1642, F. P. Verney (ed.), *Memoirs of the Verney Family* (1892), II, 64.

13.   Edward Nicholas to Sir William Campion, 9 March 1645, E. Sussex R.O., Danny MS. 49.

14.   C. Chadwyck Healey (ed.), *Bellum Civile* (Somerset Record Society, Vol. 18, 1902), 47.

15.   H. J. Moule, *Descriptive Catalogue of the Charters . . . of Weymouth, 1252-1800* (Weymouth, 1883), 77.

16.   See, for example, Nehemiah Wharton's experience in Essex's army in 1642, in H. Ellis (ed.), 'Letters from a Subaltern Officer . . .', *Archaeologia*, 35 (1853), *passim*.

17.   Cf. number of arms handed in by Oxford citizens and College members and servants, in 1643: I. Roy (ed.), *The Royalist Ordnance Papers*, I (Oxfordshire Record Society, Vol. 42, 1964), Section A.

18.   M. Prestwich, *Cranfield, Politics and Profits under the Early Stuarts* (Oxford, 1966), 572.

19.   L. Stone, *Family and Fortune . . .* (Oxford, 1973), 148-9.

20.   J. Corbet, 'The Military Government of Gloucester', in J. Washbourn (ed.), *op. cit.*, 39. Cited hereafter as Corbet.

21.   Clarendon, VII, § 157.

22.   O. L. Dick (ed.), *Aubrey's Brief Lives* (Harmondsworth, 1972), 47.

23.   P. Young and N. Tucker (eds.), *Military Memoirs of the Civil War: Richard Atkyns and John Gwyn* (1967), 7.

24.   *Calendar of State Papers Domestic, 1644*, 341; Corbet, 9, 16.

25.   B.L., Harl. MS.6804, f.118.

26.   S. R. Gardiner, *History of the Great Civil War* (1894), I, 198.

27.   Clarendon, VII, § 157.

28.   Corbet, 41.

29.   F. Madan, *Oxford Books* (Oxford, 1912), II, No. 1438; cf. Harl. MS.6804, f.114*.

30.   Corbet, 41.

31.   E. Warburton, *Memoirs of the Cavaliers* (1849), II, 262.

32.   P. Young and N. Tucker (eds.), *op. cit.*, 28-9.

33.   Clarendon, VII, § 201.

34.   *Ibid.*, § 157.

35.   For example, to Samuel Webb, clothier, of Lypiatt, 1643, Gloucestershire R.O., D 745. x4.

36.   Drafts in the hand of Edward Walker, Secretary-at-War, dated 6, 10, 12, 14 and 30 August 1643, Gloucestershire R.O., D 115, Nos. 4, 7, 8, 10, and Belvoir Castle, Lindsay Papers, QZ 23, f.32a. None of these is recorded in the standard collections of Stuart Proclamations.

37.   Gloucestershire R.O., D 115, No. 8.

38.   Aston to Rupert, 7 August 1643, Warburton, *op. cit.*, II, 276-7.

39.   G. Maxwell to Rupert, 8 September 1643, B.L., Add. MS.18980, f.117.

40.   I. Roy (ed.), *The Royalist Ordnance Papers*, II, 365.

41.   Clarendon, VII, § 206.

42.   D. Underdown, *Somerset in the Civil War and Interregnum* (Newton Abbot, 1973), 86-104.

43.   C. H. Firth, *Cromwell's Army* (1962), 214.

ARREARS OF PAY AND IDEOLOGY IN THE ARMY REVOLT OF 1647

Ian Gentles

'Constant pay' was intended to be one of the principal attractions of
the Army that was new modelled in the spring of 1645. Its finances
were centralised in London, and a monthly assessment was levied on
the counties under parliamentary control. While the soldiers were now
paid more faithfully than before, and the number of counties controlled by Parliament steadily rose, the New Model soldiers' pay fell
into arrears almost from the start. By the beginning of 1647 the Army
had built up a substantial economic grievance against its employer.
The back pay owing to all the parliamentary forces from the outbreak
of the civil war in 1642 to February 1647 has been estimated at nearly
£3 million. But at the same time as the Army was becoming restless
about its arrears, a swelling chorus of voices from all parts of the country was crying for Parliament to reduce its forces and ease the crushing
burden of taxation.[1]

Once the Scots Army had left English soil Parliament cut through
its financial dilemma by ordering the disbandment of most of the
English field army before settling a penny of its arrears. On 18
February 1647 the Commons resolved that apart from garrison forces,
only 5,400 horses and a thousand dragoons would be kept up in England. The New Model foot would be entirely dissolved. On 8 March
they purged the Army's high command by decreeing that no officer in
England except Sir Thomas Fairfax should henceforth hold rank higher
than a colonel. Fairfax himself narrowly escaped dismissal, being preferred as Commander-in-Chief over the undistinguished Presbyterian
colonel, Richard Graves, by a majority of only 159 to 147.[2] As if to
emphasise their dislike of military MPs like Cromwell, Ireton, Rainborow, Harrison, Fleetwood and Rich, the Presbyterian-led majority
further decreed that no member of the Commons should hold a military commission in England. Furthermore there would be no exceptions to the rule that all officers must conform to the Presbyterian system of church government.[3] The Commons' votes were endorsed by
the Lords, who hastened to demonstrate an equally strong desire to be
rid of the New Model.[4]

Having perceived Parliament's unconcern about their financial
plight, both officers and men resolved to take the initiative on their

own behalf. Meetings were called and petitions drafted. When a deputation from the Presbyterian dominated Derby House Committee for Irish Affairs went to meet the officers at Saffron Walden on 21 March, they were startled to be met by a united group who informed them that there would be no volunteers for the Irish Expedition until four questions were answered: 1. What regiments were to be kept up in England? 2. Who was to be the commander of the army in Ireland? 3. How were the soldiers who went to Ireland to be paid, fed and clothed? 4. What was going to be done 'in Point of Arrears and Indemnity, for the past Service in England?'[5] On the same day the officers submitted a petition to Parliament demanding satisfaction of arrears, freedom from prosecution for debt until arrears had been satisfied, an act of indemnity for actions committed by soldiers under military orders, compensation for the officers' personal expenses in raising men and supplies, and the abolition of county committees. To these military demands they appended a desire for the Church's re-establishment 'according to the word of God, and the example of the best-reformed churches', and for a guarantee of the benefit of Magna Carta and the Petition of Right for all Englishmen.[6]

Meanwhile, the rank and file had been circulating their own petitions addressed to Fairfax. According to the officers, some of the demands in these petitions extended to matters 'beyond the proper concernments of Souldiers'. In an effort to keep the unrest under control the officers took the most moderate petition,[7] removed the offensive passages and gave it their support. This edited version was similar to the officers', except that it contained no reference to religion or constitutional rights.[8] From both petitions it is clear that the level of political consciousness in the Army had not reached a dangerous point before the end of March 1647. While the soldiers cannot have been unaware of the hostility with which they were regarded in London and Westminster, there was as yet no serious thought of rebelling against parliamentary authority. While there had been a mutiny in Fairfax's lifeguard the previous month, the sole grievance had been arrears, and the men's anger had been directed at their commanders rather than Parliament. 'We shall be well paid for serving the state', they had jeered, 'we shall have liberty of conscience, and that's reward sufficient. What need yee aske for more?'[9] The soldiers were not yet politicised, for as Colonel Harley's informant told him, if Parliament would only provide money, they could do what they pleased with the Army.[10] Nor were civilian radicals yet interested in the Army's plight. At the beginning of March some young men and apprentices from London had expressed apprehension that the Army should be disbanded before the enemy had been completely subdued,[11] but the far more important Leveller *Petition of Many Thousands* of 16 March had not referred to the Army in any of its thirteen points.[12]

Nevertheless, Parliament took fright at the petitionary activity of the soldiers and ordered Fairfax to suppress it. When it was reported a few days later that the petition was still circulating, Denzil Holles seized the opportunity to submit a quickly scribbled motion declaring that the petition was 'tending to put the Army into a Distemper and Mutiny, to put Conditions upon the Parliament, and obstruct the relief of Ireland . . .' and that all those who continued to promote it would be 'looked upon, and proceeded against as enemies to the State, and disturbers of the public peace'.[13]

The Declaration of Dislike, as it came to be known, marked the first important stage in the genesis of the Army revolt. To the soldiers it was the first unmistakable sign that the majority in Parliament would prefer to crush them rather than answer their grievances. Their sense of grievance was only sharpened by Parliament's zeal to advance the Irish service at whatever cost. So zealous was the Presbyterian peace party that they were now willing to sell the royalists' estates to provide security for the £200,000 loan that they hoped to raise from the City 'for the service of England and Ireland'.[14] An active campaign was launched to induce desertion from the New Model by providing back pay for deserters and a month's pay in advance for Irish enlisters. Moreover, officers who volunteered for Ireland were offered their respited pay in rebels' lands instead of public faith bills.[15] Commissioners were appointed to go to the Army to drum up support for the Irish service, but their chances of success cannot have been enhanced by the fact that most of them were well-known Presbyterians.[16] Nor was the Irish service made attractive by the announcement of the expedition's commanders. At first it had been intended to appoint Sir William Waller as general of foot and Edward Massey as general of horse. However, by the second week of April Waller admitted his unacceptability to the soldiers and withdrew in favour of Philip Skippon, the major-general of the New Model foot.[17] Skippon was reluctant to go on the pretext of his age and infirmities, but the Presbyterians, overestimating his popularity with the soldiers, urged him to accept the appointment as a patriotic duty.[18] The soldiers were only lukewarm towards Skippon, and they greeted Massey with stony silence when he came to meet them on 17 April.[19] With the announcement that the horse regiments to be retained in England would be commanded largely by Presbyterians scarcely more popular than Waller and Massey, the soldiers realised that they were soon to be deprived of their trusted leaders in both kingdoms.[20]

The consistent hostility manifested by the parliamentary Presbyterians accelerated the army's politicisation during the month of April. By the middle of that month men in Ireton's regiment were not stickling to call the MPs tyrants, and some of them had been heard to quote Lilburne's writings as 'statute law'.[21] At the same time the soldiers were cautiously exploring the extent of public sympathy for their cause and had established correspondents in London to keep them abreast of developments there. Soon they were boasting that there was a considerable party in the City who would support them if it came to a showdown with Parliament.[22] In the counties where they were quartered, the soldiers strove painstakingly to keep political fences mended by behaving civilly towards their hosts.[23]

The growing political ferment in the army went unchecked by the higher officers, many of whom were absent from their posts during this criticial period.[24] When they began to return to their regiments in May, they found them nearly out of control. Yet there is no evidence to support the Presbyterian accusation that the grandees deliberately deserted their regiments in order to allow the flames of rebellion to flare freely, and to escape blame for having encouraged them.[25]

Despite the increasing political sophistication of the troops, in April they would still have been happy to embark for Ireland if they could have had their old commanders. Give us 'Fairfax and Cromwell, and we all goe', they told the parliamentary commissioners.[26] Instead of granting this concession the commissioners sanctioned the use of devious methods to boost enlistment. But they in turn were deceived by the overly optimistic reports emanating from their friends in the Army. Lieutenant-Colonel Kempson for example, misinformed the commissioners that Robert Lilburne's entire foot regiment had agreed to go to Ireland. They only went with him because he had carried off the regiment's colours and money saying that they would receive no pay unless they followed. When the men discovered that Kempson was taking them to Ireland, half of them broke away and returned to their quarters. In Colonel Hammond's regiment Captains Stratton and O'Hara had attempted to encourage enlistment by getting their men drunk, but their efforts were rewarded with indifferent success.[27] The result of these attempts at coercion and deception can only have been to bring the Irish service further into disrepute.

In London meanwhile, the Presbyterians were preparing another bold step which would later prove to be the second major turning point in the genesis of the Army revolt. For several months the City had been asking for control over the committee responsible for the London trained bands,[28] but not till 16 April did the parliamentary Presbyterians feel strong enough to move that their request be granted. When the motion passed, the City drew up a slate for a new committee purged of Independents, and on 4 May Parliament ratified the slate and gave the City the power to make any fresh appointments it wished in the future.[29] The new committee proceeded at once to purge

47

Independent officers from the trained bands.[30]

The purging of the London militia did not evoke a public response from the Army for more than two months, but in combination with the Declaration of Dislike and the Derby House Committee's heavy handed efforts to promote Irish enlistment, it had the immediate effect of raising anxiety to a new pitch among the rank and file. Moving to prevent what they saw as an open attempt to destroy the army, eight of the most militant cavalry regiments drew together, elected agitators, and addressed an impassioned letter to Lord Fairfax.

'To whom, next to our maker shall wee fly for shelter but to your Excellency the Patron and Protector? From what secondary meanes shall we expect our Deliverance; but from thy hand that hath so often bin ingaged with us, and from that heart that hath as often been tender over and carefull for our security? can we suffer, and you not sympathize? can we be proclaimed enemies, and your Excellency remain secure? O dear Sir, let your wonted care for us be further demonstrated, cease not to speak for us, who together with your selfe and in obedience to your command have adventured all that is deare to us for the Kingdomes safety.'

The letter witnesses to the sharply increased political consciousness of the rank and file. In Parliament, they declared, they had discovered a far more dangerous enemy than they had ever confronted on the battlefield, for '. . . like Foxes [they] lurk in their Dennes, and cannot be dealt withall, though discovered, being protected by those who are intrusted with the Government of the Kingdome'. Because they could now see that the Irish expedition was nothing else than 'a Designe to ruine and break this Army in pieces', they would boycott it until their demands were granted, and 'the just Rights and liberties of the Subjects vindicated and maintained'.[31]

Beneath the rhetoric of their letter it is evident that the cavalry regiments were still reluctant to challenge Parliament's right to take a decision that they found politically repugnant. There was no mention of the recent purge of the London militia. To have confronted Parliament on this issue would have required a major change in strategy, and for this even the agitators were unready. An intense debate over strategy was indeed pursued in the Army throughout April and May. Should the soldiers strive to remain non-political by keeping their demands strictly military, or should they take the momentous step of claiming to speak on behalf of all Englishmen and of the causes for which the Civil War had been fought? The second strategy was plainly revolutionary, since it implied that the Army had the right to sit in judgement over Parliament. John Lilburne had of course thrown his weight behind a revolutionary strategy, and sometime in May he began pressing the soldiers to make his personal struggle their own.[32] But despite the impression of some observers, Lilburne's word was not yet statute law. The agitators were still divided. The author of the 'Advertisements for the managing of the Councells of the Army' (4 May 1647) believed that they should 'Doe all things upon publique grounds for the good of the People', but another adviser cautioned them to demand 'nothing but what is relating to them as Souldiers'.[33] A letter of 20 May to the northern horse regiments shows that for the time being they chose to follow the latter advice.[34]

But at the same time there was a compelling force tugging the agitators in a revolutionary direction. The 'godly party', as the radical London Independents liked to call themselves, had begun to show interest in the Army's cause at the end of March.[35] With the suppression of their petitions[36] and the purge of the London militia in May, they turned to the Army as the only body that might protect them against Presbyterian hostility. Consequently, they made it their task to drive on the agitators to broaden the Army's demands to encompass their own. They exhorted the agitators to preserve military unity, but not to be satisfied with the simple redress of material grievances.[37] These appeals from London made a profound impression upon the Army radicals, to the extent that some of them resolved 'rather [to] suffer with the Godly party here than goe away and leave them to the mercy of their Adversaries'. A few of the fiery spirits talked of seizing the King and holding him hostage until Parliament should capitulate, but in the eyes of most of the agitators the time was not yet ripe for so drastic a step.[38]

In reality, there were still compelling reasons in favour of a conservative strategy. Unity was the paramount requirement, and the agitators never lost sight of the fact that they could succeed in nothing unless they carried the mass of the Army with them. Many regiments were still pervaded with an ignorance and inertia that could be overcome only by the slow process of political education or by a dramatic transformation of events.[39] Not only the ignorant rank and file, but the higher officers too were a conservative factor. When in May they realised what a dangerous state the Army was in they began returning to their posts to exercise a moderating influence on the fiery spirits. They set about to canvass their regiments' grievances, and then reported them to a meeting of the Council of Officers and the Parliamentary commissioners at Saffron Walden on 15 May. The papers prepared by the individual regiments had been in the officers' view, 'confused and full of tautologies, impertinences or weakenesses answerable to the Soldiers' dialect'.[40] What the officers had done therefore was to take the moderate, non-political demands that were common to all the papers and compress them into one Declaration representing the sense of the Army.

Although the Presbyterians would later charge that the officers had cynically stirred up mutinous sentiment in the Army, a comparison between the *Declaration of the Armie* (16 May 1647) and the individual regimental papers bears out the officer's claim to have exercised a restraining influence. The men of Lambert's regiment, for instance, had cried out for vengeance against ministers like Thomas Edwards and Mr Love, who used every means they could devise to make the army 'odious to the Kingdome'. Fairfax's 'Greene Regiment of foote' demanded that the laws of the land be translated from 'an unknowne tongue' into English. Sir Hardress Waller's regiment wanted liberty of conscience, and used 'scurrilous language . . . tend[ing] much to the disrepute of the Parliament'. Fairfax's horse troopers objected to having to swear the Covenant and complained 'that some who have declared themselves enemies to this present Parliament are in part become our Judges'.[41] All of these grievances were sifted out of the Declaration that was submitted to the Parliamentary commissioners, allowing Samuel Peck to report complacently that 'they meddle with nothing but what pertaines to them as Souldiers . . .'[42]

It may be that as late as the middle of May the flames of rebellion could have been quenched in the Army by a prompt attention to its material grievances, but there remains the question, would such a course of action have been practicable? Clearly, there was no way that Parliament could have found the nearly £3 million that it owed its soldiers in the spring of 1647; yet for immediate purposes a fraction of that amount would have been sufficient. It is true that the soldiers rejected the offer of a few tens of thousands of pounds, which would have eliminated only four to eight weeks of arrears at the most. On the other hand, Fairfax's own foot regiment, which was one of the most militant in the Army, stated at the beginning of June that they would have been happy with four months' pay.[43] Four months' pay for the whole New Model Army would have come to about £180,000,[44] and there is little doubt that the City would have been willing to lend as much to be rid of the army they so feared and mistrusted.[45] On 3 June the French agent Bellièvre observed that if the army revolt went unchecked and led to the overthrow of monarchy in England it would be to a large extent because 'the Presbyterians fail[ed] to act generously in the present circumstance'.[46] It was a just observation.

By the middle of May however, the Presbyterians did not feel any compulsion to deal generously with the Army. On the eighteenth the King's reply to the revised Newcastle Propositions was read at Westminster and at once accepted by both the Presbyterian leaders and the Scottish commissioners as a good basis for reconciliation. A definite prospect of coming to terms with the King was all that was needed to spur them on in their determination to dismantle the Army.[47] On 21 May promises were made that no soldier who had been a volunteer would be conscripted for overseas service; that compensation would be paid to maimed soldiers and the widows and orphans of those who had been killed; and that time in the Army would be allowed to count towards a man's apprenticeship.[48] But there was no move to shape these promises, or those of 30 April, into ordinances.[49] Meanwhile, the agitators had taken alarm at what they took to be evidence of Parliament's real intentions. The soldiers had intercepted a letter from Ashburnham to the King, counselling him not to come to terms with Parliament, 'for now that the peace beyond Seas was almost concluded the King might relye on the aid of 40 or 50,000 men'.[50] If royalists were plotting a new war, the agitators reasoned, why was Parliament so eager to disarm?

The third stage in the genesis of the Army revolt was reached on 25 May 1647 with the Commons' votes for immediate disbandment of the New Model foot, commencing with Fairfax's own regiment. The disbanded soldiers were voted £40,000 to cover the eight weeks' arrears they had been promised, but at the same time £12,000 was voted for the now Presbyterian controlled London trained bands, which were *not* being disbanded.[51]

There was no longer any need for the agitators or the Levellers to continue their efforts at political education; the job had been accomplished by Parliament. The whole rank and file was galvanised into action, and undisputed authority was handed to the agitators. Higher officers were faced with the option of following their men or being left behind, while those who were Presbyterian were either driven out or fled of their own accord.[52] Among the most radical regiments were those recently commanded by Presbyterians. The troopers who accompanied Cornet Joyce when he seized the King, for example, were entirely drawn from the regiments of Sir Robert Pye, Edward Rossiter and Richard Graves[53] while several of those who were most insistent that the Army should march immediately on London and purge Parliament were the agitators of Sheffield's regiment.[54] The regiment which reacted most violently to Parliament's votes for disbandment was Fairfax's foot, which had been commanded by the Presbyterian lieutenant-colonel, Thomas Jackson.[55]

At the beginning of June it was events more than men that swept the Army along. 'Provocation and exasperation makes men thinke of that they never intended', wrote the parliamentary commissioners on 27 May.[56] The men of Fairfax's foot regiment who basically cared only about their pay were 'carryed away . . . as in a torrent'.[57] Appeals by the 'godly party' to the Army to take up the gauntlet were now superfluous; the Army grasped it with alacrity. The soldiers quickly secured the magazine at Oxford, confiscated the money sent by Parliament for disbanding Ingoldsby's regiment, and removed the King from

Holdenby to prevent collusion between him and the Army's enemies. The horse and foot then contracted their quarters and came to a rendezvous near Newmarket.[58] Any lingering doubts about the expediency of revolutionary action had been dispelled, and the logical next step — a campaign to rally popular support behind the Army — was eagerly undertaken. Agents were sent into several counties to organise a petition campaign. This campaign soon bore fruit, for by 12 June the Army was able to forward petitions to the Commons from Essex, Norfolk and Suffolk; and by 18 June petitions had also flowed in from Buckinghamshire, Hertfordshire and Hampshire.[59] Agents were also sent into the north to win over Points's regiments and prevent them being used against the New Model.[60] At the same time a close watch was kept on the Scottish commissioners in London, and their despatches to Edinburgh were intercepted.[61]

In view of the New Model's effortless victory over its enemies between June and August, it may reasonably be asked why the parliamentary Presbyterians ever thought that they could win a trial of strength. At the time however, their conviction that they could succeed in getting rid of the Army was not as foolish as later events made it appear. In the first place, there was ample precedent for disbanding an army without its arrears. As recently as 1645 two armies — Essex's and Waller's — had been dismissed with a fortnight's pay. In the autumn of 1646 Massey's brigade was offered the alternative of disbanding with six weeks' pay or joining the expedition to Ireland.[62] When it came the turn of the New Model foot the initial intention was to pay them only six weeks' arrears, because Massey's forces 'which had been much longer without pay and had done better service' had been paid no more.[63] Under pressure from the moderates, the Presbyterians raised the offer to eight weeks, satisfied that no army could reject terms so reasonable. Indeed, they believed that if they were more generous or less insistent upon immediate disbandment, few would volunteer for Ireland, where the pay was the same and the hazards greater.[64]

When it became evident that the Army would not tamely submit to Parliament's orders, the Presbyterians were no less confident of their ability to control the Army, and if necessary, to crush it. Their first step was granting the City permission to purge the trained bands of Independents. They then set about to divide the New Model by trying to separate the foot from the horse, the officers from the men, and those who volunteered for Ireland from those who declined.[65] On 18 May Colonel Massey left the capital to secure the garrison of Gloucester for Parliament, and at the same time plans were laid to remove the magazine from Oxford to the Tower of London.[66] Major-General Points was called to London and given instructions to draw up his army in readiness to crush Fairfax's.[67] The Earl of Dunfermline was despatched to France to persuade Henrietta Maria to send the Prince of Wales into Scotland to unite all Presbyterian and Royalist forces there.[68]. Deserters from the New Model were mustered and quartered in strategic places, but their numbers turned out to be fewer than the Presbyterian officers within the Army had optimistically predicted.[69] Most of the foot soldiers that did desert were joined with other forces to form four regiments that were quartered in Worcestershire.[70] After the seizure of the King a committee of safety was appointed to recruit and organise forces from the counties.[71] Colonel John Birch's regiment in Windsor Castle was recruited and sent to Herefordshire to await further instructions. Colonel Thornton was sent to the Isle of Ely to rally the forces there.[72] The task of organising the New Model forces and integrating them with the other forces supporting Parliament devolved on the Derby House Committee, now dominated by the leading Presbyterian MPs. They secured an ordinance permitting the City to raise its own cavalry, so that the deserters from the New Model horse regiments, who numbered about 400,[73] could be joined with the trained bands and quartered close to the City. On 6 June the foot regiments in Worcestershire were ordered to advance to Reading.[74] On the same day Colonel Massey rode through the streets of London urging the citizens to defend themselves against the madmen of the Army.[75] The task of mustering the large number of reformadoes resident in and about London was entrusted to Colonel Dalbeir.[76]

On paper the Presbyterian counter-revolution was impressive enough, yet by August the strategy was in ruins and those who framed it had fled. What brought on the Presbyterians' spectacular collapse? It was less the lack of nerve with which Holles and Waller charged the majority in Parliament, than the Presbyterian leaders' own inability to inspire confidence in their direction of the country's affairs. This lack of confidence was what led Philip Skippon to waver, and Whitelocke to withdraw from the Presbyterian caucus.[77] The same motive prompted Stephen Marshall, Philip Nye, Herbert Palmer and other moderate divines to labour for a reconciliation between Parliament and the Army.[78] Two of the parliamentary commissioners to the Army, Nottingham and De La Warr, worked for the same end, warning that to levy troops in London and encourage desertion from the New Model would likely 'begett some disorder'.[79]

Some of the Presbyterians' closest friends betrayed the same lack of faith in their leadership. Sir Robert Harley, for example, dreaded an open conflict between the Parliament and its Army, convinced that it could only end in disaster. As a compromise he urged full pay and disbandment for the Army, which could then be reformed into a smaller force to defend England or embark for Ireland under the existing officers.[80] Before the end of June the City too had begun to waver, for the good reason that the trained bands had refused to obey their new Presbyterian officers. Not even the mayor and sheriffs' command to turn out 'upon paine of death' could make them budge. Boys jeered the drummers in the streets, while shopkeepers ignored the order to shut up their shops.[81] As a result, the Common Council switched its tactics and nominated three men to be a committee to reside with the Army and work for a *rapprochement*.[82] Once these men arrived at Fairfax's headquarters they gained more insight into the Army's grievances, and described them sympathetically to the Common Council.[83] Their diplomacy had the insidious effect of undermining the Presbyterians' position from within.[84]

In the north meanwhile the agitators had done their work well. The common soldiers were persuaded to ally themselves with the New Model's revolt and to ignore the commands of Major-General Points. Early in July he was arrested at his house in York and brought to Fairfax's headquarters at Reading to be tried on the charge of having striven to foment a new war.[85] Fairfax, who did not share the agitators' enthusiasm for court-martialling higher officers, released Points, but later sent John Lambert to replace him as commander of the northern regiments.[86]

Two other parties to the hoped-for Presbyterian coalition, the King and the Scots, also turned out to be broken reeds. Immediately after the seizure of the King, many London cavaliers volunteered their assistance to overthrow the New Model. But within a few days they were dismayed to hear that Charles, impressed with his courteous treatment by the Army, had ordered his supporters to stop cooperating with the Presbyterians.[87] It was commonly said that the Scots desired nothing more than to invade England and do battle with the Independent army.[88] Indeed, the Estates met several times in Edinburgh to consider such a scheme, but by 12 July all they could agree upon was that anyone who wanted to invade England was welcome to do so privately.[89] By then however it was too late for any effective assistance to be organised from Scotland.

After the seizure of the King on 3 June the parliamentary majority displayed their want of confidence in Presbyterian leadership by opting for a policy of appeasement towards the Army. The Commons hastily erased the 30 March Declaration of Dislike from their journals, and the Lords grudgingly followed suit a few days later.[90] On 7 June an unqualified ordinance of indemnity for all military actions committed during the war reached the statute book.[91] But after 3 June it was too late for gestures of appeasement to undo the damage. Concessions that might have quieted the Army in March or April were now greeted with scepticism. No longer content to press for the satisfaction of their material demands, the soldiers were now crying for vengeance on those who had plotted against them, and for fundamental changes in England's constitution. By 10 June the Army was on the march towards London, and a rendezvous had been called at Triploe Heath. The following day the grandees wrote to the Lord Mayor, warning the City not to resist their approach, while solemnly affirming that

'we desire no Alteration of the Civil Government; we desire not to intermeddle with, or in the least to interrupt, the Settling of the Presbyterian Government; nor do we seek to open a way to licentious Liberty under Pretence of obtaining Ease for tender Consciences . . .'[92]

Three days later, however, the pretended indifference to religious and constitutional matters was gone. With the publication of the *Declaration of the Army* (14 June), drafted by Ireton with the assistance of Cromwell and Lambert, the political programme of the Army was officially promulgated. The mere fact of having a political programme was excused with the observation that they were

'not a meer mercenary Army hired to serve any Arbitrary power of a State, but called forth and conjured by the severall Declarations of Parliament, to the defence of our owne and the peoples just Rights and Liberties; and so we took up Armes in judgement and conscience to those ends . . .'[93]

They offered eight reforms which, they were confident, would put the English state back on its true course: 1. A purge of all delinquent and corrupt members of Parliament; 2. A purge of all persons who had recently abused the Army; 3. A fixed time limit to the sitting of each Parliament; 4. No return to the King's arbitrary power of dissolution; 5. A guarantee of the right of all people to petition Parliament; 6. An end to the arbitrary powers of county committees; 7. A public accounting for the vast sums levied during the war; 8. Effective measures to prevent the outbreak of another war. In what appeared almost an afterthought they added a request for some provision for tender consciences.[94]

It was a minimal programme to satisfy the agitators who were clamouring for a march on Parliament to pull the Presbyterians out by their ears and return the London militia into Independent hands. Parliament's response to these demands was conciliatory enough to enable the grandees to keep the agitators under control for over a month, and even to take steps towards depoliticising the Army. On 16 June a month's pay was finally voted for the Army, and a few days later the money began to be paid out.[95] In its *Humble Remonstrance* of 23 June the Army acknowledged receipt of the month's pay, but complained that their 14 June *Declaration* had otherwise been ignored. It was not good enough to expunge the Declaration of Dislike from the record; those who had promoted it must be expelled. An ultimatum was issued that the Army would undertake 'extraordinary courses' unless certain demands were met within twenty-four hours. The demands included the annulment of the promise of arrears to those who deserted the Army, pay for the Army equal to what deserters had already been paid, an agreement not to bring the King nearer to Londdon than the Army, the expulsion of the Eleven Members, the discharge of Army deserters, the suppression of the reformadoes, and the abandonment of all efforts to raise new forces.[96] The seriousness of these demands was underlined two days later by the removal of the Army's headquarters from St Albans to Berkhamsted, and then to Uxbridge, only fifteen miles from London.[97] Although the twenty-four hour deadline was not met, Parliament did give partial satisfaction to the Army's ultimatum. The order for bringing the King to Richmond was revoked, and it was agreed that the King should not reside any nearer to London than the Army's headquarters.[98] On 25 June four companies of the London militia were ordered to guard Parliament, evidently to neutralise the swarms of reformadoes who had been intimidating MPs.[99] On the other hand, the Commons declined to suspend the Eleven Members until more substantial evidence was furnished against them. The dilemma was resolved the next day, however, when the Eleven requested, and the Commons granted, permission to withdraw from the House.[100] In response to these gestures the grandees issued a pacific *Manifesto* (27 June 1647). Satisfaction was expressed at the voluntary retirement of the Eleven Members and a drawing off from London was promised if the other demands were also met.[101] John Wildman did not exaggerate when he charged the grandees with having abandoned what they had earlier pretended to be the chief cause of their quarrel with Parliament, *viz.*, the public good.[102] The *Manifesto* was mute when it came to the broader political concerns that had been passionately voiced in the *Representation* (5 June), the *Declaration* (14 June) and the *Humble Remonstrance* (23 June). With the aid of Parliament's conciliatory measures, the grandees had evidently gained the upper hand over the fiery spirits and were succeeding in their attempts to lower the political temperature among the rank and file. This process continued for several weeks. The day after the publication of the *Manifesto* the Commons decreed that no soldier was to quit the Army without Fairfax's express permission, and the House accepted without a division the affirmation 'That they do own this Army as their Army; and will make provision for their maintenance; and will take order, that so soon as money can be conveniently raised, they shall be paid up equally with those that have left the Army.' On 29 June an ordinance was passed against tumultuous assemblies of officers or soldiers about the Houses of Parliament.[103]

These words and gestures had the effect of generating in the Army 'a general confidence of the Houses speedy and full answer to the remaining Propositions', and were matched by the removal of Fairfax's headquarters from Uxbridge to Wycombe and then to Reading.[104] But the grandees continued to be apprehensive about the dangers of counterrevolution in London, and on 7 July warned the City about the turbulent reformadoes who had not yet been dispersed, as well as the new forces that were being enlisted daily contrary to the Commons' votes and 'to the apparent hazard of a new warre'.[105] These apprehensions were partly allayed a week later by the Commons' order for the disbandment of the four foot regiments that were designed for Ireland but still stationed near Worcester.[106] On the 17th all the remaining forces in the kingdom were placed in Fairfax's hands, thus meeting a demand that the agitators had made ten days before,[107] and on the 21st all the deserters from the New Model were ordered disbanded.

On 18 July the Army broached publicly the question of the London militia committee.[108] The purge of Independents from the committee in May had created a potent grievance, and for some time the agitators had been pressing to have it reversed.[109] In their anxiety to preserve good relations with the City the grandees had managed to stave off this radical demand until the time of the Reading debates (16 July). But as soon as it became official Army policy to oppose the May purge, Parliament responded quickly. On 22 July it agreed to resume control of the militia committee, at the same time that it approved a motion against the bringing in of any foreign troops.[110] Fairfax returned the compliment by removing his headquarters again, this time to Bedford, and by scattering the cavalry over an area of southern England extending from Gloucestershire to Northamptonshire.[111] It now seemed that reconciliation had been achieved, the Army revolt contained, and a constitutional upheaval averted.

But there were still forces working vigorously to overturn any resolution of the conflict. When Parliament began to appease the Army after 14 June, the extreme Presbyterians attempted to promote a counterrevolution through other channels.[112]

The agitators were fully aware of the conspiracies that were brewing in the capital and pressed unceasingly for a march on London. In its June Manifestos the Army had officially adopted the revolutionary doctrine that *salus populi* was the highest law, and the Army had the right to define what it was. The following month the agitators had called on the Army to put theory into practice by protecting Parliament from the counter-revolutionary crowd and compelling the restoration of the London militia to non-Presbyterian control. The agitators' call for action and the grandees' reluctance to take it, were the cause of the debate held at Reading on 16 July. With unconscious irony,

Cromwell informed the agitators that as for anything obtained by force, 'I looke uppon itt as nothing'. In the end however, the higher officers did yield to pressure from below by agreeing to ask Parliament to return control of the City militia to the old committee within four days. On the strength of this promise they were able to persuade the agitators to agree to postpone the march on London.[113] With reference to the militia, the grandees' efforts quickly bore fruit in the form of a Commons motion to repeal the ordinance of 4 May. This motion unexpectedly prepared the way for the final stage in the Army revolt.

On 21 July a group composed mainly of apprentices and soldiers had met at Skinner's Hall and sworn an engagement to do everything in their power to bring the King to London and have him restored on the basis of his reply of 12 May to the revised Newcastle Propositions. They had then petitioned the Common Council to assist them.[114] This petition, together with the votes of 22 July repeating the militia ordinance of 4 May and repudiating those who would bring in foreign troops,[115] prompted the City to abandon its earlier pretence of friendship with the Army and openly to throw in its lot with the Presbyterian crowd. On the morning of 26 July the sheriffs and common councillors marched to the Commons at the head of the crowd, carrying a petition demanding the restoration of the militia ordinance of 4 May. Faced with a menacing crowd, the House hastened to comply with this demand.[116] Having obtained satisfaction the City officials withdrew, leaving the crowd to its own devices. For the extreme elements the withdrawal of the officials was the cue to bring out a more radical agenda. A number of them — 'rude boyes and meane fellows' — broke into the Commons, and keeping their hats on, compelled the Speaker to resume his chair after he had adjourned the House. No Member was allowed to leave until a motion had been passed inviting the King to come to London and treat with Parliament for peace. The MPs were encouraged to perform the task by shouts of 'vote, vote' from their captors.[117] Whoever instigated the violence of the crowd,[118] Leicester and Whitelocke were convinced that important elements in the City were behind it.[119] In any case the Presbyterians and the City government were unequivocal in approving its ends. The next day the City drafted a Declaration demanding His Majesty's return to Parliament and the readmission of the Eleven Members 'latelie driven out of the House of Commons by the violent pursuite of the armie'.[120] The prospects for a successful counter-revolution had never seemed rosier, and so the less extreme Presbyterian MPs and their friends swung into action too.[121]

But the Army had already moved to meet the challenge. The crowd's violent assault on Parliament on 26 July instantly vindicated the agitators' longstanding call for a march on London and converted the

Army's revolutionary theory into action. The scattered regiments were drawn together and preparations made to force Parliament and City to mend their ways once for all. In his own hand Fairfax wrote to the City reproaching them for their betrayal of their pledges to him and their failure to protect Parliament from the violence of the 'rude multitude'.[122] Major John Desborow was sent with a party of horse to intercept Pye's and Graves's horse, which had been commanded to leave their quarters in Kent and Surrey for the City. Desborow engaged them at Deptford, 'basely butchered' seven, took another forty prisoners, and captured sixty horses. Any dream of a foreign invasion up the Thames was quickly laid to rest by the seizure of the forts at Tilbury and the blockhouse at Gravesend, and the stationing of 2,000 troops there. It was decisive measures like these, far more than the reconciling efforts of a Stephen Marshall, that took the heart out of the City's resistance.[123] The first to see the writing on the wall were the militia officers, who threw up their commissions in increasing numbers as the Army approached, leaving the trained bands solely in the hands of 'high Presbyterians' and reformadoes.[124] The next group to waver was the crowd. As they milled around the Guildhall on the evening of 2 August their temper fluctuated with the conflicting reports that arrived hourly concerning the Army's approach. If a scout brought a piece of good intelligence — news for instance that the Army had halted — the crowd plucked up their spirits and cried 'one and all, one and all'. But if the news was bad they cried 'treat, treat'. Towards the end of the night they prevailed upon the Common Council to write a humble letter to Fairfax, imploring him to allow some kind of reconciliation.[125]

As the Army approached it sent messages to the counties requesting support for its action. The 'well-affected' in Devon obligingly wrote to Fairfax assuring him that since Parliament had shown itself to be hopelessly corrupt, they must rely on him to redeem their birthright and liberty, and prevent a new war. The inhabitants of Southwark wrote announcing that they were opposed to any design to raise a new war, and had dissociated themselves from the actions of the City. A group of Hertfordshire gentry offered two regiments of foot and two troops of horse.[126] The City itself finally reverted to its policy of appeasement, thus signalling to the 'high Presbyterians' that the game was up. A number of them slipped out of London before they could be apprehended.[127]

.The rendezvous of the Army, 20,000 strong, at Hounslow Heath on 3 August, was an impressive occasion. Fourteen Peers and about 100 members of the lower house were there to review the assembled ranks, and as they did so the soldiers flung their hats into the air shouting 'Lords and Commons and a free Parliament'.[128] Three days later Westminster was occupied, and on Saturday 7 August the Army marched through the City, without plundering or offering violence to anyone. The City's humiliation was complete.

The aldermen and common councillors tried to recoup their losses by presenting Fairfax with a basin and ewer of gold 'as a token of this Cities love', and by inviting him and all his officers down to the rank of lieutenant, to dinner. Fairfax, however, declined the invitation, and the soldiers concentrated their attention on the unfinished political struggle.[129] At their insistence the Eleven Members were expelled once again, and the votes passed after the flight of the MPs to the Army were annulled. But the grandees successfully resisted pressure from the agitators for the purge of all the Members who had chosen to sit after 26 July.[130]

Once Parliament had been tamed, the Army withdrew to the outskirts of London and debated whether to impose a religious and constitutional settlement upon the nation. The questions that were argued at Putney have understandably attained a much greater historical 'visibility' than the prosaic material grievances of the Army, but for most officers and men it was the latter that remained the most important issue in their lives. It must be remembered too that the issue of Army arrears was never settled before 1649, and that it was at all times a source of conflict and unrest. After the occupation of London, for instance, the Army issued a peremptory demand to the City to pay its overdue assessment of £64,337. It also urged Parliament to fine those delinquents who had tried to provoke a new war, and to assign the revenue to the reduction of army arrears. If money was not immediately forthcoming from these sources, the Army leaders desired Parliament's permission to raise it themselves.[131] At first, the citizens of London obstinately refused to open their purses, but after Cromwell threatened 'tumult or outrages' by the soldiers, the Commons ordered £30,000 for the Army, in addition to 'a months gratuity' and a month's pay. The month's gratuity was received and quickly distributed, but by 7 October nothing had been heard of the month's pay. This failure prompted the Army to revive a demand that had been made first in June — that arrears and respited pay be satisfied out of the Dean and Chapter lands.[132]

In its Propositions to the King of 1 November the Army requested that arrears be paid out of the revenue of the remaining episcopal land, the forest lands, two thirds of other forfeited lands, and delinquents' fines.[133] Even in that ambitiously radical document, *The Case of the Armie Truly stated*, the new agents began and ended by declaring their material grievances: there had still been according to these men, 'No securitie for our Arreers, or provision for present pay, to inable the Army to subsist, without burthening the distressed Country'.[134] The grandees were no different from the agitators in their attitude to money matters. After they had established their undisputed mastery of the Army at Corkbush Field on 15 November, they sat down to compose a *Representation* which they sent to the House of Lords on 7 December. It is interesting, though not surprising, that the grandees' white paper, which fills almost eight folio pages of the *Lords' Journals*, scarcely alluded to the Army's wider political, religious and constitutional aims. The Army's longest and most detailed attack on Parliament was devoted solely to 'bread-and-butter' issues — wages, arrears, debentures and free quarter.[135]

What this study of the New Model Army's behaviour during 1647 demonstrates is that arrears and associated material grievances, much more than ideology, were the engine behind the revolt of that year. The rank and file initiated the revolt, which was only taken over by the officers when it was raging almost out of control. The Leveller party was slow to grasp the revolutionary potential of the ferment seething within the Army after the first Civil War. They appear to have ignored the soldiers' grievances during several critical months, only attaching themselves to the cause after it had gained a considerable momentum of its own. But it was not merely the 'godly party' (as the radical Independents or Levellers liked to be known) that induced the rank and file leadership to broaden its political horizons from June to October of 1647. Disgust with Parliament, impatience with the grandees and alarm at the plottings of the 'high Presbyterians' contributed to the same end. Nevertheless, the grandees were ultimately successful in reasserting control and persuading the soldiers to focus their attention on bread-and-butter issues. It was not till after the second Civil War — after a second experience of fire and the sword, of royal treachery and parliamentary procrastination — that the whole New Model Army became authentically revolutionised. Not before the autumn of 1648 was there a united conviction among all ranks that the Army could only save itself by means of a political revolution at Westminster.

Notes

1.   Ian Gentles, 'The Arrears of Pay of the Parliamentary Army at the End of the First Civil War', *Bulletin of the Institute of Historical Research*, XLVIII, no. 117 (May 1975).
2.   *House of Commons' Journals*, V, 106-7. Hereafter cited as *C.J.*
3.   *C.J.*, V, 90, 91, 107-8.
4.   *House of Lords' Journals*, IX, 57, 66-7, 70, 71, 72, 88, 89-90. Hereafter cited as *L.J.*
5.   *L.J.*, IX, 113.
6.   British Library, Add. MS. 31, 116 (Whitacre's Diary), f. 305; *The Petition of Colonels* (27 March 1647).
7.   *The Declaration of the Armie* (16 May 1647), 4.
8.   *The Humble Petition of the Officers and Souldiers . . . to Sir Thomas*

Fairfax (21 March 1647), in *Army Book of Declarations* (1647), B.L., E 409 (25), pp. 1-2.

9. Bodleian Library, Clarendon State Papers 29, no. 2455.

10. Bodl. Lib., Tanner MS. 58, f. 16, 27 March 1647.

11. *A Perfect Diurnall*, 1 March 1647.

12. D. M. Wolfe, *Leveller Manifestoes of the Puritan Revolution* (New York, 1944), 138-41.

13. *C.J.*, V, 127.

14. *C.J.*, V, 134.

15. *C.J.*, V, 127; John Rushworth, *Historical Collections* vi (1722), 454.

16. The Commissioners appointed by the Derby House Committee were the Earls of Warwick, Lincoln and Suffolk, Lord Dacres, Sir William Waller, Sir Edward Massey, John Clotworthy and Richard Salway. *Calendar of State Papers, Ireland, 1647-1660*, 738, 741. Salway appears to have been an Independent, but he was not active on the committee. William Waller, *Vindication* (1793), 77-8.

17. Historical Manuscripts Commission, *Egmont MSS.*, I, 384, 389.

18. *A Perfect Diurnall*, 29 April 1647.

19. *Ibid.*, 17 April 1647. Skippon had evidently lost the soldiers' respect because he had tried too hard to please both sides. C. H. Firth (ed.), *Clarke Papers* (Camden Society, 4 vols., 1891-1901), vol. I, 113.

20. The first three horse regiments designated to be kept up in England belonged to the Northern Association, and were commanded by the well-known Presbyterians, Points, Copley and Bethell. *A Perfect Diurnall*, 29 March 1647. Five New Model regiments were designated: Fairfax's, Cromwell's, Whalley's, Graves's and Rossiter's. Cromwell and Whalley were Independents, but Cromwell had been eliminated by the vote of 8 March, and it was intended that his regiment should be commanded by its Presbyterian major, Robert Huntington. Waller, *Vindication*, 66. Although Whalley was later to become a staunch Cromwellian, he was at that time considered moderate and religiously orthodox. *Reliquiae Baxterianiae* (1696), 53. Rossiter was to be replaced by his major, Philip Twisleton, who was also known to have Presbyterian sympathies. Bodleian Library, Tanner MS. 58, f. 18; Waller, *Vindication*, 66. Graves was one of the Presbyterian officers who fled to Parliament after Cornet Joyce seized the King at Holdenby on 3 June. The ninth horse regiment to be kept up was drawn from local forces in Shropshire, Staffordshire, Warwickshire, Cheshire and Leicestershire and commanded by Colonel John Needham, the former governor of Leicester, whose political views are unknown. In addition, the Presbyterian major-generals Mitton and Laughorne were to command two hundred troopers each in north and south Wales. *A Perfect Diurnall*, 8 April 1647. Edward Wogan was evidently right when he said that the army left in England 'was to be all Presbyterians'. 'Colonel Wogan's Narrative', *Clarke Papers*, I, 425.

21. H.M.C., *Portland*, III, 156.

22. The first letter in the Clarke Papers from a London correspondent is dated 30 March 1647. Worcester College, MS.41 (Clarke Papers), f. 3ᵛ.

23. E. Hockliffe (ed.), *The Diary of the Reverend Ralph Josselin 1616-1683*, Royal Historical Society, Camden Third Series xv (1908), 42, 43.

24. The higher officers who appear to have been away from their regiments for a good part of the spring of 1647 include Fairfax, Skippon, Cromwell, Ingoldsby, Harley, Rossiter, Robert Lilburne, Sir Hardress Waller, Robert Hammond and Thomas Rainborow. Tanner MS. 58, ff. 16, 18, 62-3, 111, 121; H. Cary (ed.), *Memorials of the Great Civil War in England from 1646 to 1652* (2 vols., 1842), vol. I, 221, 231-2; Clarendon State Papers 29, no. 2455; *A Perfect Diurnall*, 22 April 1647.

25. Holles, *Memoirs* (1699), 84-5.

26. *A Perfect Diurnall*, 17 April 1647.

27. *Clarke Papers*, I, 14, 16, 18-19.

28. Guildhall Library, Journal of Common Council, 40, ff. 200, 207[v].

29. *Ibid.*, f. 215[v]; C. H. Firth and R. S. Rait (eds.), *Acts and Ordinances of the Interregnum, 1642-1660* (3 vols., 1911), I, 928.

30. John Lilburne, *Rash Oaths Unwarrantable* (1647), 45.

31. *Army Book of Declarations*, 7-9 (28 April 1647). The eight regiments were Fairfax's, Cromwell's, Ireton's, Fleetwood's, Whalley's, Rich's, Sheffield's and Butler's.

32. *Ionah's Cry Out of the Whale's Belly* (1647), 9.

33. *Clarke Papers*, I, 23, 24.

34. *Ibid.*, 91.

35. Worcester College MS. 41 (Clarke Papers), f. 3[v].

36. See *Gold Tried in Fire* (14 June 1647), for a history of the three petitions of March, May and June.

37. *Clarke Papers*, I, 85; Worcester College MS. 41 (Clarke Papers), f. 131[v].

38. *Clarke Papers*, I, 25.

39. Captain Rainborow recounted how at a meeting of Colonel Sheffield's regiment his troopers had joined in shouting 'Indempnity, Indempnity', and later asked him what it meant. *Ibid.*, 66.

40. *Ibid.*, 97.

41. Worcester College MS. 41 (Clarke Papers), ff. 124[v], 116[v], 117, 118[v], 109[v].

42. *A Perfect Diurnall*, 15 May 1647.

43. Tanner MS. 58, f. 129.

44. *Calendar of the State Papers, Domestic, 1644-5*, 232.

45. Journal of Common Council, 40, f. 218[v]; Jean de Montereul, *Diplomatic Correspondence 1645-48*, ed. J. G. Fotheringham (Scottish History Society, Edinburgh, 2 vols., 1898-9), II, 129.

46. *Ibid.*, 160.

47. S. R. Gardiner, *History of the Great Civil War* (4 vols., 1893), III, 253.

48. *C.J.*, V, 181.

49. On 30 April the Commons had promised speedy passage of an indemnity ordinance, payment of 'a considerable Proportion of their Arrears' upon disbandment, and issuance of debentures for the rest. *C.J.*, V, 158.

50. *A Perfect Diurnall*, 22 May 1647.

51. *C.J.*, V, 183, 188; *L.J.*, IX, 207-8.

52. *Clarke Papers* I, 113, 428; Tanner MS. 58, ff. 129, 141; Add. MS. 34,253 (Civil War Papers, 1640-1647), f. 45; *A Perfect Diurnall*, 6 June 1647. Cromwell's and Ireton's involvement in the plot to seize the King does not alter the main point that the initiative came from the rank and file and that the higher officers were swept along by their men. For a discussion of the evidence about Cromwell's role in the seizure of the King see W. C. Abbott, *The Writings and Speeches of Oliver Cromwell* (4 vols., Cambridge, Massachusetts, 1937-47), I, 452. There was nothing unprecedented about the rank and file's control of events in 1647. Almost all the major mutinies in the provincial armies during the previous two years had been controlled and organised from within the ranks. J. S. Morrill, 'Mutiny and Discontent in English Provincial Armies 1645-1647', *Past and Present*, 56 (August, 1972), 62. Mutinies in the Spanish armies in Flanders towards the end of the sixteenth century had similar grass-roots origins. Geoffrey Parker, 'Mutiny and Discontent in the Spanish Army of Flanders 1572-1607', *Past and Present*, 58 (February, 1973), 39-40.

53. *A Perfect Diurnall*, 6 June 1647.

54. Worcester College MS. 41 (Clarke Papers), f. 72.

55. Tanner MS. 58, f. 129.

56. *Clarke Papers*, I, 101.
57. Tanner MS. 58, f. 129.
58. *Clarke Papers*, I, 112; Add. MS. 34, 253, f. 45.
59. *Clarke Papers*, I, 100; *A Perfect Diurnall*, 12 and 16-18 June 1647.
60. Tanner MS. 58, f.188.
61. *Ibid.*, 290.
62. Holles, *Memoirs*, 81; S. R. Gardiner, *History of the Great Civil War*, III, 147.
63. Add. MS. 37, 344 (Whitelocke's Annals), f. 88; Holles, *Memoirs*, 81.
64. Cary, *Memorials*, I, 196.
65. *A Perfect Diurnall*, 3 June 1647; Add. MS. 10, 114 (Harington's Diary), f. 25; *C.J.*, V, 207.
66. Worcester College MS. 41, f. 132^v.
67. *Clarke Papers*, I, 168.
68. *Montereul Correspondence*, II, 164.
69. Lieutenant-Colonel Thomas Jackson had promised six companies from Fairfax's foot regiment; Captain George Drury was convinced that most of Rainborow's regiment would desert; and Colonel William Herbert was confident that the bulk of his regiment would follow him. Tanner MS. 58, ff. 62-3. In the event all three men were deceived. In April it had been estimated that 2,320 men or just over 10 per cent of the New Model were willing to go to Ireland. By June this number must have been significantly smaller. Worcester College MS. 41, ff. 18-19.
70. *A Perfect Diurnall*, 8 June 1647.
71. Add. MS.37, 344, ff. 92, 93^v.
72. *Calendar of State Papers, Ireland, 1647-1660*, 753.
73. Public Record Office, Commonwealth Exchequer Papers, S.P. 28/124, f. 337^v.
74. *C.S.P. Ireland, 1647-60*, 754.
75. Gardiner, *History of the Great Civil War*, III, 278.
76. Add. MS. 37, 344, f. 93^v. Evidence of Dalbeir's work is seen in the petitions that soon flowed in from Sir John Clotworthy's old regiment and from the commissioned officers of Massey's Brigade demanding their long overdue arrears. Order Book of the Derby House Committee for Irish Affairs, PRO, SP21/26, f. 78; House of Lords' Record Office, Main Papers, HL. (1645-1648), ff. 139-40. For another account of the Presbyterians' efforts see Valerie Pearl, 'London's Counter-Revolution', in G. E. Aylmer (ed.), *The Interregnum: The Quest for Settlement 1646-1660* (1972), 44-56.
77. Holles, *Memoirs*, 160; Add. MS. 37, 344, f. 88^v.
78. Clarendon State Papers 29, no. 2538; Holles, *Memoirs*, 160.
79. Add. MS. 34, 253 (Civil War Papers, 1640-1647), f. 59.
80. B. L., Loan 29/122, f. 16. I am indebted to Mr Michael Mahoney for this reference.
81. Journal of Common Council, 40, f. 224; Worcester College MS. 41 (Clarke Papers), ff. 79, 96^v.
82. It is significant that two out of the three had Independent leanings. Colonel Player had been eliminated from the London Militia Committee in the Presbyterian purge of April. Alderman John Warner was known as a leader of the party of compromise in the City. The third member was Christopher Packe. Pearl, 'London's Counter-Revolution', *loc. cit.*, 44, 48.
83. Tanner MS. 58, f. 355.
84. Waller, *Vindication*, 162. See also the City's petition of 1 July to the House of Commons supporting several of the Army's demands and urging Parliament to stop raising forces within the lines of communication. Journal of the

Common Council, 40, ff. 231^v-232^v.
85.   Cary, *Memorials*, I, 293; *Clarke Papers*, I, 168.
86.   Add. MS. 37, 344 (Whitelocke's Annals), f. 105^v.
87.   'Colonel Wogan's Narrative', in *Clarke Papers*, I, 428-9.
88.   *Montereul Correspondence*, II, 168.
89.   Add. MS. 37, 344 (Whitelocke's Annals), ff. 96, 98; *A Perfect Diurnall*, 12 July 1647.
90.   *C.J.*, V, 202; *L.J.*, IX, 247-8.
91.   *L.J.*, IX, 246.
92.   *L.J.*, IX, 257.
93.   *Army Book of Declarations*, 39.
94.   *Ibid.*, 40-46.
95.   *C.J.*, V, 214; SP28/42, ff. 112ff.
96.   *Army Book of Declarations*, 62, 68.
97.   Rushworth, *Historical Collections* VI, 592, 593.
98.   *Ibid.*, 592, 597.
99.   *Ibid.*, 592.
100. *Ibid.*, 592, 593.
101. *Army Book of Declarations*, 68-70.
102. *Putney Proiects* (30 December 1647), 9.
103. Rushworth, VI, 595.
104. *L.J.*, IX, 306; Rushworth VI, 596, 604.
105. Journal of Common Council, 40, f. 234^v.
106. *C.J.*, V, 247.
107. *C.J.*, 248; Worcester College MS. 41 (Clarke Papers), f. 149^v.
108. *Army Book of Declarations*, 96.
109. Cf. Worcester College MS. 110 (Clarke Papers), no pagination, 6 July 1647.
110. *C.J.*, V, 254.
111. Journal of Common Council, 40, f. 237.
112. See Pearl, 'London's Counter-Revolution', *loc. cit.*, 47-9.
113. *Clarke Papers*, I, 202.
114. Journal of Common Council, 40, ff. 238-9.
115. *C.J.*, V, 254.
116. *Ibid.*, 259.
117. Waller, *Vindication*, 182-3; Add. MS. 37, 344 (Whitelocke's Annals), f. 100.
118. Holles and Waller naturally denied any responsibility for the tumult, as did the Common Council. *Memoirs*, 153; *Vindication*, 183; Journal of Common Council, 40, f. 243^v. However, Holles and Waller were in London at the time and met together with John Clotworthy in the Bell Tavern in King Street, Westminster, on the day of the assault on Parliament. Pearl, 'London's Counter-Revolution', *loc. cit.*, 52.
119. Add. MS. 37, 344 (Whitelocke's Annals), f. 100^v; R. W. Blencowe (ed.), *Sydney Papers* (1825), 25-6.
120. The Declaration was published on the 30th. Journal of Common Council, 40, ff. 241, 244^v-46.
121. Add. MS. 37, 344 (Whitelocke's Annals), f. 101. See also Pearl, 'London's Counter-Revolution', *loc. cit.*, 51-2.
122. Journal of Common Council, 40, f. 243^v.
123. Holles, *Memoirs*, 159; Clarendon State Papers 30, no. 2565; H. R. Trevor-Roper, *Religion, the Reformation and Social Change* (1967), 327-8.
124. Clarendon State Papers 30, no. 2565.

125. Add. MS. 37, 344 (Whitelocke's Annals), f. 103; Journal of Common Council, 40, f. 250^v.
126. *A Perfect Diurnall*, 2 and 5 August 1647.
127. *Ibid.*, 3 and 4 August 1647.
128. *Ibid.*, 3 August 1647.
129. Journal of Common Council, 40, ff. 252-^{v}.
130. *The Humble Address of the Agitators* (14 August 1647).
131. Rushworth, VII, 815; Journal of Common Council, 40, f. 254^v.
132. Rushworth, VII, 825, 837-8; SP28/48, ff. 89-204; Tanner MS.58, f. 171.
133. *L.J.*, IX, 507.
134. 15 October 1647, 1-2.
135. *L.J.*, IX, 556-63.

FUTURE WARFARE: H. G. WELLS AND BRITISH MILITARY THEORY, 1895-1916

T. H. E. Travers

'The object of a military training' wrote J. F. C. Fuller, 'is to prepare the soldier for the next war, for it is the only possible war in which he can fight . . .'. Fuller went on to criticise the 'Haig-mind' of World War I, which could 'swallow the past and vomit it forth undigested', but which could not 'foresee, let alone create the future.'[1] Fuller's point about the need to anticipate was, in his case, largely prompted by the disastrous trench warfare of 1914-18. But Fuller himself did not foresee some of the particular military problems of World War I,[2] and in general it is an overworked cliche to state that the British Army as a whole was ill-prepared for the new kind of warfare presented by World War I.[3]

Yet there were some military theorists in Europe — frequently civilians — who had some success in predicting the nature of the next war in the two decades or so before 1914.[4] Perhaps the best known of this group was the Polish financier and authority on railways, Jean de Bloch, whose monumental work on future warfare and its consequences was originally published in Russian in 1898 and only partially translated into English as *Is War Now Impossible?* (1899). Bloch's work received considerable attention in the popular and military press in Britain, but his analysis of the fire power of new weapons, and of the superiority of defence over offence, while cautiously considered in British military journals, was generally rejected.[5]

Bloch's reception pointed to something of a dearth of significant professional military thought in Britain between the death of Colonel G. F. R. Henderson in 1903 and the first publications of J. F. C. Fuller (later Major-General) on the eve of 1914,[6] and especially of that branch of military thought which attempts to anticipate future tactics and weapons. However, there was one popular author who did generally accept Bloch's conclusions, and whose contribution as a serious student of warfare has been ignored — H. G. Wells. It was the political scientist Edward Mead Earle who first drew attention to H. G. Wells as a powerful military thinker, but Earle's death prevented him from completing his proposed study of Wells as a student of war.[7] This paper will concentrate, therefore, on H. G. Wells as a student of warfare within the context of British military theory between 1895 and 1916.

H. G. Wells (1866-1946) is now mainly known for his popular scientific fantasies and his romantic novels, although his over-riding interest from approximately 1900 on lay in the creation of a rational world order.[8] Wells' military thinking stems from the larger structure of his ideas on the actual process of emergence of such a world order. He believed that the pace of scientific and technological change had outstripped the ability of contemporary institutions to adapt to such changes, a situation which was all the more ominous since Wells anticipated the imminent demise of the old order through a series of devastating twentieth century wars, caused by the emotional nationalism of competing nation-states. He considered that these wars would break up the inefficient and confused governments and institutions of the time, and would result in the emergence of an elite of efficients, a ruling class capable of meeting the scientific and technological challenge of the future through the creation of a rational, planned world order. Wells therefore welcomed war, although he also feared its destructive qualities.

Wells' conviction that large scale wars were about to descend upon the world caused him to analyse the probable nature of such warfare, and, since he managed to remain a British patriot despite his internationalism, to offer advice to his countrymen on how to fight such wars effectively. Thus, Wells considered in turn, the ideal of a small and efficient elite army of technologists; the nature of technological war and the likely impact of new weapons on the offence and the defence; the problem of the most efficient social organisation for modern war; the tactical and strategic effect of two new weapons in particular, the tank and the aeroplane; and the possibility of nuclear warfare, together with the related question of graduated response and nuclear escalation.

Wells' first systematic analysis of future warfare occurs in his *Anticipations of the Reaction of Mechanical and Scientific Progress upon Human Life and Thought* (1901). Here he advanced two major forecasts, namely the likely impact of physical science upon warfare, leading to what he termed 'theoretically thorough war' or 'ideal war'; and the nature of the state most efficiently prepared to fight such a war.[9]

Wells considered that mechanisation was inexorably and inevitably creating a new kind of soldier, who would be well prepared to fight the modern 'ideal war'. The new soldier would be a sober, well-trained, 'engineering man'. This was because 'war is being drawn into the field of exact sciences. Every additional weapon, every new complication of the act of war . . . darkens the outlook of a nation of amateurs.' The old style army with its class divisions between officers and men, would be eliminated and turned into a single highly trained, homogenous force. Such a process could be helped along, but it was in any case 'the inexorable tendency in things to make a soldier a skilled and educated man, and link him . . . with the engineer and the doctor and all the continually developing mass of scientifically educated men that the advance of science and mechanism is producing'.[10]

Clearly Wells wanted an elite army of quality rather than quantity, composed of 'thousands of sober men' rather than 'hundreds of thousands of more or less drunken untrained men . . .' In fact, the key to victory in future war lay in training and scientific education – the elite would have to be recruited from, and created in, schools, colleges and universities.[11] Wells continued to pursue his ideal of soldiers as technological efficients in an essay entitled 'The Land Ironclads' (1903). This essay, whilst justly celebrated as an early consideration of the tank, was just as much aimed at the transformation of the old style army of amateurs into a small group of efficient engineers. Wells contrasts the cool rationality of the tank crews (recruited from urban centres) with their emotional and irrational enemy (recruited from the countryside).

'For the enemy these young engineers were defeating they felt a certain qualified pity and a quite unqualified contempt . . . They despised them for making war; despised their bawling patriotisms and their emotionality profoundly; despised them, above all, for the petty cunning and the almost brutish want of imagination their method of fighting displayed.'[12]

In 1912 Wells joined in the argument over a conscripted army, and rejected the idea in favour of his elite army. He argued, firstly, that a large conscripted army could neither be trained nor led, because of the lack of 'keen, expert, modern-minded *officers*' to train and lead; and secondly, that large armies were less effective than small, flexible forces. 'The experience of war during the last fifteen years has been to show repeatedly the enormous defensive power of small, scientifically handled bodies of men. These huge conscript armies are made up, not of masses of military muscle, but of a huge proportion of military fat.' And, thirdly, Wells declared that the conscript army would involve the very maximum of moral and material exhaustion with the minimum of military efficiency.[13]

Wells obviously disagreed with Lord Roberts' National Service League,[14] but was much closer to the ideas of War Secretary R. B. Haldane. Haldane also promoted the cause of a small army of quality and efficiency and opposed the idea of conscription. Protected by a powerful Navy, Haldane felt that Britain required only 'a comparatively small army', but one which was acquainted with the changes that 'science had wrought' in warfare. And while he particularly wanted the training of naval officers in science, he also admired the new school of young army officers, 'entitled to the appelation of men of science just as much as engineers or chemists . . .'[15] In fact, both Wells and Haldane belonged to a small but influential group calling themselves the 'Co-Efficients', who met on a regular basis from 1902 to 1908 to discuss Imperial affairs, and political issues generally. It is possible that Wells and Haldane compared notes in military matters: certainly Wells approved of Haldane's army reforms and expressed some regret at his departure from the War Office.[16]

Wells' concept of an elite army was still unusual, although under discussion, in the early years of the twentieth century.[17] Of equal merit was his appreciation of the kind of 'thorough' or 'ideal' war created by technology and new weapons. He believed that the arrival of improved rifles, machine guns, long range artillery, and armoured vehicles of various kinds, would have the effect of increasing the power of the defensive. Large numbers of troops could be pinned down by relatively small groups of men equipped with such weapons, so that the first phase of such a war would be indecisive trench warfare.[18] This opinion may be contrasted with the prevailing belief in Britain and the Continent that the next war would be over quickly.[19]

The state of opinion regarding the relative value of offence and defence is harder to assess. In France, the enthusiasm of Foch for the offensive *à outrance* is well known, and in Britain, Brigadier General Henry Wilson, Commandant of the Staff College from 1907-10, was reportedly influenced by Foch, although perhaps avoiding Foch's more extreme statements on the value of the offensive.[20] The general impression to be gleaned from the military journals of the day is that while most British officers were aware of the lessons of the Boer War, and the arguments of Bloch concerning defensive strength, they still sought every opportunity to refute such evidence, and to promote the value of the offensive. Nevertheless there was also a small but visible minority who expressed serious doubts concerning frontal assaults, and the offensive generally. These doubters rarely seemed to get into print in military journals, but were constantly referred to. Thus, as early as 1895 a cautious article by Lieutenant Colonel Elsdale stated that: 'while the prevailing current of opinion among military writers at home and abroad is very decidedly in favour of the offensive, we have yet a large and increasing number of capable and practical officers . . . who entirely fail to see how they can hope or expect to get their men across the storm swept zone for the close infantry attack . . .'[21]

The debate over the offensive versus the defensive during 1902-3 continued to support the power of the offensive, despite difficulties which were candidly admitted. Trenches and fire power should not prevent the surprise attack, wrote Captain Wilson in 1903. Lieutenant-Colonel Maude maintained in 1902 that the offensive was essential for victory. The editor of the *United Service Magazine* in 1903 cautioned that 'A great deal of nonsense has been written since the Boer War in condemnation of "frontal attacks" . . .', and opted for a combination of frontal and flank attacks. Captain Battine noted in 1903 that Callwell's book *The Tactics of Today* (1900) acknowledged the power of the defence over the offence, but nevertheless he himself called for offensive tactics. In 1909 Captain Johnstone admitted the problems of modern weapons and trenches, but still advocated the frontal attack, given a favourable position. And in 1910 Captain the Earl Percy thought that the extended lines of defence produced as a result of larger armies, now operated in favour of the offensive, a point 'which those writers who are continually dwelling on . . . the increasing difficulty of penetration, might do well to contemplate'.[22]

Wells' ideas on defence belonged, therefore, to a vocal minority, and in his case apparently derived from reading and largely agreeing with Bloch.[23] Like Bloch, Wells also believed that improved weapons would result in indecisive trench warfare, that the next war would involve whole populations, and that social disintegration would follow such a drawn out mass conflict.[24] But Wells also went further than Bloch, for he then argued that the first phase of indecisive trench warfare would be followed by a second, decisive phase.

The second phase would give victory to that State which was the most efficiently organised for war. This was more than a truism for Wells, since he drew upon his training in biology to conceive of the State as one organic whole, which achieved wartime efficiency in so far as the highest percentage of its members became organised and prepared for war, in fact, so far as the whole nation was transformed into one fighting unit.

'In our imaginary twentieth century State, organised primarily for war, this tendency to differentiate a non-combatant mass in the fighting State will certainly not be respected, the State will be organised as a whole to fight as a whole, it will have triumphantly asserted the universal duty of its citizens.'

Thus, not unlike Clausewitz, Wells conceived of future war as mass war, involving the total nation, as '. . . a monstrous thrust and pressure of people against people'.[25] Such national efficiency would necessarily be achieved in a somewhat authoritarian manner, for Wells believed that the class of efficients within the nation would naturally segregate from the rest of the population, and assume strong leadership of the country, while the class of irresponsible wealthy would be compelled into useful wartime functions, as Wells termed it, turning 'irresponsible adiposity into social muscle . . .' As for the working classes, the People of the Abyss, these would either be educated into efficiency, or forcibly prevented from hindering the war effort.[26] Reverting to a biological metaphor, Wells considered that such an ideally efficient State would be smoothly victorious: 'Quietly and tremendously that State will have gripped its adversary and tightened its muscles – that is all.'[27]

In practice, the manner of such a victory in the second and decisive phase of the war would require more than social organisation – it would require a breakthrough at the front, and the forcing into submission of the enemy. The latter aim would be achieved through seizure and control in one area after another of the 'vital apparatus of the urban regions – the water supply, the generating stations for electricity . . . and the chief ways used in food distribution'.[28] The former aim, the breakthrough at the front, would occur, Wells thought, when command of the air had been secured. With air predominance, the enemy's communications would be cut, his morale shattered, and a general advance would be possible.[29] Thus Wells did not conceive of the next war as being deadlocked, as Bloch had done, because an efficient nation with even more powerful weapons could break open the indecisive trench warfare.

Above all, Wells predicted that certain weapons – the tank, the aeroplane and atomic bombs – would prove decisive in future warfare.[30] In 1903 Wells had published his prophetic article on the tank, 'The Land Ironclads' in the *Strand Magazine*. The article was based partly on a suggestion from his aviator friend J. W. Dunne, and partly on a curious invention by one Diplock, of a pedrail, which consisted of iron feet attached to the rim of a wheel, and which was publicly demonstrated by Professor Hele Shaw at Liverpool in 1903.[31] Wells envisaged the ironclad as a naval vessel operating on land. Its dimensions, 80 to 100 feet long, and 10 feet high, with port holes along the side; and inside, the cabins, engine rooms, conning-tower, speaking tube, captain, and captain's orders ('half speed') – all strongly suggested a naval ship. Indeed, Wells described the ironclad as suggestive of a 'stranded vessel' and his pen portrait of the captain of one ironclad was of a man whose 'type of feature and expression . . . prevails in His Majesty's Navy: alert, intelligent, quiet'.[32] However, there the resemblance to the navy ended, for the tactics of the ironclads were firmly based on breaking the deadlock of trench warfare.

Wells' land ironclads were powered by steam, and moved at a speed of six miles per hour on eight pairs of pedrail wheels, each ten feet in diameter. Their tactical role was threefold: firstly, the transport of firepower; secondly, the crossing and destruction of trenches; and thirdly, the flanking attack on artillery placements and the destruction of the gun crews with rapid rifle fire. Wells' ironclads were equipped with searchlights, attacked at night to avoid artillery fire, and were supported by infantry cyclists who operated in conjunction with the ironclads, and who later engaged in separate sweeping-up operations once the ironclads had broken the enemy's resistance.[33] Wells' view of the ironclad's tactical role may be compared with W. S. Churchill's ideas on the tank in 1914, since Churchill also stressed some similar features: the vehicles were steam driven, they transported fire power, utilised night attacks, destroyed trenches and were used in conjunction with infantry. The main differences lay in Churchill's emphasis on caterpillar tracks (effective against wire entanglements), and the use of machine guns and grenades by the tank. But essentially both men stressed the transport of fire power and the ability of the ironclad/tank to overcome the trench deadlock.[34]

Captain Liddell Hart, in his study of the development of the tanks, pays tribute to the significance of Wells' article:

> 'This prophetic story by H. G. Wells was widely read, and had fertile effects in other men's minds — more than they consciously realised, or afterwards remembered. Among those who are known to have read it were several who played a leading part in bringing the conception to fulfilment after the outbreak of war in 1914'.

In particular Liddell Hart pointed to the impact of Wells' story upon two people who were instrumental in the development of the tank — Lieutenant-Colonel E. D. Swinton (later Major-General) and W. S. Churchill, who set up the Landship Committee.[35] It is fair to add that while Churchill acknowledged Wells' influence, he also referred to the evolution of the tank from the armoured motor car.[36] Judging by the lectures delivered to the Royal United Service Institution between 1904 and 1906, Churchill's comment appears to be accurate, and it may be useful to compare Wells' ideas with those of his military contemporaries.

At the Royal United Service Institution in 1904 Major McNalty considered that mechanically propelled vehicles could be used for transport of men, either in motor cars or as motor cyclists, and the transport and haulage of munitions and heavy fieldguns. Although Major McNalty considered various steam traction engines from the point of view of transport only, a speaker at the end of the lecture, Colonel E. J. A. Balfour, wanted some form of bullet proofing. Two years later Captain H. M. Paynter moved cautiously forward, discussing the motor car not only as transport, but also considering the protection of men and light guns with shields, and the possibility of an armoured motor car. The question period also involved discussion of armoured motor cars, and so by this date, 1906, the concept of an armoured vehicle was fully launched in military circles.[37]

However, from the point of view of concept and tactics, Wells' 1903 article predated military acceptance, and remained relevant to that post World War I school of thought which continued to see the tank as the destroyer of trenches and transporter of fire power. Nevertheless Wells did not anticipate the other major school of thought, exemplified by Fuller and Liddell Hart, which gave the tank the role of mobility, speed, and independent action,[38] because Wells' later considerations on the tank in 1916 actually made the tank into an enormous beast 'driven by engines of scores of thousands of horse power, tracking on a track scores of hundreds of yards wide and weighing hundreds of thousands of tons'. Its tactical role would apparently be that of a 'scorched earth' weapon, grinding out areas of desolation, and 'destroying the land for all ordinary agricultural purposes for ages to come'.[39]

Wells' scientific prevision had discerned some important tactical qualities in the tank, but it was the tactical and strategic consequences of the aeroplane that interested him most of all. Writing in *Anticipations* (1901), before the development of the aeroplane, Wells predicted 'aerial devices' long before the year 2000, and perhaps by 1950. These devices would act militarily as spotter planes, perhaps with searchlights at night; they would also destroy enemy balloons, fight each other *en masse* and act as a moral weapon — leading the van of a ground attack, or towering with 'pitilessly watchful eyes' over the enemy.

> 'Everybody, everywhere, will be perpetually and constantly looking up, with a sense of loss and insecurity, with a vague stress of painful anticipations . . . no apparatus or camp or shelter will any longer be safe.'[40]

Somewhat naturally Wells also commented in *Anticipations* upon the previously developed balloon — which he felt would be exceptionally valuable in war. Linking the spotter balloon to his concept of the elite army, Wells foresaw the front line held by a series of isolated companies composed of crack marksmen, and supported by artillery and spotter balloons, all of which would be commanded in an integrated fashion from behind the lines by a single individual: 'The battalion commander will be replaced in effect by the organiser of the balloons by which his few hundreds of splendid individuals will be guided and reinforced.' The balloons' reports would in effect control the front line.[41]

However, Wells' interest in air warfare frequently turned in the direction of global strategy rather than battle tactics. At a very early stage Wells had been both fascinated and appalled by the awesome strategic potential of the aeroplane — in *The War of the Worlds* (1898), Wells' hero is dismayed by the news that the Martians had developed a flying machine: 'It is all over with humanity . . . If they can do that they will simply go round the world . . .'[42] The aeroplane reappears as a military weapon, and as a form of regular transport in *When the Sleeper Awakes* (1899), where again one of the protagonists claims that mastery of the air means mastery over the earth.[43]

The theme of global war is brought to its strategic conclusions in Wells' *War in the Air* (1908), written in 1907. According to Wells the book had a serious thesis,[44] that with the flying machine, war alters its character, it ceases to be an affair of 'fronts' and becomes an affair of 'areas'; and while there is a vast increase in the destructiveness of war, there is also an increased indecisiveness. Consequently air war means complete social destruction instead of victory at the end of the war, and thus air war not only alters the methods of war, but its consequences.[45] This was because Wells was especially sensitive to, and pessimistic about, the behaviour 'of a modern urban population under warlike stresses'.[46]

Hence, Wells believed that while the airship was relatively incapable of occupying or garrisoning a captured position, yet it held an 'immense power of destruction' over the target below, both physically and morally. Indeed, so powerful was the effect of the airship upon an urban population already weakened by the shortages and economic disorganisation cause by war, that 'civil conflict and passionate disorder' would rapidly follow the appearance of an air fleet. Apart from his interesting comments on the weakness or urban centres under aerial pressure (a topic that was, of course, revived during the mass raids of World War II), Wells is concerned to point out the very *destructive* qualities of air war, and the inescapable involvement of the entire urban population in such a war.[47]

Next, Wells considered the tactics of air war. He felt that the 'early airships' were relatively ineffective against each other because of the limited weight of weapons that could be carried, and thus after the first air battle, the 'air-fleet admirals' sought the moral advantage of a destructive counterattack. Wells was evidently moving towards the conclusion that the tactical problem of air war was one of surprise, interception, and counter-interception, for otherwise airfleets tended to cancel each other out, unless one possessed unilateral numerical or technical superiority.[48]

Lastly, Wells believed that air war, although enormously destructive, was equally and totally indecisive. This was because there was no defence against air attack since there were no fronts and no natural barriers — in the air 'all directions lead everywhere'.[49] So a country, having delivered a smashing blow, was equally vulnerable to a return attack, against which there was no obvious defence. Consequently, the war became 'a universal guerrilla war . . . inextricably involving civilians and homes and all the apparatus of social life'.[50] In effect, Wells was returning to some earlier points made by Bloch, since although the aeroplane had re-established the power of the offensive, yet the results were still the same as those predicted by Bloch: mass war and prolonged indecisive conflict, resulting in chaos and social disintegration.

At another level, Wells was suggesting a somewhat extreme form of air power strategy, such as the air supremacy thesis advanced in the

1920s by General Douhet in Italy. Douhet's 'integral war', involving every aspect of life, is reminiscent of Wells' mass war, while Douhet's two main principles — that the aeroplane is the offensive weapon *par excellence*, and that the disintegration of nations brought about indirectly by land war, could be directly accomplished both physically and morally by aerial forces — again sound very like Wells' predictions.[51]

On the other hand, Wells' concern that air war, once started, would soon spread over the entire globe, and would result in the specific sequence of social chaos and panic, famine, plague and the collapse of civilisation seems somewhat apocalyptic and again owes a considerable amount to the similar pessimistic sequences of Bloch.[52] Wells' ideas on air warfare were certainly useful in drawing attention to larger strategic issues, especially the idea that command of the air was the key to the development of future warfare, and if his analysis sometimes reaches too far, one may agree with Edward Mead Earle that in 'setting the military airplane within the framework of modern society' Wells managed 'to formulate a broad statement of the influence of air power upon history'.[53]

The attempt to evaluate Wells' status as a theorist in regard to air war, should also compare the tactical and strategic thought of his military contemporaries. On at least one point all military thinkers seemed to agree — the Channel was no longer an adequate barrier to the aerial attack, or even to the aerial invasion of the country.[54] This idea was mooted as early as 1892 by Captain J. D. Fullerton, who also felt that, with aerial navigation, the value of the Navy would be reduced. Fullerton had been impressed by the industrialist and inventor, Hiram Maxim, who had written in 1891: 'If I can rise from the coast of France, sail through the air across the Channel, and drop half a ton of nitro-glycerine upon an English city, I can revolutionise the world.' Like Maxim, too, Fullerton had expected the tactical role of the 'aerial navy' to be both reconnaissance, and the dropping of high explosive bombs on enemy lines and territory. And, in common with Wells, Fullerton warned that 'aeronauts' would affect all classes and interests.[55]

Before the turn of the century, Lieutenant B. F. S. Baden Powell had also theorised on the potential of the flying machine, considering 'it probable that aerial machines will figure in any great war of the future'. Baden Powell believed that the aerial machines would observe and destroy the war material and troops of the enemy, and would ensure victory. Baden Powell went so far as to suggest, not unlike Douhet, that since the 'aerial Navy would possess an incalculable advantage', the country could do without an army or navy — although he suggested possible defences — bomb proof roofs, anti-aircraft guns, and armour plating where possible.[56]

The articles by Maxim, Fullerton and Baden Powell in the 1890s reflected the popular enthusiasm for flying experiments in that decade, and the absence of further articles until approximately 1906 reflected an equal disillusionment with the slow development of flying machines. But at this point in time, it would probably *not* be fair to say that Wells was 'far in advance of the views of professional military men . . .'[57]

From 1906 on, opinion was sharply divided upon the uses of airships — Lieutenant Colonel Capper in 1906 had something of the global vision of Wells, believing that large flying machines would be built, bringing war 'to the very door of the citizen . . . it will become amongst civilised nations a calamity far more real and far more dreaded than even at present, so that in the end the aeronaut may prove to be the great peacemaker of the world'.[58] On the other hand, Major Bannerman-Phillips in a 1908 article stated bluntly that flying machines 'remain interesting scientific toys, of little or no practical value for the purposes of war'. He went on to criticise alarmists and writers of sensational fiction (evidently Wells) who described airships bombarding towns and troops and carrying an invasion force of men over the ocean.[59] Opponents of flying machines in war tended to doubt the ability of aeronauts both to pilot and fight at the same time,[60] and to worry about the stability of the machine in windy conditions.[61] Hence the dirigible was initially favoured over the flying machine,[62] and even the proponents of the military uses of flying machines were unsure whether bombing would be permitted by the International Convention.[63]

However, by approximately 1909, the concept of air war involving flying machines was generally accepted (even by Bannerman-Phillips,[64] who contributed regularly on air matters to the *United Service Magazine*); and Haldane in the same year set up a technical Committee to deal with the military application of the aeroplane.[65] But by this time Wells' *War in the Air* had already been published, and in any case very few theorists thought, like Wells, in terms of air power, until approximately 1917 or later.[66] Wells' ability to extrapolate the potential of new weapons and new technology is even more obvious when his book *The World Set Free* (1914) is considered. Written during the summer of 1913 and projected forward into the 1950s, Wells linked together what he knew of the experiments of Lord Rutherford and Frederick Soddy on radium, radioactivity and the atomic disintegration of radioactive elements with his appreciation of the potential of the aeroplane, to envisage future atomic warfare.[67]

Wells came to some interesting conclusions about atomic weapons themselves. The atomic bombs were of a chain reaction, continuous explosive type, which emitted radiation in lethal doses. In fact, the bombs created radioactive areas, which remained dangerous for many

77

years after the war had ended. A very small number of atomic bombs (two or three) could apparently destroy a city, and there was little defence against them.[68] Since the bombs were used on urban centres, the population tended to scatter away from the cities into the countryside, a tendency which became worldwide as each nation, aware of the rapid proliferation of atomic weapons, tried for a pre-emptive strike on its neighbour.[69] Thus the re-emergence of the power of the offensive was once more making war impossible: 'Every sort of passive defence, armour, fortifications, and so forth was being outmastered by this tremendous increase on the destructive side.'[70]

As with the *War in the Air*, Wells drew much the same lessons from *The World Set Free*. Again, the atomic bomb and the aeroplane eliminated the notion of front lines; the distinction between civilian and soldier disappeared entirely; war was even more destructive and even more indecisive; and the end result was the collapse of civilisation, although Wells added to the novel his vision of a world reborn and reconstructed under a world council. However, there was one lesson that Wells may not have been fully aware of, although he mentioned it in passing — that was the question of escalation, and the qualitative change introduced by atomic warfare.

Originally, Wells had considered the concept of escalation in terms of the response dictated by new, but conventional, weapons. In *The War in the Air*, Wells noted:

'It was impossible to end a war by any of the established methods. A having outnumbered and overwhelmed B, hovers, a thousand airships strong, over his capital, threatening to bombard it unless B submits. B replies by wireless telegraphy that he is now in the act of bombarding the chief manufacturing city of A by means of three raider airships. A denounces B's raiders as pirates and so forth, bombards B's capital and sets off to hunt down B's airships, while B in a state of passionate emotion and heroic unconquerableness, sets out to work amidst his ruins, making fresh airships and explosives for the benefit of A.'[71]

Wells elaborated this line of thought in an article in 1916, while under the immediate influence of actual fighting conditions. Here Wells conducted a form of escalating war game, juggling offensive and defensive weapons, until what he called stage B2 was reached, where the offence, with the aeroplane, controlled the defence, unless stage A3 occurred, in which case the introduction of the anti-aircraft gun (proposed long ago by Lieutenant B. F. S. Baden Powell) eliminated the advantage of the aeroplane. Somewhat optimistically Wells depicted A3 as the 'final grade of war'.[72] Then, finally, in *The World Set Free*, Wells understood that atomic bombs 'were manifestly unsuitable for field use . . .'. They

were not tactical weapons, and Wells implies that they were only employed after 'Strategy and reasons of State' had failed to prevent their
use. And as the war became worldwide, Wells envisioned a worldwide
escalation of atomic warfare and the need for some form of global control of nuclear weapons.[73] However crudely, Wells did approach in
embryo the question of nuclear strategy, the idea of stages of escalation
and the problem of nuclear disarmament.

As a student of war, Wells' powers of analysis led him in several
other directions with perhaps less fruitful results. He certainly considered naval problems, opposing the Dreadnought programme with
some vehemence, since large ships were vulnerable to submarines,
torpedo boats and aeroplanes, and calling instead for a smaller, mobile
navy, composed of destroyers, submarines and waterplanes.[74] Wells
also invented a portable frontline transportation system called a 'telephrage', which he discussed with Churchill, and which was successfully
built, tested and used in 1917. To Wells' infinite disgust his system was
disregarded by the 'tin-hats' − senior army officers.[75] And in 1913
Wells published an obscure book, *Little Wars*, in which he invented a
war game, a form of *Kriegspiel*, to be played for amusement. But as
usual the book had a serious inner core, so that it attracted the attention of various military personnel (including one Colonel Mark Sykes)
who told Wells that *Kriegspiel* as played in the British Army lacked
realism. Wells offered various military suggestions in an Appendix and
observed: 'We believe that the nearer that *Kriegspiel* approaches to an
actual small model of war, not only in its appearance but in its emotional and intellectual tests, the better it will serve its purpose of trial
and education.'[76]

After the actual outbreak of war in 1914, Wells strongly supported
the British war effort, and in 1916, he visited the French and Italian
fronts as a war correspondent and wrote up what he saw, later published in his *War and the Future: Italy, France and Britain at War*
(1917). The book marks a turning point, for while Wells made a few
more remarks on the value of the tank, the aeroplane and other weapons, in general the book reflects the hope that this will be the war to
end war.[77] Wells was turning away from the analysis of war, weapons,
tactics and strategy, and towards the possibilities of achieving an enduring peace. Wells now thought that only five or six great powers had
the industrial might to pursue war in the future,[78] and thus he sought
ways to persuade these countries to end war, much as modern politicians seek agreement on the limitation of strategic weapons among the
great powers. In short, from approximately 1916 onward, Wells
devoted his time to furthering the cause of peace, and the creation of a
world government − an inter-related problem − and rarely did he
return to the study of military theory.[79]

Wells' reputation as a military theorist must rest upon the three basic assumptions that he made, and their consequences. Firstly, that scientific and mechanical progress fundamentally alters the nature of war; secondly, that modern war requires the highest organisation of the nation as one organic, efficient, whole; and thirdly, that it is both possible and desirable to extrapolate contemporary tendencies into the future.

Scientific and mechanical progress had made war both democratic and undemocratic. Democratic because old distinctions — the horse and the private soldier, the leaders and the led, had been superseded by machines, and the army connected into one homogeneous unit. However, although class differences might be erased, the new army would again become undemocratic because the 'balance of military efficiency was shifting back from the many to the few, from the common to the specialised. War . . . had become undemocratic.'[80] Apart from creating a new elite of military efficients, mechanisation also produced new weapons which inexorably applied the law of evolution and change to war. As in biology, the law was the same, adapt or perish. However, adaptation meant not only developing the new weapons, and their tactics, but understanding that such weapons, particularly the aeroplane, created mass war and worldwide war. But adaptation also meant, as Wells' professor of biology, T. H. Huxley, had taught, the opposing of natural forces in favour of the survival, not of the fittest, but of the ethically best.[81] Hence the ultimate logic of Wells' appreciation of the destructive power of mechanised, scientific war, led in the direction of controlling, and in the end, opposing and outlawing modern war altogether, through the agency of the ethically best — the rational and benevolent efficients of the world.

However, such a world government could only emerge after the imminent war-induced collapse of civilisation, so that in the meantime it behoved the British government to achieve maximum military efficiency. Here again his scientific training predisposed Wells to think in organic, evolutionary and integrated terms: the nation must evolve as an efficient whole or perish.[82] The means of achieving such integrated military efficiency were both natural and artificial. Sounding very like Herbert Spencer, Wells foresaw an evolutionary process of segregation and aggregation among the nation's population — moving from homogeneity — whereby the efficients of the nation segregated out from the mass, and emerged under the impact of mechanisation, invention and war as an aggregation of military muscle and leadership. Subsequently, it was necessary to artificially hasten the natural evolutionary process by compelling the wealthy to efficiency and helping the useless among the working classes to eventually disappear.[83]

Essentially, Wells was advancing a fundamental argument; organic national efficiency was to be achieved through the successful adaptation of the greatest number of capable people to the functional changes wrought by mechanisation, invention and war. It was a process of internal specialisation in which function replaced rank, so that the nation organised for war along functional and horizontal lines, rather than along the old vertical lines of authority.[84] Thus the elite army of the future formed just one layer of technological specialisation, interdependent with, and integrated into, the nation's remaining population, which upon the outbreak of war was equally assigned to specialised tasks according to functional ability.

Wells' prescription for the efficient war-making State, with its organic, elitist and authoritarian overtones, should obviously be seen in the context of the contemporary debate concerning social efficiency.[85] However, Wells was essentially correct in foreseeing total mechanised war, with each nation mobilising its entire resources in order to survive, and it remains to consider Wells' method of analysing such a future war. Like Major-General J. F. C. Fuller's search for a scientific method of analysing future warfare, Wells also believed that a systematic analysis of the future was possible, providing that a scientific method be found. Wells' own method was simply one of induction – the establishment of 'safe and serviceable generalisations' based upon contemporary facts and tendencies – particularly technological innovations. Although somewhat vague, Wells' method seemed sound to him because he believed in the existence of a rational world, operated by 'incessant and consistent forces', which could be discovered and extrapolated into the future.[86]

The comparison of Major-General J. F. C. Fuller and H. G. Wells becomes more interesting when Fuller's ideas on future warfare are considered. Like Wells, Fuller claimed that 'mechanisation will force the small army to the fore by rendering the mass army useless'. Thus, Fuller also proposed an elite army of technological efficients, 'of educated men, of formidable weapons and of astonishing movement, an army led by scientists and fought by mechanics – a true machine of war'.[87] Fuller was deeply impressed by the aeroplane and the tank, and by technology generally, so that future wars would 'almost certainly be decided by machine-power', and not by manpower.[88] Again like Wells, Fuller believed that emotional democracy was a war-making instrument, and that future war would be mass war, with entire populations ranged against each other.[89] Hence Fuller made suggestions similar to Wells on the need for strong national discipline and an authoritarian government capable of directing such a mass war.[90]

Both Fuller and Wells had advanced two essential theses about the war of the future: that the tactics and strategy of future war would have to be based on technological development, which in turn permitted a reasonably systematic calculation of the nature of such war: and that future war could not be fought on the basis of lessons learned from past campaigns. Perhaps the most interesting aspect of Wells as a student of war is that in the decade or so before Fuller's first publications, and the outbreak of World War I, Wells ignored the conventional method of preparing for war — the study of past campaigns and tactics[91] — and instead provided an original approach to future war based upon an understanding of the inter-relationship between science, war and society. Part of the contemporary desire for planning and efficiency, Wells had helped to focus Edwardians upon future needs rather than past triumphs, and upon the recognition of the machine as a central part of human existence, but even he grew disheartened under the impact of the mechanised war he had so successfully predicted.[92]

Notes

1. Major General J. F. C. Fuller, *Memoirs of an Unconventional Soldier* (1936), 462-3.

2. Fuller did not, for example, altogether recognise the future difficulties of the offense, Jay Luvaas, *The Education of an Army: British Military Thought, 1815-1940* (Chicago, 1964), 339.

3. Correlli Barnett, *Britain and Her Army, 1509-1970* (New York, 1970), 368. Michael Howard, *The Continental Commitment* (Harmondsworth, 1974), 57.

4. In a somewhat lighthearted vein I. F. Clarke covers some of this material in his *Voices Prophesying War, 1763-1984* (1966), especially Chapter 3. But the focus of the book naturally excludes much of the serious military writing of the authors considered, e.g. Erskine Childers' *War and the Arme Blanche* (1910), and Conan Doyle, *The Great Boer War* (1900), etc.

5. See, for example, Major General H. M. Bengough, 'A Civilian or a Regular Army', *United Service Magazine* (hereafter cited as *U.S.M.*), vol. XXIV, November 1901, 197-8. Bengough states, however, that Col. G. F. R. Henderson has been swayed by Bloch's arguments, 198. Major General C. E. Webber, 'Army Reform based on some 19th century lessons in warfare', *Journal of the Royal United Service Institution* (hereafter cited as *J.R.U.S.I.*), vol. XLV, April 1901, 379, 395.

6. This argument is supported, no doubt unintentionally, by Professor Jay Luvaas, whose selection of 'the two most prolific and influential military writers' of the period 1899-1914 turn out to be Spenser Wilkinson, a volunteer and later Chichele professor at Oxford, and Lieutenant Colonel a Court Repington, who resigned his commission in 1901. Luvaas, *op. cit.*, 251. Neither were regular serving soldiers at the time, therefore, and neither can really claim to have obtained a significant place as military theorists.

7. Edward Mead Earle, 'H. G. Wells, British Patriot in Search of a World State', in E. M. Earle (ed.), *Nationalism and Internationalism* (New York, 1950), 116-7, and particularly 117, f. 20. See also Edward Mead Earle, 'The Influence of Air Power upon History', *The Yale Review*, vol. XXXV, Summer 1946, 580-2.

8. See generally W. Warren Wagar, *H. G. Wells and the World State* (New Haven, 1961).

9. H. G. Wells, 'Anticipations', (1901) in *The Works of H. G. Wells* (Atlantic edition, 28 vols., New York, 1924-27) (hereafter cited as *Works*), vol. 4, 156, 164.

10. H. G. Wells, 'Anticipations', (1901), *Works*, vol. 4, 85, 178, 182.

11. *Ibid.*, 162, 183.

12. H. G. Wells. 'The Land Ironclads', (1903) in H. G. Wells *Selected Short Stories* (Harmondsworth, 1958), 101. (For country versus town recruits, see 88, 104.)

13. H. G. Wells, 'The Common Sense of Warfare', (1912), *Works*, vol. 20, 464-6.

14. Although Wells was not averse to compelling certain groups into war training: for example, the educated and propertied classes, together with some scholarship men from elementary schools, might serve two years in a destroyer, waterplane, airship or laboratory, *Ibid.*, 477-8.

15. R. B. Haldane speaking in Haddington, the *Scotsman*, 5 Oct. 1901; Correlli Barnett, *Britain and Her Army*, 363.

16. H. G. Wells, *Experiment in Autobiography*, 2 vols., (1934), vol. 2, 767-8. Wells wrote later that the 'Pentagram Circle' (his pseudonym for the 'Co-Efficients') certainly discussed the question of war, H. G. Wells, *The New Machiavelli*, (1911), ((Harmondsworth, 1970), 264-4. On the other hand H. C. G. Matthew considers the 'Co-Efficients' of little 'importance', and there is no mention of Wells' name in Haldane's MS. Correspondence for 1902 and 1903, the formative years of the group. H. C. G. Matthew, *The Liberal Imperialists* (Oxford, 1973), 167, footnote; R. B. Haldane papers in the National Library of Scotland.

17. For example, Captain Findlay, 'Quality Versus Quanity', *U.S.M.*, vol. XXXIII, July 1906, 380. On the other hand, Captain C. H. Wilson thought, in 1903, that talk of 'a small and efficient Army' was 'childish'. Captain C. H. Wilson, 'The "Rage de Nombres" ', *U.S.M.*, vol. XXVII, April 1903, 74.

18. H. G. Wells, 'Anticipations', (1901), *Works*, vol. 4, 153, 158-61, 173.

19. Brian Bond, *The Victorian Army and the Staff College, 1854-1914* (London, 1972), 235, 258, 299. On the other hand, Spenser Wilkinson was of the opinion that the war would be long, Luvaas, *The Education of an Army*, 283; Barnett, *Britain and Her Army*, 368.

20. Brian Bond, *The Victorian Army*, 261.

21. Lieutenant Colonel H. Elsdale, 'The Evolution of the Art of War', *U.S.M.*, vol. XI, Sept. 1895, 571.

22. Captain C. H. Wilson, 'The "Rage de Nombres" ', *U.S.M.*, vol. XXVII, April 1903, 71-3; Lieutenant Colonel Maude, 'Offensive Tactics in Modern War', *U.S.M.*, vol. XXVI, Nov. 1902, 168-78; Lieutenant Colonel Pollock (The Editor) 'The Way Round a Flank', *U.S.M.*, vol. XXVII, Sept. 1903, 672-4; Captain C. Battine, 'The Offensive Versus the Defensive in the Tactics of Today', *J.R.U.S.I.*, vol. XLVII, June 1903, 655, 672; Captain Johnstone, 'Envelopment versus Penetration', *U.S.M.*, vol. XXXIX, August 1909, 513; Captain Earl Percy, 'The Strategy of the Future', *U.S.M.*, vol. XL, March 1910, 599; see also Major General C. E. Webber, 'Army Reform based on some 19th century lessons in warfare', *J.R.U.S.I.*, vol. XLV, 379, 395.

23. Wells, 'Anticipations', (1901), *Works*, vol. 4, 223. See also the oblique references to Bloch in Wells, 'The Land Ironclads', *op. cit.*, 84-7.

24. Bloch, *The Future of War in Its Technical, Economic and Political Relations* (reprint) (New York and London, 1972), xxvi-vii, xlvii-ix, l, lxxv, 347-56. Wells, 'Anticipations', *Works*, vol. 4, 152-3, 157-9, 163-5.

25. *Ibid.*, 164-5, 161. (By 'organic' is meant that the whole is more important than the parts.)

26. *Ibid.*, 184, and 165-6.

27. *Ibid.*, 166.

28. *Ibid.*, 173.

29. *Ibid.*, 171-2.

30. This is shown below; and more generally, see H. G. Wells, 'The Collapse of Civilisation', (1909), *Works*, vol. 20, 484-4; H. G. Wells, 'The Peace of the World', (1915), *Works*, vol. 21, 275-6; H. G. Wells, 'Tanks', (1916), *Works*, vol. 26, 336, 345; H. G. Wells, 'The Grades of War', (1916), *Works*, vol. 26, 299-303.

31. Norman and Jeanne MacKenzie, *The Time Traveller* (1973), 222. Wells mentioned that Diplock's invention actually occurred in 1896, H. G. Wells, *War and the Future: Italy, France and Britain at War* (1917), 161; Major C. E. McNalty, 'Mechanically Propelled Vehicles for Military Purposes', *J.R.U.S.I.*, vol. XLVIII, Nov. 1904, 1242, 1245. However, Wells seems to imply Victoria Street Westminster, as the first place he encountered the Pedrail, presumably also in 1903, Wells, 'The Land Ironclads', *op. cit.*, 94.

32. *Ibid.*, 93, 99-101.

33. *Ibid., passim.*

34. Capt. B. H. Liddell Hart, *The Tanks: The History of the Royal Tank Regiment and its Predecessors* (2 vols., 1959), vol. 1, 25.

35. *Ibid.*, vol. I, 15-6, 22-3. Wells' ideas may also be compared with those of Captain Tulloch in 1916, 27.

36. *Ibid.*, 22-3.

37. Major C. E. I. McNalty, 'Mechanically Propelled Vehicles for Military Purposes', *J.R.U.S.I.*, vol. XLVIII, Nov. 1904, 1229, 1233, 1250; Captain H. M. Paynter, 'The Use of the Motor Car in Warfare', *J.R.U.S.I.*, vol. L, June 1906, 770-1, 775.

38. For the two schools of thought, see Luvaas, *The Education of an Army*, 331-2.

39. H. G. Wells, *War and the Future*, 165-6.

40. Wells, 'Anticipations', (1901), *Works*, vol. 4, 168-72 (Wells' penchant for seeing aeroplanes as various types of birds and fish caused him to pin the behaviour of these species onto the aeroplane, and thus to see aerial tactics in terms of hawks swooping, sharks striking, etc., 169, 170, 171. This tended to limit Wells' understanding of aerial tactics.)

41. *Ibid.*, 161-2. The value of balloons for observation and as artillery spotters, was acknowledged before and after Wells wrote, e.g. Lieutenant H. B. Jones, 'Military Ballooning', *J.R.U.S.I.*, vol.XXXVI, Feb. 1892, 271; Lieutenant Colonel Capper, 'Military Ballooning', *J.R.U.S I.*, vol. L, July 1906, 890-3.

42. H. G. Wells, *The War of the Worlds* (Harmondsworth, 1946), 162, and 180, where the hero views the dead Martians and their flying machines and comments: 'Death had come not a day too soon'.

43. H. G. Wells, 'When the Sleeper Awakes', (1899), *Works*, vol. 22, 392.

44. Much later Wells tried to analyse why he had woven together a humorous story line and a serious warning, so that the former erased the value of the latter. He concluded that it was some kind of defensive mental mechanism, H. G. Wells, *The Common Sense of War and Peace* (Harmondsworth, 1940), 65-7.

45. H. G. Wells, 'Preface to the 1921 Edition', in *The War in the Air* (Harmondsworth, 1941), 7.

46. *Ibid.*, 164.

47. *Ibid.*

48. *Ibid.*, 164-5.

49. *Ibid.*, 165-6. It is interesting to note that André Beaufre, while Director of the French Institute of Strategic Studies, made exactly the same predictions as Wells in regard to future air wars eliminating fronts and the tactical problems of interception and counter-interception. André Beaufre, 'Battlefields of the 1980s', in N. Calder (ed.), *Unless Peace Comes* (New York, 1968), 9, 15.

50. H. G. Wells, *The War in the Air*, 163-6.

51. Douhet's ideas are briefly available in Eugene M. Emme (ed.), *The Impact*

of Air Power (Princeton, 1959), 161-9; and are summarised in Theodore Ropp, *War in the Modern World* (Durham, North Carolina, 1959), 273-5. Douhet's adherence to fascism and his concept of a central warmaking authority can also be compared to Wells' idea of governments run by efficient functional elites.

52.   Wells, *War in the Air*, 231-5. Bloch thought, in general terms, that war would be followed by the moral, social and economic collapse of urban populations, leading to famine and revolution, Bloch, *The Future of War*, xxxix, xlii, xlix-l, lxii; Wells was also in an apocalyptic mood at this time: 'We have overdeveloped war', he wrote in 1909, war had now become insane because of the high expenditure on new weapons and new possibilities of destruction such as the flying machine, Wells, 'The Collapse of Civilisation', (1909), *Works*, vol. 20, 472-3.

53.   E. M. Earle, 'The Influence of Air Power Upon History', *The Yale Review*, vol. XXXV, June 1946, 582.

54.   H. G. Wells, 'The Coming of Blériot', (1909), *Works*, vol. 20, 419.

55.   Captain J. D. Fullerton, 'Modern Aerial Navigation', *J.R.U.S.I.*, vol. XXXVI, July 1892, 742, 743, 749, 720. (Fullerton cited Hiram Maxim from the latter's 'Aerial Navigation', *Century Magazine*, October 1891). Lieutenant B. F. S. Baden Powell also doubted the defensive aspects of the Channel, 'The Conquest of the Air', *U.S.M.*, vol. XV, April 1897, 57.

56.   *Ibid.*, 56, 58-9. Baden Powell made an interesting comparison of the uses of flying machines in (i) peace, (ii) strained relations, and (iii) war; as well as exemplifying the frequent tendency to visualise new weapons in naval terms, cf. Wells and the tank. For Douhet on the decrease of land and sea forces, see Theodore Ropp, *War in the Modern World*, 274.

57.   E. M. Earle, 'The Influence of Air Power upon History', *The Yale Review*, vol. XXXV, June 1946, 582.

58.   Lieutenant Colonel J. E. Capper, 'Military Ballooning', *J.R.U.S.I.*, vol. L, July 1906, 900. Fullerton, now a Colonel, was especially sanguine about the various tactical roles of 'soaring' and 'driving' machines on air, land and sea, and talked of the value of command of the air, Colonel J. D. Fullerton, 'Recent Progress in Aerial Navigation', *J.R.U.S.I.*, vol. LI, Jan. 1907, 11-54.

59.   Major Bannerman-Phillips, 'The Future of Airships in War', *U.S.M.*, vol. XXXVII, Sept. 1908, 589, 592.

60.   For example, Captain Boone, 'Aerial Navigation in War', *U.S.M.*, vol. XXXVI, Jan. 1908, 374. In 1909 Bannerman-Phillips considered that aviators needed the instinct of birds, and that a 'flying sense' would have to be developed through exposure to the risks of death and the challenge of fighting Nature, Major Bannerman-Phillips, 'Military Aviation', *U.S.M..*, vol. XL, Nov. 1909, 190, 195.

61.   Major Bannerman-Phillips, 'Progress in Aeronautics', *U.S.M.*, vol. XXXVIII, March 1909, 621, 624. (There are some unusual ideas in this article, among them that the flying machine must be able to remain stationary in one spot, that landing should be by slow parachute fall and not a glide, and an expression of surprise that it was easier to go faster than slower in the air, 623-4.)

62.   Captain Boone, 'Aerial Navigation in War', *U.S.M.*, vol. XXXVI, Jan. 1908, 371 ff.; Major Bannerman-Phillips, 'Progress in Military Aeronautics', *U.S.M..*, vol. XL, March 1910, 622; Lieutenant Crossfield, 'Airships and the Navy', *U.S.M.*, vol. XL, Nov. 1909, 141.

63.   Lieutenant Colonel J. E. Capper, 'Military Ballooning', *J.R.U.S.I.*, vol. L, July, 1906, 900; Major B. F. S. Baden Powell, 'How Air-Ships Are Likely To Affect War', *J.R.U.S.I.*, vol. LIV, May 1910, 562-3; Colonel F. G. Stone, 'Limitations of Aerial Bombardment by International Law', lecture delivered to the 44th Annual Meeting of the Aeronautical Society on 10 Dec. 1909, and cited in Harold Penrose, *British Aviation: The Pioneer Years, 1903-1914* (1967), 198.

64.   Major Bannerman-Phillips, 'The Significance of Aerial Navigation for Great Britain', *U.S.M.*, vol. XXXIX, June 1909, 278, 281.

65.   Emme (ed.), *The Impact of Air Power*, 23.

66.   1917 is the date often given as the 'Magna Carta' of Air Power Strategy, *Ibid.*, 33.

67.   H. G. Wells, 'The World Set Free', (1914), *Works*, vol. 21, 21, where Rufus, evidently Lord Rutherford, lectures on Radium and Radioactivity. See also MacKenzies, *The Time Traveller*, 298-9, where Wells is reported to have influenced the nuclear scientist Leo Szilard.

68.   H. G. Wells, 'The World Set Free', (1914), *Works*, vol. 21, 89-91, 176-8.

69.   *Ibid.*, 175, 120.

70.   *Ibid.*, 91-2.

71.   H. G. Wells, *The War in the Air*, 166.

72.   H. G. Wells, 'The Grades of War', (1916), *Works*, vol. 26, 302-4. Lieutenant B. F. S. Baden Powell, 'The Conquest of the Air', *U.S.M.*, vol. XV, April 1897, 59.

73.   H. G. Wells, 'The World Set Free', (1914), *Works*, 94, 82, 120, 185.

74.   H. G. Wells, 'The Common Sense of Warfare', (1912), *Works*, vol. 20, 137-137-9.

75.   H. G. Wells, *Experiment in Autobiography*, vol. II, 684-5.

76.   H. G. Wells, *Little Wars* (1913), 101, 111.

77.   H. G. Wells, *War and the Future*, 111-3, 153,5, 163, 8. Wells continued to stress the value of new weapons — 'the art of modern war is to invent and invent and invent'. *Ibid.*, 268.

78.   *Ibid.*, 153, 156. Wells, *Experiment in Autobiography*, vol. II, 693.

79.   On Wells' change of heart in 1916, see MacKenzies, *The Time Traveller*, 310-1. The main exception to Wells' silence on military theory seems to be H. G. Wells, *The Way the World is Going* (1928), especially the section entitled 'Changes in the Arts of War. Are Armies Needed any Longer? The Twilight of the Guards'.

80.   H. G. Wells, 'Anticipations', (1901), *Works*, vol. 4, 157; H. G. Wells, *The War in the Air*, 123.

81.   MacKenzies, *The Time Traveller*, 56.

82.   H. G. Wells, *Experiment in Autobiography*, vol. I, 210, 238, 260. At the same time Wells must have been aware of Herbert Spencer's ideal of an efficient military state:

> 'To be in the highest degree efficient, the corporate action needed for preserving the corporate life must be joined in by every one. Other things being equal, the fighting power will be the greatest where those who cannot fight, labour exclusively to support and help those who can: an evident implication being that the working part shall be no larger than is required for these ends . . . To satisfy these requirements, the life, the actions, and the possessions, of each individual must be held at the service of the society . . .'

Herbert Spencer, *The Principles of Sociology* (3 vols., New York and London, 1910), vol. 2, 600-02.

83.   H. G. Wells, 'Anticipations', (1901), *Works*, vol. 4, 87, 127, 143, 183-4, 189. For Spencer, see J. D. Y. Peel, *Herbert Spencer: The Evolution of a Sociologist* (1971), especially chapters 5-8.

84.   H. G. Wells, *Experiment in Autobiography*, vol. 2, 688; H. G. Wells, 'Anticipations', (1901), *Works*, vol. 4, 163, 178-84. The themes of horizontal and vertical struggle, the impact of invention, and subsequent specialisation, are also very evident in Herbert Spencer, Peel, *Herbert Spencer*, 209-14, 139.

85.   G. R. Searle, *The Quest for National Efficiency: A Study in British Politics*

and Political Thought, 1899-1914 (1971).

86. On Fuller's scientific method, see Luvaas, *The Education of an Army*, 349, 352; H. G. Wells, 'The Discovery of the Future', (1902), *Works*, vol. 4, 375-7, 379, *passim*. Wells went so far as to predict the future shock of accelerated change, *ibid.*, 388; and to suggest that Professorships of Analytical History be founded, in order to scientifically predict the future, H. G. Wells, *Experiment in Autobiography*, vol. 2, 646-7.

87. J. F. C. Fuller, *Machine Warfare* (1942), 8; J. F. C. Fuller, 'The Application of Recent Developments in Mechanisms and Other Scientific Knowledge to Preparation and Training for Future War on Land', *J.R.U.S.I.*, vol. LXV, 1920, cited in Luvaas, *The Education of an Army*, 347.

88. J. F. C. Fuller, *The Reformation of War* (1923), 136, 147, 154, 169,

89. J. F. C. Fuller, *Memoirs of an Unconventional Soldier*, 466; J. F. C. Fuller, *Reformation of War*, 112. For Wells on warmaking democracy, H. G. Wells, 'Anticipations', (1901), *Works*, vol. 4, 147-9.

90. Luvaas, *The Education of an Army*, 364-5. The political and military views of Wells and Fuller were so strikingly similar that it is surprising to find neither mentioned in each other's books, unless Wells' enigmatic and futuristic reference to an imaginary Fuller-Metsch, and Fuller-Metsch's book, *The Ideas of the New Warfare in the Middle Twentieth Century* (2001), be considered a parody of J. F. C. Fuller, H. G. Wells, *The Shape of Things to Come* (New York, 1933), 151 ff. Politically, also, it may be noted that while Fuller supported Sir Oswald Mosley and British Fascism, Wells came close to Fascism in the 1930s (despite his dislike of Mosley), calling for 'Liberal Fascists' and 'enlightened Nazis'. H. G. Wells, *After Democracy* (1932), 24.

91. Brian Bond, *The Victorian Army and the Staff College*, 279, 281, 286, 289, 292-3; J. F. C. Fuller, *Memoirs of an Unconventional Soldier*, 462.

92. See 'Preface to the 1941 Edition' in H. G. Wells, *War in the Air*, 8; H. G. Wells, *Mind at the End of its Tether* (1944), *passim*, although the dropping of the atomic bomb in 1945 on Hiroshima roused Wells to one last effort to save mankind, MacKenzies, *The Time Traveller*, 445-6.

ATTITUDES TO WAR IN LATE VICTORIAN AND EDWARDIAN ENGLAND

John Gooch

In their eagerness to investigate the origins of the First World War historians seem largely to have lost sight of certain important aspects of the pre-1914 *weltanschauung*. One such aspect is the degree to which British society had been conditioned to accept military activity as necessary or desirable, or both. Popular fiction undoubtedly contributed much to the formation of these attitudes of mind, and a study of the impact of such novels as those by G. A. Henty is long overdue. So too is an examination of the ideals of service and self-sacrifice inculcated at schools and universities. A third area of critical importance was the influence of non-fiction upon the reading public. An examination of this phenomenon, through a limited sample of books and journals, does make it possible to attempt an interim assessment of the educative impact of 'serious' literature (as opposed to creative fiction), of the categories into which the arguments fell and of their relative weights and merits.

The outbreak of war in August 1914 came as a surprise to many in England among soldiers and civilians alike. The future Lord Ismay, recalling his return from India in July of that year, afterwards wrote 'How extraordinary it was that none of us had any inkling that all hell was just about to be let loose in Europe'.[1] But if war was a surprise, it was not one which was entirely unwelcome. Recruits flocked to join Kitchener's New Armies and England proved sufficiently prodigal of her youth to stave off the introduction of conscription until 1916. The question which therefore arises is why war proved to be such a popular outlet for the nation's energies. A large part of the answer lies in the fact that war, although not expected, was not unconsidered by the British public. Over the previous forty years a series of debates had raged during the course of which the phenomenon of war came to be examined from a wide variety of perspectives.

In the middle years of Queen Victoria's reign England became reacquainted for the first time since Napoleon's day with the notion of armed conflict upon her own soil. One word could send a *frisson* of terror coursing down the middle class spine — invasion. Awareness of the vulnerability of England to attack from across the Channel had not been entirely unknown in the past; in 1847 the Duke of Wellington himself had remarked in print that the only portion of the British Isles secure from the attentions of an invading force was that part commanded by the guns of Dover Castle. In 1859 Palmerston had again raised the far from lifeless spectre, and had constructed a chain of forts around the south coast of England to fend off the French. But the theme was given a dramatic new twist when in May 1871, there appeared in *Blackwood's Magazine* a piece by Sir George Chesney entitled 'The Battle of Dorking'. So popular that it was quickly reproduced in book form, Chesney's story foretold the destruction of the Channel Fleet by a secret device — the precise nature of which was not revealed to readers — and the subsequent landing of 200,000 Prussians.[2] Its author went on to fame and fortune, having put war firmly in the forefront of the Victorian mind.

Chesney's work set a pattern that was copied, sometimes well and sometimes indifferently, by a myriad of scholars, servicemen and sensationalists during the next thirty years. Invasion might, however, have remained on the bookshelf had it not quickly found its way into the realms of official policy. The first stage in this translation came with the debate over the construction of a Channel Tunnel in 1882-3.[3] The second, and perhaps more significant, came five years later when Viscount Wolseley, hero of the Ashanti War and the most popular soldier of the day, broke the silence imposed upon him by his tenure of the post of Adjutant General at the War Office to inform the House of Lords of three things:

'That as long as the Navy is as weak as it is at this moment, Her Majesty's Army cannot hold its own all over the world, dispersed as it is; that our defences at home and abroad are at this moment in an unsatisfactory condition, and that our military forces are not organised or equipped as they should be to guarantee even the safety of the capital in which we are at this present moment.'[4]

Invasion had now been given an official *imprimatur*, and officialdom itself soon became as transfixed as was the public by its prospect. One important War Office official was reported as 'recasting the various schemes from the point of view of our finding the French army on our breakfast tables with *The Times* tomorrow morning',[5] and military planning grew ever more concerned with a similar, if less rapid, influx of unwelcome visitors. The Naval Defence Act of 1889, which expended £21,500,000 on new capital ships, contrived to end the immediate concern, but as a public preoccupation invasion was far from dead. It figured prominently in the tabloid press, and was called into service by Alfred Harmsworth in 1895 in his attempt to win a Parliamentary seat at Portsmouth. On this occasion, despite a luridly advertised serial entitled 'The Siege of Portsmouth' run in the Harmsworth-owned

Portsmouth Mail and figuring local worthies, the prospect of this form of war failed to win the aspiring member his seat.[6]

The literature of invasion, which had died down around the turn of the century, enjoyed a brief renaissance with the appearance in 1906 of William Le Queux's *The Invasion of 1910*. The convincing technical background to this work owed much to the advice given to the author by Field-Marshal Earl Roberts, who had only two years previously relinquished his post as the last Commander-in-Chief of the British army. Roberts' appearance denotes a change in the literature, which was now being used as a polemic by those, of whom Roberts was one, who opposed further naval construction and wished instead to see a strengthening of Britain's land forces. By 1910 invasion had all but died out in the popular press, and what remained was transmuted into the literature of spy fever.[7]

Invasion literature occupied a position halfway between fiction and fact. The crisis of the 1880s had, however, produced another form of literature which was in the long run to be more significant than the invasion novel — the serious analysis of Britain's position *vis-à-vis* the continent in terms of power politics and especially of war potential. One of the first, and probably the greatest, of such works was Sir Charles Dilke's *The Present Position of European Politics*, published in 1887. In the Jubilee Year, with the great Naval Review at Spithead and the Imperial Review in June in the forefront of the public mind, the impact of Dilke's work was more strongly felt than if it had been published either earlier or later.

In many ways Dilke's book was prophetic. Greatly concerned at the growth of Anglo-German rivalry, he correctly foresaw that the next great European war would break out as a result of German violation of the Belgian frontier in order to attack France.[8] He also realised that advances in technology meant that the next war would not be one of movement and advance since fortresses and the defensive capabilities of the rifle would halt the attack. Even though this was so, and England herself was pacific, Dilke's final consideration of her chances in war was far from gloomy:

> 'It may be noted ... that the widespread tone of peace in England to a great extent arises from the very reasons which would make us formidable in a war of long continuance: our immense wealth and resources, and that concentration of energy upon business which everywhere indisposes to war.'

Dilke's 'continentalism' provoked a strongly hostile response, chiefly because of his favourable view of conscript armies. The reaction against such unpleasant and unnecessary forces was typified by one hostile reviewer who argued that conscription produced forces too large to be handled effectively in the field, and moreover that they had 'no spirit of conquest, the rank and file have no hopes or desire of military glory . . . they detest the service to which patriotic duty compels them to submit'.[10] In the same review a notion was suggested which was to become widespread in its appeal, namely that a long war would be impossible since, with so many of the nation's wage earners absent, the economy must collapse. The general reaction to Dilke's work was to provoke a debate about the nature of war in which continental comparisons were more frequently made, together with analyses of differing forms of military organisation and of the effects of weaponry on the battlefield. This was in time to lead to consideration of war on ethical or philosophical planes.

In the first instance, the technical superseded the moral in examinations of the nature of war. Everyone appeared to be interested in war, everyone felt that certain measures must be taken against it; differences were only those of degree. As one anonymous contemporary observer remarked, 'There is no peace-at-any-price party'.[11] The monthlies and quarterlies turned ever more attention to the topic, a common approach being the glorification of war as a theatrical event of sombre magnificence. Thus an article on the Chilean Civil War began:

'On the further side of the world a great drama is being acted. The arena is a deadly unwatered nitrate plain; the background is the superb screen of the lofty Andes; the wild clang of the orchestra music is formed of booming guns and the hiss of torpedoes rushing through the waters, broken at times by a deafening crash as some stately vessel flings her burden towards the sky, then sinks with it to where it will block the stage no more; and the warships of the European Powers, stern and silent in their august neutrality, are the spectators looking on.'[12]

As far as Britain herself was concerned, the consensus of opinion rejected conscription as a solution to her military problems — and especially of the mounting possibility of a continental war — in favour of reliance upon patriotism. Since England appeared determined to sustain her 'Splendid Isolation' it was argued as being unlikely that she would have to face a continental army; conscription would in any case weaken the army by introducing into it poor physical types; and there were grave social dangers in training the populace to arms, as the Commune had demonstrated. One authority went so far as to proclaim that conscription, together with continual preparation for war, was what prevented Germany from achieving a flourishing economy. The inference, for England, was obvious.[13]

Such considerations as these tended to be submerged in the examination of the effects of technological advance upon battle, when most authorities continued to believe in the power of the offensive despite all evidence to the contrary. 'Neither smokeless powder, nor the magazine rifle will necessitate any radical change, or introduce any important modification', stated one fearless commentator.[14] The absence of clouds of smoke on the battlefield would permit the defence to be shaken by the realisation of the size of the force attacking it, or so it was thought. There was in any case a necessity to encourage offensive capability since it evoked the fighting spirit, which might otherwise be checked. This psychological imperative was grounded in the belief that men taught to fight skilfully in entrenchments would not fight gallantly in front of them. Moral force was already accepted as the key to victory. This view was summed up in 1895 by Colonel Frederick Maurice: 'We fear lest a war of mere entrenchments should reduce armies to a condition in which there will be left little of that spirit which nails victories to standards.'[15] In order to generate such a desirable quality, there was a conscious turning against the known lessons of the Franco-Prussian and American Civil Wars. Maurice himself had turned completely round from the position he had adopted four years earlier when he admitted the impact of firepower: '. . . changes in the progress of scientific discovery, which a year ago had scarcely passed beyond the experimental stage, have now arrived at a condition which forces upon us questions as to the effect they will produce in future wars.'[16]

A shrewder observer than Maurice, though one very much in a minority, did remark on the probable effects of the improvement in what he termed missile power: 'with the ever increasing perfection of missile warfare, the defence tends steadily to become too strong for the attack.'[17] The same perceptive author foresaw the advent of air power, of balloons being replaced by 'flying machines', and of the indirect attack. But his greatest foresight, and the one in which he was most at variance with his contemporaries, was in recognising that future wars would of necessity be long: 'the game will tend to become more protracted. Moreover the advantage will lie with that side which does not mobilise all or nearly all its reserves at once, but keeps them for a later stage of the war.'[18]

The discussion of war in the press during the first half of the 1890s was concerned chiefly with the nuts and bolts — questions of technical feasibility and organisation. There are signs that this began to quieten down during the second half of that decade, a development which so alarmed the anonymous 'Hibernicus' as to move him to call for a popular literature of war, spearheaded by a Zola or a Tolstoy, to keep the subject in the public mind.[19] The event which was to satisfy Hibernicus' demands, and radically to change the nature of public debate about war, occurred on 24 August 1898 when the Tsar of Russia suggested to the diplomatic representatives of the Great Powers at St Petersburg that the present moment was 'a very favourable one for seeking, through international discussion, the most effective means of assuring to all peoples the blessings of real and lasting peace, and above all of limiting the progressive development of existing armaments.'[20] The news of the Imperial Rescript and of the proposed Hague Conference at which it was hoped to implement it prompted a general call for the diagnosis of the roots of war, as distinct from its manifestations.[21] It now came to be considered as a moral phenomenon and one in which ethical considerations and social arguments were of considerable importance. Discussion was to progress onto a more generalised and theoretical plane about the place of war in human affairs.

Two closely integrated arguments were now put forward, both owing much to the popularisation and vulgarisation of the ideas of Darwin and Huxley. The first was that war was a natural state of man, and that therefore to seek to avert it was fruitless. A purely biological view was rare, though there were those who suggested that conflict occurred between species that were most similar to each other, and that Germany was more akin to Great Britain than was France: 'Here is the first great racial struggle of the future, here are two growing nations pressing against each other, man to man all over the world. One or the other has to go; one or the other will go.'[22] This notion of inevitable struggle was later to be endorsed by J. A. Cramb, professor of history at London University, whose philosophy followed that of Treitschke in believing that 'a nation's armed force is the expression of a nation's will to power, of a nation's will to life'.[23] For him, as for others, Germany and England were the twin sons of Odin, foredoomed to conflict.

Rather more common was the notion that conflict was endemic in civilisations once they had reached a certain stage of development, a stage in which they now found themselves. Consideration of the military structure of continental states was especially prone to induce despondency on this score: 'On beholding these vast European armaments, the thinker is almost led to believe, in spite of himself, that turmoil, not tranquillity, is the natural state of man.'[24] More sophisticated analysis pointed out that the military system was deeply rooted in the economic structure of a state; without armaments, industrial paralysis would ensue. Crudely put, war meant profit: 'Naval warfare is fast becoming one of the very finest processes of economic consumption.'[25] An engagement between thirty modern battleships was calculated as costing £1,000,000 an hour excluding replacement of or repairs to damaged ships. In addition war improved the labour market by siphoning off young men; to allow those now in the army to return to civilian life would be 'equivalent to the suppression of a great industry, for which nothing is to be substituted.'[26] The logical conclusion of this line of reasoning was duly pointed out by Sir Henry Howarth: that if war was both endemic and costly, then not every state could afford to indulge in it.

'The competition is necessarily one of purses and of the lasting out of resources. I have been taken to task as if I were saying something vulgar and sordid in this, but it is plain prose. The expense of modern war is what makes it a luxury, and the poorer nations who cannot afford it should desist from the competition.'[27]

Some of those who denigrated opposition to war and argued in favour of its being a natural state of man clearly felt a social spur to do so, that of the class structure as it then stood. The crudest variant of this argument was that people had always admired soldiers and that they always would.[28] A more subtle version of the thesis was that people had always admired soldiers and that they always *should*. The aristocracy had made England great, and in doing so had thrown up figures of incomparable virtue; the plutocracy was on its way to making her ignoble through middle class government, which aimed at peace and produced degeneration.[29] The belief that the military arts inspired civic virtues was one which seems to have had a widespread credence.

The second major group of thinkers on war, somewhat more dependent upon the supposed laws of natural selection than the first, held that war was to be hailed as positively beneficial to society, being a great force for social advance. They were particularly concerned to refute the analogy that war was to the nation what crime was to the individual.

'Is not war the grand scheme of nature by which degenerate, weak or otherwise harmful states are eliminated from the concerted action of civilized nations, and assimilated to those who are strong, vital, and beneficial in their influences. Undoubtedly this is so . . .'[30]

Progress was therefore held to mean struggle, security to result in deterioration and death. The theory of evolution was specifically evoked in order to prove that absolute security meant absolute decay; struggle meant strength, progress, growth and happiness. Admittedly such a belief carried with it unfortunate corollaries, the most important of which was the accepted tendency of war to breed disruptive elements: 'War is . . . a wholesale manufacturer of malcontents, revolutionaries and traitors . . .'[31] Yet this was far outweighed by the impulse that war had given to the development of art, science, learning and industry.[32]

If war was thus acceptable, so too was training for war since it fostered all that was healthy in a nation's fibre. Conscription, it was argued, would not be a burden but a blessing in disguise, improving the stamina and moral qualities of the race and counteracting the deterioration that had been brought on by city life.[33] Viscount Wolseley, not without a certain professional interest in this finding, argued strongly that such an activity was

> '. . . an invigorating antidote against that luxury and effeminacy which destroys nations as well as individuals . . . national training keeps healthy and robust the manhood of a state, and in saving it from degeneration nobly serves the cause of civilisation.'[34]

The pursuit of wealth and the enjoyment of ease appeared, at the opening of the twentieth century, to be taking on such a commanding place that 'the drastic medicine of war alone can revive . . . former manliness'.[35] Wolseley drew the attention of the public to the ruins of Thebes, Carthage, Greece and Rome and hinted darkly at the witness they bore to the disastrous results of 'unmanly vices'.[36]

Such theories offered dangerous fuel to those of a proselytising frame of mind, since they could be used to advance arguments in favour of offensive war as bringing benefits to one's defeated opponent as well as to one's self. In this light, war was seen as a justifiable barbarism because of its civilising mission.[37] It was a rare voice which argued that the strain of large wars evaporated their civilising effect and that their ultimate results were far more extreme, disrupting the economy and having longlasting effects.[38] Equally unusual was the view that war would eventually disappear through the dilution of the military instinct.[39]

The debate over the place of war in the scale of man's activity was rapidly brought down to earth in 1899 with the publication of a book which redirected attention towards the configurations of the battlefield in the light of modern technology and savagely attacked accepted views. This was the English translation of *La guerre future* by the Polish banker and economist I. S. Bloch. Bloch foresaw the nature of the next European war with uncanny accuracy.

> 'The war, instead of being a hand-to-hand contest in which the combatants measure their physical and moral superiority, will become a stalemate, in which neither army being able to get at the other, both armies will be maintained in opposition to each other, threatening each other but never able to deliver a final and decisive blow . . .'[40]

War would occupy much more time than anyone had hitherto supposed, and would be marked by entrenchments and the power of the rifle; thus the victor as well as the vanquished could expect to be exhausted. In such a struggle, Bloch pointed out, it would not be the military excellence of the armies that decided the issue but the qualities of the civilians, their reserves of 'toughness or capacity of endurance, of patience under privation, of stubbornness under reverse and disappointment'.[41]

As far as the shape of war went Bloch foresaw the use of the blockade, of submarines and of convoys, the brief life of junior officers in the front line and the dominating power of explosives. He even drew a striking picture of the no-man's-land between the two armies: 'there will be a belt a thousand paces wide, separating [the two armies] as if neutral territory, swept by the fire of both sides, a belt in which no living being can stand for a moment.'[42]

If Bloch's calculus of war were to be accepted, then the notion that it offered positive benefits to society must fall. Bloch himself could only suggest the inevitable results of the armed peace of Europe — 'slow destruction in consequence of expenditure on preparations for war, or swift destruction in the event of war'.[43] In either case, social convulsions would inevitably result.

Bloch's work appeared at the moment when Britain was harnessing her energies for the defeat of the Boers in South Africa, a task that was to prove notably difficult. The wave of popular antipathy to the Boers which swept over England added a new element in the consideration of war — jingoism. Liberal intellectuals recoiled with shock from this phenomenon, which the literature of the previous decade had done much to generate, and thus from war itself. Their foremost publicist, J. A. Hobson, provided the first and most satisfactory definition of the new term: 'That introverted patriotism whereby love of one's own nation is transformed into the hatred of another nation, and the fierce craving to destroy the individual members of that other nation . . .'[44] If Bloch's notion of the importance of social resilience was going to be accepted as a goal, then jingoism would be an important means of securing it. Hobson never fully considered this aspect of the problem, regarding jingoism as anti-rational and as a reversion to the primitive in man. It resulted, he felt, from the effect of urban industrial life in destroying individual character and from the impact of the tabloid press, which he regarded as 'a Roman arena, a Spanish bull-ring, and an English prize fight rolled into one'.[45] In the former view he stood unconsciously close to the position occupied by Lord Wolseley and others, whilst in the latter he had undoubtedly seized on one of the chief formative influences in determining the public view of war.

In regarding jingoism simply as anti-rational, Hobson failed to exhibit any understanding of the demands and strains which war placed upon society at the beginning of the Edwardian era. His was an emotional reaction against a distasteful phenomenon. He did, however, attack the 'scientific' notion of trends of civilisation that had been at the base of much earlier thought about war, with its belief that races of lower social efficiency gave way to those of higher social efficiency after the test of combat. This view he regarded simply as a mask for the 'naked iniquities of aggressive war'.[46]

Hobson's view of war came out more clearly in his study of imperialism; the relationship between this work and his earlier study of jingoism is too rarely remarked.[47] Imperialism Hobson felt to be interdependent with militarism: 'Imperialism . . . implies militarism now and ruinous wars in the near future.'[48] Imperialism was thus related to that lust for slaughter and struggle for life which Hobson so disliked.[49] This in its turn meant that the spectatorial lust of jingoism was a most serious factor in explaining the workings of Imperialism.[50] The endless chain — imperialism, militarism, jingoism, imperialism — hemmed Hobson round so that he never managed to free himself from emotion and produce a dispassionate analysis of the relationship between society and war. Nonetheless, his attack on the glorification of war marked an important stage in the development of thought about war and found several echoes. The attraction of war to the masses, seemingly an undeniable fact, was explained by a fellow liberal, G. P. Gooch, thus: 'Long immunity from the realities of warfare has blunted our imaginations. We love excitement not a whit less than the Latin races; our lives are dull; a victory is a thing the meanest of us can understand.'[51] The liberal school thus offered one more exemplar of the accuracy of Hobbes' views about the life of man, but could suggest no way of re-shaping that life so as to direct man's attention away from his popular pastime.

The environment of growing international tension after the Agadir crisis, visually personified in the naval arms race with Germany, led to a renewal of the dialectic about war, now to be found in books rather than in journals, and to a re-emergence of that school which believed war to be desirable on evolutionary grounds. It was particularly apparent in the works of an American, General Homer Lea, which enjoyed a considerable circulation in England. Lea offered his readers the thesis that war was 'but a composite exemplification of the struggle of man upward'.[52] Since the law of struggle governed man as much as it governed animals, Lea felt that any idea of international arbitration between hostile powers was ludicrous. There were in his works clear undertones of anti-democratic feeling which help to explain his ready acceptance of war: 'as the number of individuals who are in control of national affairs increases, there is a concomitant decrease of intelligence, until finally the whole nation is floundering about in the wide, shallow trough of mediocrity.'[53] The implication is clear: since war requires decisive leadership, democracies must hand over its conduct to the social and intellectual elite or else risk losing all.

Lea seized upon imperialism with the avidity that Hobson had shown, but for rather different reasons. To him the unfortunate tendencies present in peacetime democracies seemed about to meet their test as a result of the competition for empire. The inevitability of war 'now rests in the contact of nations and races, in the convergence of their expansion . . .'[54] Without preparation, he warned, Britain's empire would be lost.

Those encumbered with the 'evolutionary' view could call forth in their support the proposition that though might was not always right, nevertheless 'right always tended to create might' and that therefore efficiency at war represented God's test of a nation's soul.[55] Thus war could be portrayed as a clearing house by means of which the Almighty ensured through the operation of divine laws of evolution that sound ideas superseded unsound ones. War, with death, was 'a vital and essential part of the economy of God'.[56] The end product of this system was presumed to be 'the brief but brilliant Period of Maturity' that would represent the highest phase of civilisation and that could only occur after a struggle which would witness 'scenes of more awful suffering, of more savage cruelty, than ever heretofore in the history of the human race'.[57]

A much more convincing argument was put up by the 'rationalist' school, aided by the work of Hobson and Gooch and by a growing dissatisfaction with crude notions of social Darwinism. The strongest attack was launched against the idea that civilisation worked through the crude mechanics of natural selection in order to approach a notional ideal. Man, one important author reminded the public, was marked out from the animal kingdom by his brain, which enabled him to outstrip evolution. Thus 'civilization and cooperation have, ever since the dawn of morality, been steadily eliminating or putting into an ever-remoter background the blind forces of natural selection by death . . .'[58] Allied to this was the argument that no evidence had been set forth, nor did any exist, to prove that war was of permanent value, though it was admitted that it had had a share in the founding of nations and in displaying certain virtues in mankind. Peace, progress and the political structure were held to be intimately connected: 'Aristocracy is the normal form of militant governments, democracy is their harassing and weakening foe.'[59] War was thus seen as a device favoured by tottering governments in order to forestall revolution and silence sedition. Liberty and humanity blossomed in an atmosphere of peace.

An interesting modification of this thesis, rather less widely voiced, was that in most ways war and peace did not differ. 'Success in war requires precisely the same qualities as success in peace', or so the proponent of this view thought.[60] According to this persuasive argument, war does no more than concentrate into a short period of time changes which would normally take several decades; and violent change was for a variety of reasons undesirable.

The military's view of war, put earlier by Wolseley and now personified by Roberts and his campaign for national service, was marked out for bitter denunciation. In an introduction to G. F. R. Henderson's *The Science of War*, first published in 1905, Roberts had pleaded for 'a numerous and well trained army, such an army as we can never hope to possess unless the manhood of this country is willing to undergo a carefully considered course of physical training and tuition in the use of the rifle'.[61] He was even more outspoken in his introduction to another work published not long before his death in remarking contemptuously on 'the mass of human rottenness that thread the thoroughfares of any of our large industrial centres', the only antidote to which was conscription.[62] His repeated sermons on the virtue of war as a tonic of character were an obvious target for attack.

The most damning and direct of such attacks was the accusation, levelled by a Member of Parliament, that men 'of Lord Roberts' caste' needed hardship to arouse them to 'a serious realization of life'; the working classes by contrast had such hardships all around them.[63] The same author struck a shrewd blow against the notion that there was an inbuilt dynamic in society that tended towards war: 'a man dedicated to life-long "preparation" for war must either irrationally glorify his trade or confess that it is one which wastes the life of one set of citizens to give the others a sense of security.'[64] This was supported by a popularisation of the ideas of von Clausewitz designed to demonstrate the salient characteristics of 'absolute war' and to impress the fact that the impact of the phenomenon of a European war on the industrial state which Great Britain had become would produce 'the most calamitous results upon our internal conditions'.[65]

Deeper study is needed of the 'serious' or non-fictional press in England in the decades prior to 1914 before definite conclusions can be reached about its influence in shaping the popular consciousness of war. It is clear that many, though by no means all, of the writers involved in debating the topic of war had some connection with the services. Also the discussion appears to have begun in the pages of the monthlies and quarterlies, all of which were interested to a degree in matters military and some of which were specifically founded to cater for that interest, and then to have moved on from the world of articles into that of books.[66] More research is needed to discern whether these are accurate generalisations. Equally it is only possible to give a tentative explanation of why one mode of thought about war lost out to the other.

If the 'rationalists' had the better ground, nonetheless they appear to have been losing way to the 'naturalists' in the years immediately before the outbreak of the war. It can be argued that their literature was the less exciting of the two, and it was certainly not a popular literature in the sense that it appeared in the tabloid press. Two other explanations suggest themselves. One is that in attempting to wean men away from the notion that war offered any benefits at all they were trying to stem a major trend in civilisation towards the extravagant and the aggressive. Such a trend was discernible in most areas of contemporary activity, but perhaps especially so in philosophy where Neitzsche had given way to Bergson and to a school recognised by the application of a generic term — Futurism. One contemporary analyst thought it peculiarly apt that 'at a time when the two great brother nations of the Teutonic race are preparing their rival sacrifices for the God of War . . . the Futurists should now exalt the sublime vehemence and the aggressive fury of youth'.[67]

The second explanation is that the 'rationalist' argument failed to convince those occupying the influential positions in British society on the eve of the war. This is perhaps best typified by the case of the one man best qualified, in theory at least, to pronounce on the whole problem: Spenser Wilkinson, Chichele Professor of the History of War at Oxford University. In an essay written in 1911 and entitled 'What is Peace?', Wilkinson suggested that one of two alternatives faced man: he could sacrifice life or he could sacrifice what made life worth living. To Norman Angell and others who believed in a third alternative he stated bleakly that 'Peace cannot rationally be the object of policy'.[68]

Notes

1.   *The Memoirs of Lord Ismay*, London 1960, p. 9.
2.   I. F. Clarke, *Voices Prophesying War 1763-1984* (Oxford, 1966), 39-40. See also Samuel Hynes, *The Edwardian Turn of Mind* (Princeton, 1968), 34-53.
3.   C. 248, Report from the Joint Committee . . . on the Channel Tunnel, 10 July 1883.
4.   Hansard, 3rd series, vol. 326 (Lords), 16 May 1888, cols. 100-101.
5.   Ardagh Papers. Fleetwood Wilson to Ardagh, 15 August 1889. P.R.O. 30/40/13. The officer referred to was Colonel Coleridge Grove.
6.   Reginald Pound and Geoffrey Harmsworth, *Northcliffe* (1959), 182.
7.   See H. R. Moon, 'The Invasion of the United Kingdom: Public Controversy and Official Planning 1888-1918', unpublished Ph.D. thesis, University of London (1968), *passim*.
8.   Sir. C. Dilke, *The Present Position of European Politics*, (1887), 47.
9.   *Ibid*., 277.
10.   *Edinburgh Review*, October 1887, 553.
11.   J. A. Spender, *Life of the Right Hon. Sir Henry Campbell-Bannerman*, (1923), vol. I, 210.
12.   M. Eagelstone, 'The War in Chili', *United Services Magazine*, August 1891, 463.
13.   Lt. Col. H. Elsdale, 'Three Ruling Races', *United Services Magazine*, March 1892, 477.
14.   Anon. 'Military Criticism and Modern Tactics', *United Services Magazine*, October 1891, 60.

15.   Col. F. Maurice, 'How far the lessons of the Franco-German war are now out of date', *United Services Magazine*, March 1895, 562.
16.   Col. F. Maurice, *War*, (1891), 19.
17.   Lt. Col. H. Elsdale, 'The Evolution of the Art of War', *United Services Magazine*, September 1895, 572.
18.   *Ibid.*, 587.
19.   'Hibernicus', 'The Service and the Civilians', *United Services Magazine*, February 1896, 538.
20.   Correspondence respecting the Proposal of His Majesty the Emperor of Russia for a Conference on Armaments. Paper communicated by Count Mouravieff to Foreign Representatives, August 24 1898. Inclosure in No. 1, p. 2. Russia No. 1 (1899).
21.   Sir G. S. Clarke, 'The Tsar's Proposed Conference and our Foreign Affairs', *Nineteenth Century*, November 1898, 697-706.
22.   Chalmers Mitchell, 'A Biological View of our Foreign Policy', *Saturday Review*, February 1896. Quo. in the same author's *Evolution and the War*, (1915), xxiii.
23.   J. A. Cramb, *Germany and England*, (1914), 45.
24.   F. G. Wallace Goodbody, 'Would Conscription be suitable to England?', *Colburn's United Services Magazine*, February 1890, 418.
25.   J. McCabe and G. Darien, *Can We Disarm?*, (1899), 46.
26.   *Ibid.*, 54.
27.   Sir Henry Howarth, 'Some Plain Words about the Tsar's New Gospel of Peace', *Nineteenth Century*, February 1899, 211.
28.   Sidney Low, 'The Hypocrisies of the Peace Conference', *Nineteenth Century*, May 1899, 689-98.
29.   H. W. Wilson, 'Peace and War', *United Services Magazine*, September 1897, 602-13.
30.   W. V. Herbert, 'The Ethics of Warfare', *Journal of the Royal United Services Institute*, September 1898, 1023.
31.   Ibid., 1027.
32.   Sidney Low, 'Should Europe Disarm?', *Nineteenth Century*, October 1898, 521-30.
33.   H. Bannerman-Phillips, 'Compulsory Service', *United Services Magazine*, April 1899, 72-3.
34.   Wolseley, 'War and Civilization', *United Services Magazine*, May 1897, 564.
35.   Wolseley, *The Story of a Soldier's Life*, (1903), vol. I, 20.
36.   The report of an Inter-Departmental Committee on Physical Deterioration (1904), prompted by an article in the *Contemporary Review* in January 1902 stating that 60 per cent of all Englishmen were unfit for service in the army, seemed to bear out some at least of Wolseley's views. Hynes, *op. cit.*, 22-3.
37.   Rev. Philip Young, 'Is War Allowable?', *United Services Magazine*, October 1899, 137-41.
38.   P. Holland, 'War with Armies of Millions', *United Services Magazine*, September 1897, 631-50.
39.   A. Sutherland, 'The Natural Decline of Warfare', *Nineteenth Century*, April 1899, 570-8.
40.   I. S. Bloch, *Is War Now Impossible?*, (1899), xvi.
41.   *Ibid.*, xlii.
42.   *Ibid.*, 43, 49.
43.   *Ibid.*, 356.
44.   J. A. Hobson, *The Psychology of Jingoism*, (1901), 1.
45.   *Ibid.*, 29.
46.   *Ibid.*, 85.

47.   Thornton has perceptively remarked upon the equation of imperialism and militarism in the work of Herbert Spencer: A. P. Thornton, *The Imperial Idea and its Enemies*, (1966), 74-5. The point can be extended to include Hobson also.

48.   J. A. Hobson, *Imperialism*, (1902), 137.

49.   *Ibid.*, 255.

50.   *Ibid.*, 227.

51.   G. P. Gooch, 'Imperialism', in C. F. G. Masterman (ed.), *The Heart of the Empire*, (1901), 319.

52.   Homer Lea, *The Valour of Ignorance* (1909), 82.

53.   *Ibid.*, 137.

54.   Homer Lea, *The Day of the Saxon*, (1912), 14.

55.   G. F. Wyatt, *God's Test by War*, (1912), 9, 10.

56.   *Ibid.*, 23.

57.   V. W. Germains, *The Gathering Storm*, (1913), 290. 292.

58.   J. W. Graham, *Evolution and Empire*, (1912), 11.

59.   *Ibid.*, 38.

60.   W. M. Flinders Petrie, *Janus in Modern Life*, (1907), 98.

61.   G. F. R. Henderson, *The Science of War*, (1916), xxiv.

62.   Maj. Gen. Sir W. G. Knox, *The Flaw in Our Armour*, (1913), xi.

63.   J. M. Robertson, *Superstitions of Militarism: Essays towards Peace*, (1913), 28.

64.   *Ibid.*, 29.

65.   S. L. Murray, *The Reality of War*, (1909), 117.

66.   The problem of assessing the exact extent of the public audience for articles in the weekly and quarterly press is a perplexing one. It is best examined in A. P. Wadsworth, 'Newspaper Circulations 1800-1954', *Manchester Statistical Society*, 1955. Reviews in particular guarded their circulation figures jealously: Alvar Ellegard, 'The Readership of the Periodical Press in mid-Victorian Britain', *Acta Universitatis Gothoburgensis*, LXIII, 1957, 8, 22-7.

67.   H. B. Samuel, 'The Future of Futurism', *Fortnightly Review*, April 1913, 739-40. Hynes's assertion that 'anxiety and the expectation of war were a part of Edwardian consciousness' would seem to offer some support for this thesis. Hynes, *op. cit*, 53.

68.   S. Wilkinson, *Government and the War*, (1918), 64.

THE DEBATE ON WARTIME CENSORSHIP IN BRITAIN 1902-14

Philip Towle

The 1914-18 war concluded the great era of the war correspondent. For a hundred years before 1914 correspondents had roamed the world reporting on distant campaigns. The growth of literacy in countries such as Britain and the USA ensured a ready market for their reports, until the names of the more successful ones became household words. But in 1914 this freedom to roam was drastically curtailed. As one historian of the press pointed out recently,

> 'the war had been so well controlled that it had been for newspapermen a time of frustration. The golden age of the war correspondents was past. The machinery of government had caught up with them. They had become in effect the generals' or the politicians' or, more reputably, the private soldiers' public relations men. News could travel so swiftly that censorship had to slow it down or suppress it — often to save lives, sometimes, journalists thought, to save reputations.'[1]

It had been obvious for some time that such a *denouement* was likely. At least as far back as the Peninsular War British generals had complained about the freedom of the press to report on troop movements.[2] However, during the nineteenth century the growing body of journalists had continued to enjoy a high degree of freedom. Ever since *The Times*' correspondent W. H. Russell shocked Britain with his devastating *exposés* of the higher command in the Crimean War, his achievement had been taken as the war correspondent's ideal. Journalists thought it normal and proper to comment on and criticise the level of generalship in the wars which they observed. There were only half-hearted attempts to censor the press during the Austro-Prussian and Franco-Prussian Wars, although Bismarck and Moltke proved remarkably adept at 'guiding' it. Russell himself was treated as an honoured guest at Prussian headquarters. On the French side, the *Standard*'s correspondent in Paris was told that 'there would be a rigid surveillance, that all telegrams except those officially censored would be prohibited, that no correspondents . . . would be allowed at the front and, as Leboeuf put it shortly "on fera fusiller tous les journalistes" '.[3] In fact little effort was made to put this programme into practice and it would in any case probably have proved beyond the resources of the crumbling French administrative machine. The main danger for English journalists came from French officers who took them for German spies, but this did not stop the correspondents from crowding to the front.

These great wars in the centre of Europe were in any case exceptions. Most wars took place on the periphery of the European colonial empires where the incentive for the military staffs to impose censorship was greatly reduced. True, although journalists and war correspondents were often disliked by generals such as Kitchener,[4] they were given a great deal of freedom to report on Britain's colonial wars. After all, it was unlikely that the Sudanese or Ashantis would try to learn military secrets from the pages of the British press. The danger, as far as the generals were concerned, was that the correspondents would try to influence public opinion in England against them. The reputation of the Commander of the British Army during the Third Burma War never recovered from the attacks of one journalist.[5] More famous generals like Kitchener could shrug off such attacks, but no doubt criticisms of the treatment of wounded after the battle of Omdurman had some effect on his reputation.[6]

The war correspondents remained largely unfettered during the Boer War of 1899-1902 and journalists like Winston Churchill continued to wield a great deal of power. Some of the papers had difficulties. The correspondent of the *Manchester Guardian* was arrested after criticising the treatment of the Cape Dutch, and there were threats to cut the *Daily Mail* off from the supply of official information.[7]

However, the real change came in 1904, when war broke out between Russia and Japan in the Far East. Both powers lacked a tradition of a free press, both were autocratic and both were fighting for high stakes, the domination of Manchuria and Korea. Most important western newspapers (and particularly those in Britain and the USA where the war correspondents' tradition was strongest) had decided to send reporters to Japan even before the war had actually begun. Britain had been Japan's ally since 1902 and the newspapers assumed that the Japanese would be more willing to help them than the Russians would. They also felt that Japan had a more liberal regime than its Tsarist enemy, which had long been regarded as the bastion of European reaction, and thus they expected Japanese censorship to be milder. Nothing could have been less true. Japanese experience with western journalists had not been happy; a British journalist had described a massacre in Port Arthur, which he claimed had taken place after the Japanese had captured the town from the Chinese in the Sino-Japanese War of 1894.[8] The Japanese government was in any case far less liberal than westerners assumed and it had pressing reasons for secrecy. It began the war with a pre-emptive strike against the Russian Pacific Fleet and, once it had gained command of the sea, it was determined to preserve the element of surprise, which was the strongest weapon of the dominant naval power.

The Japanese authorities would have been only too pleased to have dispensed completely with the presence of the hundred or more correspondents, who arrived in Tokyo at the beginning of 1904. On the other hand, since most of the journalists came from England or America, the two powers on which a successful outcome of the war depended, the Japanese preferred procrastination to outright rejection. The Japanese regulations laid down that the various ambassadors should apply to the War Office in Tokyo for permission for each correspondent to go to the front. The ambassador was thus made responsible for the good behaviour of the correspondents. The British ambassador Sir Claude MacDonald did his best to see that only men he considered 'responsible' should have the support of the authorities. He refused to forward the application of the *Daily Express* correspondent because he felt that he had shown himself untrustworthy in South Africa[9] and he referred many names for prior approval to the War Office in London.

None of these minor regulations would have mattered if the Japanese had sent the correspondents to the front after they had accepted their applications, but instead they kept them waiting in Tokyo in the hope that they would go home. Most journalists were originally pro-Japanese, but their irritation increased as the months passed. This process is documented in the diary of one of the British Attaches who was in Tokyo and in the letters sent home by Melton Prior, the artist from the *Illustrated London News*.[10] On 7 February 1904 Prior congratulated the Japanese on taking on the much larger Russian forces. A week later he described his delight at learning that the Japanese had decided that the reporters 'will always have our tents pitched near H.Q.', and that the Japanese would look after their provisions. Even when he found that there was to be some delay, he felt that the Japanese 'were right not to turn us loose in Korea to telegraph news for the benefit of Russia'. But by the beginning of March he was writing 'I am sick of these men, you can never get a direct "yes" or "no" from a Jap'. The first group of reporters did not leave for the front unril 7 April and the rest did not leave until the end of July. From being sympathisers with the Japanese, they had become their bitter critics.

On the other side, the situation was quite different. Although the Tsarist regime had always maintained a firm hold on the press inside Russia, censorship on the Russian side in Manchuria was remarkably light. Once the journalists had permission from the authorities in Russia to go to the front, they were given a great deal of freedom. As a result relations between the journalists and the military censors were good.

One of the journalists, Douglas Story, dedicated his book on the war to the Russian censors and many reporters praised their tact and helpfulness.[11] There were inevitably some clashes. All the journalists were ordered to return from the front to Harbin in the rear for a time, after one of their number had signalled a Japanese victory in code.[12] Ernest Brindle, the correspondent of the *London Evening News* was expelled, according to the Russian authorities 'in view of the pernicious activity displayed in sending from Chifu false news of the capture and destruction of Port Arthur and in making use of the most offensive expressions with regard to Russian officers'.[13] Brindle however was an exception.

The Russians gained the sympathy and support of many of the journalists, but they had to forego the advantages of surprise; indeed in most cases they do not appear to have been aware of them. Kuropatkin, the Russian Commander, announced his intention of advancing before the battle of the Shaho and so the Japanese were able to prepare their position to meet him. Another correspondent was allowed to send a telegram forecasting a Russian cavalry raid behind the Japanese lines, an action which can hardly have increased its chances of success.[14] He also left the raiding party while it was on the march, so that he could send an uncensored telegram from Chinese territory and yet he later expressed surprise at Kuropatkin's anger.

The British army officers, who were also attached to the armies of the two combatants, had a good deal of sympathy with them in their dilemma about the way to deal with correspondents. They realised, as most of the journalists did not, both the tremendous advantages to be gained by secrecy and also that much of the correspondents' frustration was caused not by censorship, but by changes in warfare. Most of the reporters who went to Manchuria had been too young to see the last great European wars. Their experience was confined to Britain's frontier conflicts when the battles were fought against a compact force of primitive tribesmen. The Russo-Japanese War was fought with modern weapons and with smokeless powder, which together with trenches and concealed positions had already increased the correspondents' problems in South Africa. Above all, the numbers of troops involved in Manchuria ran into hundreds of thousands and the length of the front stretched over a hundred miles. As one of the military attaches on the Russian side commented ruefully afterwards: 'even now I cannot compile any save the most fragmentary and incomplete details of past events, as it was only by chance that we learned anything beyond our immediate zone, where fighting extended from flank to flank for eighty miles and where regiments met with generally asked for news instead of being able to give any.'[15] Such difficulties hindered the military attaches also. However their superior professional knowledge and training enabled them to interpret and take advantage of even small pieces of information.

Thus on the Japanese side, where the journalists were already infuriated by the delays in Tokyo, they tended to blame their hosts for all the frustrations of the campaign. The senior British officer with the Japanese commented later:

'the press correspondents have behaved damned badly . . . they engaged to do as they were told before they started, but as soon as they got to the front, they ignored all the orders they received and declared they would go where they liked and do what they liked. I think the Japanese have behaved to them considerately, but many of them are out of temper — God knows why — and have gone back openly boasting that they will do their best to injure Japan in the estimation of the British public.'[16]

In fact the Japanese had closely controlled the reporters even after their arrival at the front and experienced correspondents like John Fox, Melton Prior and Rupert Harding Davis had given up in despair.[17] Their sense of astonishment at the size and complexity of the war is obvious from their reports. Few reporters tried to comment on the tactics employed and many made elementary mistakes like suggesting that the range of the Japanese guns was greater than that of the Russians' or that the Japanese had more machine guns.

Despite the feelings of the war correspondents, public opinion in England was firmly pro-Japanese. Many intelligent commentators realised what Japan had gained from its policy of censorship. On one occasion the authorities in Tokyo managed to hide the loss of a battleship. They also kept their enemies guessing about the destination of their armies so that many soldiers were wasted guarding Newchwang and Vladisvostok.[18] The more information became available in England about the war, the more obvious the wisdom of the Japanese became. The British military periodicals began to call with one voice for sterner laws which would control the press were the country again to be involved in war. The *United Service Magazine* was the most outspoken campaigner in this field. One of its writers later praised the Japanese because 'the newspaper correspondents were given little opportunity of seeing important operations and they were not allowed to mention the names of places or allude to movement of troops'.[19] Another prolific writer, Lt. Alfred Dewar pointed out that the Russians appeared to have missed the importance of secrecy. The *Russki Invalid* published information from which 'a mosaic could be built up (by the Japanese) in which the whole organisation and much of the location of the Russian armies was plainly discernible'.[20] Another officer called for a ban on all war correspondents and all military attaches except those from allied countries.[21] The *United Service Magazine* dismissed Melton

Prior's complaints about the Japanese and expressed surprise that he was 'quite unable to appreciate the point of view of the Japanese military authorities'.[22]

The specialised military press was by no means alone in its belief that censorship would have to be institutionalised in wartime. The *Spectator* expressed the view that 'the war correspondent has developed into a spy of the most dangerous nature'.[23] *The Times* also warned in an editorial that

'every year that passes enhances the danger and the mischief, since every year witnesses a multiplication and acceleration of the means of communication . . . When publicity, boundless and unrestricted is the rule, insatiable curiosity, a habit of propagating rumour rather than sifting intelligence and a tendency to pander to the love of sensation . . . are sure to be among the consequences. In time of war these journalistic vices become public dangers.'[24]

A growing number of examples were discovered where press reports had damaged one side during a campaign. According to the *Fortnightly Review*, 'the untimely publication of a paragraph often times may dislocate the whole plan of campaign and may even ruin the state'.[25] The writer claimed that the whereabouts of the British Fleet was revealed in the press when it appeared that the Fashoda crisis might lead to war with France in 1898, and again when the Russian Fleet had fired at British fishing boats near the Dogger Bank during the Russo-Japanese War. 'We do not have to look beyond the Russo-Japanese War to appreciate all that publicity and all that the lack of it may mean to a nation at war' he added. According to Brigadier Aston, who was lecturing at the Staff College, the Germans had gained vital information in 1866 from watching the press.[26] Aston also believed that the Gussi expedition failed during the Spanish-American War, because the press revealed its disposition and destination.

While these arguments were being aired in the press, the government was under pressure in the House of Lords to introduce legislation on censorship. This campaign was led by Lord Ellenborough, who had fought in Afghanistan in 1879-80 and in the Boer War. In the debate, which took place on 14 July 1905, Ellenborough said 'is it not desirable to consider the arguments for having to undergo some national inconvenience as regards the dissemination of news in case of war or grave emergency . . . and whether considering the success which has hitherto attended the Japanese system of keeping secret the movement of their forces a similar system could not be introduced in England.'[27] Ellenborough quoted an article by Admiral Sir Cyprian Bridge in *Brassey's Annual* in which Bridge claimed that Japanese naval successes were largely the result of the 'prevention of the dissemination of news affecting the movement of ships'. Neither in the press nor in Parliament does there appear to have been any mention of the advantages gained by the Russians in winning over the correspondents who were reporting the war from their side. No doubt they were considered derisory by the advocates of censorship, but their opponents might have been expected to refer to them.

Official circles were also beginning to advocate tougher censorship. At the beginning of November 1904, the War Minister Arnold Forster minuted:

'has the question of correspondents in time of war been adjusted on a proper basis? I am afraid my view is that everything that has been done hitherto has been wrong and that correspondents have more often proved more of an embarassment than an aid to an army in time of war. It is difficult to make changes, because the idea that war is conducted for the benefit of newspapers has taken very firm root; but I think that the experiences of the Russo-Japanese War should prove of some assistance to us . . . I see no reason why any foreign correspondents should accompany our army in the field. I can conceive many cases in which their presence would be a great disadvantage.'[28]

the Permanent Under-Secretary of State at the War Office, Sir Edward Ward thought that the existing regulations dating from the Boer War were adequate, but his arguments were unable to stem the forces in favour of change. Already the War Office had presented a memorandum to the Committee of Imperial Defence strongly advocating reform of the existing laws.[29] 'Towards the end of 1898 when the country was believed to be on the eve of war with France, the newspapers contained exhaustive information concerning our defence and our preparations. The composition of the garrisons of all our defended ports was given', the War Office pointed out. It also believed that Major Crausé of the Prussian General Staff had managed to learn the location of all the French forces in 1870 from press reports, and that the Spaniards learnt all about the American preparations for the Spanish-American War from the American press. 'The only effective remedy is to prohibit the publication of any intelligence of naval or military interest except such as is supplied officially by H.M.G.', the War Office concluded, and the Admiralty and the India Office agreed.[30] Thus it was decided at the sixty-first meeting of the Committee of Imperial Defence (CID) that a bill should be drawn up restricting the press, which could be submitted to Parliament in an emergency.[31]

At first it seemed that the press might cooperate. The editors of the London and provincial papers were asked for their opinions and most of the two hundred who replied were sympathetic to the idea that a new act would be necessary. Lord Northcliffe, the most powerful of the press magnates, was known to be sympathetic,[32] and a subcommittee of the Committee of the Newspaper Society was set up. It agreed with the government's proposals and called a conference at the Royal United Service Institution in June 1906.[33] It was suggested by the committee that there should be censorship 'of the publication of all news with regard to naval and military matters or the movement of ships and troops at a time when the government considered it essential in the interests of the nation to put it into operation'. By this time the Conservative government and its War Minister Arnold Forster had been replaced by a Liberal one with R. B. Haldane at the War Office, but its attitude to censorship does not appear to have been markedly different to its predecessor's.

At the ninety-third meeting of the Committee of Imperial Defence at the end of 1906, Haldane argued that the act should be passed and left dormant until it was needed, but the Prime Minister thought that this would be opposed by the House of Commons.[34] However, it was the newspapers themselves which finally prevented any legal change. A conference of the newspaper representatives was summoned in February 1908 to consider a redrafted bill. But, 'the secretary of the Newspaper Proprietors Association without warning read a paper strongly condemning the proposed legislation and in view of this hostile attitude the Newspaper Society suspended all further action'.[35] This reversal surprised the government, although it admitted that 'throughout the negotiations with the press, which have continued intermittently since 1905, the journalists' body has almost unanimously agreed that some form of control is logical and necessary, but have generally objected to the statutory powers when they were set forth in detail'.[36]

Some of the opposition to legislation shown at the 1908 meeting can be attributed to the fact that the proposed legislation held the newspaper owner responsible for what was published in his newspaper. It is also possible that the immediate impact of the Japanese 'success' with censorship had begun to wear off. As the President of the Newspaper Society pointed out in an angry letter to *The Times* on 8 May 1908, there had been no opposition to the idea of such a bill at the 1906 R.U.S.I meeting. The Society had already sent an embittered letter to the Admiralty the month before, pointing out that 'from June 1906 until January 15th 1908 no intimation was ever conveyed by any of [the proprietors] to the Newspaper Society . . . that the bill was unnecessary'.[37] The Newspaper Proprietors Association had come into existence in the meantime and, although it paid lip service to the idea of having a bill, in fact its arguments completely undermined the case for censorship. 'There are occasions' it argued, 'when the publication of information concerning naval and military matters during a time of war is absolutely essential to the public interest, however distasteful such publicity may be to the naval and military authorities. For example the provisions of the bill would have rendered it illegal to publish Sir William H. Russell's letters upon the conditions of troops in the Crimea.'[38]

Nevertheless negotiations with the press continued. Security was being tightened in other ways. The threat of war with Germany loomed larger and the fear of German spies operating in England turned into a panic. In 1911 the government hastily brought the 1889 Official Secrets Act up to date to deal with German espionage.[39] Some officials suggested that a War Press Bureau should be set up, while others including Sir Eyre Crowe, the Assistant Under-Secretary of State at the Foreign Office, thought that this would be a mistake.[40] One official thought that such a bureau might extend its influence too far. 'I do not like the idea of extending its scope beyond naval and military matters. It is too much like Berlin', he wrote.[41] Conferences were organised at the Admiralty in August and October 1912 with members of the press to discuss the problem of security.[42] The War Office asked the journalists not to publish anything about the experiments which were being carried out on embarking and disembarking the new Expeditionary Force, which was being prepared for service overseas.[43] This resulted in the organisation of a system of voluntary censorship by the press which lasted until war broke out. According to one historian, 'the Official Secrets Act of 1911 provided a useful background against which a system of "voluntary censorship" could be devised'.[44]

The subcommittee of the CID which studied the problem thought that ideally the press should be persuaded to agree to an act imposing censorship, which would then be suspended until war broke out, thus reverting to the pre-1908 proposals.[45] But, because of the opposition of the press, this was impossible. In a later memorandum the subcommittee noted that the press had agreed to accept voluntary restrictions and the agreement also provided for 'the establishment in time of peace of confidential relations between the press, the Admiralty and the War Office'.[46] The subcommittee concluded that this 'cannot fail to make easier acceptance by the press at large, the establishment of a uniform censorship in time of emergency', although it admitted that legislation might also be necessary. The importance of the issue could hardly be overestimated, because, as it pointed out, 'the victories gained by Germany over France in 1807-1, by Japan over Russia in 1904-5 and by Bulgaria over Turkey in 1912-13 were due in no small measure to the secrecy which veiled operations — a secrecy that extended to the press in each case'.[47]

Many war correspondents had themselves come to accept this verdict. Shortly before his death W. H. Russell had admitted that the age of the war correspondent was over. Bennet Burleigh and Francis McCullagh, who had been in Manchuria agreed with him.[48] McCullagh pointed out that there was a 'great exodus of correspondents from the Japanese camp after the battle of Liaoyang; and of course all the aim of censorship is defeated if a correspondent having primed himself with information . . . judges it opportune to bolt for some neutral part and there unburden himself'.[49] Lord Northcliffe was so concerned that militarily useful information should not be released to an enemy in wartime that he suggested to R. B. Haldane in 1909 that 'the training of press censors might be commenced this year. One knows how Moltke and Bismarck watched the press and in those days it was only in its infancy'.[50] The Balkan wars showed that many other countries had learnt from the Japanese the crucial importance of military secrecy. The *History of The Times* notes drily, 'correspondents who tried to follow the Bulgarian armies into the field were all disappointed. An efficient General Staff kept them all out of sight if not out of sound of the firing of the guns'.[51] They had to rely on reports from the Bulgarian Staff and from the correspondent of the Vienna *Reichpost*, who was accorded a privileged position by the authorities, but was so biased that he happily invented stories of non-existent Bulgarian victories.[52]

Although the British government did not go this far, when war broke out in 1914, it was no longer prepared to rely on the voluntary cooperation of the press. Instead, like its French and Russian counterparts, it imposed censorship on all information connected with military affairs. Lord Kitchener, who became War Minister on the outbreak of war, had a long-standing distrust of all journalists, and he was largely responsible for the repressive policy which was followed. Admittedly it is doubtful whether the press would have cooperated in suppressing all the information which the government wished to avoid releasing, but Kitchener went to the other extreme and tried to prevent all correspondents going to France. As Lord Northcliffe's biographers noted, 'Lord Kitchener had an elephantine memory which did not forget that in the Boer War young Churchill had been a troublesome war correspondent . . . Set against these activities of the press, the fact that his public reputation had largely been made for him by a war correspondent, G. W. Steevens of the *Daily Mail*, was of small account. Now, well over a decade later, he resolved that the press should be kept in its place.'[53]

Thus a War Press Bureau was set up under F. E. Smith to control the flow of news.[54] Most real power remained with the Admiralty and the War Office but public criticism of censorship was conveniently diverted away from the Ministries to the new bureau. The bureau was not allowed to publish anything which it was thought might demoralise the nation, and this in 1914 amounted to most of the information about the war. As the Solicitor General explained to Parliament, the government intended to be guided by whether the publication of pieces of information 'could afford any assistance to the enemy, whether it could unduly depress our people, whether it could disclose movements and operations of our troops or our fleet or by any means whatever directly or indirectly imperil the national safety'.[55] For a time Kitchener was only prepared to allow Ernest Swinton, a serving officer, to operate as a journalist in France. The *History of The Times* argues that this 'was in depressing contrast with the practice of the German General Staff which welcomed correspondents from the neutral (particularly American) press and provided them with every facility for seeing and reporting exactly what they wanted, saving always details which the Allied Staffs would have been glad to know'.[56] As a result they were able 'to provide neutral journals especially those in Italy and the United States with full and vivid descriptions of battles of which the very existence was not revealed from the British side until some days later'. Envious British journalists believed that the Germans had in fact learnt the real lesson of the Russo-Japanese War, to control the press as the Japanese did, whilst winning it over to their side as the Russians had managed to do.

By the end of 1914 *The Times'* Military Correspondent, Colonel Repington, was arguing that 'censorship is being used as a cloak to cover all political, naval and military mistakes'.[57] The same Lord Northcliffe who had advocated censorship in peacetime, made his papers the government's most powerful critics in wartime.[58] Many journalists felt that the government's attitude towards censorship was mistaken. One of them wrote later, 'the national welfare was being sacrificed to a Japanese-bred fetish of military secrecy flogged to a dangerous finish . . . if from the beginning of the struggle in 1914 the press had been properly utilised and organised by the General Staff, what a different course our national affairs might have run!'[59] When the government relented and started to allow journalists at the various fronts it still severely limited their numbers, although this could increase the importance of individual journalists. This was most vividly demonstrated during the Dardanelles campaign, when E. Ashmead Bartlett who was one of the two authorised correspondents, did more than anybody else to damn the campaign and its leader, Sir Ian Hamilton in the eyes of the British government.[60]

Thus the debates on wartime censorship, which had taken place in England between the Boer War and the outbreak of war in 1914, did not lead to any satisfactory result. In retrospect one can see that the fears of the press magnates about the 1908 measures were partially justified, although it might have been better to accept a well thought out act in peacetime, rather than a hastily prepared and repressive system of censorship when war had actually broken out. The debate reflected the widespread view that the tolerant nineteenth century methods were no longer acceptable, but it failed to produce an acceptable alternative. Those who admired the Japanese system ignored its drawbacks, while much of the press admitted the need for wartime censorship, but thwarted it in practice. Kitchener's arrival at the War Office in August 1914 decided the issue in the most abrupt way and the old type of war correspondent almost disappeared. However, it was not just censorship which caused this disappearance. Warfare was changing and becoming too complicated for the amateur to analyse successfully and too vast to make it easy for an individual correspondent to present a balanced picture of its ramifications. The popular attitude towards warfare was also revolutionised by the Great War. On the whole, the war correspondents had romanticised and even glorified war — there was not much to romanticise about either the Russo-Japanese War or the First World War. The *History of The Times* points out that the paper censored itself deliberately, avoiding describing conditions in the trenches for fear of reducing the number of recruits.[61] This was not a consideration which had concerned the previous editor of *The Times* during the Crimean War, or any of his successors. Thanks to the brutal nature of the Great War and the demands which it made upon the manpower of the nation, the fact that literacy had become so widespread worked for the first time against the interests of the war correspondents. The forces in society which had previously acted in their favour were ceasing to do so and this change of fortunes was to become final.

Notes

1. David Ayerst, *Guardian — Biography of a Newspaper* (1971), 394.
2. David Williams, *Not in the Public Interest* (1965), 81.
3. Rupert Furneaux, *News of War* (1964), Ch. 1, Sir Henry Brackenbury, *Some Memories of My Spare Time* (1909), 87-103.
4. Kitchener Papers, Public Record Office, HH/1, Hamilton to Kitchener, 17 March 1904.
5. A. T. Q. Stewart, *The Pagoda War* (1972).
6. Ayerst, *op. cit.*, 269; Williams, *op. cit.*, 81.
7. Ayerst, *op. cit.*, 281.
8. F. Villiers, *Five Decades of Adventure* (1921).
9. Foreign Office Papers, P.R.O.: FO.46.577, MacDonald to the Foreign Office, 17 March 1904.
10. See Colonel Aylmer Haldane's Diary, vol. I (National Library of Scotland). For Melton Prior's comments see the final chapter of his autobiography, *Campaigns of a War Correspondent* (1912).
11. Douglas Story, *The Campaign with Kuropatkin* (1904).
12. Kitchener Papers, HH/16, Sir Montagu Gerard to Kitchener, 1 June 1904.
13. FO.181.805, letter from the foreign editor of the *Daily Mail*, 5 May 1904.
14. F. McCullagh, *With the Cossacks* (1906), 181.
15. War Office Papers, WO/106/38, report by Sir Montagu Gerard, 30 March 1905.

16.   Wilkinson Papers, National Army Museum, Sir William Nicholson to Spenser Wilkinson, 22 September 1904. See also Kitchener Papers, HH/30, Hamilton to Kitchener 22 September 1904 and *The National Review*, September 1904.

17.   Prior, *op. cit.*, letter dated 20 August 1904. See also John Fox, *Following the Sun Flag* (1905).

18.   See for example the printed Attache's Reports on the Russo-Japanese War by the British Naval Attaches, Admiralty Library, report by Captain Eyres, vol. 2, 24 December 1904 to 31 January 1905.

19.   Major W. S. Bannatyne, *United Service Magazine*, July 1909. See also Lionel James, *Times of Stress* (1929), 4. When James asked a British staff officer what the Army had learnt from the Manchurian campaign he replied 'how to muzzle the press'.

20.   *United Service Magazine*, April 1910.

21.   Captain H. G. Russell, 'Information in War', *Journal of the Royal Artillery* (1908), 390.

22.   *United Service Magazine*, December 1912.

23.   Quoted in Dewar's article, see n. 20 above.

24.   *The Times*, 15 July 1905. See also the *Daily Express*, 29 May 1905.

25.   The *Fortnightly Review*, March 1906.

26.   Aston's lectures were published in *Letters on Amphibious War* (1911).

27.   *The Times*, 16 July 1905. See also *ibid.*, 29 April 1907 and 24 June 1908, when Ellenborough returned to the attack.

28.   Arnold Forster Papers, British Museum, 50317, 'Office Regulations in the Event of War', minute by the Secretary of State, 3 November 1904.

29.   Cabinet Papers, CAB.38.6.100 'Control of the Press in Time of War or Threat of War', 12 October 1904, minute by the War Office.

30.   *Ibid.*

31.   CAB.38.6.119, Minutes of the sixty-first meeting of the CID 9 December 1904.

32.   Roberts Papers, National Army Museum 7101/23/46, Northcliffe to Roberts, 19 July 1909.

33.   CAB.38.12.38, Control of the Press During or in Anticipation of War, Minute by the Secretary of the CID, 9 July 1906.

34.   CAB.38.12.55, Minutes of the ninety-third meeting of the CID; 13 November 1906.

35.   CAB.38.23.6, Report and Proceedings of the Standing Subcommittee Enquiry regarding Press and Postal Censorship in Time of War, 31 January 1912.

36.   *Ibid.*

37.   Admiralty Papers, ADM.116.1058, letter dated 30 April 1908.

38.   *Ibid.*, letter read to Conference 6 February 1908.

39.   Williams, *op. cit.*, 26.

40.   Grant Duff Papers, Imperial War Museum, Diary vol. I, 2, 25.

41.   *Ibid.*

42.   See n. 35 above.

43.   *Ibid.*

44.   Williams, *op. cit.*, 81.

45.   CAB.38.25.39, Press Censorship, minute by the Overseas Defence Committee, 4 December 1913.

46.   *Ibid.*

47.   *Ibid.*

48.   F. McCullagh, 'The Question of the War Correspondent' in *The Contemporary Review*, January 1913.

49.   *Ibid.* (Lionel James was amongst those who left the Japanese Army at this

time, see James, *op. cit.*, 42.)

50.   Reginald Pound and Geoffrey Harmsworth, *Northcliffe* (1959), 363.

51.   *The History of the Times*, part I, vol. 4 (1952), 77.

52.   *Ibid*. See also *The British Review*, February 1913, 9.

53.   Pound and Harmsworth, *op. cit.*, 469.

54.   *Ibid*.

55.   Quoted in Williamson, *op. cit.*, 77.

56.   *The History of The Times, op. cit.*, 220.

57.   Roberts Papers, 7101/23/62, Repington to Roberts, 22 October 1914.

58.   See Pound and Harmsworth, *op. cit.*, 475; also *The War Memoirs of David Lloyd George* (1934), vol. I, 123, 590, 631.

59.   James, *op. cit.*, 56.

60.   Ian Hamilton, *Gallipoli Diary* (1920), 320. E. Ashmead Bartlett, *The Uncensored Dardanelles* (1928).

61.   For the inability of correspondents to understand modern war and for the voluntary self-censorship of *The Times*, see the *History of The Times, loc. cit.*, 228.

THE FRENCH ARMY AND THE SPIRIT OF THE OFFENSIVE, 1900-14

Douglas Porch

French casualties in the first fifteen months of the Great War virtually equalled those of the next three years. Desperate attacks left 995,000 casualties in 1914 and 1,430,000 in 1915, compared with 2,541,000 in 1916-18, and shattered French faith in the offensive.[1] 'It was obvious that the principles of the offensive which we tried to inculcate in the army before the war were too often misunderstood and misapplied,' wrote Marshal Joffre, army commander-in-chief in the first two years of the war.[2]

Responsibility for the ill-fated offensive has been laid at the door of a soldier elite led by Foch, Langlois and Grandmaison, working from the ideas of Clausewitz and Ardant du Picq.[3] Historians from the conservative British General Fuller to Monteilhet, a left wing republican, have seen the French offensive as the product of the *école supérieure de guerre*, accepted by the high command and the general staff and diffused in training and manoeuvres. 'When we look back on Foch's offensive *à l'outrance*, we see Clausewitz throughout', wrote Major-General Fuller, '. . . his offensives *à l'outrance* and his battles *aux allures déchaînées* became the doctrine of the French army.'[4] Monteilhet too viewed the 1914 offensive as the product of the military hierarchy. 'The professional army implies the premature offensive of 1914, and this offensive springs fatally from its very nature,' he wrote.[5] He saw the offensive as 'a theory linked in origin and in object to the destiny of the professional army',[6] and attributed its revival to the *école de guerre*'s historical approach to military science and fascination with Napoleonic campaigns.[7]

But any army as riven by political and social strife and internal doubt as the post-1900 French army was simply not capable of formulating or applying a tactical doctrine. The tactical offensive was a product of something other than professional miscalculation. To understand the genesis of the offensive, we must look more closely at the state of the army.

The offensive had for a century been part of the ideological baggage of the victorious republicans, and held sway after 1900 as the army came increasingly under their thumb and under the influence of the 'nation in arms' theory. At this point in their history, however, the offensive was also a vindication of many current military weaknesses. The theory of the offensive nicely papered over serious army cracks.

The French army had no standard doctrine, only a few officers who wrote about tactics. Joffre recognised this on his appointment in 1911 as chief of the general staff:

> '... The mass of the army, so long a defensive body, had no doctrine and no training. Not knowing what path to follow, it ceased to transmit the rough doctrine of the offensive ... To create a coherent doctrine, to impose it on officers and men alike, to create an instrument to apply what I considered the right doctrine — that I held to be my urgent duty.'[8]

In 1906, Major Driant noted that officers were free to choose among the various tactical theories of several generals,[9] and British officers watching the 1912 manoeuvres were unable to fathom the 'system' underlying them.[10] The 1912 infantry regulations, the *Porte-Voix* complained, were unclear on tactical questions and reflected 'the intellectual anarchy of the army's so-called elite'.[11]

This absence of doctrine was in part the intention of General André, an outspoken republican appointed war minister by the Radical governments of Waldeck-Rousseau and Combes. André believed that any doctrine stifled individual initiative: 'Everyone could select a system in harmony with his own character, energy, temperament, aptitudes ...' he said of his new infantry manual. 'Hoping to develop the initiative of subordinate commanders, it would have been absurd to limit the freedom of our army's leaders with formulae.'[12] On 27 February 1901, he abolished general inspections, so eliminating an important element of central control and standardisation, in the conviction that local commanders could best judge their own troops.[13]

Captain Dreyfus' 1899 retrial climaxed a bitter left wing campaign against reactionary elements in the army. Accusations of corruption and disloyalty levelled at top generals and staff officers and the resignations of several war ministers implicated in the frame-up lowered the confidence of the officer corps in its leaders. Waldeck-Rousseau formed the first Radical government in that year and immediately set out to republicanise the army. General André was called on to sweep out the old army elite and transform the caste mentality of the officer corps with policies designed to bring the army and the nation together.

André and his immediate successors sought to make the army into an institution to serve the country's social as well as defence needs. Authoritarian discipline became a thing of the past. Saint-Cyr instructor Paul Simon, one of a group of young republican officers named to reorientate army education, wrote:

'Centralized and authoritarian leadership . . . diminishes rather than raises the social worth of young men. Rather than fortify their intelligence and character, it suppresses them. It only deepened in French youth the weaknesses characteristic of our nation – listlessness, lack of initiative, irresoluteness.'[14]

Soldiers were educated to patriotic sacrifice by the officers. 'The regiment is more than a big family', André proclaimed. 'It is a school. The officer is the extension of the teacher, the nation's instructor.'[15] The officer corps spearheaded the army's social mission.

The idea of the 'officer instructor' was first mooted in 1891 by Lyautey[16] drawing on the ideas of prominent post-1870 reformers Generals Trochu and Lewal. André introduced courses on the social role of the officer in every officer cadet school and at the Ecole Polytechnique, and in 1901 ordered Major Charles Ebener's Saint-Cyr lectures castigating the officer corps for ignoring the democratic and social implications of universal conscription to be printed and distributed to every officer.

'We are the only ones not to realise that together with our role of war preparation we have to fulfil a social mission of vital importance, and that it is our duty to contribute to the spread of democracy. This is at the root of the misunderstanding between the intellectual classes and the officer corps.'[17]

Colonel Lavisse, superintendent of Saint-Maixent, the infantry school, engaged university professors to lecture to his future infantry officers on economic and social problems, while Colonel Sauret at the Artillery and Engineering School called his instructors to '. . . an ideal of democratic progress that will allow them to consider themselves government delegates for the formation of cadres for the republican army'.[18] Berteaux, war minister in 1905, demanded in a November circular that the army become 'a school of civic duty'.[19] Conscripts would return to civilian life with a high sense of civic duty, order and patriotism.[20] 'The officer is responsible for training his men', stated the provisional infantry regulations for 1902, 'but he is even more their teacher'.[21]

From 1902, the ministry churned out directives and circulars on the numerous innovations designed to heighten civic duty among soldiers of all ranks. Officers were ordered to lecture on economics, history, hygiene, morality and patriotism, agriculture and trades. They were expected to organise trips to local factories. Corners of drill fields were given over to agricultural experimentation. Regimental libraries were expanded, recreation rooms established in each regiment, and rooms with free stationery set aside for letter writing.

The reformers also set about eliminating 'immoral' and 'degrading' aspects of garrison life which they believed lowered self-respect and undermined patriotic ideals. They believed drunken, debauched nights in town would become a thing of the past if companies set up cooperative bars to serve 'hygienic drinks'. Soldiers would learn 'the moral and social advantages of social works in general and of cooperatives in particular'. Profits which once went to canteen keepers were now poured into regimental self-help societies.[22]

André boasted that his programme had transformed the caste mentality of the officer corps and convinced enough ex-servicemen to swing the 1906 elections to the Left.[23]

Republicans believed that their reforms would pay dividends on the battlefield. Only patriotic soldiers could be counted on to act bravely under fire. This conviction dated from 1793 when patriotic French troops had overwhelmed the choreographed armies of despotic states.

'The factors which push a group of men to attack the enemy despite impending death are unquestionably moral and psychological factors. They are the patriotic, personal will to conquer and a hatred for the enemy who threatens the home . . . The desire to conquer, patriotism and devotion are personal things. They must be rooted in each man's heart by inheritance or through education.'[24]

Major Grandmaison, high priest of the French offensive and a future general, commented:

'We are rightly told that psychological factors are paramount in combat. But this is not all: properly speaking, there are no other factors, for all others — weaponry, manoeuvreability — influence only indirectly by provoking moral reactions . . . the human heart is the starting point in all questions of war.'[25]

The only tactic suited to an army of highly motivated patriots was the offensive, Grandmaison proclaimed. 'A well-spring of individual initiative is a high acquisition which we must never again abandon. But to bear fruit this initiative must be applied to a positive doctrine. The study of the offensive is the only solid base for infantry training.'[26] Messimy, a retired officer and twice war minister, also tried to link democratic idealism to offensive warfare: '. . . To conquer is to advance,' he declared in his 1907 budget report. 'They must acquire the will to advance and conquer.'[27]

The theory of the offensive, supported by the victorious republicans for a hundred years, triumphed with the Radical regime. The reckless attacks of 1914 were not the result of a rational doctrine but of a 'mystique', an irrational cult[28] imposed not from the top of the military hierarchy, but evolved closer to its base under a flabby high command. 'The high command, grown old among obsolete ideas and distrustful among political agitators was sceptical and impotent,' Joffre wrote. 'Against this background, young and dynamic officers went to dangerous lengths, confident that their new doctrine conformed with war traditions and transported by their own confidence and enthusiasm.'[29]

The weakness of army leadership meant that ambitious young aides-de-camp and ministry officers had relatively free reign and could foist their views on inert superiors; Messimy complained:

> 'Too many general officers are sinking steadily into an ever deeper mental lethargy, letting their aides-de-camp think for them. Captains of industry and managing directors, whatever their age, however many their collaborators, make their own plans and themselves tell their subordinates roughly what to do. This is not the case in the army, where aides-de-camp are often all-powerful. Things run no less smoothly for it perhaps: but in the fateful hour when the leader must himself make the decisions upon which victory will depend, he will find that ability to think and plan for himself has atrophied through long idleness.'[30]

General Zurlinden complained that members of the *conseil supérieure de la guerre*, the designated army commanders, used their aides-de-camp and not their staffs to prepare for war. 'This arrangement could continue in wartime, and so undermine the general staffs,' he said.[31]

Young ministry officers were given broad decision making powers. Ministerial instability meant that young brigadiers who headed army sections made many important decisions unhindered by the *conseil supérieure de la guerre* or the chief of the general staff.[32] Promotion in the André ministry was allegedly in the hands of two captains.[33]

Without strong direction from above, many officers simply aped fashionable views. Once in power, radical republicans dusted off the offensive, and it quickly captured the imagination and ambition of many French officers. 'People probably realised that the offensive was fashionable higher up, and so did their best "to carry out the offensive" — but in what conditions!', Joffre wrote.[34]

The absence of doctrine was also attributable to malfunctioning at the top — in officer schools, the general staff and the high command.

Many military leaders had no training beyond that received at Saint-Cyr or the Ecole Polytechnique. 'We stuff our chickens and starve our horses', Messimy complained. 'With luck and *savoir faire*, a soldier can rise to the highest ranks at the age of 60 without having progressed intellectually since he haphazardly acquired more knowledge than he could possible digest at the Ecole Polytechnique or at Saint-Cyr when he was 20.'[35] Captain Jibé concurred: 'Many colonels and generals are well aware that with our present organisation they go through their career on what they learned in the military schools . . . and tactics have undergone profound changes since then.'[36]

The German army regularly returned staff officers to the Kriegsakademie for classes on the latest theory, but senior French officers had no way of keeping up to date.[37] Staff manoeuvres were infrequent. A *Centre des hautes études militaires* was established in 1910 for majors and lieutenant-colonels, but refresher courses were suspended in February 1912 after only one year because the army could not spare officers from troop commands.[38] Very few officers had passed through the centre by 1914,[39] and Messimy said that it had given the high command no 'coherent doctrine'.[40]

The quality of the officer corps declined sharply after 1900 as officer schools came under heavy fire. Radical republicans who regarded Saint-Cyr as a hotbed of political reaction and disliked the 'undemocratic' promotion of its graduates discouraged applications there in favour of NCO schools where qualified NCOs were trained as officers. Places at Saint-Cyr were slashed by fifty per cent between 1900 and 1910, but at the same time officer schools lowered their standards drastically. Saint-Cyr admitted one in five candidates in 1890, and one in two in 1913. Saint-Maixent turned almost no-one away.[41]

The resulting decline in standards has been ignored by historians. Few good applicants appeared at Saint-Cyr and the education there was considered mediocre, especially after the 1905 reforms reoriented the curriculum toward the officer's new social role.[42] Saint-Maixent boosted entrance scores for seniority, campaigns, wounds or special functions, discouraging often better educated young men who had hoped for quick promotion through the ranks. NCO candidates were prepared in their regiments by lieutenants who often had no specialised knowledge of their subjects. Four out of twenty was a pass mark.[43]

Radicals clearly hoped to equalise standards in officer schools and so overcome the main objection to their proposed amalgamation of Saint-Cyr and the NCO academies. Jaurès, who proposed a university education for officers, blasted Radical levelling as 'pseudo-democracy':

'By deflating [Saint-Cyr's] pretentions, the educational standards will suffer. In this way, officers from both schools, by becoming more similar, will soon make up . . . an honourable and democratic average, democracy being reduced in the army to the Orléanist formula of the "juste milieu".'[44]

He especially attacked the 1906 school committee report which claimed that officers needed only 'une certaine intéllectualité'. Radical 'mediocrity' would soon taint the army.

'The men who dare not candidly admit the value of higher education, a good, truly intellectual military preparation, but will not repudiate it altogether, oscillate between arbitrary combinations. They do not abolish the schools which provide it, but they undermine them and look to substitute fictitious equivalents for a solid background ... Each school must attain the highest standards possible within its given level. And if to do this the schools must be unequal, the dogma of alleged equality must not take precedence over the higher law of national security.'[45]

The most able officers went into administration. '... Our system comes down to draining off the best line officers for administrative and noncombatant jobs', Patrice Mahon wrote in 1912.[46] Candidates for the administration school at Vincennes averaged 14.5 out of 20 in the 1913 entrance examinations, compared with 7.5 at Saint-Cyr in 1912.[47] Its applicants virtually tripled after 1900, and it had ten candidates for each of its fifty places by 1910.[48] The *France Militaire* noted on 25 March 1904 that Vincennes was the only school which had escaped the general decline in standards.

The administration and the Intendance began to siphon off many of the best officers, boosted by Radical military reforms which improved their position *vis-à-vis* the combat arms.

Noncombatant officers were traditionally regarded by combat officers as professional and social inferiors, yet the technical organisation of nineteenth-century armies increasingly made support services essential. The struggle of these noncombatant officers to gain equal status − a struggle which bore many of the hallmarks of a class struggle − remains unchronicled.

In the Second Empire, doctors and pharmacists won the status and promotion opportunities of line officers. The 1882 organisation of the Medical Corps guaranteed their rights. Veterinarians and telegraphists won officer status in the early years of the Third Republic. But administration officers, under the cloud of their poor performance in 1870, were denied salutes and other military courtesies and retained their distinctive uniform and rank insignia with their second class connotations.[49]

Administration officers began to agitate for equality in the 1880s. Many contributed part of their monthly salary to support an unprecedented Paris lobby by retired soldiers.[50] These efforts paid off in 1882 with a law giving administration officers the right to enter the Intendance, formerly recruited only among captains in combat arms. This reform, however, proved largely illusory as slow promotion meant that most men reached the age limit for admittance without reaching the necessary rank. As a consequence, only eighteen administrative officers managed to step up before 1899.[51]

This semi-political agitation paid dividends when the Radicals came to power. A 1900 law placed administration officers on an approximately equal footing with line officers with identical uniforms and rank insignia. NCOs now left Vincennes with the equivalent rank of second lieutenant rather than facing five years as a 'student adjutant of administration'. They were automatically promoted to lieutenant level after two years and paralleled the combat arms to the rank of major. A subsequent 1902 law ensured all administration officers the rank of captain within fifteen years of leaving Vincennes.[52]

The Vincenneoise, a mutualist society for administrative officers founded in 1901, soon exceeded its primary role to press for full equality — military courtesies and combat ranks which would allow a first class administration officer to be addressed as 'mon capitaine' rather than plain 'Monsieur'. These demands were granted in a February 1911 decree.[53]

The new, improved status of administration officers was disastrous for the combat arms. NCOs now rushed to join the administration, drawn by a sedentary life and quick promotion. A captain in the administration could retire at 58, if he had not already been promoted to major, with a 3,450 franc annual pension. An infantry captain had to retire at 53 with only 2,400 francs.[54]

With their good knowledge of administration, administration officers found it easier to transfer to the Intendance, which virtually guaranteed a senior rank. Of officers who joined the finance section, 31.9 per cent became brigadiers and generals, compared to 9.6 per cent in the combat arms.[55] In 1912 War Minister Millerand tried to staunch the hemorrhage of NCOs from the combat arms by stripping administration officers of their combat ranks: 'It is above all a question of reviving recruitment at Saint-Maixent', the *France Militaire* wrote on 28 September. But the attraction of the administration remained strong.

The quality of the officer corps declined with the fall of the grandes ecoles.[56] The artillery was especially hard hit.[57]

The decline in officer standards was soon reflected in the école de guerre, to which the best officers applied in their fifth year of service, around the age of 25 or 26. Arès, a military critic worried by the declining officer standards, estimated in 1912 that little more than a fifth of the ninety officers could write correctly[58] and lamented the sharp decline in officer quality since 1900.[59] The poor 1913 entrance results were a matter of public concern and the War Minister complained that those of 1914 'once again reveal serious shortcomings in a great many candidates'.[60] This low educational standard soon told even in ministerial reports in which, for instance, General Lyautey frequently would not have recognised his own name.[61]

Criticism was frequently levelled at the college teaching which made much of memory and little of imagination. On 10 April 1914, the *Porte-Voix* complained that the école de guerre was gearing itself to the administrative duties required of its graduates:

'The école superieure de guerre today is not properly speaking a "school of war", but rather a special academic organization turning out good staff officers . . . It is therefore a staff school and – if brevet officers will pardon the audacity – an administrative staff school . . . Military science must not be confused with the hotchpotch of abstraction and jargon which makes up today's deplorable ESG curriculum . . . There is no real war school!'

General Pédoya complained that the école de guerre did not build military leaders or tacticians:

'It is a training school uniquely concerned with preparing officers for top commands. It does not impart the qualities or the learning needed in these commands. The instructors . . . whether because of their relatively low rank or meagre war experience, do not have the authority to make a doctrine credible.'[62]

On 28 August 1901, the *France Militaire*, a staunchly pro-government paper, also criticised the tendency to take promising young officers rather than experienced older men on the teaching staff.

The general staff should have been the army's brain. The école de guerre's top graduates were taken for immediate staff assignment while the remainder returned to their regiments as brevet staff officers, alternating every three years between a troop command and staff duty. This system centralised and systematised tactical thought and ensured staff officers the practical experience denied them in the old staff corps.

This staff system, organised on the German model, inherited many of the vices of the old corps. Staff assignments were spent performing routine administrative tasks. The law of 24 July 1880, which created the service d'état major from the independent staff corps, charged it with 'the direction and running of the administrative and medical services'. 'From his entry into the staff service', Messimy wrote, '. . . he checks charts, arranges numbers, draws up new rosters, reads and files circulars; he is very busy . . . but his imagination and judgement are never taxed.'[63] The army's 1,014 staff officers were scornfully referred to as 'leather cushions . . . a real waste of government money and of the intellectual powers of many officers'.[64] This anti-staff prejudice carried over into the Great War.

Staff time allotted to military theory was minimal. Messimy complained that morning mail duties bit into training time and that one staff ride, a compulsory training outing held annually, took place in a thick fog in Christmas week, having been delayed by the pressure of administrative work.[65] 'Find me in France a staff which sets aside a little time each week for a staff ride, any outside work, a historical study, a *kriegspiel* [war game] with a map or a garrison manoeuvre,' Charles Humbert, an ex-staff captain and senator, challenged. 'I defy anybody to name even one.'[66] He held that the government fear of an independent military leadership had stunted the growth of the general staff by encouraging a concern with minutiae.[67]

The absence of stable leadership also threw tactical doctrine into chaos and hindered effective reform. The war minister was the acknowledged army chief, but ministerial instability undermined his influence and left the army leaderless in resolving many technical questions.

Political life in the Third Republic was characterised by frequent changes of cabinet. But this image of governmental instability was deceptive. One third of the deposed ministers usually appeared in the new cabinet. 'Governmental instability, minsterial stability, these are the two inseparable characteristics of French political life', the historian August Soulier wrote.[68] Many ministers were virtually permanent occupants of their ministries.[69] Finance ministers averaged five and a half years in office and foreign ministers seven and a half years, lending much needed continuity to those offices.

No such stability was to be found at the war department, where the war portfolio changed hands more than any other in the Third Republic.[70] Only three ministers served in more than three cabinets between 1871 and 1914.

Ministerial inexperience also plagued the War Ministry in the Third Republic. Appointments often fell to generals and specialists, 27 per cent of whom served only one term and then quit government altogether. Twelve per cent of foreign ministers and only ten per cent of those who served in the Finance and Interior Ministries followed the same path.[71]

The absence of firm ministerial direction told in the rickety organisation of the War Ministry and the high command. The ministry's fourteen services and directions worked independently, while the high command counted eleven technical committees each with a considerable staff, eighteen permanent committees and 100 temporary ones, often with identical functions and little inclination to disappear. Between them the ministry and the high command employed nearly one third of France's 330 generals in 1909 in purely administrative jobs.[72] 'It is materially impossible for even a talented and diligent minister to coordinate and direct so many different sections', Gervais, a member of the parliamentary army committee wrote in the *France Militaire* on 15 February 1914. 'With only the minister to coordinate them, they work independently.' Budgets were approved by the finance section not on the basis of defence needs but according to the bargaining talents of the section chief. In this way, many vital reforms were held up.

Nor was stability necessarily an asset — Freycinet's long tenure was marked by his persistent refusal to reform the high command, while André's record four year ministry proved disastrous.

The War Ministry was seldom in the best hands. Senior army officers were reluctant to risk brilliant military careers in Parliamentary cloak-rooms. Consequently, rather junior divisional commanders were most often named, as was the case with Boulanger, André, Picquart, Goiran and others. These men had neither the authority over their more senior subordinates nor in most cases the length of tenure to impose a coherent organisation or tactical doctrine on the army. The war portfolio attracted few top politicians and usually fell to second rank men like Krantz, Lebrun, Messimy and Noulens. Freycinet and Millerand were the possible exceptions. Messimy was scathing in his criticism of the phlegmatic Brun,[73] and Monteilhet, who worked closely with Radical reformers, condemned Etienne, who served six terms as war minister, saying: 'No man more ignorant of military affairs has ever occupied the rue Saint-Dominique'.[74]

Republican fears of strong army leadership undermined the high command. Politicians refused to create a rank above that of Major General, so that division commanders, corps commanders, members of the *conseil supérieure de la guerre* and even the War Minister himself, when a soldier, held the same rank. 'Ours is the only European army where three different hierarchical strata are occupied by generals of equal rank', the *Avenir Militaire* wrote on 11 April 1893.

Chiefs of the general staff, named too near retirement to guarantee a long tenure, came and went almost as frequently as War Ministers. 'The chief of the general staff changes far too often to produce the continuity of ideas necessary for a doctrine', General Langlois wrote in 1911. 'For this reason, [tactical doctrine] can only be the product of a tradition.'[75] Between 1874 and 1914, the German army had only four chiefs of the general staff. The French army counted seventeen chiefs of the general staff between 1874 and 1914, and six vice-presidents of the *conseil supérieure de la guerre* between the creation of the post in 1889 and its abolition in 1911.

Nor was the chief of the general staff the designated wartime generalissimo. The haphazard organisation of the high command was brought home forcibly in 1911 when War Minister Goiran was questioned in the Senate on the role of the generalissimo. 'There is no generalissimo, there is only a vice-president of the conseil supérieure de la guerre', Goiran replied. On the outbreak of war, the vice-president would take command of the principal northeast army group while the chief of the general staff would remain with the War Minister in Paris.

'The government must control the overall wartime operations. The War Minister is its executor. There are army group commanders, each of whom has a mission.'[76] Senators, deputies and public opinion, shaken by the Moroccan crisis, found this answer unsatisfactory, and brought down the Monis government.

André, in his 1903 reform of the high command, had failed to define the relationshop between the vice-president of the *conseil supérieure de la guerre* and the chief of the general staff. The resulting constant friction between them sabotaged war planning. The 1911 decree abolishing the vice-presidency noted:

'The presence of a vice-president isolated and without constant contact with the chief of the army general staff has resulted in an unfortunate overlapping of duties. The chief of the army general staff who must prepare for war works independently and without direct contact with the general officer destined to command the principal army group.'[77]

In 1911, Messimy overcame republican fears of strong army leadership and appointed Joffre chief of the general staff. 'This was a great step forward', Joffre wrote. 'The long awaited standardisation of tactical doctrine could at last be realised.' The following year War Minister Millerand abolished the post of chief of the army general staff and left Joffre in unchallenged command — barely two years before the outbreak of war.[78]

Personal friction among top leaders further hindered centralisation. 'Personal clashes . . . made the situation even worse,' Messimy wrote of the high command in 1911.[79] Friction between the vice-president of the *conseil supérieure de la guerre* and the chief of the army general staff was a consistent feature of the War Ministry until 1911. Messimy's 1911 reorganisation aimed to end this friction as much as to create a more effective organisation. He abolished the vice-president expressly to axe General Michel, whom he disliked.[80] Six months later Millerand abolished the post of chief of the army general staff to end the bickering between Dubail and Castelnau, his subordinate.[81]

The *conseil supérieure de la guerre* failed to provide an army brain. Virtually moribund since its creation in 1872, it was revived by Freycinet in 1888, 'to coordinate and centralise the work undertaken to strengthen the army and national defence'.[82] The task proved a difficult one. 'They do not train the high command seriously,' Messimy wrote in 1907.[83] Among its twelve members were the designated army commanders, although neither the armies nor the army staffs existed in peacetime. On 27 February 1901, André abolished their right to inspect the corps which could make up their wartime commands, so eliminating an important element of central control and standardisation, in the conviction that local commanders could best judge their own troops.[84] Army commanders were named only provisionally and army organisation was limited to an annual meeting between the designated army leader and his staff chief for a map exercise.[85] General Zurlinden wrote in 1903:

'The [army] commanders must know their mission beforehand. They must be given the time and means to prepare for it. But in order to insure the interests of France which are threatened by these designations, to pander to republican sensibilities and to give the government a free choice, they are named only provisionally in peacetime so that the government can re-examine its choice at the beginning of each year.'[86]

But military weakness went deeper than organisation. Joffre's reforms were defeated by poor army leadership and the corrupt promotion system in the French army which frequently pushed the wrong men to the top.

The army lost control over promotion under the André ministry. The 1832 law on promotion requirements and procedures had removed promotion from political pressure. Freycinet completed this reform in 1889 by establishing a series of committees at various points of the hierarchy to assess an officer's ability. Officers were therefore judged by their immediate superiors and political and personal favouritism was greatly reduced. The war minister seldom exercised his right to add to promotion lists.[87]

But radical republicans claimed that this system perpetuated the 'reactionary cliques' which ruled the rue Saint-Dominique and worked to open promotion to outside influence. General André abolished both promotion committees and general inspections in 1901.[88] With only a seniority list before him, the War Minister was now free to promote whomever he chose, often without much attention to professional standards.[89]

Promotion now fell to officers in elite groups and to those with good political connections. Staff officers were especially favoured.[90] The surest tickets to promotion were those of an aide-de-camp or a ministerial assignment.[91] General Picquart abolished aides-de-camp in September 1908, but Joffre complained in October 1911 that the order had been circumvented by generals who cited a 1909 circular permitting the 'temporary' assignment of officers to a general's services. These temporary assignments too often became permanent.[92]

General Galliffet complained in 1900 that the promotion committees only favoured those in the chain of command and overlooked talented officers on ministerial assignment.[93] André completely reversed this situation. In 1910, 34.5 per cent of the captains serving in the infantry department of the War Ministry received discretional promotions to major, compared to 1.5 per cent in line regiments.[94] In 1911, the figure shot up to 62.5 per cent.[95] Favoured positions in military schools and other special assignments were also reserved almost exclusively for staff officers.

Promotion chances were also affected by garrison assignments. Officers in and near Paris enjoyed a higher promotion rate, while the crack Sixth Corps stationed on the German frontier ironically had the lowest rate.[96] Charles Humbert complained in the *France Militaire* on 1 February 1912 that the worst graduates of the officer schools were packed off to eastern garrisons, while generals regarded an eastern command as a punishment.

The War Ministry was now flooded with officer recommendations, between 15,000 and 20,000 annually by 1910.[97]

'When the generals were all-powerful in the classification committees, they were surrounded by crowds of courtiers. When the Minister had power of promotion for the entire army, these courtiers sought out journalists and politicians. Favouritism, therefore, has changed shape and become essentially political and open to outside influence. It has become much more commonplace. Recognising the power of political intervention, officers have become the clients of influential deputies. Name me an officer who does not know a deputy, a senator or a journalist.'[98]

'Despite my good intentions (in promoting republican officers), things sometimes went too far. Sometimes, also, one mistook an upstart for a dedicated republican because of outward signs of loyalty too ostentatious to be true.'[99]

As influence replaced ability in the promotion stakes, the quality of leadership declined. Candidates for high office had to please in high places, whether this meant putting on a republican face or simply avoiding causing their patrons embarassment. Senior Army positions were soon occupied by officers who had staked out careers in the ministry or in the corridors of parliament.

The sorry state of French military leadership was a matter of open discussion. In May 1908, the *Porte-Voix* complained that generals did not bother to visit their troops — unless it was 'to stick a spanner in the works'. On 11 February 1912 it noted:

'When you compare the generals of 15 or 20 years ago to those of today you are struck by the inferiority of the latter . . . line officers are frequently amazed by the feebleness of their appointed leaders. Ill-at-ease in the field, they are utterly incompetent and at sea in regimental service . . . In short . . . the products of the presidential and ministerial ante-chambers do not exactly shine.'[100]

An inspection report by General Dubail in November 1913, just months before the outbreak of war, said that top officers were 'timid and indecisive . . . Nowhere do they act with resolution. We must develop character, a taste for risk and responsibility.[101]

In 1911, Messimy found the top positions at Saint-Dominique in poor hands: '. . . there now was no-one at the top of this hierarchy. Deprived of real leaders, general staff officers had divided into factions, primarily according to doctrine. Little "sects" had been established . . .'[102] The generalissimo designate in wartime, General Michel, a product of the ministries and favoured aide-de-camp assignments, was 'terrified of responsibility'.[103] The chief of the army general staff, Laffron de Ladébat, was 'a perfect bureaucrat'.[104]

French generals, with an average age of 61 in 1903 against 54 in Germany,[105] were often too old or too ill to campaign. But officers refused to denounce them and they stayed on — and on.[106] After viewing the 1905 manoeuvres, Gervais wrote:

'Our leaders were obviously poorly trained . . . in practice, many generals, caught unprepared, lacked composure, judgement and common sense . . . I have no wish to enumerate all the mistakes I have seen — some of them were worse than absurd.'[107]

One of the two generals chosen to lead a manoeuvre army each year between 1909 and 1914 had reached the retirement age.[108] Autumn manoeuvres, a dry run for war, were thus transformed into an elaborate retirement ceremony. In 1912 manoeuvres climaxed on the third day when army commander General Gallieni captured his opposite number General Marion, his entire staff, one of his corps commanders and his staff, the corps artillery and four airplanes.[109] In 1913, both commanders retired soon after manoeuvres finished. Jaurès complained in 1910:

'The grand manoeuvres are nothing but a parade where military leaders hope to be noticed, not through good planning and organisation, but by the press and the politicians. The point is not who best directs his forces to achieve precise goals, but who will have the most influential newspaper editor in his car . . . The best part of their strategy goes into press campaigns against their rivals, while battalions, regiments and brigades move in a void, without firm direction or goals.'[110]

With this in mind, it is not difficult to account for the success of the modish doctrines provided by young officers like Grandmaison and Foch.

With all these problems, tactics were in confusion. Staff training exercises revealed a mass of conflicting tactical theories. General Chomer, inspecting staff *Kriegspiels* in the south in1913, noted little — if any — tactical similarity in the solutions: 'This exercise (led by a staff colonel) was so unique and based on such questionable ideas that I had to change the plans in the middle of the session and express my dis-satisfaction.'[111]

'The solutions adopted are masterpieces of ingenuity', Arès said of the exercises. 'They try for originality rather than the simple and clear ideas troops need, and the most convoluted solutions are held to be the best.'[112]

In August 1911, Messimy ordered all divisional staff chiefs and their subordinates to Paris to discuss standardisation of tactics and training.[113] But widespread staff prejudices demanded that the 'drudgery' of exercises be avoided wherever possible.[114]

Virtually insurmountable obstacles to good training also pushed leaders to approve the offensive in the hope that individual initiative would somehow prove a substitute for skill. Many also felt that emphasis on drill and formal instruction was misplaced and devalued individual initiative.

André rewrote the 1894 training regulations to simplify and cut back drill. [115] Grandmaison suggested that traditional drill should be replaced by gymnastics to encourage individual development.[116] An August 1905 regulation gave instructors more freedom in teaching marksmanship, saying: 'Each man must fire as accurately as possible without being required to shoot "Like everyone else".'[117]

Problems with training areas, short service and personnel often sabotaged training. City garrisons had no training grounds. Other regiments, especially in the cavalry, found their grounds unusable in the winter months when troops were expected to acquire the fundamentals of soldiering. Major de Civrieux complained in 1908 that his cavalry regiment's training field was nothing but clay and waterlogged for eight months of the year.[118] Autumn manoeuvres were also accused of neglecting troop training.[119]

Training camps were few and inadequate. While Germany counted twenty-six camps in 1912, of at least 5,625 hectares each, France had only seven, the four largest — Châlons, Coëtquidan, Courtine and Mailly — being between 2,000 and 3,000 hectares. Châlons was badly organised and in need of renovation, Courtine and Coëtquidan were in the throes of reorganisation after 1910, and Mailly was considered virtually unusable. The remaining three were only brigade size. French spending on these camps increased from 2,995,000 francs to 4,600,000 annually between 1908 and 1911 but still fell far short of the German investment. In 1911 alone Germany spent the equivalent of 14,346,000 francs on training camps. Only one third of regular French troops and a quarter of reservists on the second of their two training periods could hope to visit a training camp each year.[120]

The 1905 army law reducing service time from three to two years deprived the active army of a third of its combat strength and undermined training still futher, for no attempt was made to adapt a rigid and wasteful army organisation to the needs of two year service. More than half of the army was now made up of partially trained conscripts during the winter months.

The French army lived by a rigid military calendar. All conscripts arrived in October for four months basic training, leaving at the end of the year very thin on military skill. They then graduated to section training, regimental training in the spring and summer, and finally autumn manoeuvres.

To make up the numbers after 1905, conscription boards inducted men who would previously have been rejected as unfit, an estimated 35,000 in 1907.[121] Many of these were sent straight home by their regiments, but, according to some reports, continued to be counted in army strength.[122]

Training often took a back seat to the petty demands of garrison life. After accounting for inspections, sickness and duties, Major de Civrieux estimated that his cavalrymen averaged twelve hours — twelve unsteady hours — a month on horseback.[123] A soldier's second year had very little to do with training. The running sore of the French army was the 'shirker' — a man assigned to non-combat duties after his first year of service. Fully half the soldiers were employed in this way after 1905, mostly as batmen,[124] while more than 20,000 others were taken for administrative and support jobs, compared with only 7,000 in Germany's larger army.[125] Regimental strength was derisory: infantry regiments were a third below establishment, while cavalry squadrons sometimes had as few as twelve men present for training. Each infantry company of 105 men counted forty-one in noncombatant jobs.[126] 'It was not enough to have them look like Epinal Prints, with lots of NCOs, drummers, musicians, flagbearers, canteen keepers, and very few simple soldiers', War Minister Picquart wrote in the *Aurore* in 1907.[127]

Republicans looked for ways to overcome the training handicap. Grandmaison urged officers to '(1) Mingle and talk with the soldier, advise him and express opinions on current affairs. (2) Give classes on moral theory.'[128] He developed a training scheme which allowed soldiers in large measure to train themselves by drilling individually under minimum supervision: '. . . We cannot ask a young and inexperienced corporal to decide what (training) method to employ.'[129]

Critics countered that the social role demanded of officers cut further into training time. Senior officers were more concerned with administrative detail, especially the functioning of cooperatives, than with training. Humbert claimed that emphasis on moral education had made the first line of the training regulations − 'war preparation is the unique goal of troop training' − something of a joke.[130] De Civrieux remarked bitterly that inspectors were concerned not with moral and professional training for soldiers, but for civilians.[131] 'For several years, our soldiers have learned in the army everything but what they should learn − soldiering', the *Temps* wrote in 1912. 'They are taught beekeeping, mushroom growing, tree farming. They are lectured on mutual associations, civic duty, cooperatives, steel-making, and all at the expense of serious war preparation . . . The officers with the best reports in the general inspections are not always those whose troops have performed well in manoeuvres, but those who gave the most lectures on civics and morals, and who have the smartest or the richest cooperative.'[132] Captain d'Arbeaux also complained that military science took a back seat to an officer's social mission.[133]

A circular from War Minister Millerand, dated 20 January 1912, said that training was not being properly carried out and ordered generals to ensure that it was.[134] Later that year, however, British observers reported of the French manoeuvres:

'Once they were deployed, the French infantry displayed marked inferiority to our own in minor tactics. There was not the same dash or anything like the same efficiency in fire direction and control. The infantry, like the cavalry, did not seem to realise what modern rifle fire was like.'[135]

Training personnel were in short supply. Problems of NCO re-enlistment, already acute before 1905, were aggravated by the two year service law of that year. Many believed the temporary soldiers of the two year law were eager to return to civilian life and forgo an army career. Furthermore, soldiers were now encouraged to join the services as an NCO or subaltern rather than re-enlist. Reservists, not regulars, were regarded as the country's principal defence force. Old soldiers found fewer places held for them, while young short service conscripts were promoted over their heads to fill inexpertly the many NCO vacancies − and to leave after six months or so.[136]

Prospective career NCOs also found the minor civil service posts promised them after fifteen years' service never materialised. Government bureaux set age limits too low, did not publicise vacancies, or, often under political pressure, filled jobs slated for ex-NCOs with civilians.[137] Convincing NCOs to re-enlist was difficult: Messimy reported in 1907 that 2,500 places for experienced NCOs remained vacant.[138] By 1912, the re-enlistment crisis had spread even to the popular Paris garrisons.[139] The lack of experienced NCOs struck Joffre forcibly in August 1914 when he saw roads strewn with abandoned equipment: '. . . cadres, not yet in control of the situation, did not appear always to be very energetic.'[140]

The tactical offensive was also aided by the development of new techniques in modern warfare. It did not flourish, as historians would have it, in ignorance of those developments. General Fuller accused Foch of being a 'tactically demented Napoleon' and ignoring new developments in weaponry. 'Step by step', he said, 'with a few variations, he follows Napoleon in the face of magazine rifles and quick-firing artillery as if they were the muskets and cannon of Jena and Freidland.'[141] De La Gorce maintains the French 'ignored the fire-power of modern armaments, and especially of heavy artillery and under-estimated the effectiveness of defensive tactics.'[142] Liddell Hart said that: 'The new French philosophy, by its preoccupation with the moral element, had become more and more separated from the inseparable material factors.'[143] But it was those very material factors that led to the logical evolution of the offensive. Armaments development required an almost constant reassessment of tactics. Colonel Langlois wrote:

'The instability of the (tactical) regulations . . . results from the instability of our modern conditions. If formerly tactics changed every ten years, according to Napoleon, they change more frequently today, and the regulations must be constantly modified. This is a fact of life. However, the broader the terms in which the regulations are couched, the less the detail, the more durable they will be.'[144]

The republican doctrine of the offensive provided a durable tactical law. The only way to cope with the new technical developments despite poor French resources was to rely on the patriotic audacity of French soldiers.

Increased firepower was the most critical technical development in late nineteenth-century warfare. The modern rifle, machine gun and cannon compelled military pundits to re-think established tactical theory. Soldiers who once fought successfully in a relatively close order now had to spread out under fire or risk heavy casualties. With a greatly extended battlefield, officers and NCOs could no longer control or keep track of their men in combat. Simon feared that discipline would be the first casualty unless soldiers were fired by patriotic zeal:

'When a company deploys a rank, on a 290-meter front . . . many will not hear orders. The men will no longer see their leaders. They

have no-one in front to lead them, no-one behind to push them . . .
Nothing is left to keep them moving forward but the individual will
to conquer . . . History testifies that the soldiers who fight best when
dispersed are those with the strongest patriotism and will to conquer, and the strongest devotion to their leaders and comrades.
Soldiers without these feelings can be led into the attack only in
relatively close formations . . . The more armaments are developed,
the more dispersal becomes necessary and the more individual moral
strength is needed.'[145]

General Langlois advocated the offensive for the same reasons: 'In
any charge, direct commands are lost on fighting soldiers. It becomes
every man for himself. A man's individual training and his moral health
are therefore of paramount importance in modern combat.'[146] General
Bazaine-Hayter, Thirteenth Corps Commander, wrote in October 1906:

'Firepower does not weaken the offensive spirit. Never forget that a
defensive battle will seldom bring victory. However powerful
weapons become, the victory will go to the offensive, which stimu-
lates moral force, disconcerts the enemy and deprives him of his
freedom of action.'[146]

The advantages of morale in the face of modern armaments were
held to have been demonstrated in the Russo-Japanese War of 1905.
The superior moral preparation of the Japanese soldiers had more than
compensated for modern Russian armaments and those who maintained
that the Boer War had put paid to the offensive were discredited. The
devastating rifle fire of the Boer War was proof of exceptional Boer
marksmanship, but more importantly revealed the sorry state of the
British army — professional soldiers led by upper class officers.[147]
Joffre wrote later:

'The Russo-Japanese War was a dazzling confirmation of General
Langlois' view that the Boer War had not discredited the offensive.
Under the direction of Foch, Lanrezac and Bourderiat, the young
intellectual elite at the école de guerre now threw out the divisive
old doctrine [the primacy of the defensive based on Franco-Prussian
War experience]. But as always happens when established ideas are
challenged, the value of the offensive was exaggerated by this group.
People have referred to the "mystique of the offensive".'

'This is probably going too far. But it does demonstrate rather well
the somewhat irrational character the cult of the offensive took after
1905.'[148]

Moral training was placed high for a second practical reason — the
ever increasing superiority of German military strength. The French

136

birthrate had dropped after 1870 so that by the turn of the century Germany's population was larger by fifteen million. France made prodigious efforts to overcome this deficiency in army terms, conscripting 5,620 men for each million inhabitants as compared to 4,120 per million in Germany. But in 1903 she was able to muster only 459,000 men and 25,000 officers to 621,000 men and 26,000 officers across the Vosges.[149] With the approach of war, this situation worsened. The 1913 military law voted by the Reichstag gave the German army an almost two to one edge over the French, creating places for 42,000 officers and 112,000 NCOs to 29,000 officers and 48,000 NCOs in France.[150] The long term projections were even more sobering: in 1932 Germany's military resources were estimated at 5,400,000 trained men, compared with a maximum of four million in France.[151]

Although French military expenditure accounted for 36 per cent of the national budget, against only 20 per cent in Germany, in real terms the French investment fell far short of the German figure.[152] Klotz, president of the parliamentary army committee, put the 1904 defence figures at 38,256,364 francs compared with the equiavalent of 99,195,998 francs spent in Germany in the same year.[153] General Langlois calculated in 1908 that Germany spent the equivalent of 1,770 francs per soldier while France spent only 914. 'This shows the efforts our eastern neighbours have made to equip and train their army . . . happily, we still have the moral emphasis which we must consider a headstart', he said.[154]

France therefore had to look for superiority in other spheres. 'To fight in dispersed order, a soldier must compensate for the lack of material support by a more solid moral preparation', André wrote.[155] 'We want an army which compensates numerical weakness with military quality', Messimy stated in 1908.[156] 'Neither numbers nor miraculous machines will determine victory', he said in 1913. 'This will go to soldiers with valour and "quality" – and by this I mean superior physical and moral endurance, offensive strength.'[157] Patrice Mahon gauged that only drive could beat numbers: 'The truth', he said, 'is that the only possible way of overcoming Germany's more efficient mobilisation is to confront them with our offensive.'[158] With these substantial material handicaps, France had to oppose mind to Germany's main. 'It is much more important to develop a conquering state of mind than to cavil about tactics', Grandmaison concluded.[159]

The theory of the offensive was given a shot in the arm by the resurgence of French nationalism after the 1911 Agadir crisis. In 1905 the government had bowed to the Germans over Morocco rather than risk defeat with a disorganised and demoralised army.[160] But the *Panther* incident in July 1911 and the November signing of the Franco-German agreement on Morocco, the Congo and the Cameroons stoked French resentment against German bullying, even on the left.[161] War Minister Millerand exploited this new mood to encourage a martial spirit in the nation with weekly military parades in garrison towns. 'Do not think that the restored tattoo is mere child's play, it is the sign of a revival', the *Echo de Paris* wrote.[162] The subsequent raising of army morale and prestige bolstered the belief in the moral superiority of French soldiers preached by civic spirited Radicals since 1900.

A weakened army leadership meant that essential reforms were neglected. But the disorganisation caused by the application of republican military ideas was so apparent by 1913 that the government reintroduced three year service. 'It is increasingly obvious that the two year service law, the product of political and social considerations, has brought the French army very meagre advantages and massive disadvantages', the *Porte-Voix* said on 1 February 1911, quoting a German newspaper. The three year law swelled regular army strength by a third, extended training time and furnished more experienced conscript NCOs.

Historians have seen the three year law of 1913 as a defeat for the left wing doctrine of the 'nation in arms' and as the triumph of the offensive *à l'outrance*. 'In 1793 and 1870 the offensive was the lot of improvised troops', Monteilhet said. 'In 1913, by a complete reversal of the situation . . . it was the privilege of soldiers with long army service.'[163] Challener also said that the republican army was designed primarily for defensive warfare:

> 'Military theorists could argue with some plausibility that if an army was to succeed in the offensive, its troops must be skilled in the art of manoeuvre, especially competent in the handling of weapons, and particularly trained to work together. From this line of reasoning it was but a simple step to the conclusion that the reserves were unsuited for the offensive and that the existing system of two-year service did not provide sufficient training for French conscripts. Thus, . . . theories of the offensive led directly to demands for an additional year of military service on the grounds that such a change would make it unnecessary to reply upon untrustworthy reservists.'[164]

But the 1914 offensive, like that of 1793, was inextricably bound up with left wing ideas. Foch's famous equations, 'War = the domain of moral force. Victory = will,'[165] were simply lines lifted from the handbooks of republican reformers. Both Monteilhet and Challener failed to realise that it was the very disorganisation and material deficiencies of the professional army which popularised the offensive.

The three year law was designed to improve training and boost army strength. It was a first step toward remedying the basic flaws on which the republicans had built their theory of the offensive. Given time, more balanced tactical notions might have developed without the enormous bloodletting of the war's opening weeks. But the offensive of 1914, like those of 1793 and 1870, 'was the lot of improvised troops'.

Notes

1. Paul-Marie de la Gorce, *La République et son armée* (Paris, 1963), 142.
2. Joffre, *Mémoirs* (Paris, 1932), 99-100.
3. Possony and Mantoux, 'Du Picq and Foch, the French School', in E. M. Earle (ed.), *Makers of Modern Strategy* (Princeton, 1944), 222-3.
4. J. F. C. Fuller, *The Conduct of War* (1972), 128.
5. Monteilhet, *Les Institutions Militaires de la France* (Paris, 1932), 271-2.
6. *Ibid.*, 351.
7. *Ibid.*, 321, 330.
8. Joffre, *op. cit.*, 20-1.
9. Driant, *Vers un nouveau Sedan* (Paris, 1906), 139.
10. Public Records Office (henceforth P.R.O.), W.O.33.618, *Report on Foreign Manoeuvres in 1912*, 15-16.
11. *Porte-Voix*, 1 March 1912.
12. André, *Cinq ans au Ministère* (Paris, 1907), 144.
13. *Ibid.*, 141.
14. Simon, *L'instruction des officiers, l'éducation des troupes et la puissance nationale* (Paris, 1905), 431.
15. André, *op. cit.*, 17.
16. 'La Rôle social de l'officier', *Revue des Deux Mondes*, 15 March 1891, 443-58.
17. Ebener, *La Rôle social de l'officier* (Paris, 1901), 31.
18. *Archives historiques de guerre* (henceforth AHG), 5N6, 31 March 1906.
19. Sillion, *Vers l'armée démocratique* (Paris, 1907), 38.
20. Maceau, *L'Officier éducateur national* (Bordeaux, 1905), 61-2.
21. *Ibid.*, 2.
22. Sillion, *op. cit.*, 46.
23. André, *op cit.*, 108.
24. Simon, *op. cit.*, 172.
25. Grandmaison, *Dressage de l'infanterie en vue de l'offensive* (Paris, 1906), 3.
26. *Ibid.*, IX.
27. Messimy, *Considérations générales sur l'organisation de l'armée, extrait du rapport sur le budget de la guerre, 1907* (Paris, 1907), 175.
28. Joffre, *op. cit.*, 20.
29. *Ibid.*, 21.
30. Messimy, *Considérations*, 60.
31. Zurlinden, 'Les Hautes-études de la guerre et l'avancement dans l'armée', *Revue des Deux Mondes*, 15 Dec. 1904, 777.
32. *Avenir Militaire*, 19 and 26 November 1896.
33. Haroué, *La Détresse de l'armée* (Paris, 1904), 68-9.
34. Joffre, *op. cit.*, 21.
35. Messimy, *Considérations*, 137.
36. Jibé, *L'Officier dans l'armée nouvelle* (Paris, 1906), 39.
37. Pédoya, *L'Armée n'est pas commandée* (Paris, 1905), 14.
38. *France Militaire*, 9 Feb. 1912.
39. *Ibid.*
40. Messimy, *Souvenirs* (Paris, 1935), 81.

41.   *Porte-Voix*, 21 May 1912. See also 11 Jan. and 15 Sept. 1913, and 10 and 20 Jan. 1914.

42.   Arès, *La Décadence intellectuelle de l'armée* (Paris, 1912), 17, 22-3.

43.   *Ibid.*, 32-4.

44.   Jaurès, *L'Armée nouvelle* (Paris, 1932), 236.

45.   *Ibid.*, 238, 240-1.

46.   P. Mahon, 'La Loi des cadres d'infanterie', *Revue des Deux Mondes*, 1 June 1912, 655.

47.   *Ibid.*

48.   *Porte-Voix*, 1 Sept. 1912, 10 and 20 Jan. 1914. 186 candidates in 1900, 420 in 1905 and 500 in 1910.

49.   *Documents Parlementaires, Sénate*, Annexe 165, 15 June 1899.

50.   Millerand Papers, Bibliothèque Nationale, unclassified.

51.   *Documents*, 403.

52.   *France Militaire*, 21 February 1905.

53.   *Ibid.*, 5 February 1911.

54.   *Ibid.*, 15 April 1910.

55.   AHG 7N 35, report 41-2.

56.   D'Arbeaux, *op. cit.*, 113. Between 1899 and 1903, 56 per cent or 2,732 of the second lieutenants commissioned in the four combat arms were graduates of either Saint-Cyr or the Ecole Polytechnique. The remainder, 2,117, were former NCOs. After 1904 when André's reforms had begun to bear fruit the percentages were tipped in favour of the NCOs. Between 1904 and 1909, 59 per cent, or 2,459, of second lieutenants commissioned were ex-NCOs. Many of these were not NCO school graduates. After 1904, one tenth of second lieutenancies went to adjutants promoted directly from the ranks. In 1910 this figure became one fifth. See Arès, *op. cit.*, 6.

57.   The *Porte-Voix* estimated on 15 November 1909 that fully one tenth of each class left the Ecole Polytechnique because their class rank was too low to qualify them for anything but an army career. In 1900, 42 per cent of artillery second lieutenants were ex-Polytechnicians. In 1902, this figure dropped to 40 per cent, and in 1903 to 35 per cent. By 1910, only 25 per cent of artillery second lieutenants were ex-Polytechnicians and by 1913 only 20 per cent. See *Porte-Voix*, 1 March 1913. A large number of ex-Polytechnicians also resigned from the officer corps after 1900 – a full 50 per cent in 1911, according to Captain d'Arbeaux. See d'Arbeaux, *op. cit.*, 117.

58.   Arès, *op. cit.*, 73.

59.   *Ibid.*, 80.

60.   AHG, 7N 3, War Minister to Corps Commanders 27 January 1914.

61.   Students were often considered too young to make the most of the college training. 'Because of their short service and age, these candidates do not always show the professional knowledge and maturity they need to profit from the course', the War Minister wrote in 1911, echoing General Pédoya, an ex-corps commander and radical deputy. See AHG, 7N 3, War Minister to Corps Commander, 27 January 1914, and Pédoya, 14.

62.   *Ibid.*

63.   Messimy, *Considérations*, 48-9.

64.   Messimy, *op. cit.*, 48-9.

65.   *Ibid.*, 56.

66.   Humbert, *Les Voeux de l'armée* (Paris, 1908), 162-3.

67.   *Ibid.*, 164.

68.   Soulier, *l'Instabilité ministérielle sous la Troisième République 1871-1939* (Paris, 1939), 483.

69.   Ministerial careers February 1879-June 1940:

Terms of office	1	2	3	4	5	6	7	8	9	10	Total
Ministers	217	103	71	48	28	17	13	17	14	33	561

War Ministers, June 1871-September 1914:

Terms of office	1	2	3	4	5	6	7	Total
Ministers	12	12	5	–	–	1	2	32

Between 1871 and the outbreak of war, War Ministers averaged barely one year in office. Eight years – 1877, 1879, 1883, 1885, 1887, 1893, 1895, 1899 – witnessed as many as three War Ministers. In 1898, five different men occupied the rue Saint-Dominique, while 1911 and 1913, crucial years of military preparation, saw four War Ministers each. Ollé-Laprune, *Le Stabilité des ministres sous la Troisième République, 1879-1940* (Paris, 1962), 67.

70.   *Ibid.*, 41.
71.   Ollé-Laprune, *op. cit.*, 47.
72.   Humbert, *Chinoiseries militaires* (Paris, 1909), 9-12.
73.   Messimy, *Souvenirs*, 70.
74.   Monteilhet, 281.
75.   Langlois, 'Le Haut commandement', *Revue des Deux Mondes*, 1 September 1911, 65.
76.   *Ibid.*, 50.
77.   AHG, 1N 1.
78.   Joffre, 17-18.
79.   Messimy, *Souvenirs*, 81.
80.   *Ibid.*, 76.
81.   Joffre, 18.
82.   AHG, 1N 1.
83.   Messimy, *Considérations*, 70.
84.   André, 144.
85.   Messimy, *Souvenirs*, 80-1.
86.   Zurlindin, 'Le Haut commandement des armées', *Revue des Deux Mondes*, 15 June 1903, 800.
87.   Metzinger, *La Transformation de l'armée, 1896-1907* (Paris, 1909), 29.
88.   *Ibid.*, 25.
89.   André, 24-5. See also AHG, 5N 7, August 1911, letter from Lyautey to Messimy about the difficulty in assessing an officer's professional competence.
90.   In 1910, 9.6 per cent of brevet staff captains serving in infantry regiments were promoted to major, against 1.3 per cent of non-brevet captains. The 1911 figures were 9.3 per cent against 1.5, and 11.75 per cent against 1.2 in 1912. *Porte-Voix*, 1 March 1911 and 1 March 1912, 1 February 1913.
91.   Of 130 infantry captains promoted to major in 1906, 23 were aides-de-camp. Eighteen per cent of all infantry captains who were aides-de-camp were promoted while barely 2 per cent of infantry captains otherwise employed moved up. Messimy, *Considérations*, 60.
92.   AHG, 7N 3, 7 October 1911.
93.   Metzinger, 24-5.
94.   *Porte-Voix*, 1 March 1911.
95.   *Ibid.*, 1 March 1912.
96.   *France Militaire*, 8 January 1911.
97.   D'Arbeaux, 24.
98.   *Ibid.*, 22-3.
99.   André, 25.

100. See also, *Le Temps*, 4 October 1913.
101. AHG, 1N 13, 28 November 1913.
102 Messimy, *Souvenirs*, 72.
103. *Ibid.*, 74.
104. *Ibid.*, 71.
105. Archives Nationales (henceforth AN), C 7257, Messimy proposal, 90.
106. AHG, 5N 6 and 5N 7.
107. Pédoya, 19.
108. *Porte-Voix*, 1 October 1913.
109. P.R.O. W.O.33.618; and the *Temps*, 10 October 1912.
110. Jaurès, 402.
111. AHG, 1N 13.
112. Arès, 67. See also AHG, 1N 13.
113. *Echo de Paris*, 9 August 1911.
114. *France Militaire*, 12 January 1910. See also AHG 7N 2, September 1913.
115. André, 144.
116. Grandmaison, *Dressage*, 73-4.
117. *Ibid.*, 102.
118. De Civrieux, 319-20.
119. See P.R.O.: WO.33, 363, *Military Resources of France, 1905*, 20, 75;
Palat, 'Les Manoeuvres en Languedoc en 1913', *Revue des Deux Mondes*, 15
October 1913, 814-5.
120. *France Militaire*, 9 and 25 February 1912.
121. Pédoya, vol. II, 97.
122. Langlois in the *Temps*, 25 February 1908.
123. De Civrieux, 167.
124. Messimy, *Considérations*, 213-5.
125. *Ibid., Le Problème militaire* (Paris, 1913), 10-11. See also *Armée et
Démocratie*, 11 March 1907.
126. AN, C 7257, Messimy report 1903.
127. Messimy, *Considérations*, 87.
128. Grandmaison, *Dressage*, 92-3.
129. *Ibid.*, 75.
130. Humbert, *Les Voeux*, 212.
131. De Civrieux, 338-9.
132. Quoted in *Porte-Voix*, 11 February 1912.
133. D'Arbeaux, 180.
134. *Porte-Voix*, 11 February 1912.
135. P.R.O.: WO.33, 618, p. 20.
136. Humbert, 142.
137. *Echo de Paris*, 26 August 1911.
138. Messimy, 205.
139. AN, F 13330, Leroy Committee.
140. Joffre, 101.
141. Fuller, 128.
142. De la Gorce, 141.
143. Liddell Hart, *A History of the First World War* (1972).
144. *Avenir Militaire*, 4 April 1893.
145. Grandmaison, V-VI.
146. AHG 6N 41, 19 October 1906.
147. Simon, 218.
148. Joffre, 20-1.
149. De la Gorce, 82-3.
150. AN, C 7257, Messimy report, 10. German numerical superiority was

backed up by an advantage in weaponry. In August 1914, Germany counted 4,500 machine guns to 2,500 in France, 6,000 77-millimeter cannon to 3,800 French 75s, and an almost total monopoly in heavy artillery.

151. Monteilhet, 277-8.
152. AN, C 7257, Messimy report, 10. Messimy includes hidden expenses.
153. Klotz, *L'Armée en 1906* (Paris, 1906), 101.
154. *Temps*, 15 November 1908.
155. André, 117.
156. AHG, 7N 35.
157. Messimy, 15.
158. Mahon, 'Le Service de trois ans', *Revue des Deux Mondes*, 15 April 1913, 883.
159. Grandmaison, *Deux conférences faites aux officiers de l'état major de l'armée* (Paris, 1911), 34.
160. C. Andrew, *Théophile Delcassé and the Entente Cordiale* (1968), 289
161. E. Weber, *The Nationalist Revival in France 1905-1914* (Los Angeles, 1968), 97.
162. *Ibid.*, 102.
163. Monteilhet, 331.
164. Challener, *The French Theory of the Nation in Arms* (New York, 1955), 82.
165. Possony and Mantoux, 228.

WAR AND ITALIAN SOCIETY 1914-16

John Whittam

During the last hundred years one of the least bellicose of societies has
been plunged periodically into aggressive wars by the deliberate action
of its governments. On no less than five occasions Italian armies invaded
Austrian territory.[1] In 1859-60 and again in 1870 the Papal States were
attacked and partitioned. Piedmontese troops in 1860 delivered the
coup de grâce to both the Kingdom of Naples and the advancing
Garibaldini. In the 1880s, the 1890s and again in 1935, Italian columns
marched into the highlands of Ethiopia. To celebrate the fiftieth anniversary of the Kingdom of Italy, one of her most peacefully disposed
premiers launched a war against the Turks and Arabs of Libya.[2] Russia,
an unlikely foe, was twice invaded, and France, Egypt, Yugoslavia,
Albania and Greece all found themselves victims of unprovoked attacks.[3] School text books glorified the military exploits of the Risorgimento and orators, journalists and poets praised the achievements of
the heroes of unification: Mazzini, preaching a people's war; Cavour,
plotting his cabinet wars; Garibaldi, fighting his guerrilla wars; and, pre-
siding over all, the rather unconvincing figure of Victor Emmanuel II
the Warrior King. The returns on all this emotional and military investment were meagre despite a succession of carefully calculated agreements from the Convention of Plombières to the Treaty of London.[4]
Custozza and Novara in 1848-9, Custozza and Lissa in 1866, Dogali in
1887, Adua in 1896, Sciara Sciat in 1911, Caporetto in 1917, Guadala-
jeara in 1937, and, for the period 1940-43, Southern France, North
Africa, Taranto, Greece and Sicily all became known to Italians and the
rest of the world as names signifying military humiliation. Apart from
the initial phases of the Libyan War in 1911 and the Ethiopian War in
1935 none of these wars were popular. To the majority of Italians,
those who worked in fields or factories, they appeared incomprehensible or unnecessary. The practising catholics and socialists among them
had at their disposal a series of moral and political arguments against
war to reinforce their traditional distaste for military service and all the
other aspects of organised state violence. Each time, however, the
peaceful majority was outmanoeuvred by the government of the day. It
was always a case of '*I meno tirano i piu*', as Giolotti remarked in May
1915 as he contemplated the ruin of his neutralist policy.[5] But this
minority which dragged the majority along behind its war chariot was

never fully representative even of the ruling elite. Indeed in this instance, Gioletti could rightly claim that it was totally unrepresentative. Nor was opposition to war confined to dissident politicians and their followers. Within this elite there were economists, businessmen, civil servants and generals who registered their disapproval. Like the opposition politicians and the millions of peasants and workers, they too were defeated.

This is not, of course, a peculiarly Italian phenomenon, so the examination of a particular episode in Italian history can perhaps throw light on other societies struggling with the complex issues of war and peace. The episode which has been chosen is the period 1914-16, Italy's decision to intervene in the First World War and the first twelve months of fighting. Antonio Salandra, who was premier from March 1914 to June 1916, was in many ways the key figure in these crucial months. This southern conservative, despising public opinion and contemptuous of the Giolittian majority which obstructed him in parliament, was a man who liked to walk alone.[6] To a frightening degree he succeeded, almost singlehanded, in imposing his will on a reluctant nation and a badly divided ruling class. When Italy intervened in May 1915 she did so on his terms, and the war which followed was, to a large extent, his war. He aimed to fight a limited war, a *'piccola guerra'*, a final war of Italian independence to round off the Risorgimento. He found the notion of a great war, a *'grande guerra'*, particularly abhorrent. Italian intervention would, he hoped, lead to a swift victory over the central powers. The army on the northeast frontiers and the fleet in the Adriatic would fulfil their assignments. There would be no need for total mobilisation which would strain the economy and perhaps destroy the existing political and social *status quo*. By the time he fell from power in June 1916, 'Salandra's war' had become increasingly anachronistic. Two months after his fall Italy finally declared war on Germany thereby giving formal notice that she was engaged in a *'grande guerra'*. The Boselli administration, from June 1916 to October 1917 marked a transitional stage in Italy's conduct of the war. The first serious attempts were made to involve the nation and bridge the appalling gap between the concept of the *'grande guerra'* and the actual war of attrition being fought on the frontiers, the *'piccolissima guerra'* of the infantrymen defending or attacking over the same few square yards of trench and barbed wire. After Caporetto, when Italy was invaded and thrown onto the defensive along the Piave, the Orlando government witnessed the growth of a national consciousness. In fitful fashion it was still growing when the armistice was signed on 4 November 1918.

In March 1914 Salandra soon discovered that he had inherited from Gioletti not only the premiership but a political system in the process of disintegration, a deteriorating economic situation and an over-stretched and underequipped army, all this against a background of tense diplomatic activity produced by the Balkan wars and the rivalry between the two armed camps. The euphoria of 1911, when Italians celebrated the fiftieth anniversary of the founding of the kingdom and welcomed the invasion of Libya, had virtually evaporated. Indeed, the Libyan war and the granting of universal manhood suffrage had transformed the political scene and exacerbated the divisions within the country, underlining the premature nature of the unity celebrations of 1911.

The period of political balance and compromise during the previous decade began to break down under the pressure of increasing polarisation. On the left, intransigents grew more powerful in the Socialist party, the Republican party, and the trades union movement. Even anarchism began to revive and in August 1913 Malatesta, that stormy petrel of subversion, reappeared in Italy after a fifteen-year exile. On the right too intransigence became the order of the day. Contemptuous of the Giolittians, disillusioned by the conduct of the war in North Africa and frightened by the newly enfranchised masses, the young Nationalist movement, the Futurists, the admirers of D'Annunzio and the imperialists, attacked the moderates and the left in the name of patriotism.[7] Rifts within the ruling elite, the 'grand old liberal party' as it was sometimes called, and the complications arising from the implementation of the electoral law of 1912, speeded up the erosion of the political system. Mass politics required different techniques from those so successfully employed by Giolitti in previous elections, and although the Gentiloni Pact of 1913 was a clever piece of improvisation, it was doubtful if this could be repeated. Salandra had additional problems, psychological as well as political. When Giolitti retired, Sonnino was asked to form a ministry but declined when the king refused a dissolution. Salandra was summoned and he made no such conditions. Giolitti helped him by inducing the reluctant San Giuliano to stay on as foreign minister and by pledging him the support of his 360 followers in parliament.[8] Believing Salandra to be a weak man, Giolitti felt confident that he could displace him at any time merely by withdrawing his support in the chamber. The condescension of this cool northerner was bitterly resented by Salandra, strengthening his resolve to pursue as independent a policy as possible, thus complicating an already difficult situation.

Giolitti's stated reason for resigning had been the defection of the radicals, but an equally compelling motive had been provided by finance minister Facta in February 1914 when he revealed the full cost of the Libyan War, 1,276 million lire. This produced a budget deficit of 556 million, the largest since the war of 1866. Rather than increase taxation Giolitti retired from the scene. The rapid economic growth which had been such a notable feature of previous years was also showing signs of ending with a business recession. The fact that 900,000 Italians had emigrated in 1913,[9] while another 385,000 had gone on strike was unlikely to generate confidence in the economy.[10] The threat of unemployment and the presence of underemployment sharpened the unrest in the industrial north and the agrarian south.

Financial stringency also hit the rearmament programme of chief of staff Pollio and war minister Spingardi. Their previous plans had been wrecked by the Libyan War and generals and admirals clamouring for additional funds to replace the men and equipment lost in North Africa. General Porro, Salandra's first choice as war minister, quickly resigned when the treasury rejected his financial demands. His successor, General Grandi, was less exacting and agreed to accept a much lower figure which was really insufficient if the Italian armed forces hoped to play a major role in any European conflict.[11]

A European war involving Italy did not seem a remote possibility in early 1914. The Italo-Turkish war had disturbed the equilibrium in the Eastern Mediterranean and the Balkans and had helped to precipitate the Balkan wars of 1912 and 1913. Italian occupation of the Dodecanese and her concern over the fate of Albania brought about tension with Greece and strained the already uneasy relationship with her Triple Alliance partner Austria-Hungary. Italian dissatisfaction with the frontiers of 1866 which left Trieste and the Trentino in Austrian hands had tended to limit the diplomatic and military effectiveness of the Triple Alliance since its formation in 1882. Irredentism, never far below the surface of Italian politics, had re-emerged during the heightened nationalism accompanying the Libyan War and its aftermath. Nonetheless, the alliance had been renewed in 1912 and General Pollio, chief of staff since 1908, unwaveringly supported Italy's obligations to the central powers which stemmed from the military convention of 1888.[12] The Libyan War had indeed forced him to inform Moltke and Conrad that he could no longer guarantee to send an expeditionary force to the Rhine, but in March 1914 he announced that Italy was again prepared to resume her obligations and sent General Zuccari to Berlin to work out the details while staff officers in Vienna arranged for the use of Austrian railways in transporting the Italian troops to Alsace.[13] Even if Pollio had not died on 1 July there is no evidence to suggest that Salandra's government or public opinion would have sanctioned war on behalf of an aggressive Austria.

Just three weeks before Sarajevo, however, it appeared that Salandra's government was about to be involved not in a European war but a civil war. The disparate forces of the left had found in antimilitarism a far more effective rallying cry than anticlericalism or republicanism.[14] They built up a campaign in 1913-14 centred first on the case of Augusto Masetti, a conscript who had wounded a colonel in 1911 and then been declared insane to avoid untoward publicity, and then on that of Antonio Moroni, another conscript who was accusing the military of assigning known militants to punishment battalions.[15] A protest meeting on Sunday 7 June — constitution day when military parades were held throughout Italy — was held at Ancona and through mishandling by the authorities developed into yet another 'proletarian massacre'. A similar incident at Rocca Gorga in January 1913 had led the socialists and the trades unions to pledge themselves to launch a general strike if such an incident recurred. After some confusion, the strike was proclaimed and disorders broke out resulting in sixteen deaths and over 400 wounded. In Emilia and Romagna whole areas briefly became autonomous republics and over 10,000 troops had to be deployed to restore order. Red Week, as it came to be called, was Salandra's first major crisis. To his intense relief, it subsided as quickly as it had erupted. The nationalist, militarist backlash which these insurrectionary outbreaks had promoted had no time to develop fully, but had to await another crisis to present it with a second opportunity. This crisis was not long in coming for on 28 June Franz Ferdinand was assassinated and on 28 July, with German backing but without consultation with Italy, Austria declared war on Serbia.

On 31 July Salandra summoned a cabinet meeting to discuss Italy's position. San Giuliano made it clear that there was no *casus foederis*, 'nothing in the spirit or the letter of the Treaty of the Triple Alliance compelling us to join Germany or Austria over this issue'.[16] He was also convinced that public opinion was hostile to intervention on the side of the central powers, that Britain would enter the war in support of France, and that with Italy's best troops in Libya she would be militarily incapable of waging war in the immediate future. The foreign minister opted for neutrality and won the full approval of Salandra and his colleagues. Their decision was made public on 2 August and formally published the following day: it was almost unanimously accepted by the Italian people. Giolittians, socialists, catholics, factory workers and peasants were delighted, militants like Mussolini even threatening revolution if the government chose war. There were some nationalist dissenters, and, for a few weeks, Sonnino advocated loyal adhesion to the Triple Alliance,[17] a view which was at first shared by the new chief of staff General Cadorna.

Assuming his onerous duties on 27 July, Cadorna was immediately plunged into the crisis situation. Had he shown himself to be more accommodating he could have secured his appointment as chief of staff back in 1908. He was passed over on this occasion because of his uncompromising hostility to the existing civil-military power structure. Constitutionally the king was the supreme commander of the army, but in practice and in article 4, paragraph 16 of army regulations, it was the war minister who held this position in peacetime. As soon as war broke out, however, the chief of staff assumed command. Because a war minister was appointed by the politicians, sat in the cabinet and made speeches in parliament, Cadorna believed that the army was at the mercy of political manoeuvring and party squabbles. In a period of political instability, for instance, war ministers were likely to have a very short time in office and this lack of continuity of leadership would be dangerous for the army.[18] Cadorna had a good case. The disaster of 1866 could be largely attributed to divided control as General Pollio's recently published book on Custozza had clearly shown. Unfortunately, Cadorna had argued his case with scant regard for the susceptibilities of the politicians. Indeed, civilians and military showed themselves to be remarkably ignorant of each others' techniques and difficulties, a failing which was not confined to the Italians. Military debates in the chamber were badly attended and only a handful of antimilitarist socialists and 'military experts' ever participated or understood the issues being debated. On the other hand there were officers who never read the national newspapers or even knew the name of the current prime minister.[19] By 1914, political, technical and organisational developments dictated that a major war required total mobilisation which could only be achieved by the closest collaboration between the civilian and military sectors. Because of their temperament and background, the two men at the summit of their respective hierarchies, Salandra and Cadorna, were to prove incapable of effecting this fusion. Moreover, even within their own areas of competence, they both failed to inspire that sense of unity which was so essential in waging a great war.

The government's declaration of neutrality came as a complete surprise to Cadorna who had just sent a request to the minister asking for all units destined for the Rhine and the French frontier to be put in a state of readiness, and a memorandum to the king asking for his authorisation. Speed was vital because Cadorna and virtually every staff officer in Europe believed that the decisive battles would be fought in a matter of weeks rather than months. Even after the declaration of neutrality Cadorna still pressed for mobilisation as Italy's position was vulnerable with all the great powers ready for combat or actually engaged in hostilities. Cadorna's views were ignored or misunderstood by Salandra and yet both men were faced with an almost identical dangerous and delicate task. Cadorna had to revise all existing war plans and Salandra had to dismantle the Triple Alliance and reconstruct a new diplomatic framework. It would be disastrous if foreign governments and Italian public opinion became aware of these moves prematurely, but it was surely carrying secrecy to unnecessary lengths for Salandra to refuse to keep Cadorna informed about the progress of his negotiations. He was also mistaken in not asking Cadorna's advice on military affairs, or, if he distrusted him on both personal and professional grounds, in not asking him to resign.

Remaining neutral in August 1914 was a diplomatic and political decision which was taken against the advice of the military leadership. It was proof, amongst other things, that the civilians were firmly in control. The decision to intervene in the war on behalf of the Entente, taken in the autumn of 1914 and implemented in May of the following year, was also a civilian enterprise. The army, kept in ignorance of what Salandra and Sonnino were actually doing and most unjustly used as the scapegoat for Italy's delay in entering the war, was expected to act when the politicians gave the word.[20] The soldiers would finish the game which the diplomats and politicians had already won, for the pen and the mouth were mightier than the sword.

The amazing and intricate story of Italian intervention is well documented and has been told elsewhere.[21] By the beginning of 1915 there were several groups clamouring for war: the nationalists; moderates like Albertini; democrats like Salvemini; and renegade socialists and syndicalists. But the most important group never consisted of more than a half-dozen men, led by Salandra. After the battle of the Marne had removed fears of a swift German victory, Salandra cautiously began to prepare the ground.[22] This caution was dictated not only by fear of German and Austrian reprisals, but by the certain knowledge that the majority of Italians were hostile to war, and, more daunting still for a politician, that the majority of deputies – Giolittians, catholics and socialists – remained staunchly neutralist. Instead of trying to convert them to interventionism – which was attempted by the other interventionist groups – Salandra and his collaborators decided to trick them into war, to present them with a *fait accompli*. In so doing, they not only dragged Italy into the World War but dug the grave of Italian democracy as well. Sonnino, who had become Salandra's intimate even before his appointment as foreign minister, told Malagodi on 12 December 1914 that he fully realised that the majority of Italians inside and outside parliament were opposed to war, but that if the government decided on intervention it was its duty to ride roughshod over all those who stood in the way.[23] More explicit still was a letter from Salandra to Sonnino written on 16 March 1915, just two weeks after the commencement of those negotiations with the Entente which resulted in the Treaty of London. Convinced that a final break with the central powers was not far distant, he enumerated the difficulties.

They were both acting

1) without the explicit consent of the king;
2) without being sure that the country and the chamber was in agreement;
3) without the army being ready until at least the end of April;
4) without having had any pledge or any hint of a pledge on the part of the Triple Entente.

Far from being dismayed, Salandra argued that if the army was ready and a pact with the Entente concluded, or on the point of being concluded, they had nothing to fear under items one and two![24] No doubt when war became inevitable, king and country would be unable to avoid fighting for king and country. On 12 April, the director general of public security and the premier decided to sound out public opinion on the question of war and peace by sending circulars to all prefects asking them to report on 'the real feelings of the various classes of citizens' in their respective provinces.[25] It is difficult to believe that he expected massive support for his war policy. It was true that by April various interventionist groups had begun to make some headway in the cities, but to Salandra they were rather unwelcome allies. He viewed them with as much suspicion as Cadorna witnessed the growth of Garibaldian *volontarismo* and even the departure of some young enthusiasts for the French sector of the Western Front.[26] It was also true that Salandra — and the other interventionists — had been presented with a valuable gift in February 1915. This was the publication of Giolitti's famous '*parecchio*' letter in which he had remarked that Italy could gain 'quite a lot' without resorting to war. Its great importance has been succinctly put by Seton-Watson: 'The *Parecchio* letter had been a turning point. By publishing it, Giolitti unintentionally assumed the leadership of all the neutralist forces and turned the campaign for intervention into an anti-Giolitti crusade.'[27] Fighting Giolitti, 'the minister of the underworld', the agent of Vienna and the accomplice of Prince Bulow, had a far wider appeal than fighting the central powers.[28] Salandra, however, watched the growing momentum of interventionism with mixed feelings. It could interfere with Sonnino's finely balanced diplomatic game and take the initiative out of the hands of Salandra. It is possibly too bizarre to argue that Salandra was hoping to hear from his prefects that neutralism was still predominant. Whatever his reasons he called off the survey on 21 April after fifty-five of the fifty-nine prefects had replied. He had sufficient evidence to realise that the great majority of Italians were neutralist, but — and this was of crucial interest — they were largely unorganised and their neutralism could be classified as '*indifferentismo*', passive resignation to whatever God or the government decreed.[29] Six days later Italy signed the

Treaty of London.

Unlike the noisy interventionists of left and right, Salandra steadfastly refused to appeal for mass support. It was not in character for him to do so, and popular participation would also endanger his secret political and diplomatic manoeuvres. A further reason for his rejection of calls for the total mobilisation of public opinion was his confident expectation of a short war, fought by Italy for essentially limited objectives and with the minimum of commitment to other powers or to any grandiose ideology. It would be 'business as usual' while the armed forces defeated Austria in the last war of the Risorgimento. Mass mobilisation of the nation's resources would be dangerous and unnecessary.

With the signing of the treaty with the Entente there was, however, one final hurdle before Italy could fulfil her obligations and declare war on Austria. The Giolittian majority in the chamber had to be swept away by recourse to a *coup d'état* or the deputies coerced into abandoning neutrality. 'Radiant May' ensured that brute force was not required, and that the second alternative would be adopted. The events in May were the culmination of a clever and unscrupulous campaign by the interventionists to produce the illusion that the majority of Italians were in favour of war.[30] The government itself had set the stage for this confrontation between interventionists and neutralists by denouncing the Triple Alliance on 4 May. The following day D'Annunzio issued his call to arms from the new Garibaldi monument at Quarto. To the relief of his followers − and there were still over 300 of them in the chamber and 100 in the senate − Giolitti returned to Rome on 9 May. Neutralist pressure and the depressing military situation induced the cabinet to resign on 13 May.[31] Giolitti, however, declined the king's invitation to form a government and Salandra was asked to withdraw his resignation on 16 May. The following day Giolitti returned to Piedmont and his leaderless followers voted full powers to Salandra when parliament reassembled on 20 May. Mobilisation was decreed on 22 May and on 24 May Italy went to war with Austria. After the turmoil and divisions of Radiant May, there was a period which Salandra called the '*idillio nazionale*'.[32] Neutralism as an organised force seemed to disappear. The Turin strike of 17-18 May was the last great anti-war demonstration and Giolitti's departure from Rome symbolised the collapse of neutralism as a political force. Socialists declared that their policy would not be hostility to the government but '*non aderire né sabotare*'. Catholics were instructed by their priests to remember that it was a fundamental duty to obey the authorities.[33] Giolitti himself, on 5 July, called for unity and asked his followers to support king and government. But, outside the ranks of the interventionists in the larger cities, there was no enthusiasm − only the indifference and resignation which so many of Salandra's prefects had commented upon in April. For waging a short war with limited objectives, this was relatively unimportant. Cadorna, who assumed full command on the declaration of war, and over one million uniformed Italians awaiting his orders, would swiftly achieve his goals with or without popular enthusiasm.

The Italian army entered the war with grave deficiencies; there was a serious shortage of officers and NCOs, only 618 machine guns, only 112 heavy guns and no howitzers.[34] Well aware of these and many other shortcomings, Cadorna had done his best to fill up the gaps created by the Libyan War and the parsimony of the politicians. Unfortunately, he was less conscious of the problem of morale and believed that his huge army would be an effective fighting force as long as strict discipline was maintained and everyone obeyed the orders of his superiors. This attitude and the fact that the military code in force was still basically that of Charles Albert, dating back to 28 July 1840, was to create serious dissatisfaction in the months ahead.[35] In the civilian sector, Salandra's attitude was strikingly similar. Citizens must obey the laws, work hard and fulfil their various tasks unquestioningly. It was not the duty of the state – or the army – to explain what was happening, to try to take the people into partnership or institute welfare agencies.

Towards the end of June 1915, a French officer in Rome wrote: 'Unlike us the Italians do not seem to feel that this is a crucial war [*guerre à fond*] for the independence and existence of the country. They perhaps think of it as a big Libyan campaign.'[36] The authorities, civil and military, were well aware of this attitude. As the war would soon be over there was no need to propagandise either civilians or soldiers. In the summer of 1915, this belief in a short war must seem an incredible miscalculation on the part of Italy. Of course in the summer of 1914, everyone suffered from this illusion. It has indeed been argued cogently that most leaders assumed a short war. 'This assumption may have been essential to their decision for a war. Few of them would have opted for war if they had foreseen a protracted, revolutionary or unsuccessful conflict. They assumed that a short war would be decisive, limited and productive.'[37] This was understandable, but the events after the Marne must have convinced all but the most myopic that the war would be long and gruelling. In August 1915 Salandra walked along the Via Nazionale talking to Nitti. Nitti declared that the war was likely to be a long one and asked the premier if the troops had been provided with winter equipment. Salandra accused him of pessimism and was amazed that anyone could imagine the war lasting that long. In April 1915, in a room in the senate building, Cadorna explained to those who were questioning him about the forthcoming war that within a month he would be in Trieste and menacing the heart of the Austrian Empire.[38] Moreover, despite the lesson of the Western Front, Cadorna intended to achieve this through frontal assaults. He had said so in a book he published in February 1915 and he implemented it on the Isonzo front no less than eleven times between the summer of 1915 and the summer of 1917.[39] His method can only be criticised, however, by those who present a viable alternative and are prepared to denigrate all the commanders on the Western Front between 1914 and 1918, but his tenacious optimism can be condemned, as can his — and Salandra's — neglect of the morale factor. The reason for the initial optimism of both men can be swiftly explained. There was a deadlock in the west and in the east the Austrians, weakened by their losses on the Russian and Serbian fronts, appeared to be on the point of collapse. The Italian entry into the war would transform the situation in the Balkans, destroy Austria and thereby induce Germany to make peace. If Cadorna were successful, Salandra's '*piccola guerra*' — and he had no intention of declaring war on Germany — would terminate the '*grande guerra*'. The reasons for continued optimism after months of bloody and indecisive fighting on the Isonzo and stalemate in the Trentino, cannot be explained so readily.

> 'The great majority of the population . . . have in fact only the most rudimentary understanding of politics; they are unaware of the higher interests and noble ideals of the nation. They see the war therefore as a misfortune like drought, famine or plague.'

These were the words of the prefect of Teramo on 20 April 1915 describing opinion in his own rural province, but they are applicable to all but a small minority of the labouring classes in town and countryside.[40] That they apply as much to those in uniform as to those who remained at home is clear from the numerous letters and memoirs that have been preserved.[41] '*La patria*', wrote Malaparte of the ordinary soldier, 'was a conception beyond their power of understanding.' Trieste and Trentino meant little to them. When their officers explained why they were fighting against the militarism of the central powers they listened politely but understood nothing. Why did all this matter? They fought because 'there were certain paragraphs in the Regulations which they knew by heart'.[42] No doubt Cadorna would have nodded approval at this. They were perplexed by the fact that no enemy had invaded their territory, no one threatened their homes or families — except perhaps their own government. It was only after they had actually fought at the front that many of them came to hate the Austrian, a natural enough response when it became a case of killing or being killed, and this generated a crude kind of explanation for continuing to fight. Certainly the acquisition of Trieste and the Trentino seemed incomprehensible. They looked around at the terrain they were truing to conquer, the ravines of the high Alps, the Carso, that 'howling wilderness with stones as sharp as knives', and the muddy desolation on the Isonzo, and they wondered why tens of thousands were dying for acres of land which no self-respecting peasant would ever contemplate acquiring. Either they were commanded by madmen or they were being punished for their sins.[43]

There were some compensations. There was the companionship of the trenches or the alpine lookouts, and most of them did their distasteful work not for their country or for their officers, but for their companions. Slackness or cowardice would, it was true, be punished under the regulations, but it could also endanger the cohesion and therefore the lives of their comrades. Veterans and raw recruits developed their routines, knowing that deviation from them would earn the contempt and anger of their fellow sufferers. For many of them, another compensating factor was an improved diet. If supplies came through, they could expect the regulation amounts of flour, bread, meat, pasta, rice and vegetables, together with coffee, sugar, wine and tobacco.[44]

As the war dragged on, with one battle of attrition after another, the vexed question of the *'imboscati'* led to serious discontent, and underlined the widening gulf separating the war front from the home front. Essentially, *imboscati* were those who successfully avoided front line service. To the soldier in the front line trench, the *imboscati* were not only all civilians but the men in the second trench, the artillerymen, the rear formations and the general staff. As Salandra's short, victorious war began to develop into a lengthy slogging match, the continued mobilisation of men and materials became a serious problem. Indiscriminate conscription, like the volunteering movement in Kitchener's England, had a detrimental effect on the economy and particularly on the supply of arms and munitions of war. Skilled factory workers who had been called to the colours were sent back and paid high wages to keep the peasant soldiers supplied with bullets and shells.[45] The peasant soldiers, most of them from the south, were unappreciative. In December 1915, for the first time, large numbers of troops were sent home on leave. The rumours they had heard at the front were seen to be true. They passed through the northern cities, where war profiteers grew rich and munitions workers seemed to be doing well out of the war, and arrived in their villages to find their families near destitution. The price rise at the beginning of the war had pleased farmers but now the economic situation had deteriorated. The fittest peasants were drafted into the army, leaving the women, the children and the aged to run the farms. The state did little or nothing to help even when the menfolk were killed or maimed at the front. What

Turati was later to call 'the revolt of the countryside against towns' was already beginning.[46] Only in the summer of 1917 did the government and the army work out a system of exemptions and short leaves — to enable peasant soldiers to help with the sowing and harvests — for former agricultural workers, and then it proved to be totally unsatisfactory.[47] This growing anatagonism between the home and the war fronts led to the great debate on the responsibility for the increase in defeatist sentiment. This, in turn, emphasised the rift between the civilians and the military, with Salandra and the politicians accusing troops on leave of spreading alarm and despondency, and Cadorna blaming civilian agitators for corrupting his soldiers. The war, which many interventionists had seen as the answer to the divisions within Italy, regional, political and social, appeared to be tearing the country apart and Caporetto was still over a year away.

Paradoxically, it was these interventionists who were the first to be seriously disillusioned by the war. In or out of uniform they were forbidden by the military authorities to propagandise the troops. Left wing interventionists found themselves being treated with suspicion, barred from the military school at Modena, and prevented from becoming officers.[48] Volunteer corps were frowned upon by the army and the government and out of an army of over four million by 1916 only 8,000 were classified as volunteers.[49] Another shock for these enthusiasts was their reception by the liberated Italians of Friuli. Being clericals and pro-Austrian, the Italian troops were regarded as alien conquerors. For the sons of the educated middle classes, imbued with the spirit of the Risorgimento, this was a shattering blow; others were to follow. As junior officers, they found themselves unable to communicate with their men and bitterly criticised by their superiors for making the attempt. They resented the harsh discipline imposed by the regulars, and deplored their careerism and frightening lack of initiative. Cadorna and his entourage of staff officers seemed to exemplify that aloofness and cold inhumanity which treated companies and even whole divisions as expendable units in interminable battles which achieved little or nothing. Most of them marvelled at the stoical endurance of the common soldier and felt that if they could only inspire him with their own idealism the Italian army would be unbeatable. They felt the same way about the urban and rural masses but every conceivable obstacle was placed in their way by the suspicious authorities, civilian and military. Many of them joined the shock troops, the *arditi*, to escape the claustrophobic atmosphere of their units and the petty rivalries between various branches of the army. Others, particularly from the smaller provincial cities, had resented the condescension of the notables and the growing disrespect of the labouring classes, and relished the power of command given to them in the army. From these two groups sprang many of the problems of post-war Italy.

Cadorna was not unimpressed by the growing criticism of his conduct of the war. He bitterly resented the fact that the government could point to his soldiers on leave as the spearhead of defeatism. Apart from counteraccusations against subversive elements among the public at large, he promised Salandra to deal drastically with any signs of indiscipline in the army, vigorously enforcing the military code, and, if necessary, resorting to 'decimation'.[50]

Nor were the officers to remain immune. In 1919, a commission of inquiry accused Cadorna of excessive severity towards his troops and the ruthless dismissal of officers.[51] His reply was that every commander in the First World War had resorted to such measures. This was correct,[52] but there were officers – and civilians – who argued that strict discipline must be supplemented by other measures. General Capello, himself a strict disciplinarian, saw the need for propaganda among the troops and even before Italian intervention he had urged his officers to keep their men informed about the progress of the war.[53] For Capello, this was no limited war like the battles of the Risorgimento: 'It is no longer an army which fights but the entire nation, no longer a fraction of the resources of a country which is utilized but *all* the nation's resources which become necessary to obtain victory.'[54] Capello's attitude and his links with politicians like Bissolati, led Cadorna to see him as '*un generale politicante*' and his H.Q. as a political as much as a military centre.[55] Cadorna still behaved as if the millions under his command constituted a nineteenth-century garrison army engaged in a nineteenth-century war. He had never been a keen adherent of 'the school of the nation' theory and argued that by 1916 any attempt at 're-education' was doomed to failure. All the best men and officers had been killed off in the early battles, so that infantry divisions were composed basically of untrained officers and illiterate raw recruits, over half of them coming from the south and Sicily.[56] Carla Cadorna, his daughter, showed more awareness of the problem of morale by contacting Ansaldo, Fiat, Terni and the influential editor Albertini, and inducing them to support Don Giovanni Minozzi's attempts to establish '*case del soldato*', a movement which government and supreme command viewed with unjustified suspicion.[57]

It was when his personal position seemed to be threatened and rumours were spreading of his possible replacement, that Cadorna began to realise the importance of public opinion. With Ugo Ojetti as his press agent, he put his case before the public, and in the cabinet he strenuously opposed war minister Zupelli's strategic plans.[58] On 27 February 1916 he confronted Salandra and threatened to resign if Zupelli remained in office. Salandra warned him not to act in an unconstitutional manner but Cadorna sent in his resignation. The king attempted mediation but Salandra then offered to resign. The crisis was eventually resolved on 9 March by the resignation of Zupelli and his replacement by General Morrone, a Cadorna supporter. It was a signal victory for Cadorna, reinforcing his belief in his own indispensability.[59] It was also a clear indication that the implications of a *'grande guerra'* were beginning to threaten the position of both men.

Cadorna's position was so strong because on the outbreak of war the politicians — as in the other belligerent countries — had tended to leave the prosecution of the war to the military experts at supreme headquarters. Cadorna had achieved no dazzling successes but until he actually proved his military incompetence by being defeated, his dismissal was virtually impossible. To the interventionists, he was the strong man that Italy needed. To the allies, he was a general who had become convinced that he could win the war of attrition on the frontiers,[60] and was, moreover, a man who saw the Italian contribution as part of the overall war effort of the Entente.[61] The horizons of both Salandra and Sonnino were much more limited.

Following the Zupelli crisis there was a two months truce between the government and Cadorna. But on 15 May the Austrians launched their *Strafexpedition* and almost burst out of the Trentino onto the Venetian plain, which would enable them to take the Isonzo armies from the rear. A cabinet convened on 24 May, a sad anniversary, called for a meeting between leading ministers and generals, but Cadorna declined the invitation owing to a more pressing engagement on the fighting front. Salandra was uncertain what to do. He had no clear information about Cadorna's plans and was badly shaken by rumours of a retreat to the Piave. Morrone was sent to find out the truth and Cadorna confirmed his resolve to retreat to the Piave if this became necessary. Sonnino spoke darkly of betrayal and of it being a case of 'either him or us', while Salandra went to supreme headquarters at Udine to ask the king to dismiss Cadorna.[62] The king told him that it was up to the government and Salandra wavered. Meanwhile, Barrère, the French ambassador, made it clear that the allies backed Cadorna;[63] the Giolittians increased their criticisms of the government and the interventionists attacked Salandra and his *'piccola guerra'* and supported Cadorna's call for a declaration of war on Germany and support for the allies at Salonica. The cabinet approved Cadorna's dismissal on 30 May but could find no one to replace him.[64] When the chamber met early in June a series of attacks on Salandra was mounted and he proved unwilling to save his position by aligning himself with the democratic interventionists. This would have meant repudiating the stance he had adopted since Italy had entered the war. He attributed the defeat in the Trentino to badly prepared defensive positions, and this apparent attempt to shift responsibility onto the shoulders of

Cadorna resulted in a parliamentary defeat by 197 votes to 158. Salandra resigned and Boselli's government of national unity took office while Cadorna restored the military situation in the Trentino and skilfully transferred seven divisions to the Isonzo and smashed his way into Gorizia on 9 August. On 24 August war was declared against Germany and in November old Cecco Beppe, Franz Joseph, died. Since 1848, he had been regarded as the traditional foe of Italy and his passing removed yet another landmark of the Risorgimento period. Men like General Dallolio, heroically attempting to reorganise the munitions industry, and Bissolati, striving to unite military and civilian sectors, were still a long way from achieving a national war effort. But the removal of Salandra was a step in this direction. It took the defeat of Caporetto to remove Cadorna and to enable politicians and generals to call upon the Italian people to finish the war which a majority of them had not wanted to begin. The Italian people responded well, and finally won what had become *their* war. It remained to be seen whether this hard won unity of purpose could survive into peacetime.[65]

Notes

1.   Austrian Lombardy was attacked in 1848 and 1849 and, more equivocally, in 1859. In 1866 Venetia was invaded and in May 1915 Italian armies crossed the northeast frontiers.
2.   The Libyan War of 1911 was directed by Giolitti.
3.   Russia in 1855 and August 1941; France in June 1940; Egypt in September 1940 (after O'Connor's harassing raids); Yugoslavia in April 1941; Albania in April 1939 and Greece in October 1940. Italians and Austrians did fight side by side on one occasion – the suppression of the Boxer Rising in China.
4.   It is tempting to write from the Pact of Plombières to the Pact of Steel but Mussolini's agreements in the late 1930s are conspicuous because of their lack of careful planning.
5.   The fact that the prosaic Giolitti quoted Giusti's sonnet indicates his extreme agitation: O. Malagodi, *Conversazioni della guerra*, vol. 1 (Milan, 1960), 63-4. Malagodi wrote this on 18 May.
6.   *In piazza perio non ci vado, no è il mio ambiente* (16 Sept. 1915, F. Martini, *Il Diario 1914-1918* [Milan, 1966], 534).
7.   For Corradini's attempts to concert the dynamic exponents of class war into nationalists under the magic formula of 'the proletarian nation' see A. Lyttelton, *Italian fascism* (1973), 29 and 149-51.
8.   G. Giolitti, *Quarant'anni di politica italiana*, vol. III (Milan, 19.2), 102-3.
9.   This problem is dealt with in F. Mangotti, *La Polemica sull'emigrazione nell'Italia unita* (Citta di Castello, 1962).
10.   S. B. Clough, *The economic history of modern Italy* (New York, 1964), 171.
11.   G. Rochat, 'L'esercito italiano nell'estate 1914', *Nuova rivista storica*, 45, 314-5.
12.   Italy undertook to send five army corps and three cavalry divisions to the Rhine if the Triple Alliance went to war with France and Russia.
13.   Rochat, 318.

14. L. Lotti, *La settimana rossa* (Florence, 1971), 53.
15. *Ibid.*, 54-60.
16. Martini, *Diario*, 7.
17. N. Vigezzi, *L'Italia neutrale*, vol. I, 30.
18. P. Pieri, 'Les relations entre gouvernement et commandement en Italie en 1917', *Revue d'histoire moderne et contemporaine*, 15, 133-4.
19. 'Whoever concerns himself with things outside his profession', a young officer was told by a superior who learnt that he was reading a book on socialism, 'is a bad officer'. General De Rossi, *La vita di un officiale italiano sino alla guerra* (Milan, 1927), 66. General De Bono admitted that officers in the Rome garrison were interested in politics – they had to provide guards whenever parliament was sitting; E. De Bono, *Nell'esercito nostro prima della guerra* (Milan, 1931), 190-1.
20. Rochat, 295, f.2.
21. A. Monticone, *Gli italiane in uniforme* (Bari, 1972), 57-87; L. Valiani, 'La guerra del 1914 e l'intervento italiano', *Rivista storica italiana*, LVIII (1966); Vigezzi, *L'Italia neutrale*; A. Monticone, *La Germania e la neutralita italiana 1914-15* (Bologna, 1971). For sources see Martini, *Diario* and Malagodi, *Conversazione*.
22. Malagodi, I, 21. On 18 Sept. Salandra told the editor that he thought that the Triple Alliance was 'morally finished'.
23. *Ibid.*, I, 32.
24. Monticone, *Gli italiani*, 63-4. Later Salandra was to write *'Del bene e del male a noi due spetta l'onore o il biasimo'* (A. Salandra, *L'Intervento* [Milan, 1930], 79).
25. Monticone, *Gli italiani*, 67; B. Vigezzi, *Da Giolitti a Salandra* (Florence, 1969), 321-401 (containing the replies of the prefects).
26. R. De Felice, *Mussolini il rivoluzionario* (Turin, 1965), 305.
27. C. Seton-Watson, *Italy from liberalism to fascism* (1967), 439.
28. For Bülow's diplomatic mission to Rome and his links with Giolitti, see A. Monticone, *La Germania*.
29. Monticone, *Gli italiani*, 69.
30. B. Vigezzi, 'Le radiose giornate del maggio 1915 nei rapporti dei prefetti', *Nuova rivista storica*, 43 (1959) and 44 (1960).
31. Cadorna had declared that the army would be ready by the end of April and at the time of the signature of the Treaty of London the military situation seemed favourable to the Entente powers. By the middle of May, however, the Russians had been checked in Galicia, the British landings at Gallipoli and the progress of second Ypres had not produced spectacular results, and, as a result of Sonnino's diplomacy, Rumania postponed her intervention.
32. Salandra, 311.
33. Among Italian bishops, only a tiny minority were either 'nationalist' or 'neutralist'; the great majority were 'patriotic and moderate' urging obedience to the laws and cooperation with the secular power (these are the categories used by Monticone, *Gli italiani*, 145-84).
34. Ufficio storico dello stato maggiore, *L'Esercito italiano* (Rome, 1961), 205-6.
35. Monticone, *Gli italiani*, 185-6. Also in E. Forcella and A. Monticone, *Plotone di esecuzione. I processi della prima guerra mondiale* (Bari, 1968).
36. H. Contamine, 'La guerre italienne vue par des officiers francais', *Annuario dell'Università di Padova* (1958-59), 7.
37. L. Farrar, *The short-war illusion* (Santa Barbara and Oxford, 1973), 148.
38. F. Nitti, *Rivelazioni. Dramatis personae* (Naples, 1948), 183-4.
39. P. Pieri, *L'Italia nella prima guerra mondiale* (Turin, 1965), 65-6.
40. Monticone, *Gli italiani*, 72, f. 24.

41.   G. Borsi, *Lettere dal fronte* (Turin, n.d.), and especially A. Omodeo, *Nomenti della vita di guerra* (Bari, 1934). A second edition came out in 1968.

42.   P. Melograni, *Storia politica della Grande Guerra 1915-1918* (Bari, 1969), 13.

43.   Omodeo (2nd ed.), 9.

44.   A. Serpieri, *La guerra e le classi rurali italiane* (Bari, 1930), 47.

45.   The daily wage of war workers was 7.60 lire, for soldiers 0.50.

46.   Melograni, 333-4.

47.   Serpieri, 62-5.

48.   Martini, *Diario*, 486.

49.   Ministero della Guerra, Ufficio statistica, *Statistica dello sforzo militaire de nella guerra mondiale* (Rome, 1927), 28-9.

50.   For the increase in desertions and other acts of indiscipline, and for Cadorna's criticism of the leniency of officers, see Monticone, *Gli italiani*, 206-12; L. Cadorna, *Pagine polemiche* (Milan, 1950), 82 ff.

51.   *Ibid.*, Malagodi, 77.

52.   See, for instance, General Joffre, *Mémoires* (Paris, 1932), 280.

53.   L. Capello, *Caporetto, perchè?* (Turin, 1967), xx.

54.   *Ibid.*, 9.

55.   *Ibid.*, xvi.

56.   Melograni, 222. For criticism of the 'peasant army' thesis, see M. Isenghi, *Il mito della grande guerra* (Bari, 1970), 306-8.

57.   Melograni, 154-6.

58.   Concentration on the Caso and reinforcement of the Albanian front (Martini, 567 and 620-1).

59.   Melograni, 182-4.

60.   L. Cadorna, *Lettere famigliari* (Milan, 1967), 135.

61.   Malagodi, 35.

62.   Melograni, 187; Martini, 710.

63.   *Ibid.*, 714-5.

64.   Cadorna, *Pagine polemiche*, 136-41.

65.   For this, see G. Sabbatucci, *I combattenti nel primo dopoguerra* (Bari, 1974), and G. Rochat, *L'esercito italiano da Vittorio Veneto a Mussolini* (Bari, 1967).

THE CZECHOSLOVAK ARMY AND THE MUNICH CRISIS: A PERSONAL MEMORANDUM

Brigadier H. C. T. Stronge, C.B.E., D.S.O., M.C.

In recent years I have studied much of the literature on the subject of the Munich crisis, including the scholarly works of many of our contemporary historians and the Official Documents On British Foreign Policy 1919-39, third series, which incidentally includes several of my own reports, submitted as required to H. M. Minister in Prague, Mr Basil Newton. Most of the authors whose works I have read have analysed in detail and with great skill the political factors bearing upon the period in question, and they have concluded in the light of all the knowledge now available that Britain and France played a truly deplorable part, whether or not inevitable, in the rape of Czechoslovakia. The intrigue, bordering on dishonesty, which has become apparent in much of the official correspondence can hardly justify any other verdict.

My purpose here is not to comment upon or question the views of the historians whose research work in the political field has been far more extensive and penetrating than my own, but to place on record certain facts, and my opinions deriving from those facts, concerning the military situation in the Czechoslovak Republic before and during the crisis of 1938. In none of the histories which I have read has this subject received the attention due to its relevance in an issue of peace or war. In fact, as I hope to show, the faulty judgement which was made at the time concerning the potential of the Czech army to offer effective and highly damaging resistance to the invading *Wehrmacht* is, in the accounts of most historians, either under-rated or ignored. The assumption inherent in this treatment cannot be allowed to go unchallenged. Before attempting to do that, however, I should endeavour to indicate the circumstances leading to my appointment as military attache.

I was born in 1891 of parents both of whom had been partially educated in Germany, though of pure British stock, and had cultivated friendships in leading military circles there. After nine years schooling in England I was sent to a state school in Germany for two years during which time I became deeply interested in the German army and its recent history. In 1910 I was gazetted from Sandhurst into The Buffs. From August 1914 I served throughout World War I as a regimental infantry officer in three separate theatres of war, finishing as a battalion commander (temporary Lt. Col.) in France in 1918. After graduating from the Staff College I was appointed in 1928 G.S.O. third grade at the War Office in Military Intelligence, during which tour of duty I and another officer completed a special reconnaissance in a part of north-west Germany. The MI section in which I worked was also responsible for France, Belgium, Spain and Portugal and their overseas possessions. I had already visited all the French colonies, except one, in West and North Africa. After a period of secondment in Nigeria I was appointed military attaché in Czechoslovakia and Yugoslavia in 1936 when tension was building up in Europe. When selected I had just completed two years as G.S.O. second grade in charge of MI I at the War Office, administering our attachés abroad and foreign attachés in London, all of whom I knew at the time. In June 1940 I was appointed G.S.O. first grade in Military Operations, and from 1941 until the end of the war I had administrative commands, first at Aldershot, then in North Africa, Sicily, Corsica, France and Holland. I retired from the army in 1946.

For reasons of protocol it was decided that I should reside in Belgrade rather than in Prague and visit the latter from time to time as required. My predecessor in the appointment had found that arrangement satisfactory, albeit in a period of relative tranquillity. Early in 1937, a few weeks after my arrival in Belgrade and as soon as introductory formalities had been completed there, I went to Prague for the first time to repeat the initial procedure in Czechoslovakia. To my great surprise I was told on arrival that I was to be received the following morning by the President, Dr Benes, a formality which I had understood to be normally confined to Heads of Missions. Indeed, in Belgrade I had called on the Chief of the General Staff but there had been no suggestion of my seeing the Prince Regent as Head of State. Neither our air attaché, resident in Prague, nor the Legation could account for this departure from custom.

In the event President Benes received me cordially and alone. In the course of more than half an hour he touched on the history of the Republic since its formation, its present problems, external and internal, the latter with special reference to the Sudeten territory, and briefly also that of the army. The interview, which must have been meant as a compliment, was in fact the first of other favours to come. No doubt also it was designed as a form of indoctrination against anti-Czech propaganda likely to be encountered in the course of my work.

During the early spring, summer and autumn of 1937 I paid four visits to Czechoslovakia, each one having a particular purpose in view. For instance, on one such occasion I visited the great national arsenal, the Skoda works at Pilsen, the small arms factory at Brno, the chemical warfare factory and depot, and other military establishments including the Staff College. In August I toured virtually the whole Republic in a Prague taxi (my own car being under repair), in order to familiarise myself with the physical nature of the country, its strategic and tactical possibilities, and to make some occasional contacts with the ordinary people of the land, my driver acting as interpreter throughout, except in German, wherever we made a halt. In September I attended army manoeuvres. Reports on all these activities had to be written before returning to Yugoslavia, including details of interviews with the General Staff, foreign attaches and other special contacts. But apart from an inspection of artillery units and attendance at a display of armoured vehicles near Prague, I came into less close touch with troop formations in 1937 than in 1938, by which time I had acquired much useful background knowledge of the general military situation in the Republic.

The following is a summary of my impressions at the end of 1937, the first year of my tour of duty as military attache in Prague:

a. I was greatly impressed by the Skoda works at Pilsen and the other factories visited, especially by the zest of the workers themselves. They showed an obvious sense of purpose and awareness of the importance of their job.

b. In no part of the Republic was any anxiety as to the future noticeable, neither in civilian nor in military circles, as yet. The general feeling was, however, that a showdown with Germany must come some day. The tendency at that stage was to place some reliance upon the country's allies and friends, but above all upon their own gathering military strength and efficiency. My early impressions in regard to this were favourable.

c. My relations with the Chief of General Staff, General Crejci, and the Director of Military Intelligence were very good.

d. I had got to know my colleagues, the other military attaches fairly well, in particular General Faucher, head of the French military mission who had spent some years in the country and was most helpful in giving advice; also Colonel Toussaint the German military attache, a non-Nazi at heart but loyal to Hitler. He was well liked by most of us and by members of the Czech General Staff.

Early in 1938 the treatment by Hitler of the Austrian government was becoming increasingly arrogant and threatening. He was even claiming to have received tacit support from Lord Halifax for any action he might take. However, the actual invasion of Austria by German forces on 11 March was almost totally unexpected. Certainly none of my fellow military attaches in Belgrade (including the Austrian and German attaches), present at a party in our house, had any foreknowledge of the event. The first reaction to this ruthless act was to turn one's attention towards Czechoslovakia. I was surprised therefore on arrival in Prague soon afterwards to find much less concern than I had expected as to what was likely to happen next. There were two reasons for this composure; in the first place the General Staff were fully alive to the impossibility of an immediate follow up operation, and secondly, incredible though it seems, Göring's assurance 'on his honour' that Germany had no aggressive intentions towards their country was taken at its face value by Dr Benes and his government, for the time being at any rate. But within the next few weeks that mood was to change to one of mounting apprehension.

After conversations at the Ministry of National Defence with the Deputy Chief of the General Staff, the first Assistant Chief and the heads of the various bureaux, I was able on 29 March to submit a memorandum to H. M. Minister dealing with the whole question of the defence of the Republic. My main impressions were summed up as follows:

a. An attack by Germany within the next few years was probable as it was impossible to negotiate satisfactorily in connection with the Sudeten problem, though a declaration by Britain to stand by France, upon whose good faith as an ally so much depended, might well prove to be a sufficient deterrent to ward it off.

b. The General Staff maintained that the Czechs would fight it out. For my part I believed that to be a fact provided they were supported by France and Soviet Russia, but was less sure otherwise. Also they might be unable to resist effectively if the defences were pierced or turned before mobilisation was complete.

c. Although it was recognised that eventually, if left totally unsupported the Czech defence must be overwhelmed, it was capable of offering protracted resistance especially in Bohemia and Moravia.

d. Strategic planning was based for the most part on the assumption that France at the very least would mobilise her army.

e. The fortifications along the northern frontier with Germany were well advanced. Sabotage was a real danger but seemed to be largely discounted by the plans designed to deal with it. There were as yet no permanent defensive works in the south.

Before passing on I must stress that the foregoing summary was the result of my first meeting with senior members of the General Staff within three weeks of the Austrian *Anschluss*. In the months to come I was to form more definite views upon many factors relevant to the worsening situation.

At about this time I enquired of Colonel Hajek, Director of Military Intelligence, whether any facts concerning the frontier fortifications could be given me for the information of our War Office as a matter of M.A.s routine. Such a request was entirely in keeping with normal procedure in any country. In fact all official information on service matters is obtained by formal enquiry. It came as a surprise, however, when some days later I was informed that General Crejci, Chief of the General Staff, would himself give me the answer to my question. In the event he told me that I had full permission to go wherever I liked in the fortified zone and that the Director of Fortifications would accompany me during a three day tour and answer any questions. The only conditions were that I should inform nobody at all apart from H. M. Minister and the authorities in London about my visit, and that I should meet the Director at a prearranged point in the Sudeten area, and in plain clothes. No other military attache had or would be accorded the same privilege, I was informed, including General Faucher, though he had visited certain sectors. As I rose to leave, having thanked him and given the undertakings required, he remarked that although Britian was not bound by treaty to come to his country's defence, we were in fact allied to France and he had complete confidence in our integrity as a nation.

As there would not be time to cover the whole area of the fortifications in three days, I selected certain sectors which seemed to me to be of crucial importance, between a point in the line northwest of Prague and Moravska Ostrava (Märisch Ostrau), far to the northeast. The Director was most helpful in explaining the fire plans and other relevant tactical features at places where we stopped, indicating also what still required to be done. On returning to Prague I reported in general terms to Mr Newton and in more detail to the War Office. I had been greatly impressed with the defensive strength of the whole system, the skill with which it had been designed, permitting economy of force in garrison formations. Even at that comparatively early stage the works would constitute, if manned, an obstacle of some delaying power to an attacking force. By the autumn it was to become truly formidable, a fact freely admitted by German officers and by the *Führer* himself, it was reported, after the Czech surrender to the Munich *diktat* and the abandonment by their allies had made a free inspection possible. However, another six months was needed for the completion of extra refinements in the nature of casemate accommodation, extended minefields, turrets, etc. After the *Anschluss* the General Staff had been counting upon just such a reprieve.

The line of fortifications along the northern and western frontiers with Germany was the key to Czech defensive strategy. It closed the otherwise open access to the vital area of Bohemia, and acted as a shield for mobilisation and the manoeuvre of counterattack formations. In the south where communications for an invading force were poor the pattern of a highly fortified defence bastion was unnecessary.

The hope of a six-month reprieve was presently to be wrecked. On 19 May, information was received in London and Prague, emanating from Germany, that troop concentrations had been observed in Saxony and at other localities near the Czech frontiers. The details are now fully recorded in official and sundry historical accounts. I visited the Ministry of Defence the following morning where the Director of Intelligence explained to me in some detail the reported movements of certain *Wehrmacht* formations. They were considered, he said, to be a threat to Czech national security. He did not vouchsafe the source of his information, which I assumed to be the secret service. At first sight the situation looked serious but within a few days Colonel (later Lt. General Sir Frank) Mason-Macfarlane, our military attache in Berlin, and Major (later Major General Sir Kenneth) Strong, his assistant military attache, both reported that extensive personal reconnaissances by them independently had been unable to establish any evidence of troop movements other than those normally taking place at that time of year. We know today that there were in fact no grounds for alarm, but we are still in doubt, as far as I am aware, as to whether the scare was started with a definite purpose in view, and if so why and by whom, or whether it resulted from a genuine mistake by someone who, having seen troops on the move, assumed the worst. Tension in the Sudetenland had already been mounting sharply, creating a likely source for rumour and intrigue.

As soon as Colonel MacFarlane's report reached our Legation in Prague I ceased to have any doubts that the affair was a deception, whether intended or not, especially as the Director of Intelligence had nothing further to say on the subject. I have always been inclined to suspect the Czechs as they were the only party to benefit from the scare at that time. Britain and France were embarassed as they were forced to come into the open, the very last thing they wanted to do, and administer a warning to Hitler (shortly to be smoothed over by Sir Nevile Henderson), whilst Hitler himself was angered at being bluffed by the small country he was hoping shortly to destroy.

In Czechoslovakia however, the action taken by Britain and France received general approval; it was taken as an implied rebuke to the Germans. Moreover, the alleged troop movements in Saxony were assumed to justify the calling up of one class of reservists as a precautionary measure, affording a useful trial in mobilisation procedure; it also acted as a morale booster for the sorely tried Czech officials in the northern and northwestern areas of Bohemia, where local elections were due to take place on 20 May. All in all the whole episode served a seemingly useful purpose for the Czechs at that particular time. They were not to know that on that very day the enraged *Führer* dictated his wishes as to how 'Case Green' was to be prepared and implemented.

In mid June I went to London for the annual conference of military attaches at the War Office, lasting four days. At this conference which was opened by General Lord Gort, the CIGS military attaches spoke in turn about the military situation in the country to which they were accredited, and this was followed by a general discussion.

We had been issued on arrival with a General Staff paper on the later developments in our own army (not an encouraging picture but one which I knew well having recently attended our manoeuvres in southern England as a conducting officer for foreign military attaches accredited to the UK). In view of the existing threat to Czechoslovakia the conference was particularly attentive to what I had to say. I gave it as my personal opinion that the morale of the Czech army was good, that its organisation was sound and that its preparedness for war was well advanced, in fact a favourable all round report. During this period I was summoned for separate interviews with the CIGS, with the Secretary of State for War, Mr Hore-Belisha, and with Lord Halifax, Foreign Secretary. To the CIGS I was able to give the views of the Czech General Staff, as told to me, of the most probable plan of attack by the *Wehrmacht*. Mr Hore-Belisha was particularly incisive in his questions, whilst Lord Halifax asked about the will to resist in the ranks of the Czech army and of its ability to repel a full scale invasion. At these several interviews I gave it as my opinion that the army would fight it out if allowed to do so by the Prague government, and that the degree of resistance it was capable of achieving in the early stages of a campaign might well have a decisive effect upon its further course. I could not of course advise on the probable attitude of the government, a political issue, nor was I anxious to be drawn into forecasting in terms of weeks or months how long the army might be able to hold the *Wehrmacht* at bay single-handed as that depended upon many diverse factors. However, when pressed on one occasion to indicate an approximate minimum period I hazarded an estimate of three months. It seemed obvious, and it was generally agreed, that Germany with her population of 75 million must ultimately win in a protracted struggle. On the other hand if both France and Britain, and possibly Russia, were to come to the aid of the Czechs, a greater war, possible a world war, would result and upon the issue of that would depend the ultimate fate of all engaged in it. The three months minimum estimate agreed incidentally with that of General Faucher and, I understand, with views expressed by German officers some months later after they had inspected the fortifications.

Returning to Belgrade after a few days leave in Britain, I hoped to catch up on my duties in Yugoslavia, spending part of July in that country. On 27 July, the War Office instructed me by cable to proceed at once to the area north and northwest of Vienna south of the Czech frontier, as a concentration of German troops had just been reported there. My wife and I were staying at an hotel in Bled, a lakeside resort in Slovenia where the diplomatic corps, including H. M. Minister Sir Ronald Campbell, spent the hot month of July. The Minister authorised my immediate departure and we were able to reach Vienna the first night. The following morning I explored the whole area in question by car but saw no troops nor any signs whatever of them having been there recently. The only minor and not very significant occurrence that day was the fact, first noticed by my wife, that we were being followed by another car at some distance. Any 'stop-go' movements on my part were at once reflected by a similar movement on its part. However, eventually it stopped and ceased to follow. The whole affair had clearly been a false alarm.

On returning to Prague after an absence of a few weeks I found that the pending arrival of the Runciman Mission, with a brief to investigate and mediate in the Sudeten question, was the main topic of talk in diplomatic and political, though to a lesser degree in military circles. When first approached by Mr Newton on the subject, Dr Benes had been so upset that he even hinted to him of resigning the Presidency. However, he was quickly induced to change his tune by a combination of adroit British diplomacy and advice from Dr Hodza, Slovak President of the Council, enabling Mr Chamberlain to announce in the House of Commons that a request for the Mission had been received from the Czech government. It had in fact been his own idea from the start, not quite what the House was led to believe, but the project was accepted more or less cordially by the governments in London, Paris, Prague and Berlin as well as by the Sudeten leaders (SDP). It was viewed with some distrust by the army and a large section of the Czech people. The Generals felt that their government had already gone as far as it was militarily safe to go towards meeting the demands of the SDP under Herr Henlein, and that the Mission would probably press for even more. Lord Runciman and the members of his team were all men of undoubted integrity and ability, qualities which, combined with a charm of manner, readily ensured their acceptance wherever their duties might take them. But they were set an impossible task initially, a factor which could not be known at that stage and was only to become apparent later.

The Mission resided at the Alcron Hotel where my wife and I also happened to be staying. Lord Runciman occasionally spoke to me about recent events in the Republic, though never of course in the form of consultation but only as an enquiry as to facts. I was glad to be able to help in a small way, whilst my wife did her best for the ladies of the party. It was not long before I became acutely aware through my own fairly numerous contacts, civilian as well as military, that mistrust of

169

the Mission by the Czech people as a whole was steadily increasing. The physical movements of 'The Lord' as he was commonly referred to, and of the members of his team, were obviously matters of general interest, so that the close relations established by them with some of the wealthy aristocratic families (Hohenlohe, Kinsky, Czernin, Schwarzenberg and others), mostly pro-Sudeten in outlook, was duly noticed. However, the main concern of the general public centred upon the news being leaked that Drs Benes and Hodza and the Council were under increasing pressure from the Mission for far-reaching concessions to the SDP. This was in fact the case, and by the time Lord Runciman felt obliged to admit that his function as mediator had come to an end, in mid-September, nothing short of a transfer of territory to the Reich had become acceptable to Hitler or to his minions in northern Bohemia. Britain and France had already obtained the consent of the Czech government to the principle of a liberal measure of autonomy for the Sudetens, as much as it could possibly concede within the framework of its own sovereignty. The formerly genuine grievances of the Germanic minority had long since been put right but were still constantly and viciously exploited throughout the summer months under Nazi direction so as to afford a potential *casus belli*.

In retrospect one must in fairness admit the dedicated effort of the Mission to succeed in its task of mediation. It failed, as it was bound to do from the start and as any other Mission would have failed. For the Czechs this was sheer tragedy. Having only accepted the Mission under pressure, and then consented to comply with its biased advice acutely affecting the structure of the state, they felt at least entitled to some moral support when the impending crisis actually came. Instead they were betrayed. The army with every reason to be apprehensive became greatly disturbed when it was known the way things were going. I was even informed at one point in early September that the government would not resist invasion if abandoned by its allies. That mood, however, quickly changed, and I came to regard it as a *ballon d'essai* to draw some positive reaction from our side, similar perhaps to the one they achieved in May. I have no doubt whatever that later in the month when general mobilisation took place, the army as a whole, officers and other ranks alike, was not only prepared to fight but inclined to want to fight and settle the affair once and for all. Much took place behind the scenes in those pre-Munich days when even General Syrovy, the father figure of the armed forces and hero of the Czech Legion in World War 1, later to become, albeit unwillingly, the counterpart of Pétain in the Czechoslovak Republic, still insisted upon fighting it out. Most of the other generals were equally resolute, in particular Crejci (CGS) and Ingr, a senior Corps commander.

It would be irrelevant to discuss in this memorandum the political poker game which characterised the final ten days of the crisis, with its bluffs, degradations and hypocrisies, leaving Hitler the outright winner. Almost all of our leading British historians of the period have exposed as a result of diligent research into the now known facts the falsity of the doctrine of appeasement. They have mostly been able to show that in spite of our own unreadiness for war, even more acute than in 1914 as I can personally testify, we did not in fact stand in danger of defeat in 1938, nor did France if both countries had gone to war. Neither could we have won a war, then, unless Germany — also unprepared by her own high standards — had broken her back in a desperate attempt (*blitzkrieg*) to knock out the Czech army of one million well trained and well equipped men, fighting for their country on their own territory, with all the strategic advantages afforded by interior lines.

Such an attack, by Hitler's own orders, would have to succeed at the first attempt or fail. There was to be no question of a war of attrition. This vital fact was not then known outside Germany, it is true, nor was the actual strength of the *Wehrmacht* and its important deficiencies, especially in officers, realised in London and Paris in spite of the well informed reports by our military attache and assistant military attache in Berlin upon the views of the German General Staff. The full extent of the several warnings to Hitler by these senior officers has only been revealed since the capture of the German documents. These papers have also confirmed what was at the time widely suspected from numerous secret reports emanating from Berlin, but rejected by Whitehall as lacking in authenticity — that Hitler's ultimate political weapon was that of blackmail carried out by threat, falsehood and bombast; it amounted perhaps to one of the greatest bluffs in history, a card played adroitly to the relief of many, notably the people of the German *Reich*, to the shame of others and to the despair of the Czechoslovak Republic.

My purpose in writing this memorandum has been to record my personal opinions and conclusions upon the military situation confronting Czechoslovakia before and during the Munich crisis. The views I then held have been modified to a certain extent as a result of knowledge since acquired. Only, however, in the matter relating to the actual strength of the *Wehrmacht* were my earlier estimates in a marked degree at fault. I had been deceived like so many others, close observers of events in central Europe, and had supposed the number of divisions in the German army to be considerably larger than we now know to have been the case. As to the state of morale and general military efficiency of the Czech armed forces, I had kept an open mind in 1937 although my predecessor had assured me that all was well. The more I saw of the troops in 1938, the General Staff and the whole of the military ensemble, the more convinced did I become that here was a force capable of defending its frontiers and willing to so so at any cost.

The question which naturally arises in the case of armies composed of diverse national elements such as existed in Czechoslovakia, with minorities speaking different languages and nurturing grievances against the majority governing party, is the extent to which men can or will endanger operations in time of war. As I have already mentioned, the General Staff had studied the matter very carefully and devised ways and means to counter sabotage and subversion, especially in the Sudetenland. It must not be supposed that all the German speaking people were disloyal; far from it, though most anti-Nazis did not declare themselves as such. In my view, the loyalty of the troops of Slav origin, in fact the bulk of the army, was never in doubt, whilst interference with military measures on a large scale by minority groups would be both difficult and dangerous. Some desertions and individual acts of sabotage were of course liable to occur.

Details regarding the strength, efficiency and organisation of the Czech air force were never directly my concern, but that of the resident air attache in Prague, with whom, however, I worked in close association. There is no doubt that in number of aircraft and in modernity of equipment the *Luftwaffe* surpassed the combined air forces of France, Britain and Czechoslovakia at that period, but it is fair to say in the light of later experience in war that air power alone could not inflict a mortal blow upon the adversary. I mention this fact because some critics have envisaged Czechoslovakia, its cities, its arsenals, its communications and even its fortifications being subjected to such a pounding as to render the army in the field unable to fulfil its vital role of defence. That is an entirely false picture.

Thus in my view the assumption of Germany's ability to invade, conquer and retain control the the Czech Republic in the autumn of 1938 is unrealistic. That, however, was the solution to the question almost universally taken for granted at the time, and still maintained by some students and writers of history today. To add stress to my own conviction in the opposite sense I will summarise, and in some cases further develop, my reasons.

In the first place, several of the leading generals in the *Wehrmacht*, whose knowledge of their army was factual and unrivalled, had warned Hitler on more than one occasion that a war with Czechoslovakia could not be won quickly and that the army was not yet ready for one which might involve France and Britain, and possibly develop into a world war.

Secondly, although the *Wehrmacht* at the start of hostilities would have been the stronger of the two contestants, especially in armoured divisions, the disparity would only have become serious at a later phase of the campaign.

Thirdly, the balance of strategic advantage lay almost entirely with the Czechs. They would benefit by operating on interior lines, by having precise and detailed knowledge of the country and its resources, by short lines of communications to their supply depots and arsenals, and by working amongst a generally loyal and cooperative population.

Fourthly, the strong protective screen of fortifications along much of the northern and western boundaries of the state, though still not completed, would greatly restrict the potential points of penetration. It would also ensure cover for mobilisation and all internal movement of troops.

Fifthly, the important element of surprise which had served Hitler so well at the time of the Austrian *Anschluss*, and it was hoped to achieve again, had already been forfeited by the end of September when the attack was due to start, as the mobilisation of the Czech army of thirty-eight divisions (more than a million men) was complete and the fortifications fully manned. Moreover, 'Case Green', the invasion plan approved by Hitler at Nuremburg on 9-10 September, involving a pincer movement from the north and southwest on Olomouc and Brno respectively, was substantially the plan envisaged by the Czech General Staff as the soundest strategic concept, the one therefore, most likely to be followed.

Finally, and perhaps most importantly, the 'cause' for which the Czechs and Slovaks would be fighting was their very existence as an independent sovereign nation. Thus the morale of the army was high, inspired alike by confidence in their own efficiency and leadership. By contrast, the *Wehrmacht*, albeit equally and rightly self-assured of its own military prowess, had little beyond its sense of discipline to sustain it in its allotted task, one which the mass of the German people were anxious to avoid.

On two occasions during the crisis period Colonel Mason-MacFarlane, military attache in Berlin, came through Prague. On his second visit he called on me in my office. There was blood on his face caused by barbed wire at the frontier, which he had crossed on foot. He told me he had formed a poor impression of Czech army morale. It appeared that a young soldier at the place where he came through seemed nervous and indecisive as to what to do about the Colonel and his companion, a Czech. I explained that at that stage the actual frontier was kept under observation by men of a paramilitary formation, non-regulars, and that any members of that body might well have been perplexed at seeing him arriving in that fashion, but I was unable to counter his opinion about army morale. After both his visits, Colonel MacFarlane sent in adverse views to the War Office. I did not see the first report (which was highly inaccurate in other respects also), but on seeing the second, I took steps at once to contradict his opinions. Mason Mac, as he was generally known, had a distinguished record in both World Wars, and was, I believe, an excellent military attache, but was known at times to act impulsively. It is unfortunate that his views on Czech army morale would seem to have been accepted in Whitehall rather than mine, as a factor affecting official policy.

The reasons I have advanced for discounting the theory that the Czechs would have lost if Hitler had carried out his threat to invade cannot of course be regarded as proof. They merely indicate probability. In war, as everyone knows, the unexpected often occurs. A false strategic move, for instance, by either contestant might well have a vital effect on the outcome. History has many examples of this.

Postscript

There are certain matters partly related to the main theme of this memorandum upon which I also hold firm opinions, and will attempt to clarify now.

There appear to have been two main reasons why it was generally assumed by politicians and most foreign correspondents in 1938 that if the *Wehrmacht* were to invade Czechoslovakia there was nothing that France and Britain could do to save her from defeat. The first was the perfectly logical reason that however valiantly and tenaciously the Czechs might fight, they would be overpowered eventually by sheer weight of numbers. Secondly, because of our own state of unpreparedness and France's disinclination for a similar reason to honour her treaty obligation, neither country would be able to offer timely and effective support to the hard pressed Czechs.

With regard to the first point, it was not known then for certain, as it has since been revealed in the German documents, that although Hitler was confident in the success of the *blitzkrieg* planned for 'Case Green', he nevertheless made specific provision for possible failure. On no account, he decreed, was there to be a war of attrition in which his armies might bleed to death. That was a wise precaution in view of his later and more ambitious designs incorporated in the *Drang nach Osten*. It is also a pertinent factor in refutation of the theory of inevitable success.

As to the presumption that France and Britain could render no useful and timely help to the Czechs, it can safely be said that a positive declaration of war on their part must have involved an immediate despatch of several divisions of the *Wehrmacht* to man the Siegfried line in the west, thereby reducing substantially the number available for invasion. We know that provision was in fact made for this purpose. The inability of our two countries to mount a major offensive on land in the early stages of a campaign was of course well known to Hitler, but the fact of the very great disparity in numbers between the French and German armies, to the advantage of the former, the ascendancy of the British navy, together with the mobilisation of the entire armed forces of the two nations would surely have exerted pressures on Berlin and have been of moral support for Prague. Indeed, such a declaration of intent by us would have denied Hitler his main incentive to march, the conviction that we would stand aside.

If Dr Benes had rejected the Munich terms in defiance of the advice, and even threat of abandonment, given to him in the names of France and Britain, would Hitler have actually carried out his oft repeated intention of invading Czechoslovakia, in those circumstances?

I believed in October 1938, and continue to believe today after much reading and study of the issue, that in the last resort and in face of a final challenge, Hitler would have yielded to reason and stayed his hand, temporarily at least. It is a subject which has been debated fully by professional historians with whom I cannot compete in dialectic nor in research. I will try to be brief.

First, a personal note. One day in October 1938, an important German industrialist called at our Prague legation and asked to see the military attache, a seemingly odd request. To explain the purpose of his visit he said he wanted 'our people' to know that if we had stood firm at Munich, Hitler would have climbed down. He claimed to have positive evidence of the fact. To my objection that such a course must involve serious loss of face, he denied that that was so, maintaining that the *Führer*'s prestige would have been much enhanced as a true man of peace and a statesman of world stature. He pointed out, further, that the Sudetens had already been offered, and Benes had agreed to give, all that had been asked for, short of annexation. Honour was therefore satisfied. My visitor's personality and manner as well as his reasoning impressed me favourably.

Next, it is only right to point out that Hitler for his part had much to gain in delaying by a year any further recourse to arms, enabling him to reach an improved, and more typically German, state of military preparedness together with a radical swing of popular morale in the *Reich*, before embarking on his master design for *Lebensraum* towards the east. The fact that these great benefits, and more, were actually 'handed to him on a plate' after Munich by his erstwhile appeasers and future enemies only highlights the great tragedy which immediately followed, and is a scar in the memory of those who lived through it.

In conclusion, some reference must be made to the follow up period linking Munich with the outbreak of World War II in September 1939. The disparity of effort made by the two sides to prepare for a threatened future conflict reflected disastrously the lack of real purpose and awareness by our two nations, Britain and France, of the mortal danger lying ahead. The graphic account of this sorry state of affairs by Winston Churchill in the first volume of *The Second World War* shows how the superiority in military strength, in its overall aspect, with which we faced the confrontation of 1938 was being overtaken month by month in 1939, so that Germany's chance of winning a possible world war had greatly increased by September of that year. Incidentally, Hitler had by then won his battle of wits and daring against his General Staff.

The loss of Czechoslovakia as an ally with her powerful military component and its arsenals, together with her entire economic wealth, was Europe's greatest setback since Hitler became leader of the *Reich*. It reversed at one stroke the balance of armed strength and economic potential in the entire continent, and that event more than any other determined the course of world history in the years immediately to follow.

It is in my view inconceivable that, if Hitler had been faced in 1938 with the certainty of French and British, and possibly Russian, intervention on behalf of the Czechs, he would have dared, or been permitted, to make war in defiance of the sound professional advice of his generals. Indeed he is known to have assured them on at least one occasion that he would not invade Czechoslovakia unless he was convinced of the passive inactivity of those Powers.

It is idle to speculate at length upon what might have happened *if* we had stood firm at Munich, and the Czech Republic had been saved, at any rate temporarily on a basis of Sudeten home rule. But of one fact there is little doubt, namely that Hitler was determined, come what may, to invade Soviet Russia in his own time, a project envisaged years before in *Mein Kampf*.[1] I firmly believe that whenever that situation should occur, and provided the Czech commitment was no longer an issue, neither France nor Britain would march in support of the Soviet Union. They were not bound by treaty to do so.

Finally, could Britain and France have in fact abandoned the Czechs to their fate if Dr Benes had, on his own initiative, rejected the Munich *Diktat* which both countries had bade him accept, and if Hitler had actually launched his attack? The answer must surely be NO!

Note

1.   In the course of a private talk I had with Colonel Toussaint, German military attache, during the summer, he told me that whatever the ultimate solution of the Czech question might be, he had heard Hitler himself say that he intended to attack 'that abominable communist state Soviet Russia' at some later date. That possibility had of course been fully considered in political circles, but Mr Newton, H. M. Minister in Prague, to whom I had reported the talk, thought that perhaps this was the first time that it had come 'straight from the horse's mouth'. It would seem also that the acquisition of *lebensraum* was not to be the sole objective of the operation!

FROM BOULANGER TO PETAIN: THE THIRD REPUBLIC AND THE REPUBLICAN GENERALS

David B. Ralston

The attitude of the political leaders of France towards the military during the seventy-year history of the Third Republic has usually been depicted as one of distrust, even antagonism, or at best cordial incomprehension. Such negative sentiments would appear to be an inevitable consequence of conflicting principles of organisation, with an authoritarian, hierarchical army on the one hand, and a libertarian, increasingly democratic regime on the other. So evident has been this ideological and organisational imcompatibility, that a concurrent but contrary tendency among the republican politicians has been obscured, for many of them did in fact, along with their devotion to liberal principles, also harbour a real sympathy for the army and for military ideals. The coexistence of these two incongruent sentiments within the personnel of the regime may help to explain why it was that, despite the clearly civilian character of the Republic, certain generals were still able periodically to utilise the resources and the machinery of the regime to attain political prominence.

Republican sympathies towards the army did not disappear even at the time of the Popular Front, but they were more clearly in evidence during earlier decades, as can be seen from the first official celebration of the anniversary of the fall of the Bastille in 1880. Having been designated as the French national holiday only a few weeks before, 14 July in many of its manifestations was meant to be a *fête populaire* but in Paris the culmination of the day's festivities was the great military review at Longchamps. The government obviously intended to give to this first review of the Paris garrison to be held on 14 July a special significance, since it was made the occasion for the presentation by Jules Grévy, President of the Republic, of new regimental flags to the army. These were to replace the colours which most of the regiments had lost ten years before at Sedan and Metz.[1] Following a short speech by Grévy on the profound sympathy felt by the Republic for the army, and a moving ceremony of presentation, the banners were paraded past the reviewing stand. According to reports in the republican press, it was an imposing and splendid patriotic ceremony,[2] although the conservative journals professed to be scandalised at this commemoration of an armed uprising against the crown,[3] the association of the army

178

with it. Indeed, there was, as the *Journal des débats* pointed out, something anomalous in a celebration whereby a government 'civilian in essence and popular in origin seals . . . a pact of union with an army whose memories and traditions are attached through the centuries to the Monarchy'.[4]

The interest displayed by the populace in this and subsequent 14 July reviews, and indeed in any military ceremony or spectacle, was symptomatic of the profound patriotism of the era. Born paradoxically enough of the defeat of 1870, this sentiment found its most natural focus in the army. For at least two decades, all sectors of French society, divided as they may have been over fundamental political and religious questions, were united in their fondness for the soldier and in their fervour for things military. Although the republicans, under the Empire, had been antimilitarist, Léon Gambetta in the Belleville Programme of 1869 having gone so far as to call for the abolition of standing armies,[5] their attitude after the defeat underwent a radical change. In a speech delivered in 1878 at a banquet celebrating the 110th anniversary of the birth of Hoche, Gambetta now claimed for the republicans the credit of being the one party which was truly devoted to the army, seeking its betterment in every way.[6] The military patriotism of the republicans had perfectly valid historical antecedents, for the Republic of 1792 did, after all, initiate one of the more splendid eras of French martial glory, its armies led by such heroes as Hoche, Jourdain, and Masséna.

Gambetta and the republicans of his generation were doubtless sincere in their admiration of the army. They were also politicians engaged in the difficult task of founding the regime on some kind of permanent, stable basis, and to achieve this end, they were ready to utilise the newly reawakened military patriotism of the French people. The military review is one example of this tactic. Another is to be seen in the educational policies of the Republic. In the curriculum of the state run primary schools, religious instruction of one form or another was replaced by courses of an overtly propagandist nature. Students were meant to develop a sense of patriotic pride, through a highly chauvinistic approach to history which emphasised the great feats of French arms and the deeds of her military heroes.[7]

Courses in civic education were also introduced, one of whose chief purposes was to prepare young Frenchmen for their military service.[8] In the estimation of Paul Bert, the leading figure of the period in French educational circles and Minister of Public Instruction in Gambetta's *Grand Ministère* of 1881, military education in the schools and in the army was the most important single element in the 'preparation of the complete citizen', for it was upon the military abilities of her sons that France would have to depend for 'her existence and her honour . . .'9 Even the daughters of France had a role to play here. According to an article in a semi-official publication of the Ministry of Public Instruction, it was the duty of the school mistress to explain to the young girls in her charge why their brothers had to do their military service and to teach them 'to appreciate courage, to scorn cowardice . . .'10

There can be no doubt that the Republic, in its cautious, pragmatic approach to the problems besetting the nation in the years after 1870 was in accord with the fundamentally unadventurous, conservative spirit of the country. There can also be no doubt that the Republic of Grévy, Ferry and Freycinet had little about it to capture the imagination of the average Frenchman. It was in fact somewhat drab. Like every prior regime in nineteenth-century France, the Republic lacked legitimacy in the sense that it could not rely on a longstanding, unquestioning popular acceptance of either its existence or its exactions. It was just this kind of quality which the army, its roots extending far back in the history of the monarchy, possessed, and which the republicans hoped in some way to appropriate for themselves. In so doing, they may have been appealing to the militarism which the noted Italian sociologist, Gugliemo Ferrero, writing in the 1890s, considered to be one of the essential traits in the French national character at that moment.11

For all the outspoken patriotism of republican politicians of the generation following the Franco-Prussian War, they could not overcome a deep-rooted and not entirely groundless distrust of the army. France's first two essays in republican government had both been cut short by *coups d'état* in which a few ambitious soldiers had either, as in 1799, taken an active role or, as in 1851, been utilised by civilian conspirators, and it was common knowledge during the first crisis of the nascent Third Republic, the so-called *Seize-mai* of 1877, that many conservatives would have welcomed the army being used in a similar attempt against the regime. Uncertain as they still were of their mandate, republican politicians exaggerated the danger, but their fears were at least understandable in the light of recent history.

The officer corps, in general, maintained a reserved but correct attitude towards the Republic, the fears of the politicians notwithstanding. Even if the military recognised the good intentions of the government and all that it was now doing for the army, 'no subtlety of reason and no oratorical eloquence would ever be able to make identical concepts of liberty and hierarchy, individualism and cohesion, sovereignty of number and the authority of a chief . . .'12 As a body, the military behaved towards the Republic as they had towards every other regime during the nineteenth century. The periodic political upheavals of the time had shown them the wisdom of not being too closely attached to or identified with any particular regime. The disciplined and obedient servants of each, the soldiers were in no way compromised by its eventual collapse. The typical French professional soldier of the era may well have agreed with General du Barail, Minister of War under MacMahon, in his stated preference for a military monarchy,[13] but this did not interfere with his loyally and obediently serving the Republic.

According to spokesmen for the military, an apolitical stance, by protecting the unity and cohesion of the officer corps, furthered national defence. Whatever the validity of the argument, the Republic wanted something more than this disciplined, obedient and possibly disdainful reserve. If the efforts of the republicans to assume the great military heritage of the nation were to be plausible, along with their claims to be the patriotic party *par excellence*, there had to be at least a few officers who were overtly republican, or who by their unpretentious manners, their relatively humble origins, or their religious attitude, i.e., non-attendance at mass, might be considered as such. The fact that there were a number of republican officers also served to allay the latent fears of the regime with regard to the army, as to whether in an outbreak of civil violence the soldiers would defend the existing institutions with the requisite determination. These officers could expect favourable treatment from the Republic. In the lower ranks, where promotion was generally regulated by the military themselves and where the civil authorities only infrequently intervened, it would have done an officer little good to have openly espoused republican sentiments. Things changed as he neared the summit of the military hierarchy. Here the government was more likely to intercede, and a reputation as a·good republican could do something towards furthering a career, which, on the discernible military merits of the man in question, might well have been arrested.

Despite what has been written about the generally monarchical or Bonapartist sentiments of the officer corps in the first decades of the Republic,[14] there were still a number of men in the upper ranks of the army known to be avowed partisans of the new regime.[15] A few of them were already generals at the time of the Franco-Prussian War; others would be promoted to that rank over the next ten or fifteen years. Certain important posts tended, of necessity, to be reserved for such men. During most of the three decades following 1870, the Minister of War was a general on active service. Although a soldier, he was still expected to display at least a modicum of sympathy for the Republic. Parliament could hardly have given its confidence to a cabinet containing someone reputed for his anti-republican opinions.[16] Another post almost always bestowed upon a republican general was that of Military Governor of Paris. As the commander of the troops of the Paris garrison, he was the man upon whom the government would have to rely to repress any outbreak of anti-republican violence in the streets of the capital. For obvious reasons, the government expected there to be no equivocation in his political loyalties.

There was no set pattern as to how and why an officer became an overt supporter of the Republic. Generals Faidherbe, Saussier and Campenon had been republicans before 1870, while Generals de Galliffet and Clinchant, having been disenchanted at the incompetence displayed by the imperial regime in the recent war and moved by admiration for the spirited efforts of Gambetta and his cohorts,[17] had thereupon rallied to the Republic. Clinchant was Military Governor of Paris in 1880-81, while Saussier held the post from 1884-98. Then there were officers such as Billot, Carrey de Bellemare and Chanzy who had served under the Government of National Defence. Many of them had been rapidly promoted due to the exceptional circumstances prevailing under that emergency regime and were henceforth considered to be republicans.[18] They were to have manifestly successful careers over the next few decades. Whatever the origins or sincerity of his republican connections, Carrey de Bellemare, among others, was not hesitant in reminding the government of past sacrifices made for the Republic, in return for an expected favour.[19]

The most notable example of political opportunism utilised to further a military career was furnished by General Boulanger. Although he was considered a fervent republican at the time of his nomination as Minister of War in 1886, a few years before his sentiments had apparently been of a quite different kind. During the late 1870s, while still a colonel, Boulanger commanded a regiment which was part of the Seventh Army Corps. The fact that this corps was stationed in a strongly Catholic region and was commanded by the Duc d'Aumale indicated the proper tone for an officer interested in his career and Boulanger reacted accordingly. He was assiduous both in the court he paid to *Monseigneur*, the general commanding the army corps, and in his religious duties, going so far as to institute in his regiment a military mass with music. All of this led to his being noted by his superiors as a good officer, one who was '*bien pensant* . . .'[20] Having been promoted to the rank of general, Boulanger was in 1880 given command of a brigade at Valence in the republican department of Drome. There followed a political about face and within a short while he was beginning to be known as an outspoken partisan of the Republic.

His career already founded on his qualities as a soldier, as they had been demonstrated on the field of battle, Boulanger now began his spectacular and rapid ascent to the summit of the military hierarchy. He was sent in 1881 as representative of the Minister of War to the celebration of the centenary of the Battle of Yorktown, after which he served for two years as Director of the Infantry. Having been promoted to the rank of General of Division, he was made Commander of the Expeditionary Corps at Tunis, before the final step, his nomination as Minister of War in the Freycinet government of January 1886.[21] All the while Boulanger's reputation as a vigorously republican soldier was being nurtured through a series of dramatic gestures and a propensity for patriotic speeches. It received its final consecration in the great review of 14 July 1886. Meant to honour the troops returning from the conquest of Tonkin, the review became a personal triumph for the Minister of War. Boulangism as a movement had been born and the purely military career of its protagonist came to an end.

In the years when Boulanger's star was rising, there can be no doubt that the republicans were enchanted with him. Boulanger displayed all the qualities supposedly possessed by a good republican soldier in the style of the Year II — bravura, youth (relative to the other generals, anyway), and outspoken Jacobin patriotism. The fact that the most dashing and popular soldier of the era was evidently an ardent republican could only enhance the prestige of the regime in the eyes of the average Frenchman. The inconveniences presented by so political a general were, however, not long in becoming apparent. His republicanism had its origin in his unbounded ambition, and Boulanger was perfectly capable, once he believed his career to have been thwarted by the government, of lending his name to a movement mounting an attack on the Republic.

The style appropriate to a republican general was not a static thing. As the Republic evolved over the years between 1870 and 1900, its centre of gravity shifting to the left, so also did its relations with the army change, and along with them, the somewhat ambiguous concept of what constituted republican generalship. In the 1880s, the chief concern of such men as Gambetta and Jules Ferry had been to endow the new political institutions of France with some degree of stability, creating as wide a base of support for the Republic as possible. All that had been demanded of its adherents, both civilians and soldiers, was loyalty to these institutions, without too much worry about ideology. The Republic of René Waldeck-Rousseau and Emile Combes was more stringent. The Radicals, coming to power towards the turn of the century, in the wake of the Dreyfus Affair, believed the Republic to embody a specific, well defined set of political doctrines and ideals. As the radical politician Léon Bourgeois declared to a right wing group: 'You accept the Republic of course, but do you accept the Revolution?'[22] An officer could with little hesitation give his allegiance to the essentially non-doctrinaire regime of the Opportunists, but he would have little liking for the Republic as defined by the Radicals.

Then, too, the soldiers were increasingly exasperated at the government as it reluctantly moved to reopen the case of Captain Dreyfus, thereby rejecting the verdict of a court martial and calling into question the principles of military justice.[23]

Where the Dreyfus Affair angered and ultimately alienated the military, its effect on the personnel of the Republic was one of alarm. The adamant refusal of the soldiers to admit that the Dreyfus court martial may have erred inexorably led to a major political crisis. Before it was over, the republicans found themselves obliged to reconsider the question of whether an authoritarian army could coexist with a democratic regime. Turning away from the splendours of the French military tradition, the Radicals as the new political masters of France now envisioned a reshaping of the spirit and ideals of the officer corps, to bring them into accord with current democratic concepts. That such a programme could be contemplated is indicative of a decline in the naive military patriotism of the generation after the Franco-Prussian War and also of a new self-confidence on the part of the personnel of the regime.

Republican politicians in the years after 1900 felt less of a politically motivated need for the army because their sense of the legitimacy of the regime was stronger than at any point in its 70-year history. Its adversaries having discredited themselves through their participation in the Boulangist adventure and by their excesses in the Dreyfus Affair, there was no one left capable of seriously disputing its right to govern. As David Thomson has remarked, the Republic had by 1905 managed to dispose of the great political issues which it had inherited from the nineteenth-century history of France; the social and economic problems of the twentieth century had yet to arise.[24] The result was that republican politicians for the moment displayed unwonted consistency of purpose and firmness of policy. The agent of the Republic for the execution of its policy with regard to the army was General Louis André, Minister of War from 1900 to 1904 in the governments of Waldeck-Rousseau and Combes and one of the few generals whose republicanism met the strict standards of the Radicals.[25]

The advent of General André signified that it was no longer sufficient for a republican officer simply to announce his belief in the soundness of the present regime. He was now expected to give witness to his convictions by deeds, to be the advocate and even the instrument of a specifically political programme with regard to the army, the republicanisation of the officer corps. Nor was the defence of the national soil against the foreign enemies of France meant to be his sole, or even his primary professional concern. Rather, it was now the defence of the regime against those, especially within the ranks of the army, who supposedly had hoped and worked for its overthrow.

184

The implementation of General André's programme of republican defence involved the use of the freemasons, in particular the network of lodges associated with the rite of the Grand Orient, as a source of information on the political opinions of the officer corps.[26] The promotion of an officer could depend on this information. When in late 1904 the nature of the connection between the freemasons and the Ministry of War was revealed before parliament, the so-called *Affaire des Fiches*, the resulting scandal led first to the departure of André from the Combes government[27] and soon thereafter to its fall. Already badly shaken, the morale of the officer corps, and along with it, the efficacy of the army as an instrument of national defence, was further damaged by the revelation that a number of officers had been zealous enough in their political beliefs to be able to overcome the usual notions of military solidarity and camaraderie, and to denounce their comrades to the government for their political opinions.[28] With the government defining republicanism according to these new, more narrow criteria and employing some rather unorthodox methods to enforce its views upon the army, a precipitous decline in the number of republican officers of all ranks was only to be expected.

The increasingly troubled state of international relations in the decade preceding the outbreak of war helped to bring about a change in the French political climate. Patriotism, temporarily in eclipse, came back into fashion as France was again faced with the possibility of war with Germany. The Radicals had no choice but to take the requisite steps to assure the defence of the country, and despite the Dreyfus Affair to place their confidence in the loyalism of the officer corps. This meant conferring positions of responsibility on men with connections in reactionary and Catholic circles, as when in 1908 the government named General Foch to the command of the Ecole de Guerre.[29] The 1911 decree on the reorganisation of the high command provided even more striking evidence as to the change in attitude of republican politicians towards the army. By this measure, the offices of Commander-in-Chief and Chief of Staff were combined and the incumbent was given more independent authority over the functioning of the French Army than any commander since Napoleon. Still, in the question of who should be assigned to this extremely puissant office, General Joseph Joffre owed his nomination, in part, to his *petit bourgeois* origins and to his reputation as a republican officer, albeit an unostentatious one.[30]

Although the Republic may, in the decades between 1871 and 1914, have intervened for political reasons in such fields as promotion and conscription, on balance it allowed the soldiers almost complete autonomy in their own professional sphere. Nowhere was this more true than in the development of French strategic and tactical doctrines.

185

Concerning these arcane matters, no politician, and indeed, no civilian would presume to have an independent opinion. About the only political figure of any significance who was an exception to this rule was Jean Jaurès. His theories on the reorganisation of France's military institutions along socialist lines and on an appropriate strategy for these armed forces were presented in his study, *L'Armée Nouvelle*. For the rest, various conflicting theories on the efficacy of the offence as opposed to the defence, and vice versa, were debated within the confines of the army and they had few repercussions in any civilian milieu. To the degree that politicians took an interest in these matters, they tended to favour the predominantly offensive theories of the General Staff.[31]

The views of the different military chiefs with regard to strategy and tactics were largely independent of their political leanings. In 1911, when General Michel, the man designated to be the wartime Commander-in-Chief of the Army, and a person known for his republican views and his connections among the more advanced elements in parliament, drew up a basically defensive plan of deployment for the French army, the attack on his ideas was led by General Galliéni, also a republican, and Adolphe Messimy, the Minister of War and a leading figure in the Radical Party. Michel subsequently resigned, to be replaced by General Joffre, a good republican. Joffre chose as his immediate subordinate, General de Castelnau, called the *capucin botté* because of his ardently Catholic opinions, and the two men collaborated closely in drafting the thoroughly offensive Plan XVII. As one authority, Henry Contamine, points out: 'Generals who dared to attend mass could still have the same views as those such as Joffre who did not care to.'[32]

When war broke out in the summer of 1914, Plan XVII and its German counterpart, the Schlieffen Plan, both recipes for a rapid decision in the field, proved inadequate. Following the Battle of the Marne, the war quickly came to assume a form and be waged on a scale unforeseen by pre-war thinkers. To break the stalemate which developed on the Western Front the two adversaries had to commit an ever increasing portion of their total resources to the struggle. The result was a war in which 'the nation in fact merged itself with the army, in which the whole vital energies of France were mustered within the military machine . . .'[33] In the process, problems of tactics and strategy, formerly the domain of the General Staff and the Ecole de Guerre, could not help but become more than military issues. The deputies and senators found it difficult to treat the theories of the high command concerning the superiority of the offence as a purely technical matter, when these theories were apparently causing the deaths of hundreds of thousands of Frenchmen.

As the struggle continued and the huge sacrifices undergone by the
nation led to no decisive military advantage, opposition to the conduct
of the war grew. By the end of 1916, this opposition was strong enough
so that the government dared to prevail upon Joffre, virtually unassailable following his victory at the Marne, to relinquish effective
command over the French armies on the Western Front and to accept
as recompense for his sacrifice elevation to the rank of Marshal of
France. As for the successor to Joffre, General Nivelle, the government
sacked him in the wake of the collapse of the April 1917 offensive
associated with his name.[34] In thus asserting its authority *vis-à-vis* the
high command, the government did no more than to go along with the
mood of the great mass of the army and of the country at large, for the
poilus had already rejected the offensive conceptions of the General
Staff. Whole divisions of front line troops had in fact mutinied.

The nomination of General Pétain to the command of the French
armies at the moment of the mutinies signified a new phase in the
management of military operations. For almost a year the French stood
resolutely on the defensive as he set about rebuilding the morale and cohesion of the troops.[35] Pétain, unlike most of his contemporaries, had
been sceptical before 1914 as to the 'virtue' of the offence. He had
taught a course at the Ecole de Guerre along those unorthodox lines,
emphasising the strength of fire power and the importance of defence
in modern war.[36] Long the exponent of a style of warfare which circumstances now imposed upon the army, he was to remain in command
until the end of the war.

The drawn out dispute between the government and the high command over the conduct of the war reawakened latent republican suspicions concerning the army. Vigorous and hardy chiefs such as Foch,
Castelnau and Mangin, all outspoken exponents of the offence, were
practising Catholics. None of them had ever made any display of their
republican sympathies. It was all too easy to see in their 'reactionary'
political attitudes a reflection of their 'reactionary' and therefore unsound military theories. In this politicisation of strategic and tactical
ideas, the defence, of necessity advocated by the government after the
Nivelle disaster, came to be considered as 'republican' or 'leftist'. The
generalised enthusiasm of most politicians for the theories of the
offence in the years immediately before 1914 was forgotten. In actual-
ity, the experiences of the war tended to convince both the civilians
and the soldiers alike of the efficacy of the defence in modern war,[37]
but only the left gave a political colouring to this military theory. As
one author has noted: 'After 1918, a Radical or Socialist would have
had to be possessed of a great deal of audacity to recall that for the
soldiers of the Year II the offense had been revolutionary, and that in
1871 certain chiefs of the Armies of the *Défense Nationale* had looked

upon the defense as "reactionary".'38

The unprecedented scale of the hostilities and their unforeseen lengths also contributed to the spectral fears of the politicians. The military chiefs had always occupied a prominent place in the life of French society, but in time of peace their power and freedom of action were rigidly circumscribed through a variety of legal and administrative measures. It was different in time of war, for the military chiefs necessarily were allowed a wide measure of discretionary power and authority, including control over the fate of what was virtually the whole of the young manhood of France, and the politicians felt threatened. Clemenceau may have been jesting, when in restoring the temporarily eclipsed Mangin to a field command, he reminded him of the supremacy of the civilian power and admonished him not to play any tricks, but Poincaré, unaware of Pétain's sardonic style, took with deadly seriousness the latter's intimations of his scorn for constitutional niceties in time of war, seeing here the avowal of 'a candidate dictator'.39

If republican fears of some kind of *coup d'état* at the hands of the generals were unwarranted, the politicians did have other grounds for their equivocal feelings towards the military. Under the stress of the gigantic conflict, the line between the policy making and the purely technical military spheres became blurred, and there was real uncertainty as to the extent of the respective prerogatives of the civil and military chiefs. During the first year of the hostilities, Joffre, with the firm backing of the Minister of War, Millerand, was able to exercise a virtual dictatorship over the conduct of the war, going so far as to attempt to forbid members of the army commissions of the Senate and the Chamber to visit the 'Zone of the Armies' without his express and reluctantly granted permission.40 There was little that parliament could do about this apparent usurpation of its prerogatives until Joffre's prestige had been somewhat eroded. In the closing months of the conflict, Clemenceau was constantly embroiled with Foch over the latter's position as Supreme Commander of the Allied Forces. The Tiger sought to make Foch give direct orders to the allied generals nominally subordinate to him, while Foch saw his powers as permitting him not so much 'to give commands, but simply to suggest'.41

The confusion and uncertainty over the boundary between the civilian and military spheres, particularly in the minds of the soldiers, which existed by the time the Armistice was signed, persisted after the end of the war. Foch, by forcefully advocating at Versailles and elsewhere what he considered to be a sound and militarily defensible territorial arrangement on the eastern frontiers of France, was, in the estimation of Clemenceau, trespassing in the realm of policy making, a matter in theory beyond the competence of a soldier, and he was being insubordinate to boot.[42] Another notable example of a soldier seeking to promote a specific political and diplomatic programme was provided by Mangin. Tempestuous and irascible, Mangin more than any other of the military chiefs, possessed a *condottiere*'s temperament, although he had acted as a disciplined soldier during the war.[43] Following the Armistice, he commanded one of the French armies of occupation, enjoying virtually a viceregal situation with regard to the Rhineland. On his own initiative, although almost certainly with the knowledge and the tacit consent of the French government, Mangin vigorously encouraged the activities of the Rhineland separatists. The failure of their efforts to organise a Rhineland Republic in the spring of 1919 led to Mangin's being relieved of his command and prematurely retired from the army.[44]

The Republic never liked its leaders, be they civilian or military, to be strong personalities. Clemenceau, after all his eminent services to the country, was refused the Presidency of the Republic because he frightened the typical, timorous politician. The politicians were wary of the military chiefs now that they were clothed with the prestige of an unparalleled victory. This may be the reason why few of the more noted wartime commanders were given positions of any direct influence or power within the post-war army. Some — Joffre, Fayolle and Castelnau — were retired because of age. Lyautey and Franchet d'Esperey held important posts, but outside of France, while Foch was commander of the allied occupation forces in Germany. Pétain was the only one of the *grand chefs* to be given a position of significance in the army of Metropolitan France, being in 1920 named Vice-President of the Conseil Supérieur de la Guerre, and thus the designated Commander-in-Chief of the French army in case of war,[45] and as shall be seen below, his qualifications were more than merely military.

Renewed republican suspicions of the army may have been understandable, given the wartime and immediate post-war experiences of the government, but they also indicated a persistent, nagging doubt among the politicians as to the legitimacy of the regime in the eyes of the French people. Thus it was that fifty years after the advent of the Republic and twenty years after the last futile attempt to unseat it, they still found a reassuring resonance in the phrase 'republican general'. In 1924, Edouard Herriot, the President of the Council of Ministers, speaking at the annual banquet honouring the birth of Hoche, lauded the virtues of this republican general, and noted that he had never betrayed the Republic. In Herriot's words, Hoche was one of 'those, too few, in number, alas, who never overstepped the legitimate boundaries assigned to the warriors . . .'[46]

The criteria for denoting a republican general were never very clear, but in the early years of the Republic a definition was in some degree facilitated by the putative preference of most officers for one of several alternative political visions, i.e. Bonapartist, Legitimist or Orléanist. With the progressive fading of these alternatives and the growing unlikelihood of any regime but the present one, the phrase 'republican general' tended to be emptied of any substance insofar as it referred to a specific political preference on the part of a given soldier, especially since the military were denied the vote under the Third Republic. One of the few who stood as an exception here, whose republicanism signified the adherence to a particular set of political principles, was General Sarrail.

The reputation of Sarrail as a republican general of intense convictions dated from the year he spent as a member of the military cabinet of General André during the latter's term as Minister of War. Although he appears not to have been involved in the more questionable practices of the André ministry, he was for the rest of his career in bad odour with his comrades and a favourite of the left.[47] In July 1915, when at the behest of Joffre he was removed from command of an army on the Western Front and sent out to virtual exile in Macedonia to lead a small French expeditionary force, serious political repercussions were only narrowly avoided.[48] During his two years of command in Macedonia, Sarrail was frequently at odds with his own government and those of the allies over various military and diplomatic issues. He was finally recalled in December 1917 and placed on the retired list.[49] Sarrail may not have been a militant republican at the start, but the stormy incidents of his career conspired to push him in that direction. After the war he stood for parliament, unsuccessfully, as a Radical candidate, before becoming a member of the central committee of the League for the Rights of Man. Convinced that he had been persecuted for his political opinions, Sarrail wholeheartedly 'entered into the character imagined for him by both his friends and his enemies, considering himself to be the standard bearer of a hard and pure republic, the last representative of a great epoch, lost in an army reconquered by the forces of reaction . . .'[50]

With the victory of the Cartel des Gauches in 1924, restitution was made and Sarrail was reinstated in the army. It was as a republican general that he was sent to Syria to serve as High Commissioner, replacing Weygand, the protégé of Foch and therefore suspect in the eyes of the newly triumphant left.[51] Sarrail may have been a republican, but he was also overbearing and peremptory in his dealings with the indigenous population. Within a year his methods of administration provoked a revolt by the Druzes, which was repressed with exemplary brutality. In the wake of the outcry this caused, the chagrined government of the Cartel recalled Sarrail and quietly dropped him.[52]

A general with the pronounced political views of a Sarrail, and the

190

willingness to proclaim them, was a rarity. Usually the republicanism of a general tended to lie as much in the eye of the beholder as in the stated opinions of the man in question. The same could also be said for the supposed anti-republicanism of an officer, as may be seen from the career of General Weygand. By having served as chief of staff to Foch during World War I, Weygand automatically inherited some of the aura of his *patron*. His reputation for political 'unreliability' was increased by the role he assumed at Versailles, that of Foch's *éminence grise*, endeavouring behind the scenes to promote the views of the Marshal.[53] This and other incidents, both during the war and after, provoked the celebrated outburst from Clemenceau that Weygand might some day assume an overt political role.[54] He was sent as head of the French military mission to Poland in 1920, and his share in planning the victory over the advancing Red Army in the Battle of Warsaw only increased his stature in the eyes of the right, as did also the circumstances of his replacement by Sarrail in Syria.[55] When in 1930 Weygand was nominated to the post of Chief of Staff of the Army at the insistence of Marshal Pétain, the left objected vigorously but could hardly over-rule the wishes of the venerable Commander-in-Chief.[56] There did take place, however, an interpellation in the Chamber concerning his supposed anti-republican sentiments.[57] In reply, André Maginot, as Minister of War, read a public statement from Weygand to the effect that although he was a Catholic, he was also republican, and that he could conceive of no other regime for France than the Republic.[58] 'Alone of the inter-war supreme commanders, Weygand was forced to do penance, in a public confession, for the High Command's suspected loyalty.'[59]

General Gamelin differed little from Weygand in terms of social background, education and religious belief, but he was entirely acceptable to the political chiefs of republican France. This may in part be attributable to his marriage to the sister of General Picquart, the hero of the Dreyfus Affair.[60] Gamelin had also been the protégé of Joffre, who despite his predilection for the offence both before and during the war, was more republican than Foch. His position in the good graces of the left was shown when Sarrail chose him on the suggestion of Painlevé to be his assistant in Syria.[61] Gamelin's acceptability to the left, and indeed to all shades of political and military opinion, was a tribute to his undeniable qualities of intellect. It was also indicative of his sense of tact, his courteous and debonair personality, which allowed him to get along with everyone – Pétain, Weygand, Daladier, Blum.[62] Where the politicians were reassured by the personality of Gamelin, they looked upon Weygand, brusque and authoritarian in all things pertaining to the welfare of the army and contemptuous of most of them, as factious. In his memoirs, Gamelin goes so far as to chide Weygand for his attitude towards the parties of the left and their chiefs, and in particular for his open ridicule of Paul-Boncour, Minister of War, reminding him that while it is easy to mock a public figure, 'not everyone has the right morally to do so'.[63]

When Weygand was named Chief of Staff, the left insisted that Gamelin be made his immediate subordinate, to serve in some fashion as a political counterweight.[64] Upon the retirement of Pétain in 1931, Weygand became Vice-President of the Conseil Supérieur de la Guerre and Commander-in-Chief while Gamelin became Chief of Staff. Finally, in 1935, Weygand retired to be succeeded by Gamelin, who also retained his post as Chief of Staff. This joining together of the two highest posts in the military hierarchy recreated for Gamelin the situation which Joffre had assumed in 1911, and which for a variety of reasons had been terminated after the war. However pressing the military grounds for the creation of so potentially formidable an office, it would have been politically impossible so long as its incumbent was likely to be Weygand. As Commander-in-Chief, Gamelin represented no threat to existing institutions, but his debonair style and his flaccid leadership were to prove tragically inadequate, both in preparing the army for the coming war and in the conduct of operations once the German assault was loosed on France in May 1940.

Generals on active service were named as Minister of War far less frequently than before 1914, but if the occasion arose, it was assumed that they would be republican. Thus when Herriot, as the head of the first leftist government since the war, found it politically expedient to have a general in the post, in order 'to protect his right flank . . .', among the qualifications of his nominee, General Nollet, was his reputation as a republican.[65] According to an article in *L'Ere nouvelle*, the Cartel newspaper, this was of primary importance, since one of his chief tasks would be to block the 'reactionary' tendencies of the 'rightist' clique at the War Ministry.[66] General Maurin, Minister of War on two different occasions in the 1930s, was also known as a republican. It may not have been entirely fortuitous that during the Chamber debate of 15 March 1935, he gave the most explicit public statement of any military figure in a position of responsibility during the interwar years as to France's devotion to a defensive strategy, spelling out her disinclination to consider the possibility of launching an offensive in the event of hostilities.[67]

Of all the leading men of the army in the interwar years, the one whose reputed republicanism was most reassuring to the politicians was Marshal Pétain. A colonel on the verge of retirement in 1914, his qualities as a chief had been quickly demonstrated in battle, particularly during the defence of Verdun, and had by the summer of 1917 led him to the command of the French army, a post he would retain until 1931. Imposing as Pétain's military qualities may have been, they were not necessarily any greater than those of the other Marshals of France,[68] none of whom played a role comparable to his in the French army after the war. The paramount situation of Pétain stemmed above all from his having been the original advocate of the defence, revealed in the heat of the combat to be the republican style of warfare. More than just a military technician, this prudent and unadventurous soldier was in fact that personage whom the French Republic of the interwar years could most readily accept as the 'symbol of an army managed according to its deepest inclinations'.[69] Pétain had about him little of the disquieting aura of a Foch, a Mangin or a Lyautey, to stir in republican hearts uneasy feelings about the army. He was, in short, 'the republican marshal'.[70]

How much greater confidence the Republic had in him than its other *grand chefs* was to be seen during the 1925 rebellion of Abd-el-Krim in Morocco. Well aware of the threatened uprising, Lyautey had been requesting reinforcements from the government for several months, to no avail.[71] Suddenly alarmed at the extent of the rebellion when it broke out, the government despatched Pétain to Morocco on a tour of inspection and then sent him out again, this time at the head of massive reinforcements with orders to quash the revolt and to restore order, which he proceeded to do. Lyautey was deeply offended at having been so highhandedly dispossessed of his military powers and prerogatives and asked to be relieved as Resident-General.[72] The episode reflected no great credit on either Pétain or the *Cartel des Gauches* government, but it was nonetheless symptomatic of the persistent distrust felt by the Republic towards a soldier of Lyautey's stamp: aristocrat, crusader, romantic adventurer, 'civilizer of the infidels',[73] and its corresponding sense of security *vis-à-vis* Pétain.

Pétain did not owe his pre-eminent situation solely to the acceptability of his military views or to his capacity to inspire an attitude of trust within the government. His role as the saviour first of Verdun in 1916 and then of the army in 1917 had also won for him an especial place in the estimation of the French people. The horrors of modern warfare as they had been revealed in the trenches to a generation of Frenchmen had certainly lessened their enthusiasm for things military, but it had not done away with their fundamental patriotism.[74] The *poilus*, who in their grimy uniforms of horizon blue had selflessly and stoically defended the national soil, were filled with a grim pride at what they had endured and ultimately overcome. Far more than any of the other leading generals, Pétain was after the war identified with the wartime experiences of the *poilus*.[75] Joffre may have been admired for winning the battle of the Marne in 1914 and Foch for the final victory in 1918, but towards Pétain people felt something bordering on reverence. As Léon Blum wrote panegyrically of him in 1931, at the moment of his election to the Académie francaise, Marshal Pétain was 'of all the *grands chefs* of the war . . . the one whose modesty, whose seriousness, whose sensitive and thoughtful scruples demand our respect . . .'76 It is significant that, despite the distasteful memories inspired by World War I, the most idolised figure in the nation was still a soldier, even if Pétain represented a very different kind of military glory from a Boulanger, or indeed any dashing general of the pre-1914 era.

Pétain stepped down from the command of the French army in 1931 at the age of 75, but he did not by that token disappear from the public eye. Rather than letting him retire Cincinnatus-like to his recently purchased farm in Provence, the republican politicians, by bestowing upon him a number of honorific posts, sought to 'associate him in their administration of the state'.77 In point of fact, the Republic needed Pétain and for primarily political reasons. The decade of the 'thirties witnessed a drastic decline in the prestige and the authority of the Republic, as successive ephemeral governments grappled ineffectually with the effects of the worldwide economic depression. Not only were the social and economic problems of the era particularly intractable, the political leaders lacked stature. The nadir for the regime came with the Stavisky scandal and the subsequent riots of 6 February 1934.

In the Government of National Union which the former President of the Republic, Gaston Doumergue, formed in the wake of the riots, Pétain accepted the post of Minister of War. As a Marshal of France, he represented the non-political legitimacy embodied in the army and thus contributed significantly to the authority which Doumergue hoped his cabinet would possess. The parties of the left would have accepted no other military chief but him in the government, even if it was a matter of 'a national union'.78 At the same time, the presence of Pétain could be expected to have a calming effect on the men who had rioted on 6 February. Most of them were war veterans and formerly under his command. As one enthusiastic commentator declared, all that was necessary to bring them back to order was to announce: 'Pétain is there.'79 Pétain was to be called upon once more to join a Government of National Union, the one formed in May 1935 to deal with the devaluation crisis. This government fell, however, in the course of its first confrontation with the Chamber.

The inefficacy of the republican regime at this juncture led many in France to consider the viability of some more 'modern' form of government. Taking their cue from the apparent success of Hitler and Mussolini, some spokesmen for the right wondered if a strong regime under a leader untarnished by participation in politics might not be the solution for France. An obvious choice for the role was Pétain, as Gustave Hervé suggested in a series of articles, 'C'est Pétain qu'il nous faut', which in

February 1935 began to appear in his paper *La Victoire*. The articles created something of a stir but had few real repercussions.[80]

The various Fascist leagues of the 1930s had many connections and considerable influence within the officer corps, and Pétain could not have been entirely ignorant of their activities. Two officers in his personal staff belonged to clandestine organisations, and one in particular, Commandant Loustanau-Lacau, was the founder of the Corvignolles network, dedicated to the discovery and elimination of Communist subversion in the army. It is highly probable that Pétain agreed with the traditionalist conservative ideals of such organisations as *La Croix de Feu* and with their condemnation of the way the republican political system was working, especially after his 1934 experience in government,[81] but unlike Marshal Franchet d'Esperey, who made no secret of his involvement, he prudently kept his distance from the leagues.[82] Where on at least two different occasions during the interwar years, Lyautey and then Franchet d'Esperey contemplated taking an open stand against the policies of the regime, Pétain refused even to think of such a course of action. He was, as he informed Franchet d'Esperey, 'a republican marshal'.[83]

Hervé and those on the right were not the only ones who envisioned a political role for Pétain in this period. Men with a similar point of view were to be found all across the political spectrum. In an article appearing in *Figaro* just after the Rhineland coup of 7 March 1936, Wladimir d'Ormesson called for an immediate truce in France and re-establishment of national unity under the leadership of Pétain.[84] A referendum organised by the independent republican *Petit Journal* revealed a similar current of opinion.[85] These theories also had an echo on the left. Writing in a special 1936 issue of the magazine *Vu*, which was devoted to the subject of the Fascist leagues, Pierre Cot, future Minister of Aviation during the Popular Front, advocated the bestowal by the President of the Republic of emergency political powers on Pétain in the event of a Fascist *coup d'état*, so as to ensure the loyalty of the army. He admitted that his idea might sound strange to many but he was sure that it would be approved by all those 'who have seen that remarkable thing, the gaze of Marshal Pétain'.[86] Prominently featured in this issue of *Vu* was a photograph of the Marshal with a caption to the same effect, stressing his 'perfect loyalty, his absolute political independence'.[87] This was, as one author has noted, the classic *appel au soldat*, but in a reverse sense in that Pétain would be a kind of anti-Boulanger, polarising around himself the enthusiasm of the war veterans, damping their revolt and restoring calm. 'Since he had put down the mutinies of the Left in 1917, so now he would put down the mutinies of the Right in 1935.'[88]

The attitude of the left towards Pétain continued sympathetic even after the end of the Popular Front. As late as March 1939, when he was named ambassador to Madrid, Léon Blum lamented that in sending the 'noblest, the most humane of our military chiefs' to establish diplomatic relations with the Franco regime, the French government was bestowing too much prestige on the 'apprentice dictator . . .' while *Humanité* was angered at the humiliation inflicted on France of having 'her most honoured soldier wait upon the good will of the traitor Franco'.[89] In the estimation of Paul Reynaud, all sectors of French public opinion bore some responsibility for the 'deification' of Pétain before the war, but it was the left which contributed to it in the greatest degree, by believing that 'the only strategy reconcilable with democratic principles was that of systematic defense . . .', a doctrine incarnated in the person of Pétain.[90]

When in September 1939 France resignedly went again to war with Germany, Edouard Daladier as President of the Council of Ministers made a gesture in the direction of *union nationale* by asking Pétain to join the government. Pétain refused stating that he wished to remain in Madrid until he was sure of Franco's neutrality,[91] but when the same request was made some eight months later by Daladier's successor as premier, Reynaud, Pétain accepted. By now the *drôle de guerre* had come to a violent end and the German breakthrough of 13 May had placed the French army in a desperate situation. Reynaud called upon Pétain to become Vice-President of the Council of Ministers, while at the same time he removed Gamelin as Commander-in-Chief of the French army and confided the post once again to General Weygand, who had held it from 1931 to 1935.

By bringing the nation's most honoured soldier into the government Reynaud was obviously seeking not so much to take advantage of his military abilities but rather to utilise his enormous prestige in an effort to restore the badly shaken morale of the country.[92] If the enthusiasm displayed in the press and in parliament are indicative of the real feelings of the French people,[93] Reynaud succeeded, at least momentarily. Unfortunately, more was needed than the arrival on the scene of the eighty-four year old Pétain or of Weygand, the supposed recipient of the 'secrets of Foch', to retrieve the catastrophic military situation. Within a few days, Pétain realised the full extent of the French collapse. and with his usual equanimity accepted the situation. He thereupon gave his full support to Weygand's efforts to obtain an armistice, efforts which were capped with success on 22 June.[94]

The defeat of the French army led directly to the collapse of the regime. On 10 July both houses of the legislature sitting together as the National Assembly voted by an overwhelming majority a proposal by which Pétain was given full powers to govern the country and to revise the Constitution as he should see fit. With this act, the Third Republic effectively brought about its own demise. Pétain had no innate will to power, no overwhelming drive to dominate men or events, but rather a detached, passive confidence in himself. He may well have come to believe that he was a kind of foreordained saviour, if for no other reason than that everyone else seemed to look upon him as such. It was this particular quality in Pétain which various governments at moments of crisis during the 'thirties had sought to employ in an effort to mobilise public support for their policies.

Pétain was the last and most eminent of those military chiefs in whose republicanism, alleged or certified, the politicians sought reassurance. That they did so is indicative of their ambivalence towards the army. By its reputed unity and cohesion, by its supposedly selfless devotion to patriotic ideals, the army stood in marked contrast to a parliamentary regime rent by factional dispute and for that reason apparently incapable of defending the national interest. Where the republican mandate was weak, founded more on the implausibility of any other regime than on the commitment of the French people to the ideals and institutions of the Republic, the army, even after World War I, continued to enjoy a measure of public acceptance and even legitimmacy. Understandably enough, republican politicians might well see it as posing an implicit threat to the regime. Given the realities of France's international situation, the politicians dared not reduce its strength or attempt a radical transformation in its structure. Rather they could only try to neutralise the army as a rival, if latent, political force by associating it with the Republic in the minds of the French people, hoping thereby that a prosaic regime could be made somehow to partake of the attractive and emotive qualities of the military. The coexistence of these two complementary, but also contradictory sentiments in republican breasts, a conscious, politically motivated need for the army on one hand and a wariness of it on the other, helps to explain why periodically a reputation for republicanism could become an important factor in a successful military career.

On 14 July 1940, the traditional military review was held at Vichy in the presence of the new Chief of the State. In contrast to the splendid ceremony of sixty years before when at the first official celebration of the *fête nationale* the President of the Republic had presented new regimental flags to an army full of pride and confidence in the future, Marshal Pétain presided at the parade of a few hundred soldiers, forlorn troops of 'miserable appearance . . .'[95] The Republic may have been ignominiously despatched four days before at the hands of its confused and despairing representatives, but the army still went through the motions of providing, as it had done so regularly in the past, a military aura for this notably republican national holiday.

On the same day, some hundreds of miles away in London, another review of French troops was held in the presence of a recently promoted and as yet relatively unknown brigadier general, Charles de Gaulle. These soldiers, however, along with their leader, were in open rebellion against the authority of what was considered by the great majority of Frenchmen to have become the legally constituted government of France. At this crucial juncture in French history, no republican statesman, championing the great ideals of *Liberté, Egalité, Fraternité*, came forward to organise or to lead the continuing struggle against the Germans. Rather it was a general who, determined to carry on the war in defence of the permanent interests and ideals of the French nation, refused either to obey the orders or to accept the authority of the Vichy regime. De Gaulle claimed that by this act of resistance he assumed French sovereignty and legitimacy.[96] The civilian leaders having by the vote of 10 July 1940 abdicated their functions, the political future of France would now depend on the outcome of a struggle between two governments, both organised around the person of a soldier.

For the history of the Third Republic to have come to such a denouement merely confirms the enduring importance of the military as a political force, albeit a tacit one, in French society. It would be one of the greatest ironies of the modern history of France if General de Gaulle who had lived within the military milieu for some three decades before uncertainly entering upon a political career at the age of forty-nine, should ultimately prove to have exerted a more profound influence on the evolution of republican institutions than any civilian politician or statesman.

Notes

1. *La République francaise*, 15 July 1880.
2. *Ibid.*, 16 July 1880.
3. See *La Revue des deux mondes*, 15 July 1880; *Le Gaulois*, 9 July 1880; *Le Figaro*, 12 July 1880.
4. *Le Journal des débats*, 15 & 16 July 1880.
5. Charles Seignobos, *Le déclin de l'Empire et l'établissement de la IIIe République*, vol. VII of *Histoire de la France contemporaine*, Ernest Lavisse (ed.) (10 vols., Paris, 1920-22), 75.
6. Léon Gambetta, *Discours et plaidoyers politiques de Gambetta*, vol. VIII, ed. Joseph Reinach (Paris, 1888), 212.
7. Raoul Girardet (ed.), *Le nationalisme francais* (Paris, 1966), 23.
8. Paul Bert, *L'instruction civique a l'école* (Paris, 1883), 11-32.
9. Paul Bert, *De l'éducation civique* (Paris, 1883), 19.
10. Quoted in Girardet, *Nationalisme*, 77-8.
11. Gugliemo Ferrero, *Militarism* (1902), 217-30.
12. Jean Perré, 'Les officers de carrière et la Nation', *Ecrits de Paris*, January, 1957, 32.
13. General du Barail, *Mes souvenirs* (3 vols., Paris, 1894-96), vol. II, 497.

14.   In such works as David Thomson, *Democracy in France* (1946); Richard W. Hale, Jr., *Democratic France* (New York, 1941); or Francois Bédarida, 'L'armée et la République; Les opinions politiques des officers francais en 1876-1878', *Revue historique*, July-September 1964.

15.   For this and the three following paragraphs, see David B. Ralston, *The Army of the Republic* (Cambridge, Mass., 1967), 78-82.

16.   *Ibid.*, 149.

17.   Paul Gheusi, *La vie et la mort singulière de Gambetta* (Paris, 1932), 172-3.

18.   H. Contamine, *La Rèvanche* (Paris, 1957), 32.

19.   See correspondence between General Carrey de Bellemare and Gambetta, and also between General Ferron and Joseph Reinach in the Joseph Reinach papers in the Nouvelles acquisitions francaises, Bibliothèque Nationale, Paris.

20.   Louis Garros, *L'armée de Grand-papa, de Galliffet à Gamelin* (Paris, 1965), 71-3.

21.   Adrien Dansette, *Le Boulangisme* (Paris, 1938), 17-24.

22.   Albert Thibaudet, *Les idées politiques de la France* (Paris, 1932), 225.

23.   Ralston, *op. cit.*, 220-3.

24.   Thomson, *op. cit.*, 170-3.

25.   For this and the two following paragraphs, see Ralston, *op. cit.*, 260-77; also Jean Karl Tanenbaum, *General Maurice Sarrail* (Chapel Hill, N. Carolina, 1974), 9.

26.   Tanenbaum, 15-17.

27.   *Ibid.*, 21-2.

28.   Denis Brogan, *The Development of Modern France* (1940), 383.

29.   Ralston, *op. cit.*, 322.

30.   *Ibid.*, 331-4.

31.   *Ibid.*, 351-2. Also, Pierre Bourget, *Un certain Philippe Pétain* (Paris, 1966), 44.

32.   Contamine, *op. cit.*, 87.

33.   Raoul Girardet, *La société militaire dans la France contemporaine, 1815-1939* (Paris, 1953).

34.   Jere C. King, *Generals and Politicians: Conflict between France's High Command, Parliament, and Government, 1914-1918* (Berkeley and Los Angeles, 1951), 168-9.

35.   Richard Griffiths, *Pétain* (Garden City, N.Y., 1970), 49-52.

36.   Jean Plumyène, *Pétain* (Paris, n.d.), 14. Also, Bourget, *op. cit.*, 38-41.

37.   Richard D. Challener, *The French Theory of the Nation in Arms, 1866-1939* (New York, 1955), 140-1, 216-7.

38.   Jacques Nobécourt, *Une histoire politique de l'armée: De Pétain à Pétain, 1919-1942* (Paris, 1967), 185.

39.   J. R. Tournoux, *Pétain et de Gaulle* (Paris, 1964), 343.

40.   King, *Generals and Politicians*, 53-62.

41.   Clemenceau, *Grandeurs et misères d'une victoire*, 74, quoted in King, *Generals and Politicians*, 222.

42.   Jere C. King, *Foch vs. Clemenceau* (Cambridge, Mass., 1960), 13-16, 50-6.

43.   Georges Wurmser, *La République de Clemenceau* (Paris, 1961), 343.

44.   Nobécourt, *op. cit.*, 81-94, 108-9.

45.   Griffiths, *op. cit.*, 100-3.

46.   *L'Ere nouvelle*, 29 June 1924. The annual banquet at the end of June honouring the birth of Hoche was organised by the various republican groups in Versailles, the town of his birth, and was in most years an unexceptional event. Still an affair commemorating so unimpeachably republican a soldier did provide an ideal occasion for the leading politicians to address the politico-military questions of the moment, either to remind the soldiers that they should emulate the example of Hoche, and be absolutely loyal to the regime, as did Herriot in 1924, or conversely,

to reassure them of the good intentions of the Republic and its good works for the army, as did Gambetta in 1878. This forum was especially useful at moments when relations between the army and the regime were subject to some kind of strain. Thus in 1904, General André spoke of Hoche as a model of political loyalty and as 'a republican officer par excellence', (*La France militaire*, 28 June 1904) while a year later following the scandal of *L'Affaire des fiches*, the new Minister of War, Maurice Berteaux, chided those who denigrated the military state of France and noted the sacrifices sponsored by the Republic for the well being of the army (*La France militaire*, 27 June 1905). In 1924, just after the victory of the Cartel des Gauches, there was, in addition to the above mentioned address by Herriot, one by Paul Painlevé, who as Minister of War, praised the civic virtues of the 'republican general' Hoche (*L'Ere nouvelle*, 30 June 1924). In 1936, Daladier, as Minister of War in the government of the Popular Front, spoke of the army as the 'emanation of the whole people . . . animated by the most splendid spirit of duty and discipline . . .' (*La France militaire*, 30 June 1936).

47. Nobécourt, *op. cit.*, 127-8.
48. King, *Generals and Politicians*, 70-88. Also, see Tanenbaum, 55-74.
49. Tanenbaum, *op. cit.*, chs. V-IX.
50. Nobécourt, 129.
51. Philip Bankwitz, *Maxime Weygand and Civil-Military Relations in Modern France* (Cambridge, Mass., 24-5). Also, Tanenbaum, *op. cit.*, 189 ff.
52. Nobécourt, *op. cit.*, 132.
53. Bankwitz, *op. cit.*, 19-20.
54. *Ibid.*
55. Nobécourt, *op. cit.*, 220.
56. 'Chronique Francaise', *La Revue militaire suisse*, February 1930, 90-93.
57. *Journal Officiel de la Chambre des Députés: Débats* (1930), 81-2.
58. *Ibid.*, 84.
59. Bankwitz, *op. cit.*, 39.
60. Garros, *op. cit.*, 114.
61. General Maurice Gamelin, *Servir*, vol. II (Paris, 1946), VIII-IX.
62. Nobécourt, *op. cit.*, 201-2.
63. Gamelin, *op. cit.*, 75. Gamelin is faithful to this precept in his memoirs, where he has little but good to say of the leading political figures of the day. He admires Paul-Boncour as a 'gallant man and a distinguished mind', praises Herriot for his 'elevated mind and his radiant qualities', (*ibid.*, 76), and even discerns in Flandin 'very considerable qualities as a statesman' (*ibid.*, 138-9). He thinks of Daladier as being profoundly patriotic and notes his integrity, a quality, according to Gamelin, he shared with most of those in ministerial positions 'in a milieu where temptations are extremely frequent' (*ibid.*, 88-9). Such affirmations of confidence in the honesty of the average minister were highly unusual coming from a soldier under the Third Republic.
64. Nobécourt, *op. cit.*, 198-9. See also, Guy Chapman, *Why France Collapsed* (1968), 14.
65. M. Soulie, *La vie politique d'Edouard Herriot* (Paris, 1962), 151.
66. *L'Ere nouvelle*, 18 June 1924.
67. *Journal Officiel de la Chambre des Députés: Débats* (1935), 1045-6.
68. One of Pétain's salient qualifications may have been that he *looked* as a Marshal of France ought to look. Loustaunau-Lacau in his *Mémoires d'un Francais rebelle* aptly and wittily depicts the imposing appearance of Pétain compared to that of the other Marshals. Quoted in Bourget, *op. cit.*, 140. See also the comment of General André Beaufre, *1940: The Fall of France*, trans. Desmond Flower (New York, 1968), 40.
69. Plumyène, *op. cit.*, 62.

70. Griffiths, *op. cit.*, 98.
71. Wladimir d'Ormesson, *Les vraies confidences* (Paris, 1962), 133-4.
72. Nobécourt, *op. cit.*, 147-50.
73. Plumyène, *op. cit.*, 60.
74. See Carlton J. H. Hayes, *France, a Nation of Patriots* (New York, 1930), for an account of the various manifestations of French patriotism.
75. Griffiths, *op. cit.*, 88.
76. *Le Populaire*, 25 January 1931. Quoted in Plumyène, *op. cit.*, 66-7.
77. Bourget, *op. cit.*, 15.
78. Nobécourt, *op. cit.*, 147-50.
79. Pierre d'Hugues, 'Le Parti de Pétain', *La Grande revue*, March 1934, 11.
80. Bourget, *op. cit.*, 154-5.
81. Griffiths, *op. cit.*, 158-95, especially pp. 194-5.
82. J. R. Tournoux, *L'histoire secréte* (Paris, 1962), 24-32.
83. *Ibid.*, 33. See also, Bourget, *op. cit.*, 151-3.
84. D'Ormesson, *op. cit.*, 141.
85. Griffiths, *op. cit.*, 172-5.
86. *Vu*, 30 November 1935, 18-19.
87. *Ibid.*
88. Nobécourt, *op. cit.*, 248.
89. *Le Populaire*, 3 March 1939 and *L'Humanité*, 24 March 1939. Quoted in Plumyène, *op. cit.*, 89.
90. Paul Reynaud, *In the Thick of the Fight*, trans. James D. Lambert (New York, 1955), 340.
91. Henry Lémery, *D'une République à l'autre* (Paris, 1964), 222.
92. Camille Chautemps, *Cahiers secrets de l'armistice*, 1939-40 (Paris, 1963), 86.
93. Reynaud, *op. cit.*, 345-6.
94. Griffiths, *op. cit.*, 227-43.
95. Paul Baudouin, *The Private Diaries of Paul Baudouin*, trans. Sir James Petrie (1948), 168.
96. Charles de Gaulle, *The Complete War Memoirs of Charles de Gaulle*, vol. II, trans. Richard Howard (New York, 1964), 665.

THE DANGER OF BOMBARDMENT FROM THE AIR AND THE MAKING OF BRITISH AIR DISARMAMENT POLICY 1932-4

Uri Bialer

The danger of a 'knock out' blow by air attack was an immediate concern which critically affected the making of British defence and foreign policy in the 1930s. A devastating bombardment from the air aimed at vital parts of the country and, above all, at the capital was — within the British government, and indeed almost universally — expected to be a decisive blow in a future war against Britain. Much has been written on the special apprehension about the danger of aerial bombardment in Britain in that period. However, most of these writings deal with the issue as an important, but background element for the account of British air rearmament and the buildup of air defence at that time. This article thus attempts to fill a gap by focusing on the fear itself and on the question of how far was it shared by those responsible for shaping the national policy. It tries to trace the impact of this apprehension on the process of formulating some key decisions in British foreign policy long before the Munich crisis of 1938 when the impact of that fear became apparent and well known. It suggests that obsession with that danger greatly influenced the making of British air disarmament policy at the International Disarmament Conference in Geneva in 1932 and subsequently.

The problem of air disarmament cannot be separated from the basic problem confronting the British government in its policy towards the Conference. This problem may be summed up as a lack of a means to achieve a desired aim.[1] A successful international disarmament conference ending with a substantial disarmament convention would have served the British government well. From the point of international politics it could have eased the tension between France and Germany by reconciling German demands for *Gleichberechtigung* and what the British considered as an excessive French demand for keeping the Versailles Agreement intact.[2] A disarmament agreement might have eased the way for American cooperation on debts and other economic issues. Considering British defence, an all-round disarmament could not but improve the relative position of her armed forces. At home the government faced a wide and very active public campaign for disarmament which the existence of the Conference aroused. The campaign and the

202

general public expectation about the Conference were taken very seriously by the national government at that time. A deep sense of electoral insecurity existed within the government throughout these years as the impact of the by-elections of 1933-4 was to show.[3] In view of the public campaign, the declared British adherence to the disarmament cause and the part played by the disarmament issue in the Conservative defeat in 1929, failure to achieve a substantial disarmament convention was considered to have grave political consequences.[4]

The *sine qua non* of reaching such a convention was the reconciliation of French demands for security and German demands for equality of rights. The most obvious contribution the British might have made to this cause was a further commitment to French security. This however contradicted a focal point in Britain's position, since one may find at the time of the Disarmament Conference a very firm and consistent line that under no circumstances could she increase her commitments abroad. The British did not have the capability to implement such a commitment nor the will to strengthen their own armed forces.[5] There were many strands to this policy: the financial exigencies of the economic crisis, the reluctance of the Dominions and the United States to be pulled by the British into any European commitment, the perilous state of British armaments themselves, and the myth that armed camps and an armaments race had led to war in 1914.

The government had been placed in a position of considerable tension. On the one hand were those factors, political, economic, military and imperial, whose effect was to impede any bold line of policy and restrain any risk-taking abroad. On the other hand were the internal political pressures demanding a governmental success especially in this subject of disarmament. The implication of this inability or lack of will to give a substantial lead in the Conference by means of contributing to French security had been clear to the government even before the opening of the Conference. As put by Vansittart, the Permanent Under-Secretary of State for Foreign Affairs. 'The result of breaking no eggs is admittedly not an omelette, but may well be a mess.'[6] In contrast to the public enthusiasm there had been great pessimism within the government early in 1932 as to the possibility of reaching a successful agreement in Geneva.[7] At the same time the government could not for obvious political reasons extricate itself from the search for a formula which could prove to be a basis of agreement; nor could it admit failure when failure was evident. The result had been continuous efforts to find what Eden, who led the British delegation at the Conference, called 'Intermediate Positions'[8] designed to obviate the criticism of silence and to provide some basis for negotiations without tackling the basic problem.[9]

This, then, is the essential background for understanding the pressures under which the British government had to formulate its general policy towards the Conference.

Three important elements have to be taken into consideration in analysing how British air disarmament policy was made. All three had a considerable influence and all were connected with the concept of the 'knock out' blow from the air. Public opinion on the specific subject of air disarmament, the personal views of some prominent decision makers on the danger of air attack, and the attitudes and opinions of some Departments of State on this subject, are all essential to the understanding of the internal process by which the policy had been made.

To some extent it may seem artificial to refer to public opinion on the specific subject of air disarmament and to separate it from the context of the general public attitude towards disarmament. Yet the problem of air disarmament has specific characteristics so that a distinction can be made between public opinion on this problem and on others. The danger air bombardment posed to the civilian population seems to have been far more obvious to the British public than the dangers from other means of warfare. Ordinary citizens were aware that air warfare tended to nullify the distance between the military background and the civilian theatre. The short, but impressive, experience of the aerial bombardment of London in the First World War, and the fast and tangible progress of aircraft technology provided a fertile ground for popular writings on the subject of air warfare. These writings stressed especially the immense destructive capability of air bombardment. The difference between the 'professional' analysis on the impact of air attack in a future war and the 'Science Fiction' of that time seems to be very small in this respect.[10] The vision of a desolated city and its mutilated inhabitants which was common in these writings underlined a widespread belief that bombardment from the air could destroy big cities like London within a matter of hours. The fact that Britain was an island could no longer protect her from the danger of direct and intense involvement in a future war. This realisation seems to have been the main reason for the particular interest which the public showed in the problem of air disarmament.

Consequently it is hardly surprising that this problem was prominent in the campaign launched by various organisations at the time of the disarmament Conference. The League of Nations Union, one of the most powerful pressure groups in this campaign was well aware of the sensitivity of the British public to the air disarmament issue[11] and constantly used the 'air peril' theme in its disarmament campaign at the time of the Disarmament Conference.[12] There was little doubt at that time that Baldwin's speech of November 1932 was accepted as a firm strengthening of the League's campaign for air disarmament.[13] The declaration that 'the bomber will always get through' seemed to strengthen the concentration of public attention on the problem of the 'air menace' and gave precious ammunition to the campaign for air disarmament. In his analysis of British attitudes towards disarmament in the 1930s, John Kyba comes to the conclusion that the problem facing the Conference which united the press to demand, suggest and plead for the acceptance of *one* proposal was the abolition of bombing and the internationalisation of civil aviation.[14] And indeed, there is only a difference in style between *The Times* leader of 11 November 1932 and the *New Statesman* of 18 November emphasising that 'the supreme menace and the supreme horrors of war come from the air and unless Mars can be dethroned in the sky, there will be small gain in pin-pricking him on the earth and sea'. When the Earl of Halsbury said in the House of Lords that the way to tackle the danger was, paradoxically, to make civil aviation bigger, 'so that people can understand that they can get here, there and everywhere directly before anybody can stop them',[15] he only showed the extent of the popularity of the concept which had been expressed by Baldwin's speech.

The League of Nations Union and other pacifist organisations had not been the only ones to be aware of the interest which the British public showed in the problem of air disarmament. Early in 1933 when the Labour Party started to use the alleged failure of British policy at the Conference as a major element of attack in Parliament, it was air disarmament which was chosen to be the central theme of attack.[16] Moreover, the Parliamentary criticism was not made only by the Labour Party. Conservatives such as Vyvyan Adams and Austen Chamberlain stressed the same points which the opposition had made.[17] Consequently, it was this particular issue of air disarmament, stressing the concept of the 'knock out' blow from the air, which helped keep disarmament alive in British politics and the press in 1933 when the hope of reaching any agreement in Geneva faded away.[18] This proved to be an important pressure on the government to achieve an international convention which would minimise or eliminate the danger of air attack on Britain.

Public opinion is not a quantity which can be measured with great accuracy in the inter-war period. Apparently obvious indications like the East Fulham by-election of 1933 and the Peace Ballot of 1934-5 remain open to debate.[19] What is most important for a study of decision making is an analysis of the evaluations which decision makers gave to opinions publicly held on various subjects. These evaluations of opinions need not necessarily reflect what in retrospect seems to have been the true state of affairs, yet they influenced the decisions made, and as such are of particular importance. Thus, even if the East Fulham by-election had not been fought on disarmament at all, it would still have a considerable influence on the issues of rearmament and disarmament. Baldwin's personal evaluation of what this election indicated rather than what it actually implied was critically important for his conclusion as to the political advisability of starting rearmament. There can be little doubt that public opinion had an important influence on the making of British policy at the Disarmament Conference. In formulating policy at the Conference the government aimed *inter alia* at satisfying or at least not contradicting what seemed to them a very firm public advocacy of disarmament. MacDonald the Prime Minister was well aware of and very sensitive to the Labour attacks on him in matters of policy at the Disarmament Conference.[20] Simon, the Foreign Secretary, admitted in a private letter to his Permanent Under-Secretary his personal apprehension as to the consequences to the national government of a failure of the Disarmament Conference and concluded, 'The loss of credit which the British government will suffer in the eyes of the public if there is no international agreement which can be called a Disarmament Conference will be something tremendous . . . I feel in my bones that we are digging the grave of elder statesmanship if we cannot do better than that.'[21] The whole controversy surrounding Baldwin's speech in the House of Commons on 12 November 1936 underscores one factor − his deep personal conviction of a strong pro-disarmament public opinion in Britain in 1932-4.[22] Other members of the Cabinet clearly shared this conviction.[23]

Thus a clear consensus seemed to exist among decision makers about the intensity and importance of the pro-disarmament campaign in the early 1930s. They seemed to be well aware of the particular public urge for and interest in air disarmament. Hankey, the Cabinet's Secretary, whose long experience in his office taught him to judge very accurately the opinions which influenced decisions, had been aware of the influence which this specific public interest had on the Cabinet. In a note he wrote to Simon he said, 'Compared with bombing aeroplanes the public interest in such matters as heavy guns or whether a battleship should be 35,000 or 25,000 tons is almost negligible.'[24] The need not to contradict the popular demand to abolish the bomber was an important element which was taken into consideration in discussions on the problem of air disarmament. Thus MacDonald was worried, 'Lest public opinion might become restive if we adopted a purely negative attitude to the one form of disarmament which might affect the man in the street in this country.'[25] Simon and Baldwin shared these views and, on various occasions, referred to the importance of satisfying, and not contradicting, this *specific* public demand.[26]

The opinions held by some of the decision makers on the essence and significance of the danger of bombardment from the air is of particular relevance to the understanding of the extent to which concern about the 'knock out blow' from the air had been established within the government. This was perhaps the most important element behind the efforts to reach an air disarmament agreement at that time.

Much has been written about Baldwin's obsession with the danger of bombardment from the air.[27] His speech in the House of Commons on 10 November 1932 in which he expressed a deep fear of air attack was the first time the public came to know his opinions on this issue. The Cabinet, however, had been well aware for many months of the extent to which he was obsessed with this danger. His obsession with Britain's liability and vulnerability to air attack and his deep revulsion against war turned him into the most fervent advocate of air disarmament within the government. Being one of the first within the Cabinet to point to the specific danger of German air power[28] he struggled for a convention prohibiting bombing even after an informal recognition by the government that such agreement could not be achieved in Geneva.[29]

Baldwin was not the only one within the government to hold these ideas. MacDonald seems to have shared his apprehensions. Reaching an air disarmament agreement had been considered by MacDonald to have priority over any other agreement since, as he explained, '. . . it might prevent a full blown offensive being developed at zero hour which was in fact the real danger to which London might be exposed'.[30] Simon, who won his reputation more as an analyst than an effective decision maker, defined in clear terms one of the basic characteristics of the fear of a 'bolt from the blue' by air attack. This was the fear of what may be called a 'progressive unknown'. He said, 'The fact remained that until something was done to stop the menace, the prospect of a future war . . . was appalling, particularly to civilians in crowded places. *If civil and military aviation were in a position to do what they could do after fifteen years of evolution what were the prospects fifty years hence?*' This was the fear which was making them all so much concerned to get some remedy.[31] The Foreign Secretary saw particular importance in the problem of tackling what he considered to have been a very serious danger to British security, and in a private letter he claimed that 'it would be the ending of a *nightmare* if the great powers had the sense to agree to abolish military and naval aviation'.[32] Other prominent Ministers such as Herbert Samuel, who had been greatly influenced by his experience as the chairman of the Air Raids Precautions subcommittee of the CID, and Samuel Hoare, who had been under the strong personal influence of Lord Trenchard, the prophet of the 'knock out blow', shared the same anxiety.[33]

The contention is then, that discussions within the government at the time of the Disarmament Conference disclosed the fact that although Baldwin had been the most prominent in his personal obsession with British liability to air attack, his views on this issue were widely shared within the Cabinet.

The last element to be discussed in connection with the decision making process by which British air disarmament policy was made is the consistent opinion if some Departments of State on what this policy should have been. On the one hand, there was the policy advocated by the Foreign Office, the Admiralty and the War Office and, on the other, the policy suggested by the Air Ministry. They all based their different conclusions on the same common concern and apprehension about British vulnerability and liability to air attack.

Throughout the period of the Disarmament Conference the Foreign Office advocated acceptance of substantial air disarmament. There were two reasons for this. The first was the difficulty in which this department had been put by the Cabinet's reluctance to give any further commitment to French security. The Foreign Office considered such a commitment to be the main means by which Britain could have solved the basic problem of the Conference and thus secured the desired international convention.[34] At the same time, it had been pressed to formulate concrete plans on which to base British policy at the Conference. Being well aware of the popularity of the proposal to abolish bombing from the air, the Foreign Office held the view that efforts to achieve substantial air disarmament agreement presented a decisive British contribution to the Conference.[35] The second reason for the Foreign Office's particular interest in and advocacy of air disarmament was the obsession with the danger of German air rearmament which its Permnent Under-Secretary seemed to develop as early as 1932.[35] Vansittart was one of the first within the government to draw attention to the special danger of the newly born German air power. Early in 1933, before the establishment of the Luftwaffe he came to a definite conclusion about the prominence of the danger of German air rearmament and in a letter to Hankey he wrote, 'The speed and ease with which new types of aircraft are being developed makes it [German air rearmament] a far more formidable danger than anything in the way of naval or military armaments'.[36] Vansittart had a dominant influence within the Foreign Office at that time and this is reflected in many of the Foreign Office's assessments which found their way to the Cabinet. Until March 1933 when there had still been some hope of achieving a substantial air disarmament agreement in Geneva, the Foreign Office (which warned the Cabinet that 'Germany will rely for their military power above all on military aircraft'),[37] advocated the acceptance of drastic air disarmament plans as the best means of tackling the danger of air attack. When this hope faded away, it was air rearmament in which this department seemed to be most interested.[38]

Throughout this period the Admiralty and the War Office put before the Cabinet the same ideas as to the desirability of abolishing bombers as the best way of tackling the problem of British vulnerability to air attack. They had not accepted the Air Staff's theory that counter attack would be the best means of defence against bombardment from the air.[39]

Public opinion, prominent decision makers and important Departments of State saw in a substantial air disarmament agreement a means to solve the problem of British vulnerability to air attack. All these forces put the Air Ministry under serious pressure at the time of the Disarmament Conference. The acceptance of a substantial air disarmament plan calling for the abolition of the bomber threatened to destroy what the Air Staff considered to be its *raison d'être*. The material consequences of acceptance of any disarmament convention prohibiting bombing were too obvious to be overlooked by the Air Ministry. Consequently, they vehemently opposed the general trend in the Cabinet and were one of the important obstacles to any British initiative in air disarmament at Geneva. Some of the arguments put forward by the Air Ministry about the practicability of various air disarmament plans raised difficult problems for the Cabinet. Among these were the implications of the plan to abolish bombing from the air. In the east a cheap means of British military control was by 'police bombing'. However the main and unbeatable argument which the Air Ministry put forward was the problem of civil aviation. The problem here was the impossibility of preventing the misuse of civilian aircraft after an international air disarmament agreement was signed abolishing the bomber or the act of bombing. The ease with which civil aircraft could be transformed into military planes was the main point raised by the Air Ministry. British reluctance to accept any international control of civil aviation (not to speak of a League of Nations air force) was a complementary reason for what proved to be a permanent deadlock. The various air disarmament proposals all failed to beat these arguments and this strengthened the point made constantly by the Air Ministry: that if it was desired to achieve security from air attack by international agreement it would have to be by outlawing flying altogether.[40]

Inability to define any agreed British line of policy towards the Disarmament Conference characterised the various deliberations within the government up to the actual opening of the Conference in February 1932. Substantial air disarmament plans which became a much discussed subject towards the middle of that year were only superficially dealt with at that time. The main reason for this was the fact that the Disarmament Conference was originally to base its discussions on the Draft Disarmament Convention which had been agreed to in 1930. This Draft Convention was a very general framework for future discussion which was to have solved the real problem of principles and numbers of various categories of armaments. Although the Draft Convention could not possibly solve the basic problem of the Conference, it still provided an easy solution to the British search for a policy. The Draft Convention based the air disarmament schemes on limitations according to numbers and horsepower, and thus prepared a rather narrow and techcical basis for the deliberations on air disarmament at Geneva.[41]

The supposition that the Draft Convention would be the basis for discussions in Geneva was proved wrong when the French launched their independent plan, known as the Tardieu Plan, in February 1932. This plan recommended *inter alia* the prohibition of bombing from the air and the creation of a League of Nations air force.[42] The British government could not then afford to delay the formulation of a definite plan which would be recognised as a specific British contribution to the Conference. The Foreign Office had to find some formula on which to base this plan, and found it in the principle of qualitative disarmament. The principle had to be implemented by precise air disarmament proposals. The Foreign Office suggested a formula calling for the prohibition of bombing from the air on the territory and shipping of another sovereign state.[43] This proposal aimed at avoiding two pitfalls: the civil aviation problem and the British interest in keeping its air force for 'police' purposes in the east. The pressure of public opinion led to the acceptance of this proposal by the Cabinet early in April 1932.[44] However the vehement opposition of the Air Ministry delayed a final decision until early in May.[45] The problem came to a head in the Cabinet meeting of 4 May. In the discussion Baldwin put forward his proposals to scrap all military aircraft and to abolish subsidies to civil aviation as the best way to tackle the problem of air disarmament. He explained to the Cabinet that he had been impressed with the appalling consequences of a future war conducted from the air, and that his hopes had been that such a proposal would remove one of the main elements of a fear that was such a disturbing feature in the international situation.[46] Later in a private letter to the Prime Minister he explained the motive and rationale behind his drastic and seemingly absurd proposals: 'I am not at all sure that the shock that such a proposal, coming from us, would make, would not be a good thing for the statesmen of Europe.'[47]

Baldwin's proposal and the Foreign Office formula had been referred to the Coast Defence Subcommittee of the CID which had been called to consider them particularly from the point of view of the defence of London. The well stated arguments of the Air Staff accompanied by many technical examples could not but impress that Committee which discussed first the Foreign Office plan on 6 May. In the absence of the Chief of Imperial General Staff and the First Sea Lord, the Air Staff's representatives did not encounter any serious technical objection. They succeeded in emphasising the vulnerability of London to air attack even after a hypothetical adoption of the Foreign Office formula.[48] The decision reached by the Committee proved the impracticability of the Foreign Office formula as a means to minimise the danger of bombardment from the air.[49]

The implications of this decision, although not recognised at that time, had been far-reaching. For the susceptibility of various other substantial disarmament proposals to the counter arguments of the Air Staff had been much greater than that of the Foreign Office plan. Thus the decision of 6 May 1932 had been a major potential obstacle to any other substantial air disarmament initiative in Geneva.

A special Committee which had been appointed to deal with Baldwin's radical proposals and which was not represented by the Air Staff, presented the Cabinet early in June with a paper strongly recommending the acceptance of these proposals.[50] The Admiralty and the War Office presented papers which indicated that from the broadest view of national defence, an effective total abolition could not but be advantageous.[52] Prominent Ministers such as Baldwin, Simon, Samuel, MacDonald and Hailsham advocated the acceptance of the proposals which implied a dissolution of a national air force in order to tackle what was considered by them to be a very serious peril to British defence. Even if one assumes that there was some scepticism among them about the practicability of the acceptance of this proposal by the Disarmament Conference, one must still be impressed by the deep conviction shared among them about the essence, meaning and importance of the 'air peril'. Facing this opposition the Secretary of State for Air, Lord Londonderry, could not but warn the Cabinet that the Air Staff might lose their confidence in the government and that his personal position would become untenable.[53] The Cabinet could not therefore reach a definite conclusion, but authorised the Prime Minister and his colleagues to enter into private and informal conversations embracing these air disarmament proposals with the French Prime Minister at their coming meeting in Paris. This meeting proved fruitless. The French refused to accept any of Baldwin's drastic proposals.[54]

This brought to an end the first stage of the British search for a substantial air disarmament plan which came to a halt in July 1932. The firm demand by the Germans for *Gleichberechtigung* and their threat to leave the Conference should such a demand not be seriously dealt with, led to the reopening of the problem of British air disarmament policy in October on that year. The new plan which had been decided upon by the Cabinet after successive meetings during the end of October and the beginning of November 1932 recommended the reduction of the air forces of the leading powers to the level of those in Great Britain and a cut of 33 per cent of the air forces of the world thus reduced. These resolutions faced the same objections as other plans, and were unacceptable to other nations, and especially to France.

What was recognised and advocated publicly by Britain for the first time was that the ideal solution to the problem of air disarmament was the complete abolition of all military and naval aircraft combined with an effective control of civil aviation.[55] New factors seemed to justify an adoption of this principle at that time. By the acceptance of this principle Germany could be given complete equality of status without being allowed to rearm. However the Cabinet's records point unmistakably to a growing 'air anxiety' within the government by the end of 1932. One of the main reasons for the adoption of this formula was a growing obsession with the danger of bombardment from the air, 'Certain peculiarly terrible potentialities which recent experiments had shown the aircraft clearly possessed. *The only way to check such a development was to take the edge out of the national organisation whose business it was to explore them intensively.*'[56]

The crux of any proposal to abolish military and naval aircraft was the question of civil aviation. The problem of how to tackle this obstacle was only superficially dealt with in the various committees and the Foreign Office up to February 1933.[57] The advocating of the principle of abolition of the air forces, and a working proposal which was submitted by Britain to the Conference late in January 1933 confirming this principle, made such an enquiry essential. On 17 February the Cabinet Disarmament Committee started to discuss these matters. The object as defined ironically by the future Secretary of State for Air, Cunliffe Lister, had been 'to make the world safer from the terror of bombing . . . the problem was how to prevent a 100 tons of bombs per day being dropped on London.'[58] Lister himself, with his experience in international cartels and organisations, had been asked to prepare a scheme for the control or internationalisation of civil aviation which would fulfil two basic conditions: to prevent the resources of civil aviation from being used for military purposes in the event of an outbreak of war, without hampering the fullest development of aviation in every country for civil and commercial purposes. Such a scheme – the most serious effort by the government to tackle the problem – was suggested by Cunliffe Lister late in February 1933. However the Cabinet rejected the plan because it could not fulfil the two basic conditions, namely to provide a really effective barrier to the employment of civil aviation for military purposes without hampering the growth of the aircraft industry.[59] For internal political considerations British policy makers could not admit their absolute despair of the various air disarmament proposals which they themselves put forward after March to the Conference.[60] However they clearly lost hope of achieving an air disarmament agreement in the context of the Conference by the beginning of March 1933.

Two suggestions may be made in conclusion. The first concerns the concept of the 'air peril' and the Disarmament Conference. Apprehension about the danger of air attack was of particular importance in influencing the government's struggle for air disarmament in Geneva. The anxiety had been built on many widely shared concepts and beliefs as to the nature of the 'next war', the actual and potential capability of aircraft to achieve a decisive 'knock out blow', and the impact of bombardment on civilian population. These clearly influenced the formulation of British air disarmament policy in 1932-3. An international air disarmament agreement abolishing the bomber or prohibiting the act of bombing seemed to be the most efficient way of tackling the danger. Discussions within the government exposed the futility of these air disarmament plans as a means to tackle the problem of British vulnerability to air attack. The failure, however, had not destroyed hope within the government of reaching some air disarmament agreement after the breakdown of the Conference. The danger of bombardment from the air continued to be the main force behind constant efforts on the part of Britain up to 1939 to secure some international air disarmament agreement.

The second remark draws attention to the uniqueness and importance of the attention given by British decision makers to the subject of the aerial 'knock out blow' in 1932-3. The growing concern and apprehension as to the danger of air attack was not, at that time, a reflection of actual development and change in the military map of Europe. Up to the end of 1933 the theoretical basis for the discussion on the danger of bombardment from the air was the French air force, yet war with France had for long been considered to be a very remote and unacceptable possibility. Thus discussions on the 'air peril' at that time lacked the element of pointing to an actual enemy. The particular attention which many politicians gave to the problem of the danger of air attack in 1932-3, even before the establishment of the Luftwaffe, has two implications. Not only does it highlight the extent to which anxiety and concern about British vulnerability to bombardment from the air was established within the government at that time, but it also has a far reaching implication for a new perspective on decision making in the following year, 1934, and in 1935. For the discussions in 1932-3 which anticipated the emergence of a potentially hostile air force in Europe prepared the way for, indeed one might say biased, the discussions of the Cabinet and the Cabinet Disarmament Committee in 1934-5 which resulted in decisions to base early rearmament largely on air rearmament.

Notes

I am grateful to Mr John Barnes for his helpful comments on an early draft of this article.

1.   On British policy at the Conference and on the Conference itself, see E. B. Segel, 'Sir John Simon and British Foreign Policy: The Diplomacy of Disarmament in the 1930s', Ph.D. thesis, University of California (1966). R. A. Chaput, *Disarmament in British Foreign Policy* (London, 1935); A. C. Temperley, *The Whispering Gallery of Europe* (1938); A. Eden, Earl of Avon, *Facing the Dictators* (1962); C. Loosli-Usteri, *Geschichte des Konferenz für die Herabetzung und die Begrenzung der Rüstungen 1932-1934. Ein Politischen Weltspiegel* (Zurich, 1940), and J. W. Wheeler Bennett, *The Disarmament Deadlock* (1934).

2.   See N. Waites, 'British Foreign Policy Towards France Regarding the German Problem from 1929 to 1934', Ph.D. thesis, University of London (1972).

3.   For a useful analysis of public opinion see J. Kyba, 'British Attitudes towards Disarmament and Rearmament 1932-1935', Ph.D. thesis, University of London (1966), and also James K. Thompson, 'Great Britain and the World Disarmament Conference 1932-1934', Ph.D. thesis, University of North Carolina (1961). The impact of the by-elections is still controversial but the literature still centres on East Fulham. See M. Ceadel, 'Interpreting East Fulham', in C. Cook and J. Ramsden (eds.), *By-Elections in British Politics* (1973), 118-40.

4.   See conclusions of the Cabinet Disarmament Committee on 19 January 1932, CAB. 24. 227.

5.   See MacDonald's analysis in July 1931 in CAB. 21. 346.

6.   1 January 1932, CAB. 27. 476.

7.   On the British efforts to delay the opening of the Conference see CAB. 63. 44.

8.   Eden, *op. cit.*, 29.

9.   For an analysis of British position as seen by the government see Hoare's private letter to MacDonald, 4 February 1932, MacDonald Papers 2/6.

10.   Compare for example the professional assessment of A. E. Blake, 'The Future of Warfare', and B. Liddell-Hart, 'The Next War', *Fortnightly Review* (September 1930), 29-40, 585-98 with Wyndham Lewis, *The Danger of Youth* and *Filibuster in Barbary* (1932). For an analysis of the image of the 'next war' in the fiction of the 1930s and the danger of air attack see I. F. Clarke, *Voices Prophesying War 1763-1964* (1966), 170.

11.   See the Cecil Papers, vols. 51107-51108.

12.   See, for example, Noel-Baker's private letter to Cecil, 31 August 1931, Cecil Papers, vol. 51107.

13.   See Gilbert Murray's letter to Simon, 14 November 1932. FO. 800. 287.

14.   Kyba, *op. cit.*, 173.

15.   See House of Lords debate on 14 November 1932, Cols. 1279-1286.

16.   See House of Commons debate on 13 June 1933, Col. 270.

17.   *Ibid.*, Cols. 280, 354.

18.   See *inter alia, Manchester Guardian* leaders, 24 June and 4 August 1933, *Daily Herald* leader 29 May and the *Economist* leader 3 June 1933. *The Times* and the *Saturday Review* were among the few that had not followed suit in this campaign.

19.   See R. Heller, 'East Fulham Revisited', *Journal of Contemporary History*, vol. 6, no. 3 (1971), 172-96.

20.   See Segel, *op. cit.*, 265.

21.   23 December 1933, CAB. 21. 387.

22.   See B. C. Malament, 'Baldwin Re-restored?', *Journal of Modern History*,

44 (1), March 1972, 87-96. Also K. Middlemas and J. Barnes, *Baldwin, A Biography* (1969), 970-3.

23.   See Viscount Templewood, *Nine Troubled Years* (1954), 114.

24.   6 May 1932, FO. 800. 286.

25.   5 April 1932, CAB. 27. 505.

26.   See *ibid.*, Air 8/151 and FO. 371. 16431 W/8178/10/98.

27.   K. Middlemas and J. Barnes, *op. cit.*, 732.

20.   7 March 1933, CAB. 27. 505.

29.   *Ibid.*

30.   5 April 1932, CAB. 27. 505.

31.   1 June 1932, CAB. 23. 71.

32.   9 June 1932, FO. 800. 287.

33.   See Samuel's speech on 6 June 1932, CAB. 21. 354. For Hoare's opinions see C.P. 44 (32) and Templewood, *op. cit.*, 117.

34.   See Foreign Office Memorandum dated 1 January 1932, CAB. 27. 476.

35.   See FO. 371. 17380 W/2322/117/98.

36.   CAB. 63. 46, M (33) 6.

37.   C.P. 52 (33).

38.   See U. Bialer, 'Some Aspects of the Fear of Bombardment from the Air and the Making of British Defence and Foreign Policy, 1932-1939', Ph.D. thesis, University of London (1974), 84-9, 273-81.

39.   C.P. 164 (32) and C.P. 176 (32).

40.   See D. Carlton, 'The Problem of Civil Aviation in British Disarmament Policy 1919-1934', *Journal of the Royal United Service Institution*, 664 (November 1966), 307-16.

41.   Chaput, *op. cit.*, 339-43.

42.   Wheeler-Bennett, *op. cit.*, 14-15.

43.   FO. 371. 16429 W/3359/10/98.

44.   On this see discussions of the Cabinet Disarmament Committee in CAB. 27. 476 and CAB. 27. 505.

45.   CAB. 23. 71 and AIR 8/151.

46.   CAB. 23. 71.

47.   1 June 1932, MacDonald Papers.

48.   CAB. 16. 106.

49.   *Ibid.*

50.   C.P. 164. 32.

51.   C.P. 176. 32 and C.P. 183. 32.

52.   CAB. 23. 71, see also FO. 800. 287.

53.   FO. 371. 16462 W/7043/1466/98.

54.   CAB. 23. 72 and FO. 371. 16432 W/10837/10/98.

55.   CAB. 23. 72 (italics added).

56.   See FO 371, 15705 W/8457/47/98 and FO. 371. 16430 W/5916/1466/98.

57.   CAB. 27. 505.

58.   D.C. (M) (32) 37.

59.   Bialer, *op. cit.*, 57-61.

60.   *Ibid.*, 125-220.

TOTAL WAR IN THE TWENTIETH CENTURY: PARTICIPATION AND CONSENSUS IN THE SECOND WORLD WAR

Michael Howard

In 1925 the University of London sponsored a series of lectures by distinguished civil and military leaders with the title *The Study of War for Statesmen and Citizens*.[1] This course was designed to bring home to the general public the extent to which war had become a matter, not simply for military specialists, but for society as a whole. The experience of what was still known as The Great War had shown that in the twentieth century wars had to be fought with the full resources of the entire community. Even in the midst of the profoundest peace societies thus had to be conscious of the possible demands which a future war might make on those resources and be prepared to meet them. The emphasis therefore was on the measures which the community might have to adopt, the sacrifices it might have to make, the dangers it might have to undergo, if war were ever to occur again. But as yet there was no serious academic study of the way in which society itself would be transformed, and indeed had been transformed, by the demands of total war. The material for such a study had existed, at least for Great Britain, in the remarkable collection of documents collected and housed by Miss Caroline Playne in the University of London Library, which provided the basis for her own pioneer studies.[2] For other nations monographs of uneven quality had been produced under the auspices of the Carnegie Endowment for International Peace.[3] But none of this was yet made the basis for any sustained or coherent scholarly examination.

The Second World War awoke a new interest in the relationship between war and social change. Not only did it accelerate, within all the societies involved, the processes of change catalysed by the Great War, but it brought social involvement in belligerent activity to a new level of intensity by eliminating the distinction between 'front line' and 'base'. This distinction had characterised not only the 1914-18 war but the great majority of wars in Europe since the seventeenth century. During the First World War heavy and prolonged pressures had been brought on civilian populations to find vast and continuous resources of men and material for the Front — a word which itself became heavy with sombre meaning — and these pressures were in themselves highly catalytic of social change.[4] But the pressures arising from a situation in which the Front was *everywhere*, whether because of air bombardment as in Britain, Germany and Japan, or because of invasion and occupation as in continental Europe and the Soviet Union, were of a different order of magnitude altogether. It has taken us a generation to get these pressures into perspective and perhaps we have not done so yet. Certainly the experience made it difficult for anyone involved in them to maintain the serene assumption of the Enlightenment that war had not been a major factor in social development but a barbarous aberration which man had outgrown. It also made it difficult to believe, however wrongly and pessimistically, that it would not in some form or another continue to be so.[5] The experience may or may not have made us better political scientists and sociologists, but I have no doubt at all that, by improving our insights into the tragedies and dilemmas of the past, it made us better historians.

This total involvement of society in warfare had not developed evenly. Over the past thousand years in Europe the process had rather been one of ebb and flow. During the period of the 'barbarian invasions' from the fourth to the tenth centuries war was certainly total; a savage struggle for survival between impacably hostile and alien tribes. Then for almost four hundred years – the period which historians were subsequently to term 'feudal' – warfare became a lifestyle among a warrior elite, a recognised and regulated way of settling disputes about property, inheritance and status in which much of the population played little active part. Then from the fifteenth until the end of the eighteenth century these disputes about property and inheritance between ruling families were transformed into disputes about wealth and power between sovereign states. The warrior elites were transformed, first into mercenary contractors doing jobs for anyone who would pay them, and then into professional soldiers maintained full-time by their states with a distinct ethos and subculture of their own. By the eighteenth century a clear distinction has emerged between the concept of 'the military' and that of 'the civilian'; a notion of the warrior as distinguished by function rather than by caste and of war as a specialised activity in which the rest of society was only marginally involved – an activity indeed not only specialised but beginning to be considered as barbarous, foolish and unnecessary.[6]

Then came the French Revolution and with it that ferment of change which Clausewitz was to analyse so definitively in his massive work *On War*. The 'cabinet wars' of the eighteenth century were transformed into the 'absolute wars' of the nineteenth. This transformation was itself a function of the transformation of society which occurred when the narrow social basis of the states-system was broadened by the political participation of new layers of the population – a process

217

which continued ineluctably throughout the nineteenth century. Armies became 'peoples in arms' for whom the professional soldiers provided training, organisation and leadership. The First World War appeared to validate all too aptly the grim lesson which Clausewitz had drawn from his study of the wars of the French Revolution; military achievement depended on maximising the amount of manpower and material one could put into the field. But this in itself depended on achieving the widest possible basis of consensus within society — consensus which it was difficult to achieve without maximising participation or at least a sense of participation. So the broadening of the political basis of the state and the increase in the fighting capacity of the armed forces went hand in hand — from the time of Scharnhorst until that of Lloyd George.

In the First World War the first states to collapse were those where the relics of a feudal political and social structure prevented the full development of democratisation: Imperial Russia, the Habsburg Empire, Wilhelmine Germany — states which succumbed to the contradictions of trying to manipulate the full resources of their communities without either adequate coercion or total consent.[7] This certainly was the lesson which Adolf Hitler drew from that war in the passages of *Mein Kampf* where he developed his theory that both military and political success lay in the successful manipulation of the masses. The model for the conduct of total war he saw in the leadership of David Lloyd George, whose charismatic appeal he contrasted bitterly with 'the futile stammerings of a Bethmann Hollweg'.[8] Only a comparable appeal, he considered, could evoke the full, the inexhaustible response of the German *Volk*.

The requirement for the total participation of the entire community in national war had thus become, by 1918, very clear indeed. But so had the full horror of the result. One must bear in mind that it was not the front line soldiers, with their cheerful reunions and their increasingly nostalgic memories of *Grabenkameradschaft*, who led the revolution against war. (Wilfred Owen, Henri Barbusse and Erich Maria Remarque, with their bitter denunciations of the war, were by no means typical figures, as the documentary material now being accumulated at the Imperial War Museum does much to attest.)[9] Rather it was the civilians who had lost husbands and sons and lovers, the intellectuals of a new generation who read about it, and everyone who remembered the ordeal of shortages and deprivation at home. To all this was added, in the 1930s, the increasing dread of the new horror of bombardment from the air. The growth of this mood made it difficult in any European country for the leadership to obtain that readiness for total participation which the conduct of another war demanded. The outbreak of war in 1914 had been widely welcomed with an ecstasy comparable to that which had greeted the French Revolution. In 1939 it is doubtful whether, except for a limited number of highly indoctrinated German youths, anyone in any nation went to war with any feeling other than sick apprehension.

The sterile destructiveness of the First World War on the Western Front led military thinkers themselves to seek new solutions to the problem: how could war again be made an economical and effective instrument of state policy if it *had* to be fought? There were the prophets of air power who saw the solution in direct attacks on the centres of will and decision in the civilian population who would, they believed, 'after a few days of bombardment rise up and demand an end to the war'.[10] The technological and sociological *naiveté* of this doctrine was to be revealed when in the first part of the Second World War air forces were found to lack the capacity to deliver destruction on anything like the scale predicted as necessary; and in the second part when such destruction was found to be far more effective in consolidating civilian morale than in destroying it.

Others hoped that the development of armoured warfare might lead to a return to the age of 'limited wars' fought purely by professionals; conflicts which, without involving mass conscript armies, could achieve rapid and decisive results.[11] Exaggerated expectations of this kind assumed too readily that the change in the nature of warfare had been due rather to developments in weapon technology or even to 'styles' or 'fashions' in military philosophy than to irreversible and fundamental changes in social consciousness and organisation. So long as twentieth century societies were reasonably coherent, so long as their value systems were evenly shared, their bureaucracies efficient and their elites self-confident, they could still survive the defeat of their professional forces; and indeed respond to the challenge, as was the case with Great Britain and the Soviet Union, with a heightened awareness of their solidarity, an enhanced efficiency in performance.

On the other hand if such societies were *not* reasonably coherent, if they were socially polarised and torn by political strife, it would not take much of a political shock to destroy them. Because the French army in 1940 was so genuinely the French people in arms, a thoroughly citizen force of short service conscripts, it embodied at every level the uncertainties, the divisions and the pessimism of French society as a whole; and it was thrown off balance and destroyed by military setbacks barely comparable with those it had overcome so triumphantly in August and September 1914. No amount of skill in German generalship can explain the events of May and June 1940 if one leaves out of account the political and social confusion of French society as depicted so brilliantly in the work of Marc Bloch, *L'Etrange Défaite*;[12] a confusion to be deepened and embittered by the experience of occupation, liberation and resistance. Nevertheless it *was* an experience in which the seeds of future renewal began to germinate, to an extent which the bitter polemics among French scholars and publicists have hitherto concealed. Not all the heroes were in the Resistance. Several of the measures of the Pétain government were salutary, overdue and have since been quietly consolidated.[13] The time has come perhaps when we can expect a full and definitive study by a major historian of a new generation of the real significance of the Second World War for French society and the structure of the French State.

France fell, not because there was too little participation by society at large in the waging of the war but because there was almost too much. Hitler, on the other hand, owed much of his initial success to his skill in avoiding this: in laying as light a burden as possible on the shoulders of a civilian population which he knew did not share his enthusiasms, to whose loss of morale a quarter of a century earlier he attributed the loss of the First World War and which, he very well knew, expected butter as well as guns. Hitler's *Blitzkrieg* did not require mass participation. His campaigns were fought by armed forces with few reserves either of men or of material, and the diversions from civilian consumption were limited to the specific needs of the campaign in question: armour for the attack on the west in 1940, aircraft and submarines for the war against Britain, tanks again for the attack on Russia in 1941.[14] Like Napoleonic warfare, *Blitzkrieg* assumed instant and total victory as a condition of its success: it predicted the avoidance of prolonged stalemate, of a *bataille d'usure*, of a *Materielenschlacht* such as had brought Germany to her knees in 1918.

This required a very fine tact of judgement; not simply of his enemies' military capacity but of their social cohesion. Hitler had boasted before the war that he would never strike until he judged his adversaries politically ready to fall.[15] His insight was triumphantly justified in May 1940, when it enabled him to take military risks which his military advisers regarded as insane. (He would have preferred indeed to have taken them six months earlier, which they regarded as yet more insane but when they might have been more successful.) It was justified also, negatively, by his reluctance to launch an invasion of the United Kingdom: whatever the military problems involved, Britain was not politically ripe for the plucking. His disastrous mistake lay in his assessment of the Soviet Union, but it was one shared by nearly all western observsers. Hitler believed not only that the Soviet armed forces would be defeated but that the Soviet State, rotted with internal dissension under Stalinist rule, would thereupon disintegrate.[16]

The Soviet armies were indeed defeated, but the Soviet State did not disintegrate. And this political miscalculation, combined with comparable miscalculations about a United States which he did not begin to understand, landed Hitler with that *guerre d'usure*, that total war which he had tried to spare German society and which he knew he must lose. Yet once the German people were confronted with the requirements of total war in 1942 they responded with dour determination. German society remained cohesive until the bitter end. Why? Partly because all possible major *foci* of dissidence had already been tidied away into concentration camps — all save a handful of courageous but ineffectual conspirators within the governing class whose attempted *coup* on 20 July 1944, even if it had succeeded, might well have been crushed by the SS within two or three days. Partly because the *Parteiapparat* provided a most effective instrument both of encouragement and of coercion. Partly because aerial bombardment, until it became truly unendurable at the end of 1944, created a sense of enhanced group solidarity at every level of society. And partly because from 1943 onwards the Germans believed that they were fighting not just for national but for personal survival, against a threat from the east which embodied all the atavistic fears which had lurked in their collective subconscious, renewed by myth, history and indoctrination over a thousand years. Anglo-American attacks in the Mediterranean and France, western demands for 'unconditional surrender', were minor irritations and irrelevances compared with the gigantic menace advancing on them from the east.[17]

And the Russians believed that they were fighting not just for group but for personal survival, with very good reason. In the first place the Soviet peoples had been taught ever since 1921 to consider themselves in a state of siege, surrounded by hostile reactionary states bent on destroying the achievements of the Revolution. Their leaders believed not only that any future war would be total but that sooner or later it was bound to come. Russian military training, indoctrination and organisation were devised accordingly.[18] In the second place, whereas German propaganda may have misrepresented Soviet intentions towards the German people, the Soviet government needed only to state the stark truth of what the Germans intended to do in the Soviet Union and indeed did do in the areas they occupied.[19] One might have considered it difficult to present the peoples of the Soviet Union with an alternative more disagreeable than the regime which they had endured for the past twenty years, but it was a difficulty which the Nazi leadership very successfully overcame.

Thus the Germans squandered all the political advantages with which they began their campaign in 1941. Probably at that time, in the aftermath of the Great Purges, Soviet society was as confused, divided and pessimistic as the French had been a year earlier, and, like the French, the Soviet armed forces faithfully reflected this confusion at every level. Yet underlying all this there evidently remained a deep sense of social cohesion, if only on a local basis, which had *time* to develop and *space* in which to operate. Society in the areas over-run coagulated again in great partisan movements.[20] In the territories which still resisted the Party provided both an iron skeleton and a nervous system supporting and initiating activity at every level, military, agricultural, industrial and recreational. Even the most politically apathetic or reluctant Soviet citizens accepted its claim to primacy and obedience as perhaps they never had before. Even Joseph Stalin, that entirely uncharismatic figure whose exercise of power had hitherto been as unobtrusive and conspiratorial as it was vindictive and ruthless, emerged in the uncharacteristic role of a great national leader hobnobbing on the world stage with other great national leaders. Hitler's attempt to smash Soviet communism, or reduce the Russian people to the status of serfs, thus had the effect of endowing the party structure and the party leadership with a strength and a legitimacy such as it had never previously possessed; which enabled the Soviet Union not only to survive the German attack but to emerge after the war as one of the most formidable powers, if not the most formidable, in the world.[21]

It was the same sense of absolute threat to personal and group survival, although perhaps less well grounded, that evoked total if belated participation in Britain once the war began in earnest in the summer of 1940. In spite of its rigid class structure — perhaps indeed because of it — Britain was probably still the most socially cohesive major nation in Europe between the wars; but it was a cohesion increasingly eroded by political and industrial conflict. The governing classes were divided and unsure of themselves. The intelligentsia exhibited all the symptoms of a culture in decline, turning inward to esoteric art forms and the cultivation of privacy and nostalgia in socially exclusive cliques. Only the weakness of a Labour Party which never recovered from the split of 1931 obscured the widespread doubts as to the competence of the 'National' government as a whole — though one must not under-rate the degree of personal support enjoyed by both Baldwin and Chamberlain throughout the country. There was in short at the end of Auden's 'low dishonest decade' a very general sense of self-mistrust, almost of self-disgust, which betrayed a widespread social malaise.

Under pressure in the spring of 1940 it became clear how very little support in the nation as a whole the Conservative leadership commanded. If Churchill had not been available one can rack one's brains in vain to think of one of its members who could have provided a focus for national consensus. That Churchill *was* there was providential, and on his role as a charismatic national leader, his remarkable capacity for blending the aristocratic with the demotic, one hardly needs to dwell. But that a national consensus did exist to be focused, that the bewilderment and apprehension with which the British entered the war was blown away almost overnight, was due not to Churchill but to Hitler and the direct sense of menace — a sense almost invigorating after the vague nightmares of the 1930s — created by the German conquest of Western Europe in the summer of 1940, by the threat of invasion, and by the air attacks which followed.[22]

Angus Calder in his brilliant study *The People's War* (1969) has made — and perhaps overstressed — the point that it was not the efficiency of governmental organisation but its inefficiency, its lack of appropriate preparation, its ignorance of great areas of social life throughout Britain through lack of information and the means of gathering it, that evoked the spontaneous, improvised and really almost total participation of all sections of British society in the organisation of the country for war. Such matters as the evacuation of cities, settlement of refugees, organisation of rescue and welfare work in air raids, job allocation in factories, entertainment and other morale building measures, and allocation of scarce goods were necessarily done as cooperative efforts between the authorities and local communities, and communities virtually created themselves to do it. Suburbs hardly conscious of having an identity became, with their ARP, their WVS and their Home Guard as proud and self-conscious as the embattled London boroughs in G. K. Chesterton's novel *The Napoleon of Notting Hill*.

The sense of total participation was all the greater because for most of the war Britain was not simply providing a base for armed forces who were fighting overseas. The greater part of the army and the air force remained at home until 1944, mooching disconsolately around training camps and air bases, shuttling to and fro on leave in their cumbrous equipment in cold, ill lit, overcrowded trains, crowding into dance halls at week-ends, not only part of society but society itself. Moreover (and this of course applied to all the belligerent powers) because of the enormous demand for ancillary services in the armed forces, a great proportion of servicemen were doing jobs indistinguishable from civilians: driving and maintaining trucks, working in hospitals, running stores depots, working nine to five jobs in offices, plying their civilian trades as engineers, doctors, musicians, schoolteachers. Generals had to acquire entirely new managerial skills. And finally, perhaps most important, the physical danger for civilians was no less than for all but a tiny minority of the armed forces. Of the 360,000 UK citizens killed in the Second World War — which was perhaps one fiftieth of the number of Russians who died — one in four was a civilian. one in ten a seaman in the Merchant Navy.[23] The armed forces were in fact only one group — or three groups — among others no less vital to the war effort — miners, dockers, steelworkers, farmers — among whom increasingly scarce resources of man (and woman) power had to be allocated.[24]

For British society as a whole, the lasting results of the Second World War were threefold. First, there was a great and accepted increase in both governmental power over the community and sense of responsibility for the community; a dedication to the goal of what Sir William Beveridge called 'Full Employment in a Free Society', and an acceptance of the ideas of John Maynard Keynes as the means of achieving this. Whereas in 1918 there had been a strong desire to return to prewar conditions of 'normalcy', in 1945 it was common ground between all parties that the experience of war should be used to build a new and better Britain, the foundations of which had already been laid under the coalition government. Secondly the United Kingdom emerged as socially a far more homogenous society than she had been in 1939 – a continuation of the general trend traced by Professor Arthur Marwick in his work *Britain in the Century of Total War* (1968). And third, she emerged far poorer, with all her overseas assets liquidated: in a word, broke. The British people may have had far greater aspirations towards social welfare and equity but they had far fewer resources to accomplish them with; and few of them realised, then or since, the extent to which, since 1940, they had been pensioners of the United States.

As for America, her position had been remarkably similar to that of Britain in the First World War. Like the British government before 1914, Roosevelt's administration before 1941 had realised the need, in terms of power politics, to be prepared to fight Germany, but did not see how this could be done without hopelessly dividing a nation profoundly unprepared, psychologically as well as materially, for any kind of war. Like the British in 1914 their problem was solved for them by a surprise military *coup* on the part of their adversaries that affronted all shades of opinion and created a sense of unity that made total participation possible. Like Britain in 1914-18, American forces fought entirely outside their own country; so the Americans did not suffer that experience of war in depth which was so traumatic an experience for all other belligerents. And finally, like Britain in 1914-18. the war made possible and necessary for the United States an increase in governmental power at home which was irreversible, and the assumption of responsibilities abroad which were unavoidable.

But unlike Britain, who fought the First World War with an economy which was already on the decline, the United States emerged from the war richer and not poorer, with a people prepared as never before to endorse its government's claims to act as a world power. For most of the American people the Second World War was not seen as a time of suffering in any way comparable to the Great Depression ten years earlier. The unemployed got jobs and businesses boomed. Only a small minority considered either at the time or in retrospect that

America had been mistaken in getting involved in the war; the mistake had been, by ignoring the world outside, to allow it to happen at all.

And, finally, the Americans became conscious of themselves as a military nation. Previously the archetypes of the American military man had been such quasi-civilian figures as Stonewall Jackson and Ulysses S. Grant. Now they had fully professional military heroes, George Patton and Douglas MacArthur, who could rank with Wellington or Marlborough; and a great military organiser in George Catlin Marshall who could hold his own with Carnot or Moltke. So 1945 was not for the United States what 1918 had been for Britain, the end of an almost insupportable ordeal. Rather it was what 1871 had been for Germany; not an end but a beginning. The American leadership stood ready to shoulder the burden of world responsibilities. The American century had, in their view, now really begun.

Notes

1. Sir George Aston (ed.), *The Study of War for Statesmen and Citizens* (1927).
2. Caroline Playne, *Society at War 1914-16* (1931) and *Britain Hold On, 1917-1918* (1933).
3. Perhaps the only serious sociological study in the series is that by A. Mendelssohn Bartholdy, *The War and German Society* (New Haven, 1937). The remainder tend to deal narrowly with economic issues.
4. The process has been well analysed by Arthur Marwick, *The Deluge: British Society & the First World War* (1965).
5. For a staunch American defence of the liberal and optimistic view against such European pessimism see J. U. Nef, *War and Human Progress* (1950).
6. This *tour d'horizon* is based, as all such surveys must be, on the first four volumes of Hans Delbrück, *Geschichte der Kriegskunst im Rahme der Politische Geschichte* (Berlin, 1908-20). But on the eighteenth century and the beginnings of military specialisation see especially E. Léonard, *L'Armée et ses problèmes au XVIIe siècle* (Paris, 1958).
7. It is arguable that in the case of Germany at least this backward social structure accounted not for Germany's defeat, which was due rather to the realities of the military situation once the United States had entered the war, but for the fact that defeat was accompanied by revolution. A 'democratised' Germany might have made peace sooner; but also it might, if presented with unacceptable terms, have attempted to prolong the struggle as did France in 1870.
8. Adolf Hitler, *Mein Kampf* (1939), 156-63, 396.
9. For a study far more indicative of the phlegmatic mood with which the mass of British soldiers endured the war see George Coppard, *With a Machine-Gun to Cambrai* (1969).
10. Giulio Douhet, *The Command of the Air* (1941), 52. For seminal discussions within the Royal Air Force see Sir Charles Webster and A. N. Frankland, *The Strategic Bombing Offensive Against Germany* (4 vols., 1961), IV, Appendix I.
11. Although British thinkers took the lead in studying the tactical and strategic possibilities of armoured warfare, its political and social possibilities were most imaginatively examined by Charles de Gaulle, *Vers l'armée de métier* (Paris, 1934).

12.   Marc Bloch, *Strange Defeat* (Oxford, 1949). For the general background of French military policy see Richard D. Challener, *The French Theory of the Nation in Arms 1866-1939* (New York, 1965).

13.   See the seminal article by Stanley Hoffman, 'The Effects of World War II on French Society and Politics' in *French Historical Studies*, I (April 1961).

14.   Alan Millward, *The German Economy at War* (1965).

15.   Hermann Rauschning, *Hitler Speaks* (1939), 14-21, 208-10.

16.   For Hitler's plans and intentions towards the Soviet Union see Barry A. Leach, *German Strategy against Russia 1939-1941* (Oxford, 1973).

17.   See especially Albert Speer, *Inside the Third Reich* (1970).

18.   See John Erickson, *The Soviet High Command 1917-1941* (1962), esp. ch. X.

19.   Alexander Dallin, *German Rule in Russia 1941-45* (1957) and Norman Rich, *Hitler's War Aims: The Establishment of the New Order* (1974).

20.   John A. Armstrong, *Soviet Partisans in World War II* (Madison, Wisconsin, 1964).

21.   Alexander Werth, *Russia at War 1941-45* (1964).

22.   Henry Pelling, *Britain and the Second World War* (1970) is a balanced account by an expert political historian.

23.   *Statistical Digest of the War prepared in the Central Statistical Office* (1951), 13.

24.   H. M. D. Parker, *Manpower* (in *History of the Second World War*, Civil Series, 1957).

226

NEITHER HEROES NOR TRAITORS: SUGGESTIONS FOR A REAPPRAISAL OF THE YUGOSLAV RESISTANCE

Stevan K. Pavlowitch

'If a man will begin with certainties, he shall end in doubt: but if he will be content to begin with doubts he shall end in certainties' (Francis Bacon). Basil Davidson, who begins his *Old Africa Rediscovered* (1964) with this quotation, goes on to write in the introduction to his book: 'I have tried to steer between the rock of prejudice and the whirlwind of romance.' The history of Yugoslavia during the Second World War has, in the twenty-five years following the end of the war, generally been moored to the rock of prejudice whenever it was not sailing through the whirlwind of romance, for most of the skippers — its chroniclers — began with certainties.

In Yugoslavia itself, political reasons have dictated the official line of post-war historiography — that there had been no civil strife between the Yugoslavs at the time of the occupation by the Axis powers, but just a war waged by the communist led partisans under Marshal Tito on the side of the Allies against the Axis forces and their native auxiliaries, the chief of whom was General Mihailović.[1] Outside Yugoslavia, the narration of her wartime experiences has been the quasi-preserve of British writers. Former liaison officers with Yugoslav guerrillas, and one time officials of various special departments, executives and other services have written their narratives.[2] Most of them were either with Tito's partisans, body and heart, in the *maquis*, or in sympathy with them, from London, Cairo and Bari. Some are quite simply autobiographical and tell us what they saw; others, more ambitiously, attempt to reconstruct the whole story. Two of the latter, because of their academic positions and of their access to the Yugoslav leader, have become particularly known for presenting the unblemished image of heroes to whom they are emotionally attached: Phyllis Auty and F. W. D. Deakin, who have also published papers and articles in Yugoslavia, in Serbo-Croatian. Constantly and anonymously reiterated by *The Times Literary Supplement* in the early 1970s,[3] such an attitude has acquired — at least in this country — virtually the standing of an 'authorised version'. At the same time, in the obscurity of the *émigré* underworld, Mihailović has been revered as a martyr. Nobody in their senses listens to the survivors of the losing party, but in so far as the

227

one sided story told by right wing exiles reached the British public, it could only serve to reinforce the other, the chic, one sided version.[4]

The lapse of three decades is now slowly beginning to set these events in perspective. There are memoirs and diaries, apologetic and inquisitorial interpretations from all sides.[5] Many Yugoslav documents have been published, under official auspices in Yugoslavia, and at haphazard all over the *émigré* world. Simply by collating all these, impressions can be gained of the kaleidoscopic chaos of the period, which do much to destroy the deceptively neat simplicity of most published British narratives. American and British war archives have recently been made available, although the records of many special services have not been released or have actually been destroyed. German and Italian documents enable us to see that what the Allies believed was happening did not always coincide with what was really taking place.[6] And scholars in America and in Germany are actually becoming aware of the inadequacy of the existing descriptive literature.[7]

In Yugoslavia too, a hesitant, though perhaps premature, start was made a few years ago by more scholarly minded historians who criticised the 'sclerosis' of an official historiography monopolised by a set of amateurs personally involved in the events they describe. President Tito himself admitted on Yugoslav television on 12 May 1972: 'It was really a fully fledged civil war, but we did not want to admit it at the time, because it would have been detrimental to our cause.'[8]

The Second World War in Yugoslavia was not a neat story of resistance and collaboration, but a messy tale of civil strife and revolution. Populations speaking more or less the same language, living more or less the same way of life, drawn together yet drawn apart through history, had been precipitated into unification by the First World War. The common enterprise would have been a difficult one even if attempted under the best possible conditions. The difficult times of the twenties and thirties did not make it any easier. Serbs and Croats were the two largest historically conscious groups in Yugoslavia, and the nearest to each other, both culturally and territorially. The former, however, reacted as a satisfied majority, for the new state had inherited many of the characteristics of their own limited pre-war kingdom. The others reacted as a dissatisfied minority, for the united state had not turned out as they had envisaged it, and they were not numerous enough to change its structure through constitutional means. Feeding on the disillusionment of most Croats, a faction — the *ustasa* movement — turned to separatism and violence. It had taken a world war for Yugoslavia to come prematurely into the world, yet however shaky its conditions, it was to take another world war to destroy the Kingdom of Yugoslavia.

Caught half prepared by the German attack in April 1941, ill equipped and outnumbered, the Yugoslav army was quickly surrounded

228

and cut off from the outside. Croatia seceded under the ustashas. The King and government left the country. The Yugoslav state was said by the enemy to have been annihilated along with its army. The Italians claimed Dalmatia, and also wished to supervise a string of vassal states on the other side of 'their' Adriatic sea. The Germans, for their part, did not want much more than to control the important communication lines, and to thoroughly crush the Serbs, whom Hitler considered to be the main disturbers of the European order. All territorial demands at the expense of regions inhabited by them were accepted, all possible separatisms encouraged, all tensions pushed to paroxysm. As for the Croats, it was hoped to be able to bring them over to the Axis. Their fascist type ustasha fringe was allowed to set up a nominally independent yet client state of Croatia — better known by its initials, NDH (Nezavisna Drzava Hrvatska) — over all the territories inhabited by Croats, except that Mussolini insisted on keeping most of the coast, and that the ustashas found themselves with almost as many 'aliens' as Catholic Croats. The problem of the Orthodox Serbs in the NDH would be solved — it was openly announced — by conversion, expulsion and extermination.

The reactions of the country to the destruction of the Yugoslav state were many and various. They can be grouped under four headings: 1. To take advantage of it in order to realise sectional dreams under the Axis umbrella. 2. To take advantage of it in order to destroy the whole existing structure, and to prepare the way for a new revolutionary order. 3. To try and keep the pre-war fabric from altogether falling to pieces while the going was bad, and to prepare for the day when the country would once again play an active part in international affairs. 4. To organise locally in order to survive.

Resistance could mean to oppose the enemy occupation, or to oppose any of the reactions listed; more usually a mixture of the one and the other. Resistance, furthermore, was not necessarily military: it could also be political, moral or psychological. Three facts, however, were to facilitate guerrilla action: 1. The rapidity with which the Yugoslav army had been defeated. The greater part had not even seen action. Many officers and men had gone into hiding, or simply home. Vast quantities of arms lay about, which people had been concealing. 2. The fact that the Balkan peninsula was strategically important for the Axis powers only in so far as they held the main communication lines and mineral deposits. Because the enemy also had other lands to occupy, as well as to fight on the African and Russian fronts, it could not afford to control physically the whole Yugoslav territory. 3. The constant friction between Germany and Italy, each with her own interests, policies, clients, and her own zone of occupation.

For most people, the principal worry was to survive, and insurrection could only be an act of hope, or of hopelessness. So dissimilar were the conditions in each of the sections of partitioned Yugoslavia, that in the summer of 1941 there was a series of independent risings, in different regions, for different reasons, against different enemies. The most important took place in the 'Independent State of Croatia' and in the 'Territory of the German Military Commander in Serbia' (*Gebiet des Militärbefehlshaber Serbiens*). In the former, the ferocious racialism of the ustashas caused the Serbian peasantry to rise in self-defence, against extermination. In the latter, an upsurge of pro-Allied enthusiasm at the time of Hitler's break with the USSR caused a rising against the Germans.

It was this rising which gave two groups the chance to set themselves up above all others with aims which were more than strictly local. One, around the debris of the regular army under Mihailović, tried to ensure the continuity of the Yugoslav state by organising a clandestine network linked to the government that had taken refuge in London. The other, around the Communist Party cadres under Tito, wanted to promote their revolutionary aims at a time when conditions suddenly seemed to have become particularly favourable.

By the end of 1941, the Germans had crushed the insurrection in Serbia. They had come to within a hairsbreadth of capturing the two rival leaders who escaped literally by taking to their heels.[9] Mihailović went underground but remained in Serbia, a region of great homogeneity, ethnically, religiously and even socially with its relatively prosperous smallholding rural population dominant. But it was also a region closely watched by the Germans, for through it ran the Belgrade-Salonika line. Mihailović was saved by the active support of important sections of the peasantry, the bourgeoisie and the former military. Thereafter, he concentrated on organising a network which enabled him to follow events, and prepare for an insurrection he would launch when the Allies were near enough to make it useful without turning it into a holocaust. The losses of 1941 (of the April war, of the ustasha massacres, and of the German repression in Serbia) could not be forgotten, nor could the direct German control of the territory he was in.

Tito, on the other hand, went to the other end of the country — to Serbian inhabited western Bosnia, in the NDH. The war there had been more an instance of paranoiac ustasha racialism than of German and Italian oppression. For the survivors of this desperately poor region, there was often less risk in joining the armed bands than in remaining in the villages. Communist guerrillas were left relatively undisturbed there by the occupation forces, so long as they did not get too near the river Save communication line, or did not become too important. Tito was saved by his 'long march' to western Bosnia, where he could concentrate on organising a revolutionary guerrilla.

Although both these movements bore Yugoslav labels, they were expressions of an essentially Serbian resistance, for it was the Serbs alone whom the Axis treated collectively as vanquished foes. Few Croats could be attracted to either Mihailović or Tito, for few of them wanted either a restoration of the pre-war regime, or a communist revolution, however disappointed most of them were with ustasha 'independence'. If the Axis powers had set the components of Yugoslavia against each other in an unprecedented way, the dismembered country also set Germans and Italians against each other. The strength and determination of the Reich offered scant possibilities of action to the insurgents of the German occupation zone. Italian commanders, on the other hand, had no clear idea of the role they were expected to play in the Balkans, but they realised that a purely military solution was, in the long run, impossible in regions where the population on the whole sympathised with the Allies. Since their German and Croatian partners were against the Serbs, the Italians soon took to using the Serbian armed bands of their zone as a counterweight to ustashas and Germans, all the more so since this stratagem was effectively to divide the Serbs themselves.

The insurgents first called themselves 'chetniks' (*cetnik*, pl. *cetnici*), after the popular irregulars of earlier wars against the Turks. If the bands were taken over or organised by communists, they became 'partisans', after the Soviet irregulars fighting the Germans behind the lines. Starting with the harsh winter of 1941-2, they divided increasingly into communists and anti-communists, popularly known as partisans and chetniks, and they were taken over by, adhered to, or simply made use of the name of one or other of the two more ambitious movements, Mihailović's and Tito's, who preferred to use the names respectively of Yugoslav Home Army and of People's Liberation Movement. For all guerrillas in occupied Yugoslavia, whatever their original aims and their publicised slogans, to survive, and then to eliminate native opponents, quickly became more important than to fight the foreign occupants. Henceforth the Germans were able to concentrate their efforts on one of the two movements, while the other looked on, or even took advantage in order to fall upon its rivals from the rear. Sporadic fighting alternated with a 'legal existence', the latter to obtain food, equipment, funds and information, to attend to the wounded or to comrades otherwise in trouble, to look for recruits, to infiltrate collaborationist administrations and armed forces, or simply to lead a normal existence when the *maquis* was inactive.

In the rugged and mountainous western regions, poor and disorganised Serbian peasants had taken up arms to defend their lives. The armed bands which had sprung into being under improvised leaders retained their identity after they had achieved their first immediate aim, often without realising where this would lead them, whom it would eventually help, and whom they were really fighting. The occupation forces and their ustasha *protégés* had not been able to eliminate the chetniks. They had to agree to sharing power with them, on the basis of unofficial, local, non-aggression arrangements, and they had set rival bands against each other, for there was disagreement among them as how to best 'save Serbian lives'. Italian commanders had stepped in to protect the victims of ustasha activities, and were ready to parley. Their attitude, the arrival of the communists from the east, and harsh economic reasons, were leading the improvised chieftains of 1941 in the Italian zone to forms of collaboration with the Italian army against ustashas and communists. In those areas where some sort of insurgent authority had established itself as a buffer between the Orthodox peasantry and the ustashas of the foreign occupants, communists could do little as yet. But elsewhere there were even more bereft and bereaved Serbian peasants. The Croats themselves were increasingly disappointed by the chaotic ustasha regime, whose very nationalism had had to give in, first to its Italian protectors, then to the Serbian 'bandits'. They could not turn to Italy, and they were afraid of Serbian vengeance. For the insurgents had responded to the fanatic and terroristic anti-Serbian Croatian nationalism of the ustashas with narrow anti-Croatian Serbian nationalism. The communists were thus able to increase their influence in Croatia in 1942, by harnessing the plight of the western Serbs for revolutionary aims, and by infiltrating the apathetic administration and army of the NDH.

The chetnik leaders of the Italian zone had taken up arms independently of Mihailović, and for other reasons. They had then come to terms with occupation authorities without asking for his advice, but in the summer of 1942 they were anxious to acknowledge him as a nominal supreme authority. They considered their arrangements with the Italians as a temporary expedient, and saw no contradiction in this double acting. There is evidence, as yet indirect, that the British shared this view. As for Mihailović, he took the risk and accepted the link. He knew that these chetniks would never fight with Axis forces against the British. They kept the communists in check, and they made his movement appear more widespread, which was important now that he had been acknowledged, by the Yugoslav government and by the Allies, as leader of the Yugoslav resistance. He believed the Western Allies would one day land in the country, and in the meanwhile — with support from abroad — he hoped he could influence the local chetnik captains to change their tactics and their ideas, or that he could get rid of them if necessary. He also hoped to be able to destroy the NDH through them, for they were still involved in countless clashes with Germans and ustashas. But they had already achieved all that they could achieve, and where his authority was not direct, he was not able to impose it. He was the organiser of an underground movement in one particular region. In the conditions in which he operated, his conceptions were the nearest to those of the Yugoslav government and of the Western Allies. Where his influence was strong, his was a movement in resistance to occupation forces and their native auxiliaries, and one that, by defending the peasants, offered an alternative to seeking the protection of occupation armies. At the same time, he was now nominal overall commander of armed formations over which he had no effective authority, and which were increasingly dependent on the Italians. His was a gamble that he lost. It was used by the communists in propaganda against him, it made it difficult for him to find an audience among the Croats, and no Allied landing took place on the Yugoslav coast.

Out of the complex pattern of 1942, Tito's communist movement, after it had been almost destroyed, emerged like a phoenix. Its sudden development in the mixed western regions after its defeat in the homogeneous Serbian lands of the east, where the populations had turned against it, was due to a number of reasons. It penetrated the desperate struggle against extermination started by the Serbs in the NDH; it prevented that struggle from turning to generalised vengeance against the Croats; and it gave it a belief in a better world to come no longer immediately identifiable as Godless collectivism.

The object of SOE, the British 'Special Operations' Executive, had been, originally, to organise in every occupied country of the Continent a disciplined network grouping the different political tendencies of the resistance. Its operations would, when the time came, be coordinated with those of Allied armies. In the meanwhile, it should aim at a level of activity which kept its members busy, and inconvenienced the occupying powers, without risking the destruction of the organisation, which was to act under British tutelage. This balance had been upset that summer in Yugoslavia by the premature rising of communists and of remains of the regular army. The Germans having crushed it, British (and Soviet) interest in the Yugoslav resistance lessened. Left to their own devices in 1942, the insurgents survived by mimicry and mobility, extending and fighting each other.

At the end of that year, with the crisis over in North Africa, interest in Yugoslavia increased. The enemy was to be misled about the whereabouts of an Allied landing in Europe. Even if this were not to be on the Yugoslav coast, the evacuation of Axis troops from the peninsula to another European front had to be blocked. The sudden threat of a Balkan front made the Germans want to destroy all rebels, and for them, Mihailović was the greatest potential danger, for they feared the possibility of his linking together numerous other formations which, as Hitler believed, were biding their time to strike a blow against the Axis when the Allies landed. Italian generals, however, were not enthusiastic about the German plan. Quite apart from the fact that they did not believe in the success of large scale anti-guerrilla action, they wanted to get out of the Yugoslav quagmire, not deeper in. Defeatism was ripe in their army. Moreover, some of them now more than suspected the local chetniks' links with Mihailović, and they were anxious to keep contacts which could have been extended to the Anglo-Americans when they landed. The Italians participated only halfheartedly in the great German directed operations of January-March 1943, the communists managed to squeeze out of the trap, and the anti-communists were not destroyed, yet both suffered heavy losses.

The entanglement of antagonisms and arrangements between different sides became increasingly complicated and bloody. At the end of 1941, there had been contacts between the Germans in Belgrade and Mihailović.[10] In the spring of 1943, it was the turn of Tito and the Germans in Zagreb.[11] In 1941 as in 1943, one of the Yugoslav rebel leaders was in dire need, fighting against superior Axis troops and native opponents simultaneously, with no help from the Allies. German intelligence realised what Hitler did not realise: that the guerrillas were at the end of their tether, but that short of killing everybody, the rope could not be cut. Local German commanders feared that, bu pushing things to extremes, they would achieve what the Allies could not: a common front of the rival factions. Hints of a possible accommodation were probed into. Mihailović in 1941 and Tito in 1943 had the same message for the Germans. Neither intended to capitulate, but in so far as each wanted to concentrate on fighting his native opponents, he was ready for a ceasefire with the Germans, and wished to suggest respective territorial interests. The motives of the partisan leaders were complicated by the fact of their determination to oppose a landing on the Yugoslav coast by the Western Allies. In both cases, the talks came to nothing.[12]

From the British point of view, arrangements with the Italians were no longer justified as 1942 came to a close, especially as they turned the local guerrillas to fighting mostly against each other. By that time, SOE was beginning to discover the partisans as well, but they were unable to get them and the chetniks to work together, so it was decided to contact the communist leader, and at the same time to demand increased activity from Mihailović. In order to oblige, however, the latter wanted to know why these demands were made on him, and he wanted to be sure that he would obtain effective backing. Just as the British were, from that time, opposed to arrangements between chetniks and Italians, so were the Russians angry when they discovered something of

the contacts between partisans and Germans. The Yugoslav rebels tried
to hide such embarassing facts from their Allies, because they needed
their material support, and they said so, at the same time as they tried
to exploit the powers' exasperation with their political rivals.

Mihailović had tried to take advantage of the Sovier exasperation
with the partisans' premature revolutionary zeal in 1941, but his
movement had remained predominantly military. Tito's was essentially
political, and he was quick to take advantage of British exasperation
with the chetniks. Although a landing in Yugoslavia was no longer contemplated, the Allied invasion of Italy, early in July 1943, made it
necessary to exploit every opportunity of involving the enemy on the
other side of the Adriatic. The Axis powers still believed that Mihailović would turn out to be the leader of a nationwide movement as soon
as the Allies came anywhere near Yugoslavia, and so considered him the
greatest *potential* danger, but the Anglo-Americans came to be convinced of the *effective* superiority of Tito's organisation. Thus it was
that SOE, in order to get more out of it, stopped insisting on British
tutelage, and even came to accept the communist version, that the
People's Liberation Movement was the only real resistance, no longer
just the more effective.

With the Italian armistice, Italian troops in Yugoslavia were instructed to surrender to the partisans. This was the first opportunity
that either of the two movements had of arming and equipping itself
properly. The collapse of Italy brought about the deflation of the local
chetnik formations, and all those who wanted to join the victorious
Allies in what had been the Italian occupation zone threw in their lot
with the partisans. The early autumn of 1943 was a period of euphoria
for Tito. The Allies were more interested than ever in the possibilities
of Yugoslav resistance but, paradoxically, by the time they had definitely turned to Tito, in November, their advance had been slowed down
in Italy, and the Germans in Yugoslavia once again had the situation in
hand. By that time, also, Mihailović's position had become distinctly
weaker.

By the turn of 1943-4, the expected victory of Yugoslavia's allies
meant that the country would be restored as an independent and
united state after the war, whatever the regime, and this simplified the
nature of the civil war. Its ethnic aspect was receding. The separatists
who had, willy nilly, thrown in their lot with the occupying powers,
were fast declining. The resisters, on the other hand, even if they had
not always fought locally with that aim in mind, were led by people who
wanted to maintain a unified Yugoslav state. The average Yugoslav,
whether he sympathised with the one or the other movement, or with
neither, did not wish a return to the past, but did not think in terms of
revolution, which forced the one side to radicalise its appeal, and the

other to moderate its image. The longer they resisted, the more both came to look at the occupation as a temporary phenomenon, the more they became concerned with one another – one side with the threat of a Soviet backed communist revolution, the other with the menace of the moderates coming to power supported by the English and Americans. As much blood was thus shed in fighting between Yugoslavs for the restoration of Yugoslavia as had been let earlier in the fighting between Yugoslavs that had threatened to destroy Yugoslavia beyond repair.

More than ever, the Germans aimed at controlling those areas which they considered of decisive importance. This they were able to achieve even without Italy, but only at the price of giving the rest over to guerrillas, and of resorting to political warfare with even greater emphasis. To fan the flames of civil war, German propaganda depicted one set as sinister agents of Red terror, the other as deluded hangers-on of the perfidious Anglo-Saxons. There was now also a tendency locally to try out what had been the Italians' policy of using anti-communists against communists, but it was kept in check by opposition from Berlin and by the unabated pursuance of reprisals. The net result was to drastically reduce resistance to the Germans over the winter of 1943-4. The contenders could tie down a certain number of German troops. They could not hope to free Yugoslavia from German control.

In the spring of 1944, the Germans made one last major effort to disorganise all insurgents, and to capture the heads of both movements. Once again, Mihailović and Tito just managed to escape capture, but the latter actually had to be rescued from Yugoslavia for a while by the Allies, who definitely and completely dropped the former. Because the communist leader had most profited from the collapse of Italy, and because he was obtaining more and more help from the Allies, he was able not only to successfully hold out against the Germans, but to extend his movement. We can see him defending himself, fighting against Mihailović, but doing as little as his rival to help the Allies destroy the military structure of the German occupation, or thwart the evacuation of the Balkan peninsula. During the politically crucial summer of 1944, when the British were trying to obtain a compromise between King Peter and Tito, there was, generally speaking, no large scale resistance against the Germans in Yugoslavia.

The communists had a clear political aim. In spite of numerous tactical errors, they had quickly established an overall unity of strategy. This enabled them to exploit the situation, and to show a bolder, single face to the world outside. There was no such unity of purpose among the anti-communists, not even among those who were staunchly pro-Allies. Mihailović had attempted to impose some form of military unity, and had failed. The government abroad had also imposed a political role on him, and that had failed.

The NDH had been well suited for Tito's movement to grow in. The more obvious the coming defeat of Germany, and the nearer the break-up of the satellite ustasha state, the greater the number of Croats who wanted to leave that sinking boat. The People's Liberation Movement provided a way out, and it was in such an atmosphere that it grew, especially as Allied support (which had been symbolic until the end of 1943, for both left and right) was generous since the end of the winter, and forthcoming to Tito alone.[13] Nevertheless, he still did not cut much ice in the east generally, where the population was, on the whole, antagonistic to the partisans. Serbia in particular — Mihailović's base and the bastion of his Yugoslav Home Army — was still out of bounds. While the Germans carried out a well directed gradual evacuation, there was fighting between the partisans trying to force their way into Serbia, and the chetniks trying to fend them off. September 1944, when the Red Army reached Yugoslavia's eastern borders, saw a sudden rise in the military operations of the resistance forces against the Germans. Soviet forces helped the partisans free Belgrade, and went on to Hungary, leaving the Yugoslavs once again to liberate the rest of their country by themselves, and fight their civil war to an end. The war against Germany in Yugoslavia was to continue for another seven months after the fall of Belgrade, and for a full week after the end of the war on other European fronts.[14] As for the civil war, it dragged on until after Mihailović's capture in March 1946, and eventually petered out in the 'fifties.[15]

'Resistance' in Yugoslavia during the Second World War was resistance to the *Neuordnung* imposed by the Axis powers, but it was also resistance to the 'new order' which the revolution was seen to be bringing, so that the opposition between *resistance* and *revolution* was at least as important as that between *resistance* and *collaboration*, and the two grids always have to be superimposed, even if the operation produces patterns difficult for Western European eyes to read. Resistance to the occupation forces was efficient to the point of destroying the possibility of a long term military solution over the whole area, of bogging down important enemy forces. On the other hand, the forces thus paralysed were not as strong as the Allies believed.[16] The Germans could always go through and occupy any portion of territory, and no native force was ever able to effect a lasting interruption of traffic on the main communication lines.

All the native armed formations — legalists, revolutionaries, and the endless range of bands locally recruited to protect different sections of the population — whatever their aims, claims and colours, all of them, in order to survive, had to adjust themselves to hard realities. Whatever

the official policies at national level, all of them appealed to, or antag-
onised, the population, locally and temporarily, by politically or
ethnically motivated actions. And because these changed in order to
come to terms with more important realities, there were many shifts
of allegiance, both individual and collective.

The Allies, according to their needs, had glorified first Mihailović,
and then Tito, exaggerating the importance of their champion, closing
their eyes to his accommodations. The propaganda which helped the
one, then the other, also created misunderstandings between the Yugoslavs and their allies. Each one of the two movements, at one given
time, felt the need to appear stronger to the Allies than it really was.
Hence their tendency to exaggerate exploits, to accept into their ranks
ex- or quasi-collaborators, to round off numbers and make them look
bigger. The Allies wanted to help those who seemed stronger, but also
those who were deemed more compliant. Hence the innumerable
difficulties of both British and Soviets, with those proud and independent leaders who needed all the help the Allies could provide, but were
reluctant to accept their directives, if these did not coincide with their
own conceptions of the interests of their country and/or their cause.

There are so many dimensions to this story that all words used to
describe it turn out to be too simple. In destroying existing super-
structures, the Second World War in Yugoslavia threw the individual
back to older and more intimate structures. Between 1941 and 1945,
the land of the South Slavs survived at the lowest level of its components — historical, geographical, ethical, ideological, religious, individual. Beneath the enthusiasm brought about by the great cause —
whether revolutionary or traditional — and alongside it, there was the
behaviour generated by narrower or less noble causes, and permeating
it all was individual behaviour. All Yugoslavs were not *either* traitors *or*
heroes. Many were *both*, at different times or even at the same time,
and most were *neither*. But in order to understand this, it is necessary
to go beyond the unidimensional narratives, the set pieces, the epics,
the lives of saints and heroes, and all the fashionable literature. It is
necessary to know the framework in which individuals lived, and their
mentality, to work with a microscope, and in many dimensions. It is
necessary to be interested not only in the progress of societies, but also
in the individuals tossed about by such progress. One must sympathise
with the individual shabbily wagging and fidgeting, rather than with the
hero posing, *post partum*, for posterity.

One day, perhaps, in 150 years' time, the Yugoslav Revolution
may end up with its Richard Cobb, and there may be an Oxford don (if
the breed survives) to write a Yugoslav counterpart to *Reactions to
the French Revolution*. For the time being, we could 'begin with
doubts', give up a thirty-year-old attempt to impose a new 'Whig

interpretation of history', and start a more complex reappraisal.

Notes

1.   A. Dzonlagic, Z. Atanackovic and D. Plenca, *Yugoslavia in the Second World War* (translated by L. Edwards, Belgrade, 1967), is the drastically abbreviated translation of the Serbo-Croatian original which puts forward the official view of the People's Liberation War.

2.   In chronological order: Basil Davidson, *Partisan Picture* (1946); Jasper Rootham, *Miss Fire: The Chronicle of a British Mission to Mihailovich, 1943-1944* (1946); Christie Lawrence, *Irregular Adventure* (1947); Stephen Clissold, *Whirlwind: An Account of Marshal Tito's Rise to Power* (1949); Fitzroy Maclean, *Eastern Approaches* (1949); Maclean, *Disputed Barricade: The Life and Times of Josip Broz-Tito, Marshal of Jugoslavia* (1957); Bickham Sweet-Escott, *Baker Street Irregular* (1965); Clissold, 'Occupation and Resistance', in *A Short History of Yugoslavia* (edited by Clissold, Cambridge, 1966); Phyllis Auty, 'The Rise of Tito', in *History of the Second World War* (IV/5, 1967, published in weekly instalments by Purnell and Sons Ltd in cooperation with the Imperial War Museum); Auty, *Tito: A Biography* (1970); F. W. D. Deakin, *The Embattled Mountain* (1971); Julian Amery, *Approach March: A Venture in Autobiography* (London, 1973); Donald Hamilton-Hill, *S.O.E. Assignment* (1973).

3.   Reviews of Phyllis Auty's *Tito* ('From Partisan to President', 21 August 1970), of F. W. D. Deakin's *The Embattled Mountain* ('With the Partisans of Tito', 22 October 1971), of Stevan K. Pavlowitch's *Yugoslavia* ('the Mihajlovic Myth', 25 February 1972), of Julian Amery's *Approach March* ('Resistance, not Change', 16 November 1973), and subsequent correspondence.

Much of what J. B. Kelly has to say about the anonymous *T.L.S.* reviewing of books on the history of the Near East during and after the First World War ('TLS in the Desert', in *Journal of Imperial and Commonwealth History*, I/3, 1973) could be applied *mutatis mutandis* to the history of Yugoslavia during the Second World War. The mystery men of Yugoslav reviewing (if, indeed, they were more than one) shared the same moralising ardour, the same sectarian spirit, the same emotional phraseology. Apparently old boys of some wartime special service dealing with the Yugoslav partisans, they continued to fight the good fight in favour of the side that had won the Yugoslav civil war, contemptuous of those who, in the higher spheres of their own government, were slow to follow their advice, not to mention those Yugoslavs who were not in the right camp. They dogmatically stated what books had laid down the truth on the matter once and for all, and were impatient of authors whose reading differed from their own.

4.   Berlioz's Lelio complained of 'ces jeunes théoriciens de quatre-vingts ans, vivant au milieu d'un océan de préjugés et persuadés que le monde finit avec les rivages de leur île; ces vieux libertins de tout âge qui ordonnent à la musique de les caresser, de les divertir, n'admettent point que la chaste muse puisse avoir une plus belle mission'. Admittedly by now less chaste than Euterpe, Clio should nevertheless be protected, as far as possible, from such libertine treatment.

5.   Vlado Strugar, 'Apercu bibliographique sur la Yougoslavie', in *Revue d'histoire de la Deuxième Guerre mondiale* (22e année, 87, Paris, 1972) analyses the literature published on the subject in Yugoslavia itself. K. W. Böhme, 'Die deutschen Kriegsgefangenen in Jugoslawien', in *Zur Geschichte der deutschen Kriegsgefangenen des Zweiten Weltkrieges* (edited by Erich Maschke, B and 1/2, Munich-Bielefeld, 1964) covers the German literature to that date. Janet Ziegler lists *World War II: Books in English, 1945-1965* (Standford, California, 1971). Andreas Hillgruber, *Südosteuropa in Zweiten Weltkrieg: Literaturbericht und*

Bibliographie (Heft 1, Stuttgart-Frankfurt/M., 1962), and Alfredo Breccia, 'Le fonti per lo studio delle relazioni internazionali dei paesi jugoslavi nel periodo 1870-1945', in *Storia et politica* (Anno IX-X, Fasc. IV/1970 and 1-2/1971, Milan), are more comprehensive though far from exhaustive. At a different level, a beginner's tasting is to be found in 'Suggestions for Further Reading; Chapter 3: The Chaotic Gap' at the end of my *Yugoslavia* (1971).

6.   'The point is what the Allies believed *at the time*', wrote a former SOE officer in a letter to *The Times Literary Supplement* of 26 May 1972. Well – is it? Some politicians may, in the opinion of Bernard Levin, be 'convinced that what things *look like* is more important than what they are', but historians should try and do better.

7.   The Germans, having occupied Yugoslavia and lost the war, usually had their ears nearer the ground, and were less prone to fashionable interpretations. Walter R. Roberts, *Tito, Mihailovic and the Allies, 1941-1945* (New Brunswick, N.J., 1973) is the first book in English to attempt not to espouse a cause. The author, in no way a participant in the events he describes, is dispassionate. Several young American scholars are engaged in research on various aspects of the war in Yugoslavia.

8.   E.g., the considerations on the civil war published in the Zagreb philoso-phical Marxist bimonthly *Praxis* (1971, 3/4), silenced since, or the round table discussion organised by the Belgrade periodical *Gledista* at the beginning of 1972 on 'Historiography and the Revolution', excerpts from which appeared in *Nin* (Belgrade, 13 February 1972). Tito's interview also appeared in the daily press (*Politika*, 24 May 1972, p. 6, *i.a.*). The challenge was more recently taken up by Yugoslavia's permanent dissident, Mihajlo Mihajlov, in an unscholarly and quixo-tic, but obviously brave, plea ('The Mihailovich Tragedy', in *The New Leader*, New York, 3 February 1975) which has earned him yet another prison sentence.

9.   Tito himself has described how he had to run out of a hiding place on the wayside of a country lane, after he had left Uzice on 29 November 1941, in order to get out of the way of a German patrol coming up on him (extracts from Presi-dent Tito's unpublished war memoirs, in the illustrated Belgrade weekly *Front*, 5 May 1972). Pavle Meskovic has described how, a week later, on 6 December, Mihailovic jumped out of a window of a house in the village of Struganik in the nick of time, as German soldiers entered the courtyard ('Misiceva ztrva', in *Knjiga o Drazi*, edited by Radoje L. Knezevic, Windsor, Ontario, 1956, I, 196 *et seq.*).

10.   Phyllis Auty (*Tito*, 192 *et seq.*) has described these on the evidence of J. Marjanovic, 'Cetnicko-nemacki pregovori u selu Divci, 1941', in *Zbornik Filosof-skog fakulteta*, X/1 (Belgrade, 1968), the published minutes of the Mihailovic trial, and interviews with J. Matl. the German *Abwehr* officer who arranged the meeting. Deakin (*The Embattled Mountain*, 144) refers to them from Marjanovic alone. B. M. Karapandzic (*Gradjanski rat u Srbiji, 1941-45*, Cleveland, Ohio, 1958, 128 *et seq.*) has obtained a fuller account from Matl, and has confronted it with that of Colonel Pantic, who acted as go between, and of a German NCO who accompanied the German representatives. Roberts (*Tito, Mihailovic and the Allies*, 35) uses another source, Gert Buchheit, *Der Deutsche Geheimdienst* (Munich, 1968). Yet another printed source is *German Anti-Guerilla Operations in the Balkans, 1941-1944* (US Department of the Army, Pamphlet 20-243, 1954, 22, *et seq.*).

11.   I summarised the evidence available in 1970 in *Yugoslavia*, 141. Roberts has since given a much fuller story (*op. cit.*, 106 *et seq.*) based on further German evidence.

12.   In the case of Mihailovic's contacts in 1941, we can compare the records of the conversations from both sides, and the discrepancies relate to details only.

The hard evidence on the conversations held by Tito's representatives in 1943 – Djilas, Koca Popović and Vladimir Velebit – comes from the German side only. No available Yugoslav source mentions them, except in so far as they related to usual guerrilla truces for prisoner exchanges. Phyllis Auty has written to *The Times Literary Supplement* (27 December 1970): 'Tito and his chief negotiator in 1943 have denied categorically to me (interviews in 1968) in response to specific questions that these negotiations had any purpose other than a truce for exchange of prisoners. I see no reason to doubt Tito's word on this, and know of no credible evidence to refute it.' Tito, his chief negotiator in 1943, and Miss Auty were thus implicitly denying the evidence contained in the despatches of General Dippold to General Glaise von Horstenau, and of Minister Kasche to Foreign Minister von Ribbentrop.

13.   This is now confirmed by British Foreign Office records. Between June 1941 and June 1943, twenty-three tons of material were dropped to Mihailović, and six and a half tons to Tito. Then in the third quarter of 1943, more than 2,000 tons were landed on partisan-held islands, in addition to 125 tons of airborne supplies to both movements. During the first quarter of 1944, over 6,500 tons were either landed or dropped, increasing in the second quarter to some 8,500 tons. 'The following figures for supplies during 1944 give some idea of the scale on which the Western Allies were now heping the partisans: over 100,000 rifles; over 50,000 light machine guns and submachine guns; 1,380 mortars; 324,000 mortar bombs; 636,000 grenades; over 97,500,000 rounds of small-arms ammunition; 700 wireless sets; 175,000 suits of battledress; 260,000 pairs of boots' (Maclean, *Eastern Approaches*, 461).

14.   Berlin had fallen on 2 May 1945, on the same day the German surrender in Italy had taken effect, on 9 May the German terms of general surrender had been ratified in Berlin, but in Yugoslavia, German forces held out until 15 May, reluctant to surrender to 'irregulars'.

15.   Right down to the 1950s, special security forces were kept busy dismantling the remains of Mihailović's wartime network, and local Party bosses were still being killed in rural areas. *Cf.* the revelations of a serial in the Belgrade daily *Politika* (28 March to 14 April 1969), and in *Ilustrovana Politika* (17 November 1970). The subject of Lawrence Durrell's *White Eagles over Serbia* (1957) is the same. Durrell was press attaché at the British Embassy in Belgrade in 1951.

16.   For instance, Churchill told the British chiefs of staff on 23 June 1943 that thirty-three Axis divisions were being held in Yugoslavia (*The Second World War*, V, 1952, 410). The figure was provided by the Minister of Economic Warfare from an SOE 'appreciation': 'Altogether the Partisans and Mihailović between them are containing the following Axis Divisions – Italian 18, German plus Croat 10, Bulgarian 5: total 33' (Selborne to Churchill, 18 June 1943, in the papers of the Prime Minister's Private Office: Prem. 3-510/7643, 153). Incidentally, Lord Selborne goes on: 'Since this appreciation was written . . . we have just heard that Tito's Partisans H.Q. and Army between Kalinovik and Zabljak have been disintegrated by the current Axis drive . . . This Axis move may alter the whole 'set-up''.'

     From a non-specialist (and far from exhaustive) reading of German and Italian military records, I would venture to suggest that, in the summer of 1943, the ten 'German plus Croat' divisions comprised no more than seven low-strength German divisions (most of them two regiment *Jäger* formations, the rest being training formations or much reduced ones back from the Russian front), an SS foreign volunteer division, and two NDH divisions, and that there were no more than fourteen Italian divisions (mostly two regiment formations). Earlier in the year, when the SOE 'appreciation' was being compiled, there were a few more Italian divisions, but only four German divisions in Yugoslavia.

     The impressive figure of thirty-three was thus probably slightly inflated.

Eight were native Balkan divisions of doubtful value. Italian morale was more than low, and that of Bulgars and Croats perhaps even lower. Some thirty Axis divisions, all of low strength, some of poor quality, most of bad morale, were being held in Yugoslavia, by distrust in one another as much as by the resistance.

WAR AND THE AMERICAN EXPERIENCE:
SOME NEW PERSPECTIVES*

Reginald C. Stuart

As these books reveal, the Macmillan 'Wars of the United States' under the editorial direction of Louis Morton is becoming a most valuable series. Despite minor blemishes and occasionally mixed critical reaction, the previously published volumes have all been solid, well researched, have displayed an impressive command of their subjects, and have represented the most up-to-date synthesis in each case.[1] The works under review do not deviate from this general pattern. When completed, this series will constitute a basic library in American military history.

Douglas Leach, Don Higginbotham, and Russell F. Weigley are all accomplished scholars with extensive publications to their credit. They have moved beyond the 'battles-and-leaders' approach which has made military history seem narrow in the past. Higginbotham and Weigley in particular paint on a broad conceptual canvas. Leach adheres to a more traditional format, but at the same time he does not neglect the non-martial aspects of war.

Leach's history of the colonial wars is the most complete single volume work on the subject. He goes far beyond Howard Peckham's smaller and earlier work covering the same material but to a great extent, however, he only amplifies and echoes some of Peckham's broader conclusions.[2] He shows, for example, that while the colonists did indeed place much emphasis on their local militia, they also relied upon British regulars and men-of-war, at times actively seeking them. Both authors stress the colonial particularism which made long range expeditions so difficult to mount and sustain when the requisite effort was beyond the resources of a single colony. Leach confirms Peckham's point that

---

*   Douglas Edward Leach, *Arms for Empire: A Military History of the British Colonies in North America, 1607-1763*. New York: The Macmillan Company, 1973, pp. xviii, 566. Notes, Glossary, Bibliography, Maps, Illustrations, Index, $14.95.

Don Higginbotham, *The War of American Independence: Military Attitudes, Policies, and Practice, 1763-1789*. New York: The Macmillan Company, 1971, pp. xviii, 509. Notes, Bibliography, Maps, Illistrations, Index, $12.95.

Russell F. Weigley, *The American Way of War: A History of United States Military Strategy and Policy*. New York: The Macmillan Company, 1973, pp. xxiii, 584. Notes, Select Bibliography, Maps, Index, $12.95.

the colonial wars contributed to an American feeling of separateness, and both authors assert, although they do not prove, that the Americans had a sense of 'coming of age' by 1763 which was directly traceable to their wartime experiences.[3] Leach parts company with Peckham when he says that the Americans were a military people in many ways and he does not believe that the wars helped to bring Americans together. From Leach's perspective, particularism reigned until the end of the colonial period.

Actually, Leach does not appreciably add to our understanding of the colonial wars, but he does bring together and synthesise an enormous amount of material. He also produces a well paced narrative which brings the experiences of the colonial wars — the sudden terror of a frontier raid, the bucolic conviviality and clumsiness of militia day, and the drama of the battlefield — into vivid life against the shifting backdrop of the imperial contest. But, like Peckham, Leach peers ahead at the American Revolution and as a result abstruse foreshadowings of the future Anglo-American clash periodically darken his otherwise bright literary landscape with mildly pompous phraseology. Granted that each historical epoch lays the foundations for its successor, continuity is one thing, predestination quite another.

Leach suspends his story with a chapter on the militia and a well conceived discussion on the social, economic, political and intellectual impact of the wars which should have been taken much further. Here is where Leach might have made a more original contribution, comparable to his enlightened understanding of Indian-white relations. As it is, Leach presents a dominantly operational history, with occasional forays into planning and logistics and frequent sallies into international diplomacy. These are twice told tales, but Leach's great service here is clear compression and synthesis.

Several themes emerge clearly The influence of the wilderness on European tactics is well presented. The colonials adopted the Indian raid and deliberate terror, descending into brutality as they did so. Savagery became a fixed pattern and colonial zeal even transformed the limited nature of native warfare into more total conflicts which sought the eradication of the enemy. At the same time, the influence of the eighteenth century was evident because many campaigns and sieges were conducted by regulars, with their chivalric code and manuals. The crescendo of the imperial struggle, the dramatic clash on the Plains of Abraham before the walls of Quebec, was a stand up battle between professional troops. Actually, the British adapted better to the wilderness than legend would suggest. The incompetence of second rate officers explains more than doctrinaire adherence to military orthodoxies in Leach's view. Commercial interests — land speculation, the fur trade, privateering, the supply of imperial expeditions — were inextricably woven into the fabric of the colonial wars as well. The paradox of the militia is made apparent. While it was a politically acceptable military institution because of its localism, this same quality made it fractious and recalcitrant when it came to larger expeditions and for the most part it proved unable to protect frontier settlers. It could only retaliate for raids. Even when warning was sufficient for it to assemble, this was often in the shelter of a stronghold where it witnessed the destruction of crops, buildings and livestock.

The grand theme is the struggle for empire and the centrality of war for the colonial experience. But Leach suggests that two sets of wars took place, at times simultaneously, between 1706 and 1763. Local friction between the English and the Indians, Spanish or French produced local tensions. These often erupted into local feuds which merged into the larger imperial endeavours. The brutal facts of power and force governed the colonial world, irrespective of policy from London, Versailles, or Madrid. Often, local imperial officers engaged in their own private ventures, and attempted to utilise the militia or recruit Indian allies to fight wars by proxy. Apart from this imperial theme, Leach's story lacks cohesion. Howard Peckham saw the wars produce the triumph of modernism over feudalism when France was defeated. Daniel Boorstin saw in them the beginnings of an American perspective which eschewed wars of policy in favour of war strictly as a defence of home and hearth.[4] But Leach goes no further than to echo the imperial theme, stress the beginnings of the American traditions of civil supremacy of the military function, and emphasise the evolutionary transition to the Amercan Revolution. Apart from his main themes he provides us with no interpretive tool.

Other problems emerge. A final appraisal of the militia is absent. When the contribution of regular British forces increased in the later wars, the militia fades from view. Leach treats all the antagonists in the wars fairly, especially the Indians, but an expert on the French experience in colonial America has taken him severely to task for ignoring the 'enemy's side of the hill'.[5] The several themes which were raised and developed throughout the book are not brought together at the end and as a result the story seems incomplete. But these caveats cannot outweigh its merits. It tells a magisterial story with grace and humanity, provides an excellent bibliography, and will without question become the standard work on the subject.

Don Higginbotham takes the same military promontory for his view of the American Revolution. Then he gazes into diverse historical corridors and antechambers to relate the military history of the period to social, intellectual, political and economic trends. There is enough smoke, bayonets and broadsides to satisfy those interested in the details of campaigning, just as there is enough strategic and logistical analysis to satiate the hunger of the more demanding military students. Higginbotham argued in 1965 that historians should 'regard things military within the context of society as a whole', just as they 'should eschew the notion of warfare as something distinct or compartmentalized from other segments of the Revolution'.[6] He followed his own advice and in the process clearly demonstrates the validity of his two primary assumptions — that armies are projections of the societies from which they spring and that civilian institutions of a country are produced by the interaction between warfare and society. As a result, only one third of the book deals directly with campaigns. The story has few surprises, but it does impress the reader anew with the importance of the military perspective for a proper understanding of the causes, process and consequences of the American Revolution.

Higginbotham argues that the Revolution produced a war between a people on the one hand and the army of a government on the other. The fact that American nationalism was only in embryo form does not preclude such a view. The militia, which the author sees as 'close to being the nation in microcosm', was therefore of crucial importance. It combined social, political and military functions on a local level, thereby disarming the intense anti-militarism embedded in American thought and society. At the same time it rendered vital military service, despite its sometimes dubious performance in the field. For example, when George Washington's first army disintegrated in December 1775, the militia filled the void until new forces could be assembled. Even in battle it could perform well.

The Continental Army mirrored the militia in many ways, and despite Washington's efforts to create a professional eighteenth century force, no 'New Model' army emerged from the American Revolution. Recruiting difficulties, unauthorised leaves during planting or harvest times, and the lenient American military code all suggest the popular nature of Washington's army. Yet, the war was conventional in many ways. At Princeton, Monmouth, Brandywine and Cowpens, the Americans,and British had stand up fights. Yorktown was a formal siege, with trenches and salients. In fact, two wars were fought from 1776 to 1783 — one at a local level by the militia and the other at a national-international level by the Continentals and later their French allies. In both cases, the struggle was as much political as military, and many times, the two conflicts overlapped and were mutually reinforcing. It was the combination of success at both levels which led to American Independence.

American anti-militarism emerges as a major theme in this study which was characteristic of both levels of the war. It was evident in the prelude to independence by the American reaction to the presence of British regulars in the colonies in peacetime.[7] It carried on with the concern displayed by the Massachusetts Provincial Congress over the control of its many bodies of militia, with the sporadic and uneven efforts by the Continental Congress to control Washington, his officers and the army, and finally in the military control clauses of the Federal Constitution of 1787. Civil-military tensions were ever present, although Congress left strategy to the generals while retaining command of policy when it could obtain the cooperation of the states, since it directed a form of coalition war rather than a unified effort. The final solution for American military problems was the creation of two armies — a local militia and a federal force.[8]

The fact of war explains much to Higginbotham and he reveals an occasional flash of patriotism in his analyses. He is scrupuously fair to the British and the loyalists but he too easily excuses the state violation of civil liberties of all citizens by means of insistence on stringent loyalty oaths as a form of naturalisation. The exigencies of war also explain the questionable financial measures adopted by the Americans. He seems on firmer ground here, but is only suggestive when he argues that the war stimulated nationalism at a local level.

This faint hue of patriotism pales before Higginbotham's solid research, sound judgement and fair treatment. The American invasion of Canada clearly was too ambitious and could not have succeeded given the circumstances. The ultimate result of the war probably would have been favourable to the Americans, even without French assistance. Clearly, neither side monpolised atrocities in the savage frontier warfare, as a glance back to Leach confirms. Congressional military policy clearly was inadequate during the war and a failure during the peace that followed. The British receive the same comprehensive and judicious treatment as the Americans, and this juxtaposition is then placed in a broad geographic and temporal framework. While paying meticulous attention to detail, Higginbotham never lets his reader forget the broader and less substantial aspects of history. He has produced military history as it needs to be written, the kind of integrated synthesis of the study of war that may not have been possible with Leach's subject because of the state of research. Seldom have war and society been so clearly related in American historiography as they are in Higginbotham's book.

Russell Weigley combines the scope of Leach's work with the integration of Higginbotham's. He begins his well documented survey with the Revolution and carries it forward to include the Vietnam era. He argues that 'the direction taken by the American conception of war made most American strategists . . . strategists of annihilation'. American wealth and the 'adoption of unlimited aims in war' made the annihilative approach the characteristically American way of war. A secondary theme is the perpetual lack of preparedness on the part of

Americans which is reminiscent of the militia response to frontier raids described by Leach. Consistently, Weigley argues, Americans neglected strategic planning and refused to relate political ends with military means. Only the threat of international communism in combination with the destructive potential of the atomic age produced a shift in this fundamental pattern. After World War II Americans engaged in formulation which was 'not merely a military strategy but an all-inclusive planning for the use of the nation's total resources to defend and advance the national interests . . .' Weigley takes his themes from Clausewitz, and he clearly approves when Americans began to ponder and understand the real relationship of politics and war. As Leach and Higginbotham showed, this story began with the founding of the colonies and was given a dramatic impetus with the Revolution. Weigley brings it up to date.

Weigley also places American military concepts in a broad framework. Democracy, nationalism and the rise of industrial mass production are all related to the nature and conduct of war. This story has been told before by Walter Millis, but Weigley expands on Millis' earlier study.[9] The logic of the American experience pointed toward the annihilative approach, but it was only the massive exploitation of wealth, productive capacity and manpower reserves in combination with rising national emotion and a realisation of these forces by American military thinkers that produced the American way of war in the twentieth century. Prior to the Civil War, Weigley argues, Americans were shackled by attitudes of mind and relative poverty which had prevented the flowering of their national tendency to wage total war.

It is here that Weigley's argument sticks slightly. His discussion of the American odyssey to total war is more convincing for the period after 1865 than before 1861. Few would quarrel with the Civil War as a watershed. But Weigley implies determinism, and borders on the contradictory when he argues that attitudes of mind and lack of resources prevented Americans from waging total war on the one hand, and that military logic and political objectives beckoned toward annihilative war on the other. Weigley may have been seduced by Clausewitz here. For the colonials, total war was a logical development, but they managed to live comfortably enough with limited victories for specific objectives. It was the British who initiated the drive for the destruction of French power with the accession to office of William Pitt. Weigley suggests that given the circumstances, Americans should have thought in terms of total war by 1776. But the Americans did not, They remained firmly entrenched in the age of limited war until after 1861. George Washington and the Continental Congress had, as Weigley admits, 'never sought to wage a "revolutionary" kind of war'. Americans accepted a continued British and Spanish — then Mexican — presence in

North America. Historians now seem to agree that the cry for the total expulsion of Britain in the War of 1812 was a blind. Canada was a convenient British limb for the Americans to gnaw upon, and not an object of conquest. Even in the Mexican War, James K. Polk had limited territorial objectives. The Americans were drawn into the heart of Mexico more by the Mexican refusal to treat than by the beckoning hand of annihilative war. After 1861, 'rich in the manpower and resources to make war, the caution and restaint hitherto predominant in American strategy gave way . . .' One could more accurately argue that historical circumstances shifted, as Weigley most assuredly does in part, rather than create the impression that Americans were at last freed of bothersome constraints on their natural tendencies.[10] The development of the American way of war was not inevitable, although the evolution of history creates a tendency to see it that way, just as Leach was unable to resist seeing the American Revolution as a necessary consequence of the colonial wars.

But if the American way of war changed after 1861 in one sense, in another it remained the same. Americans still refused to relate military means to political ends. Planning remained essentially improvisational, however successful, until the atomic age. The period after World War II thus witnessed a revolution in Weigley's second theme. He is persuasive here as he shows how concepts of war and realisation of the need for planning at last became symbiotic. Circumstances continually change, however, and Weigley concludes that in light of the Vietnam experience and the current balance of destructive power, 'the history of usable combat may at last be reaching its end' in a new age of limited and indecisive wars.[11]

This is a thoughtful conclusion to a fine study. Interpretive caveats notwithstanding, Weigley's mastery of his sources and his sound judgement are apparent throughout. He is a fluent writer and has put American military thought into perspective with such force and clarity that this work will remain required reading for future students of the subject, although one might wish that Weigley had investigated civilian thinking more extensively in the early period. When civilians became prominent contributors to planning, Weigley moves easily into their work, demonstrates their significance, and reminds us that in America war has always been planned and conducted by the elites, however much it has been 'democratised' over the past three and a half centuries.

Together, these volumes demonstrate the continuity of the American military experience, with its retaliatory character and strong civilian flavour. They also reveal how central war has been for the history of the United States, and how important it is that martial conflict be understood within a broad framework of social, political, economic and intellectual events and trends. Finally, these studies reflect the fact that military historiography has taken new directions in the past decade which bid fair to elevate the study of war to new and more sophisticated levels of interpretation. Historians and others can only await new volumes in the Macmillan 'Wars of the United States' with high expectations. If the past is anything to judge by, they will not be disappointed.

Notes

1.   Previous volumes are Russell F. Weigley, *History of the United States Army* (1967), Robert M. Utley, *Frontiersmen in Blue: The United States Army and the Indian 1848-1865* (1967), Harvey A. DeWeerd, *President Wilson Fights His War: World War I and the American Intervention* (1968), Francis Prucha, *The Sword of the Republic: The United States Army on the Frontier 1783-1846* (1969), Clarence C. Clendenen, *Blood on the Border: The United States Army and the Mexican Irregulars* (1969), Robert M. Utley, *Frontier Regulars: The United States Army and the Indian 1866-1891* (1973), and K. Jack Bauer, *The Mexican War, 1846-1848* (1974). DeWeerd has been taken to task for a misleading, if not deceptive title since he focuses on the war in Europe to the exclusion of not only the American home front, but even of Woodrow Wilson himself. See reviews by Arthur S. Link, *Journal of American History* 56 (1969), 173, and Richard W. Leopold, *American Historical Review*, 75 (1969), 945-6.
2.   Howard Peckham, *The Colonial Wars 1689-1762* (Chicago: The University of Chicago Press, 1964).
3.   *Ibid.*, 214-21. Compare with Leach, *Arms for Empire*, 504-8. Peckham's general conclusions emerged in an earlier essay, 'Speculations on the Colonial Wars', *William and Mary Quarterly*, Third Series, 17 (1960), 463-72.
4.   Peckham, *Colonial Wars*, 216. Daniel J. Boorstin, *The Americans: The Colonial Experience* (New York: Random House, 1958), 352, 360-2.
5.   See W. J. Eccles' review in *William and Mary Quarterly*, Third Series, 31 (1974), 501-3.
6.   Don Higginbotham, 'American Historians and the Military History of the American Revolution', *American Historical Review*, 70 (1964), 33. A similarly broadly conceived study is John Shy, 'The American Revolution: The Military Conflict Considered as a Revolutionary War', in Stephen G. Kurtz and James H. Hutson (eds.), *Essays on the American Revolution* (Chapel Hill: The University of North Carolina Press, 1973), 121-56.
7.   Higginbotham relies heavily on John Shy, *Toward Lexington: The Role of the British Army in the Coming of the American Revolution* (Princeton: Princeton University Press, 1965), for his arguments.
8.   The story of these two armies has been traced by Russell F. Weigley, *History of the United States Army*, the first volume published in this series. See Marcus Cunliffe, *Soldiers and Civilians: The Martial Spirit in America 1775-1865* (1969), for a discussion of American attitudes toward the military prior to the Civil War. Both Higginbotham and Weigley underscore the clear and sharp contrast

between acceptance of local, amateur militia units and suspicion of the professional military service documented by Cunliffe. Arthur A. Ekirch, *The Civilian and the Military* (New York: Oxford University Press, 1956), is an earlier wotk with a similar theme.

9.   Walter Millis, *Arms and Men* (New York: G. P. Putnam's, 1956).

10.   John Shy, 'The American Military Experience: History and Learning', *The Journal of Interdisciplinary History* 2 (1971), argues that American experience has encouraged the tendency toward total war by continued military success which has reinforced previous predilections.

11.   Louis J. Halle, 'Does War Have a Future?', *Foreign Affairs*, 52 (1975), 20-34, concludes on a similar note.

NOTES ON CONTRIBUTORS

Uri Bialer was awarded his doctorate at the University of London in 1974 and is now teaching political science at the University of Tel Aviv.

Ian Gentles was educated at Toronto and London Universities and is currently Dean of Students, Glendon College, University of York, Toronto. He has published several articles on the English Civil War and the Interregnum.

John Gooch took his B.A. and Ph.D. at King's College, London, and has been a Lecturer in History at the University of Lancaster since 1967. His publications include *The Plans of War: the General Staff and British Military Strategy, 1900-1916* (1974).

J. R. Hale was formerly a Fellow of Jesus College, Oxford and Professor of History at Warwick University, and is currently Professor of Italian at University College, London. His numerous publications include *Renaissance Europe, 1480-1520* (1971).

Michael Howard was formerly Professor of War Studies at King's College, London and is at present a Fellow of All Souls College, Oxford. His books include *The Franco-Prussian War, Grand Strategy* vol. IV and *The Continental Commitment.*

Stevan K. Pavlowitch was educated at the Universities of Paris, Lille and London and is currently a Senior Lecturer at the University of Southampton. He is the author of *Yugoslavia* (1971) and is currently working on a study of Italian policy regarding Yugoslavia during the Second World War.

Douglas Porch took his doctorate at Cambridge University and is now a Lecturer in History at the University College of Wales, Aberystwyth. He is the author of *Army and Revolution: France 1815-1848* (1974).

David B. Ralston is the specialist in modern French History at the Massachusetts Institute of Technology, and is the author of *The Army of the Republic* (1967). Since 1973 he has been a Visiting Professor in the Strategy Department of the US Naval War College.

Ian Roy was educated at St Andrews and Oxford Universities. He is the editor of texts on the Habsburg-Valois Wars and the English Civil War, and is preparing studies of aspects of the Civil War.

Brigadier H. C. T. Stronge was British military attache in Belgrade and Prague from 1936 to 1939.

Reginald C. Stuart took his B.A. and M.A. degrees at the University of British Columbia and his Ph.D. at the University of Florida. He is currently Assistant Professor of History at the University of Prince Edward Island and is preparing a book on American thought on war in the late eighteenth century.

Philip Towle took his B.A. at Cambridge and his M.A. and Ph.D. at King's College, London. After teaching at the Royal Naval College, Dartmouth, he is at present working in the Arms Control and Disarmament Research Unit of the Foreign Office.

T. H. E. Travers took his doctorate at Yale in 1970 and is currently Assistant Professor of History at the University of Calgary. He has published several articles on nineteenth-century history and is preparing a book on *The British Anarchists 1883-1896*.

John Whittam is a graduate of Oxford and London Universities and has been a lecturer in History at Bristol University since 1964. He is now completing a book on *The Politics of the Italian Army 1861-1918*.

253

BOOKS RECEIVED

Robert O. Paxton.   *Vichy France: Old Guard and New Order, 1940-1944* (Barrie & Jenkins, 1972).

Piers Mackesy.   *The Strategy of Overthrow 1798-1799* (Longman, 1974).

Peter Padfield.   *The Great German Naval Race: Anglo-German Naval Rivalry 1900-1914* (Hart-Davis, MacGibbon, 1974).

Arthur J. Marder.   *From the Dardanelles to Oran: Studies of the Royal Navy in War and Peace 1915-1940* (Oxford University Press, 1974).

T. A. Heathcote.   *The Indian Army: the Garrison of British Imperial India 1822-1922* (David and Charles, 1974).